D0895352

The Transformation of
Corporate Control

The Transformation of Corporate Control

Neil Fligstein

Harvard University Press
Cambridge, Massachusetts
London, England
1990

Copyright © 1990 by the President and Fellows of Harvard College
All rights reserved
Printed in the United States of America
10   9   8   7   6   5   4   3   2   1

This book is printed on acid-free paper, and its binding materials
have been chosen for strength and durability.

Library of Congress Cataloging in Publication Data
Fligstein, Neil.
    The transformation of corporate control / Neil Fligstein.
        p.   cm.
    Includes bibliographical references.
    ISBN 0-674-90358-7 (alk. paper)
    1. Trade regulation—United States—History. 2. Antitrust law—
United States—History. 3. Big business—United States—History.
4. Consolidation and merger of corporations—United States—History.
I. Title.
HD3616.U46F57 1990   89-15586
338.6′048′0973—dc20   CIP

For Christine

Acknowledgments

First, I wish to acknowledge the work of Alfred Chandler. While much of what I say is antithetical to his work, his penetrating insights into the history of American business are the starting point for any serious work on this topic. Those who are familiar with his work will see its influence on mine.

Over time, I have benefited from the comments of a large number of people. In particular, I would like to thank Doug McAdam, John Meyer, Harrison White, and Mayer Zald, all of whom read the manuscript in its entirety. Thomas McCraw read the manuscript twice for Harvard University Press and gave serious comments that have reshaped the manuscript and pushed it toward its present form. I owe an extremely large debt to his unrelenting criticism. The other anonymous readers of the manuscript also provided invaluable help. I thank Gerhard Arminger, Jim Baron, Paul DiMaggio, Ken Dauber, Roger Friedland, Stan Lieberson, Jim Lincoln, Don Palmer, Charles Perrow, Jeff Pfeffer, Woody Powell, and Dick Scott for useful comments along the way. Michael Aronson, General Editor at the Press, has helped with substantive comments and good advice on the overall structure of the book. Naomi Lamoreaux and Ralph Nelson graciously gave me their data on the industries and firms involved in the turn of the century merger movement.

The Department of Sociology at the University of Arizona has proved a congenial location for my work. My colleagues have listened to me discuss this book, first at a faculty seminar in 1982 when I had just begun to write it, and later at an ongoing series of lectures. The Department has also provided material support without which I could not have completed this book. I have had a number of research assistants and would like to thank Peter Brantley, David Chang, Cam Counters, Beverly Lanzetta, Erin

McBryde, and Sherry Sinclair for their help. Barb MacIntosh helped type and retype the manuscript. A series of grants from the Social and Behavioral Sciences Research Institute at the University of Arizona made it possible for me to travel to collections and gather data.

Numerous libraries and archives aided my work tremendously. At various times, librarians and archivists at the University of Arizona Library (particularly in Government Documents), the Library of Congress, the Baker Library at the Harvard Business School, the National Archives, the Justice Department Library, the Federal Trade Commission Library, and the National Archives branch containing the Nixon Presidential Papers helped in my search for primary documents.

I acknowledge the kind permission to use tabular material from Michael Gort, *Diversification and Integration in American Industry,* copyright © 1962 by National Bureau of Economic Research, published by Princeton University Press; and excerpts from Alfred Sloan, *My Years with General Motors,* copyright © 1963 by Alfred P. Sloan, Jr., reprinted by permission of Harold Matson Co., Inc.

Finally, my thanks to Christine Breit Fligstein, who has never known me when I was not finishing this book. Well, now it's done.

Contents

The Transformation of
Corporate Control

1

Introduction

Bemoaning the state of the American economy has become commonplace. Critics seek to explain how and why the dominance of American business in the world has decreased. Some have argued that American culture with its emphasis on the individual has raised expectations to such high levels that people are no longer self-sacrificing enough for the common good. Others blame workers, who they say lack a work ethic and demand more in wages and benefits than is justified by their productivity. Still others point to inadequate technological innovation and improvement in productive capital stock. Some view the federal government as the key problem with its intrusiveness into the workplace and high tax rates. And some have taken American executives to task for favoring policies that may raise short-term profits, but ignore the long-term possibility of decline.

While there appears to be little consensus as to the cause of this decline, the consequences are evident everywhere. The United States has rapidly moved from an exporter of goods and capital to an importer. The country's industrial base has diminished, and there are now fewer manufacturing jobs as a proportion of all jobs in both absolute and relative terms.

I propose a different way to understand how the American economy has been transformed in the past hundred years. Since the current tendencies are the product of long-run strategic interactions between key actors in the firms and the government, the causes of any decline must be located in that interaction. These actors have interpreted their environments, both inside and outside their organizations, and created new solutions to recurring problems. Their innovations have been adopted by other firms and become accepted business practices. American managers may pay inordinate attention to short-run policies, but this is the result of the implementation of a certain conception of the firm within a set of existing institutions. From this perspective, the actions of managers are explicable only in the context of a long-run structural view oriented toward discovering how, when, and why changes have taken place.

My central thesis is that the viability of the large industrial enterprise in the United States is most related to the long-term shifts in the conception of how the largest firms should operate to preserve their growth and profitability. These shifts have occurred in response to a complex set of interactions between the largest firms, those who have risen to control those firms, and the government. They originated with managers and entrepreneurs who sought more control over their internal and external environments. When one solution was blocked by the actions of the government, new solutions were created and diffused. The result was a shift to a new conception of the large corporation and hence a new set of strategies and structures.

These changes were not the product of profit-maximizing actors in efficient firms working to become more efficient. Managers and entrepreneurs were not optimizers or satisficers. Instead, they constructed new courses of action based on their analyses of the problems of control they faced. The new conceptions and the strategies and structures that resulted were successful to the degree they allowed firms to survive and grow.

Consider, for example, the finance conception of the firm: the purpose of the firm is to increase short-run profits by manipulating assets in order to produce growth through mergers and diversification. This conception has come to dominate the world of the largest firms and for those firms has generated a successful strategy for growth. Indeed, between 1947 and 1985, the asset concentration of the 500 largest manufacturing companies increased from 42 percent to 76 percent. Most of this increase occurred through diversified mergers. This conception, however, has had the ironic effect of promoting the health and growth of the largest firms, while impeding expansion of manufacturing facilities. For those who control the largest firms, their actions have been profitable and sensible. For the economy as a whole, the effects have been less positive.

The current system has come about in a complex, yet explicable way. It emerged under a certain set of rules and as those rules changed, the system changed. These changes were driven by managers and entrepreneurs seeking tactics for survival in the face of economic crisis, instability in their relations with competitors, and the restrictions of antitrust laws. The finance conception of the large corporation, consequently, is the historical product of a dynamic system.

In the scholarly literature, there exist two opposing images of the large, modern corporation. The first stresses the success of the corporate form as a vehicle that deploys capital efficiently to maximize returns. The heroes of this version of the corporation are the top managers who maintain control through decentralized administration and detailed financial reporting. These tools allow top managers to assess problems and react quickly to shifts in markets, technology, and consumer preferences.

The second version focuses on the failure of the modern firm as inefficient with low-quality production leading to an inability to compete in world markets. Managers, rather than being heroes, rule over bloated bureaucracies that do not produce sufficiently high returns on investment to stockholders. Instead, these managers concentrate on their personal aggrandizement by surrounding themselves with large staffs and perquisites. This poor performance is measured by the fall of a firm's stock price below the book value of its assets.

These descriptions evaluate the firm primarily in financial terms. Both accounts place too much responsibility for the success or failure of the corporation on managers. While managers have played a central role in the transformation of the large corporation, they have done so in ways that are much more subtle and constrained than either point of view would acknowledge. Neither version theorizes the context of production or allows for the interaction between managers' ideas about appropriate corporate behavior, how the firms actually work, and what is occurring in the organizations surrounding the firm. In any given moment, there exists a conventional wisdom that guides action and managers face pressures to conform to that view. The internal strategy and structure of existing firms reflect organized power and interests. Managers, as part of those organized interests, behave to preserve what is. The organizations that surround the firm provide constant clues as to what is occurring in the firm's product markets. This information is filtered and interpreted and greatly affects what actions are possible.

Neither point of view considers the state's effect on corporations. For instance, corporate charters were granted by the various levels of government and the rights and privileges of the corporate form have depended on legislatures and courts. The state also drew the boundaries of appropriate corporate behavior in defining how markets were to be constructed. The antitrust laws defined the limits of competitive behavior and had a great effect on possible courses of action. In these ways, the worlds of top managers have always been highly structured and their actions shaped by social and political contexts.

Finally, neither point of view takes the problem of constructing managerial courses of action seriously enough; the motives of managers are taken to be somewhat obvious. In the first description, managers act as maximizers for the benefit of the stockholders, and in the second they act against those interests and narrowly for their own. The problem is that courses of action are constructed not with reference to the manager and the issue of self-interest (whether it be that of the shareholder or the manager), but rather in terms of the social context in which managers operate. The existence of conceptions of the firm and the strategies and structures they imply, the example of competitors' behavior, and the actual experiences of the managers in the firm make plotting a course of action depend on what is viewed as appropriate or normative in their worlds. Managers may seek profits, but the ways they choose to do so will tend to be consistent with the existing distribution of power in their organization and similar organizations.

Courses of action are determined by a legal framework and a self-conscious version of the world that make both old and new courses of action possible and desirable. Like everyone else, managers tend to see the world in a certain way and the framing of action often takes place in a context where the action taken was the only and obvious one. New courses of action require risk takers with alternative conceptions of the world. Some succeed and others fail, but if the winners outnumber the losers the course of action will spread through the business community and become the new obvious tactic. Given the high cost of failure, it should not be surprising that there have been relatively few conceptions of the corporation and few accepted courses of action.

In the neoclassical theory of the firm, the motives and actions of managers and entrepreneurs presume that firms must maximize profits. What I will examine is how they have chosen to do so. I claim that the central goal of managers in the past hundred years has been to make sure their firms survived. To promote survival they proposed various forms of control, both inside and outside the firm. Internally, control was oriented to ensuring that organizational resources were deployed so that top management could be confident that their directives were being executed. Externally, this control was oriented toward establishing stable relations between competitors to promote the survival of their organizations. This search for control had other constituencies: boards of directors, labor, and middle management on the inside and the state on the outside. It was difficult to construct courses of action leading to stability. Once in place, these conceptions tended to remain stable for relatively long periods of time. Nevertheless, the concern with survival and control did not produce one solution that held sway forever. Indeed, shocks to stable structures meant that managers and entrepreneurs had to analyze their problems differently at various points in time and then construct new solutions.

Organizational Theory

In my organizational history of the large modern corporation over the past hundred years I use a distinctly sociological framework that originates in current organizational theory. To support the arguments I also use the tools of both the historian and the economist.

Organizational theory focuses on three relevant institutional contexts in which the transformation of organizations takes place.[1] First, organizations are embedded in larger groups of organizations which are called organizational fields that may be defined in terms of product line, industry, or firm size. The other organizations are most frequently competitors, although sometimes they are suppliers, distributors, or owners. Second, the state sets the rules that define what organizations can do and what the limits of legal behavior are. Third, organizations have in place a set of strategies, structures, technologies, and physical limits that shape and constrain their patterns of growth and change.

The existence of organizational fields is established by the mutual recognition of actors in different firms of their interdependence. These actors share a similar conception of legitimate action and the place of each organization in that field. The function of organizational fields is, first and foremost, to promote stability. They are the basic mechanism of control of the external environment available to managers and entrepreneurs.

Organizational fields are not generally benign and cooperative arrangements held in place by a sense of duty or honor, although the rhetoric and ideology of their proponents might lead one to think so. Instead, they are set up to benefit their most powerful members. These firms have often organized the rules and have the power to enforce them. The most important determinants of that power are the size of the firms and the ability of actors in them to prevent other organizations from entering their fields. Large size implies they have resources to undercut possible competitors. The most common barriers to entry are patents, technologies, and large initial investments.

From the point of view of actors in less powerful organizations in the field, the reasons to support the dominant organizations all revolve around survival. Direct challenges to the leading firms may result in persecution of the smaller or weaker firms. The conditions that promote the stability of the organizational field also lead to stability for the less powerful members of those fields. Being a member of the field, albeit a dependent one, is one way to survive. While competition continues to exist, it is no longer predatory. For these reasons, once stable organizational fields come into existence, it is in the interest of all organizations in the field not to upset them.

The actual formation of organizational fields requires a high level of social organization. Managers or entrepreneurs in leading firms must articulate a set of rules to control the field and be willing and able to enforce those rules. In order to do this, actors in one firm must have the ability to observe their competitors. For these reasons, organizational fields are more likely to form where the number of leading organizations is small or where some form of trade association exists. Through observation of one another managers construct courses of action and find market niches for themselves. The problem is deciding who to watch and how to interpret their actions.

There have been many extensively constructed organizational fields. The first were built around single products, but as time went on and large firms diversified, reference groups changed. By the 1930s managers in the largest firms viewed their organizational fields as industries, not just product lines. In the past twenty-five years managers of the largest firms have come to define their organizational fields in terms of the group of the largest firms, as well as entire industries. Many of the largest firms are highly diversified and the firms their managers watch are naturally those whom they most wish to resemble. This means that the dominant conception of the large corporation is generally held by all of the largest firms.

The largest firms have the most influence on the stability of their organizational fields. They also provide examples of success to the constituent members. Actors in organizations exist in murky worlds where the consequence of any given action is unclear and the definition of any given situation is open to interpretation. Because of this they mimic what they perceive as successful strategies and organizational innovations in their fields. The dependency on and example of successful large organizations cause actors in less powerful organizations to conform to the patterns and expectations of their more powerful neighbors. Fields define normative behavior, but they depend on the relative power of the largest, most successful firms to enforce those norms.

Organizational fields can be destabilized by a number of forces. Most frequently, organizations from outside the field upset the status quo and create new rules. Often, innovative behavior occurs in newly emerging organizational fields, fields whose structures and rules have yet to coalesce. If their behavior is observed as producing relatively successful results, it can spread to neighboring fields. Macroeconomic and political shocks can produce crises that destabilize the power structure of an already existing field. In such a situation, actors in leading organizations within a field can respond to internal or external crises by changing their behavior and thereby altering the rules. This kind of transformation is somewhat rare, as it involves great risks and potential undermining of their control.

The state is made up of the organizations, institutions, and practices that constitute the political function of any given society. The organizations each have agendas that are determined by the political actors that control them and the economic and social forces that lurk behind the political process. The organizations of the state are driven by actors who have interests shaped by different, and often conflicting, purposes.

The state is an important force in the economy in several ways. It defines the rules by which actions in the economy are carried out. It is one thing to say you are in favor of free markets, and quite another to actually define what a free market is. That definition has shifted over time and the dispute has primarily been between firms and the state. Laws regarding incorporation, antitrust, and the regulation of various industries are important aspects of state definitions. The state also affects the economy by consuming products, intervening in the business cycle, and providing for the redistribution of income through taxation and social expenditures.

State actions can have both intended and unintended consequences. A state action may be to limit the power of the large firm, the intended consequence. For example, if the state decides to outlaw monopolies, and its actions are effective, no monopolies will exist. However, the state's actions may have unintended consequences. By foreclosing the possibility for monopoly and collusion between firms in a single market, the state opens other possibilities for firms. In the United States, for example, two alternative courses of action emerged when monopolies were outlawed: oligopoly conditions in a number of industries where one or several firms shared a large portion of a given market and maintained stable prices, and product diversification, where firms achieved stability by spreading their risks across products. Neither of these results was intended by the state. But by eliminating possibilities, the state encourages organizations in society to innovate. It places limits on legal behavior so that firms must find new courses of action given those limits. Once new tactics are taken by firms, actors in the state have to decide on what subsequent course of action to take. This sets the cycle in motion again.

Perhaps the most pressing theoretical issue in political sociology today is the relative autonomy of the state. This issue basically turns on the question of how and in whose interests policy is made. Marxists view the state as controlled by the interests of capital while pluralists see the state as the arena where political conflict between groups is adjudicated. Max Weber proposed that the state is a structure controlled by actors with their own interests in organizing society. In this sense, the state can be viewed as a set of organizations that act autonomously from the economy.

The relationship between the state and large firms generally has been to serve the interests of the firms. At times, state agencies have been captured by corporate interests and policies are made for their benefit. The state can, however, act as a mediator between interests and in its own interests, and the problem of deciding what is occurring is an empirical question. For instance, antitrust laws and their enforcement are deep-rooted issues concerning the legitimacy of the entire system. It is not surprising that firms resist their implementation while the electorate generally favors them. Antitrust efforts have a bureaucratic constituency in the Justice Department and the Federal Trade Commission. The concern over the issue has waxed and waned in both the legislative and executive branches, however, depending on who has held power in them.

The internal structuring of the organization is the final arena to consider. As it turns out, there have not been many organizational innovations in the past hundred years. This reflects the fact that managers in organizations are generally highly constrained and that to change the course of the large firm requires taking huge risks. Equally important, managers and entrepreneurs have a stake in what exists. They have an organizational story about what the organization does and how it does it. Those who are in control generally base that control on existing organizational strategy and structure. This illustrates one of the central insights of organizational theory: organizations tend not to change what they are doing because of deep-seated interests to continue business as usual. Only when those interests can be changed do organizations strike out on new courses of action.

The major impetus toward such change can be generated internally or externally. In either case it will rely on a perceived crisis. The crisis can be that the company is losing money, or only that actors in the company want to achieve more growth or profits. Either way, certain actors in key organizations must interpret their organization's problems and propose a solution, which can follow practices of other organizations in their field or be novel. But in order for the solution to be carried out, the actors must have the power to act. Organizational innovation will often occur in new organizations where there is not an established set of practices or power relations between key actors or in organizational fields where rules are not firmly established.

All large organizations have an internal power struggle over the goals and resources of the organization. Those who control the resources use them to force their view of appropriate organizational behavior. In the largest firms, there are two bases of control: formal ownership and authority. Those who own the firm control by virtue of ownership. Authority relations embedded in the organizational structure legitimate how managers can control organizations. In the large modern corporation, the set of managers who control the organization has changed over the past one hundred years. Structural position is determined by observing the subunit in the organization from which the president or chief executive officer (CEO) originates. Aside from entrepreneurs, the subunits of power represented are manufacturing, sales and marketing, and finance. The basis for claims on organizational power concern the ability of executives in these three functional subunits to propose solutions to organizational crises.

Actors who control organizations, be they in the employ of the state or firms, must interpret their organizational fields and then make policy based on their reading of those fields. This policy, by necessity, will be bounded by the internal logic of their organizations, what those actors know, how they perceive the world, and what they define as appropriate organizational behavior. The perspective that managers and entrepreneurs develop can be called a conception of control. This term refers to the fact that these actors want to control their internal and external environments. The way in which they try to achieve and exercise control is dependent upon their perspective of what constitutes appropriate behavior. Conceptions of control are totalizing world views that cause actors to interpret every situation from a given perspective. They are forms of analysis used by actors to find solutions to the current problems of the organization. At the center of conceptions of control are simplifying assumptions about how the world is to be analyzed.

A distinction can be made between a conception of appropriate organizational action and organizational strategy. The conception of control refers to a totalizing world view of managers or entrepreneurs that causes them to filter the problems of the world in a certain way. This means that two individuals with different conceptions will perceive a given organizational crisis differently and indeed one of them may see no crisis whatsoever. It also means their analysis may lead them to propose different solutions to the problem. An organizational strategy refers to the actual goals of the organization and the policies put in place to reach those goals. The conception of control refers to why managers view those strategies as appropriate for what the firm ought to do. Differing conceptions generally imply a small set of strategies which will be consistent with the orientation of each conception. Different conceptions of control may implement the same strategy, but they will interpret the efficacy of that strategy in their own terms.

To illustrate this distinction, diversification is one organizational strategy. It reflects a policy of the organization concerning its product mix. But the conceptions of control that support diversification give different reasons for pursuing that course of action. For example, a sales and marketing executive may diversify product lines in order to have a full line of goods to sell customers. A finance executive will view the same diversification as a way to spread risk for the firm. The strategy of increasing the number of products is the same for both executives, but the meaning each attaches to the action is quite different.

Managers' and entrepreneurs' conceptions create different views about how control is to be achieved. Their actions will be justified as ways to extend their control over the situation at hand. These conceptions are not static, but depend on interaction with the world. The model of action proposed is not to be mistaken for either the rational or bounded rational actors of economic theory. Actors are assumed to construct *rationales* for their behavior on the basis of how they view the world. Their goals and strategies result from those views and are not the product of an abstract rationality. The construction of courses of action depend greatly on the position of actors within the structure of the organization, which form the interests and identities of actors.

Setting the Stage

In my study I concentrate on the 1000 largest industrial enterprises in the United States since 1880. Since membership in this group has been fluid (indeed, it would be hard to identify the 1000 largest corporations in 1880), my goal is to understand how the group was transformed in terms of conception, identity, strategy, and structure. Most of the quantitative data presented actually refer to a much smaller group, the 100 or 500 largest firms. The manufacturing and mining sector of the economy is my central focus, although I also discuss firms engaged in retail and entertainment. I do not consider the financial sector, however. My emphasis instead is on the goods producing and distributing sectors of the economy.

I use a number of key constructs throughout this book. These terms reflect the theoretical arguments just made, but apply more precisely to the large modern corporation. My analysis revolves around six key notions. *Conception of control* is a perspective on how firms ought to solve their competitive problems and is collectively held and reflected in their organizational fields. Constructs that concern the internal organization of the firm are its *strategy, structure,* and *subunit power base.* The *state* and the *organizational field* constitute the firm's external environment.

The primary question is how the *conceptions of control* in the largest U.S. firms have been transformed in the past one hundred years. The strategies, structures, and organizational fields that have emerged embody these different conceptions. Once in place as control perspectives, they are widely shared ways of reducing the complexity of the world. They come into existence in a piece-meal fashion and are articulated by representatives of the largest, most successful firms. They are propagated by the business press and informal links between organizations and then are supported by those organizations and their organizational fields.

Since 1880 there have been only four conceptions of control used by the leaders of the largest firms: direct control of competitors, manufacturing control, sales and marketing control, and finance control. These conceptions are not disembodied, idealist constructs. They emerged from the interaction among leaders of large firms and are conditioned by the state. They become successful by helping create organizational fields and by being accepted as principles to guide action within those fields. Once they prove successful, they disseminate across organizational fields. Each conception of control make use of a small number of consistent actions, or strategies. *Strategy* implies an explicit understanding of the goals of the organization and the construction of appropriate courses of action for reaching those goals.

The conception of the firm that emphasizes direct control of one's competitors became dominant in the late nineteenth century. At the time there were no rules governing behavior among competitors and there were no stable organizational fields. The intent of the conception of the firm that emerged under these chaotic conditions was to lessen competition. Managers and entrepreneurs, in an effort to achieve stability for their firms, attacked their most important competitors. Since there were few laws or rules guiding behavior, almost anything was acceptable. There were only two ways to protect one's firm: attack others before they attacked you or if this failed unite with your competitors to stop competition. Often firms moved from confrontation to cooperation. Within the direct control conception of the firm, three strategies were evident: predatory trade practices, cartelization, and monopolization.

The first strategy consisted of engaging in different forms of predatory competition. These included price competition, making it difficult for competitors to obtain raw materials for their production processes, and disrupting competitors' sales through legal and illegal means. Patents were another way to control competitors. Another tactic was secretly to purchase a competitor's stock and continue to operate the firm as a separate entity. An extension of this was for firms under common ownership to form what were called "communities of interest" to control competition. A large proportion of the antitrust suits in the early part of the twentieth century were directed toward these predatory trade practices.

The second strategy to directly control competitors was cartelization. Cartels involved elaborate written agreements to divide territory, assign production quotas, or set prices. Trade associations were often the vehicle for making these arrangements. Cartels were always defined around product lines and represented the first step toward establishing stable organizational fields.

The third control strategy was to try and create monopolies. Managers and entrepreneurs reasoned that if all of the productive forces of a given product line could be concentrated under a single ownership, then production and prices would stabilize. The merger movement at the turn of the century reflected the desire of managers and entrepreneurs to organize holding companies that would control a substantial portion of product lines.

The problem of controlling competition persisted well into the twentieth century. The manufacturing conception of control then attempted to solve it by stabilizing the production process and creating oligopolistic pricing conditions in organizational fields.

The central goal was to manufacture a product without interference from competitors by controlling inputs and outputs through the vertical and horizontal integration of production. These defensive measures tended to make the production process operate more effectively and lessen costs. Another part of this conception was to protect the firm by making it larger than its competitors. Once this control was achieved, then competitors would have less incentive for direct confrontation because they did not want to risk becoming engaged in a price war that would threaten everyone. From the manufacturing perspective, a firm's best way to control was stable, reliable, and cost-effective production.

The strategies pursued to achieve this control were backwards and forwards integration of production, mergers to increase market share, and the creation of oligopolistic product markets. Vertical integration meant that managers and entrepreneurs extended their control by absorbing suppliers and marketing functions into their organization. This protected them from the predatory acts of their competitors who would attempt to disrupt their suppliers or customers. It also lowered the overall cost of production and allowed firms to compete only with other large firms. A large market share obtained through mergers protected the production process of the firm by making it able to threaten competitors who might engage in price wars. Once a small number of large vertically integrated producers existed in a given organizational field, they used their market power to set up oligopolistic price structures. They would publicize their prices for a given commodity and because of their influence most of their competitors followed suit.

The sales and marketing conception of the firm began with the marketing revolution of the 1920s and came to dominate the largest firms in the post–World War II era. This conception of control emphasized that the key problem for firms was the selling of goods and therefore the solution was to expand sales. The sales and marketing conception focused the firm's attention on finding, creating, and keeping markets. The strategies that this conception inspired were oriented toward growth by nonpredatory competition. The view of what the corporation should be was radically altered from one focused on the destruction or control of competitors, to one concerned with its continuous expansion.

The sales and marketing perspective created a number of strategies: differentiation from competitors in terms of product quality and price; more advertising to increase market share; new products to stimulate growth; and expanded markets for existing goods, particularly overseas. Advertising was the major way in which firms were able to differentiate products from competitors and guarantee market share. Advertising also meant that price competition lessened as qualitative differences between products became important to their success. Expanding markets nationally and internationally allowed firms to continuously grow without cannibalizing their competitor's market share. The diversification of firms provided some security that when one product line faltered, another would emerge to take its place and produce growth. The organizational fields of the largest firms shifted from those based on products to those based on whole industries as firms diversified their product lines.

The finance conception of the modern corporation, which currently dominates, emphasizes control through the use of financial tools which measure performance according to profit rates. Product lines are evaluated on their short-run profitability and important management decisions are based on the potential profitability of each line. Firms are viewed as collections of assets earning differing rates of return, not as producers of given goods. The firm is not seen as being a member of only one industry. Consequently if the prospect of an industry in which it participates declines, the firm disinvests. The problem for management from this perspective is to maximize short-run rates of return by altering product mix, thereby increasing shareholder equity and keeping the stock price high.

The key strategies are: diversification through mergers and divestments (as opposed to internal expansion); financial ploys to increase the stock price, indebtedness, and ability to absorb other firms; and the use of financial controls to make decisions about the internal allocation of capital. The product mix of firms is less important in the finance conception because each of the firm's businesses are no longer product lines, but profit centers. Since the goal is to increase assets and profits, the organizational fields of the finance driven firms are no longer industrial based. Once large firms began to pay more attention to one another than to industries or products, strategic innovations that reflected the finance conception of control spread more rapidly across the population of the large firms. Currently, leveraged buyouts, stock repurchases, and corporate restructuring, which all reflect the finance conception, have disseminated throughout the largest firms as appropriate strategies for growth and profits.

The successive conceptions contain elements of their immediate predecessors: each was built on the insights and successes of what came before. The search for price stability was the central motivation of those who tried direct controls. Firms with the manufacturing perspective tried to achieve that price stability through the internal control of the production process and the creation of organizational fields based on oligopolisitic pricing. The sales and marketing conception lead to the realization that without sales, production ground to a halt. But the sales and marketing perspective was predicated on the ability to produce goods consistently and reliably for a mass market. The sales and marketing conception provided the impetus for developing the multiproduct, multidivisional firm. The basic insight of the finance conception was that such a firm could be more tightly controlled by strict accounting. This progression does not imply, however, that one conception of control caused the emergence of its successor. New conceptions of control evolved out of key interactions among firms and between firms and the state.

Structure refers to the design of the organization and the lines of authority that link the divisions of the organization and the divisions with the central office. In order to execute strategies, it is necessary in the large corporation to have a sound structure. To the degree that a given structure helps implement the strategies, it will vindicate and strengthen those strategies.

Five structures have been utilized for the large modern corporation: the trust, the holding company, and the unitary, functional, and multidivisional forms. The trust existed for only a few years in the late nineteenth century and represented a loose confederation of corporations. A holding company owns the stock of many companies which are operated from a small central office. The constituent firms often maintain their identities and are generally independent of one another. The unitary and functional forms are quite similar in design. The functional form organized production into departments that reflected the sequential movement of products through production stages. An oil company might contain drilling, shipping, refining, and sales departments, with a central office for financial matters. The unitary form is a simpler version of the functional form. It contains manufacturing, sales and marketing, and finance departments.

The multidivisional form organizes the large firm into product divisions. Each division is responsible for its manufacturing, sales, and financial performance. The central office monitors the divisions through financial controls and makes long-term decisions on investment for the firm. The multidivisional form attempts to distribute day-to-day decision making to executives who are close to production, while holding those same executives accountable for their performance. Almost all large modern corporations are organized into some version of the multidivisional form.

The power struggle within the firm determines which conception of control will dominate and how that conception will be translated into concrete strategies. The winners of this struggle will push the organization in a certain direction and maintain that direction as long as their strategies bring positive results. I use the term *subunit power base* to refer to the group in the organization that currently has claim on its strategy and structure. The power struggle in an organization over its goals takes place within the existing structure. A key position in the structure supplies actors in the struggle with a number of resources, the most important of which is authority. To the degree that owners and managers control their subordinates and can use their subordinates to deliver valuable goods, they can influence higher levels of the organization.

A powerful position in the structure provides actors with access to resources and continued input into the strategies of the organization. When the power relations are stable, then the structure and existing strategies will remain the same. When actors in key positions mobilize themselves and others, they can force strategies and structures to change.

Powerful positions can be characterized not just in terms of structure but also in terms of ideology and function. Actors in different subunits in the organization will think about the world differently. Their formal schooling and on-the-job training will make them see the organization and its problems in a particular way. Managers in charge of production will tend to see the problems of the firm as problems of production, while those in charge of sales will emphasize selling instead. These experiences will shape what organizational goals will be supported by subunit members and define in any given power struggle how members will act. Not surprisingly, the subunit in control will tend to pursue goals consistent with their subunit's view of the organization's critical problems.

Three significant subunits of any company involve its manufacturing, sales and marketing, and finance functions. Representatives of each subunit will organize criteria of success that will allow them to claim that a course of action did or did not achieve success. Their ability to take power will depend on how their conception of control operates as a convincing analysis of the firm's problems. That in turn will depend on what is occurring in the firm's organizational field and in its relations to the state. Once in power a subunit will implement strategies and structures consistent with their perspective. Fundamental change in a firm's direction will generally require a new resolution of the internal power struggle as those in established positions will not want to take actions that would undermine the status quo.

These three ways of analyzing the corporate world imply radically different courses of action. Indeed, executives with these different points of view will analyze any given situation in quite different terms. Since this suggests different interpretations of reality, the problem of deciding when a strategy is working or whether a competitor's strategy is superior is always going to be difficult. I use the term *successful* or *efficient* in this book to signify when actors perceive that a course of action produces superior results over some alternative course of action. Success is a qualitative construct that actors must come to agree about. In the world of managers, there are no profit maximizing or even satisficing actions. This is because such success is impossible to define strictly from the actor's point of view. Criteria of success are always relative to the organization and its field.

When managers pursue strategies which in the end are not profitable, it is because those actors with power have a limited view of the world. For example, the conglomerate strategy of merging unrelated firms to achieve growth spread quickly through the population of the largest firms. Yet most economic studies show that conglomerates did not earn higher profits than samples of similar size firms that were not pursuing that strategy.

The strategy spread and persisted for two reasons. First, conglomerate mergers produced spectacular rates of growth for firms. Executives in sales and marketing and finance pursued growth for its own sake, as that appeared to increase the stability and status of the firm. As long as profits were at acceptable levels and the stock price remained high, managers pursued growth. Competitors observed this and decided to emulate those actions. Second, once this view of mergers for growth became established, it became an institutionalized myth and accepted as one appropriate way to do business. While disinvestment occurred in the 1970s and early 1980s of many firms that pursued the conglomerate strategy, the largest firms have remained highly diversified despite the lack of evidence their performance was superior.

Organizational fields have shifted in definition from those based on product lines to industry to the population of the largest firms. These shifts have coincided with the shifts in the conception of the largest firms. Organizational fields depend on the actions of the largest firms for their stability. They also allow firms to monitor competitor's actions. They present like firms with evidence of appropriate strategies and structures and define acceptable courses of action for them. Managers may switch organizational fields in order to supply themselves with a new reference group, one that embodies a new strategy or structure and new possibilities for growth. When firms invade existing organizational fields or a firm in a given field develops a new strategy or structure that produces positive results, then executives in other firms follow those examples. One way to determine the existence and boundaries of organizational fields is to assess the limits of the spread of given conceptions, strategies, and structures.

The *state* has been the central arbiter of legal and illegal market behavior on the part of firms. The American government has influenced the American economy in a unique way. The practices that emerged in the largest firms were a response to the state's perception of a need to control markets. These practices reflect only one way of responding to the situation and, as such, are not provided by an a prior reading of the logic of markets. Rather, they are best viewed as a result of the strategic interaction between actors in the state and actors in firms. In this sense, markets in the abstract do not suggest anything about how to organize production. That organization is an outcome of social processes whereby firms interact with one another and the state to produce what can be called a market.

Periodization of Strategies, Structures, and the State

In order to see the historical changes that occur, one cannot begin by claiming that those changes have produced the best, that is, most efficient, organizational forms. This is an extremely teleological way to view history and one that would require comparative historical analysis to sustain. Given the state of our economy today, it would be hard to argue that the large diversified American firm is the most competitive organization in the world. Hence, to argue that the most efficient is what survived is to misunderstand the actual historical process by which the large firms emerged.

An organizational and institutional history reads history forward, not backward. In this book I will attempt to analyze developments from the point of view of the actors involved. By pursuing this strategy and using the organizational theory of the state and firms just proposed, we can recover a nonfunctionalist history of the large modern corporation.

New conceptions of control emerged where stable organizational fields had not existed. A new conception proved its worth by providing stability and profits for its leading practitioners. Once established, new fields remained in existence for long periods of time. Their construction was the solution to the problem of control and helped create norms that guided action in their fields and neighboring ones.

The preconditions for a new conception of control to emerge were two-fold. Some form of economic crisis often provided a stimulus for innovation. In the case of unstable organizational fields, that condition was chronic. The economic depressions of the late nineteenth century proved pivotal in the emergence of direct control. Similarly, the Depression of the 1930s proved the worth of the sales and marketing conception. The transition from manufacturing control to sales and marketing control resulted when firms were relatively more successful with diversified product strategies.

The state provided the second precondition for the construction of a new course of action. This worked in two ways. First, the state had to decide whether or not the conception of control was legal. Second, the state often took actions that blunted the course of a given conception and thereby opened up the possibility for a new course of action. The state was crucial in the shift from direct control to manufacturing control and the shift from sales and marketing control to finance control. In the first case, it ruled that all forms of direct control were illegal. In the second, the state encouraged mergers for diversification indirectly by banning vertical and horizontal mergers.

The conception of control through direct means had its origins in the post–Civil War era. In this period there were no established organizational fields, no rules to guide trade practices, and no established way to do business. The economy of the period was characterized by periods of growth, followed by inevitable decline because of too much competition. With a rapid expansion of markets and relatively high profit margins, the quantity of goods available increased dramatically. But markets quickly became saturated and there was downward pressure on prices. Many firms were caught with too many goods, too few buyers, and too low prices. Bankruptcies occurred, firms started laying off workers, and demand fell. This situation produced three substantial depressions between 1870 and 1895.

Economic theory predicts that a firm will produce until it no longer can make a profit. Unfortunately, in the nineteenth century world, firms continued to produce well beyond the point of zero profitability. This was because entrepreneurs incurred substantial costs in shutting down their plants. An idle plant meant their investment was worthless. If they had borrowed money to open the plant, then they were pressured by creditors to keep the plant running to prevent bankruptcy. As long as production continued the firm might lose money, but it might outlast its competitors and eventually begin to make money again.

Leading executives of the time all decried the cutthroat competition. What they desired was price stability and a fair return on their investments. But, there was no way to achieve such goals. There were no rules governing competitive behavior, so firms engaged in many ruthless practices to destroy their competition. Aggressive trade tactics failed as frequently as they succeeded, which forced managers and entrepreneurs to consider cooperative forms of organization. The formation of trade associations or cartels to divide market share, assign production quotas, and set prices were the first attempts at cooperation.

The impetus toward direct forms of control was most strongly felt in the rapidly expanding sectors of the economy where capital investment was the greatest: railroads, steel, oil, and the emerging chemical and electrical machinery industries. The effort to directly control one's competitors was felt most acutely where there was the most to lose. For instance, cartels formed in capital intensive industries where profits were falling. But cartel arrangements were inherently unstable. They were not enforceable by law, hence, there was no legislated consequence for cheating on the agreement. Further, firms who were not party to the agreement could choose to enter the market and undersell the members of the cartel.

While managers and entrepreneurs were trying to regulate competition, the politicians and judges who controlled the state and federal governments consistently opposed such arrangements. This was despite the fact that the state and federal governments generally favored economic development and passed laws granting railroads, merchants, and capitalists great latitude, including creating the limited liability joint stock corporation which was already common by 1870.

The relationship between the state and the emerging large corporations, however, was complicated by a number of factors. The fragmented character of the political system granted the federal government authority to regulate interstate commerce and gave the states power only over intrastate commerce. Firms had to conform to the rules of the state where they did business and that state had the right to grant them corporate charters. Corporate activities could be strictly limited by state actions, which would appear to have given the states a great deal of power over corporations. But as interstate commerce expanded states lost their ability to control corporations from a different state. They could not interfere with interstate commerce and the courts consistently ruled against the states and for interstate corporations. Since the states did not have uniform incorporation acts, it was advantageous for firms to incorporate in states with the most favorable policy. Managers and entrepreneurs of the largest interstate firms became capable of dictating the rules by which they did business.

Managers and entrepreneurs never got the upper hand when it came to directly interfering with the operation of competitive markets. There was a long tradition in Anglo-American law to make restraints of trade illegal. Almost every state had laws preventing agreements between parties to restrict production or control prices. Firms formed cartels in spite of these laws as they were willing to do anything to control competition. The long-standing stricture against cartels was formalized in the Sherman Antitrust Act of 1890. The act was most successfully used against arrangements that involved a "conspiracy in restraint of trade."

In Europe during the nineteenth century the governments were generally more favorable toward collusive behavior. Laws existed that made cartel agreements enforceable contracts. As a result they became the major strategy for coping with competition. Representatives of large firms would gather and divide markets by product and region. These cartels had the effect of providing a market for everyone and made even the smallest firms viable. Firms would be sanctioned by other firms for breaking cartel shares by either being denied raw materials or having their markets taken over by other cartel members. Since the cartel agreements were legal, firms had great incentives to comply with them.

Given that cartels were unenforceable contracts in the United States and therefore inherently unstable, there were three alternative strategies of control over competition and prices. First, firms continued to engage in predatory trade practices to destroy their competitors through any means possible. Second, firms tried to have the federal government regulate industries in order to stabilize prices and profits. In the nineteenth century only the railroads tested the strategy and only in the twentieth century did it succeed. Third, firms could end competition by combining the assets in a given product line.

The issue of how to control one's competitors legally was paramount in the late nineteenth century. The trust was formed in the late 1880s as an attempt to avoid the laws that prohibited cartels. Managers and entrepreneurs gave ownership in their firms to a collectively held trust, which was administered by a board of trustees who most often were the same people who operated the constituent parts of the trust. In return they received shares in the trust equal to the assets they brought to it. The trust was short-lived, however, because state government officials used existing statutes to sanction them. The courts ruled that corporations that formed trusts were restraining trade and that continued participation in the trust would nullify their corporate charters. In the face of these problems the trust form disappeared and was replaced by the holding company.

The holding company was a financial device whereby individual firms were bought by one company with controlling stock in each of them. The firms ran semiautonomously with only financial control emanating from the central office. Since holding companies incorporated in states that allowed corporations to hold stock in other corporations, there was little that state governments could do to prevent their existence. Cases against violators of the Sherman Act in the mid- and late 1890s upheld the right of holding companies to produce near monopolies, yet cartels were ruled to be illegal.

The legality of the holding company and the desire of managers and entrepreneurs to control competition produced the merger movement at the turn of the century. Since, cartels were illegal and holding companies were not, firms jumped on the merger bandwagon. Between 1895 and 1905, 35 percent of the assets of American manufacturers were involved in mergers. Industries that had tried cartels were now most likely to engage in consolidation.

The attempt to create monopolies did not end the problem of competition, however. By 1919, about 60 percent of the large mergers had failed. Businesses achieved no economies of scale by consolidating into large corporations. In fact, production costs often increased because firms were difficult or impossible to manage. Many of the industries were easy for other firms to enter and using predatory trade practices to stop them could prove grounds for an antitrust suit.

In the late nineteenth century state governments protected competition in the American economy. But during the first twenty years of this century the federal government assumed this role. The Progressive era in American politics can be interpreted in two ways: as a liberal era when middle-class reformers adopted populist ideology and attempted to ameliorate some of the worst qualities of the emerging industrial order, or as the triumph of big business. Both interpretations have merit. On the one hand, liberal reformers were not trying to destroy the large firm. On the other hand, legislation such as the Federal Reserve Act furthered the interests of one fraction of capital. The major pieces of legislation to regulate firm relations were the Clayton Act and the Federal Trade Commission Act.

The Clayton Act was an attempt to outlaw specific types of competitive behavior that were thought to lead to monopoly conditions. These included purchasing a competitor's stock to control its actions, tying agreements to force customers to buy nonessential materials in order to get essential materials, and predatory pricing behavior. The authors of the Clayton Act had no intention of attacking already existing corporate concentration, but were oriented toward preventing unfair advantages of one firm over another. The Federal Trade Commission (FTC) was set up to control unfair trade practices, especially price fixing. Its actions were consistent with an economic ideology that defined anticompetitive behavior as collusive direct control of prices. Both acts were consistent with the theory of "restraints of trade" and neither was meant to undermine the power of large firms.

The Sherman Act was also used to great effect during the Progressive era. Starting with the Northern Securities decision in 1904, enforcers pursued the firms that most closely approached predatory monopolies. The Supreme Court forced Standard Oil, DuPont, and American Tobacco to divest a substantial portion of their businesses. The laws against price fixing, cartels, monopolization, or other forms of direct control were enforced consistently. The problem of competition for the large firm, therefore, persisted well into the twentieth century. Without collusive arrangements, prices, profits, and market shares were always threatened. Indeed, before World War I the economy continually drifted in and out of recession. The war then provided a market for goods and caused wages, prices, and profits to rise. After the war, prices and wages remained high and that fueled a great period of growth in the 1920s.

The only stable solution to the problem of competition was the manufacturing conception, which emerged when all of the more direct strategies of control were made illegal. The manufacturing conception of control developed in fields of single products or industries and those tended to be the highly capital-intensive industries, that is, steel, oil, and electrical machinery. The key managers in this endeavor were those engaged in manufacturing the product, since they had the most knowledge of the production process.

Two features of these fields worked together to bring them stability: large firms that were willing to be price leaders and a successful organizational structure, that is, the unitary and functional forms. Large market share gave the leading firm sufficient influence to set prices and the integrated production apparatus gave it the ability to enforce them by undercutting competitors. The holding company had not been able to coordinate the day-to-day activities of a large number of plants because the central office could not effectively regulate the flow of products. Indeed, single plants could often adapt more easily to changes in supply or demand. Hence, the functional and unitary forms solved the problem by controlling the flow of production.

This tactic of controlling prices was not illegal because there was no direct collusion. One of the leading advocates of the new manufacturing conception was the U.S. Steel Company, which had been formed during the merger movement. Indeed, the antitrust suit against U.S. Steel was decided in its favor: the firm had not intentionally used its large size to damage its competitors. Once it became evident that large vertically integrated firms could control prices legally as oligopolists, the manufacturing conception began to spread. The peak for the manufacturing conception of control was reached during the merger movement of the 1920s.

There were two major reasons why the second merger movement occurred. Mergers were profitable in key industries such as steel, oil, electrical equipment, and chemicals; and the federal government was lax in enforcing the antitrust laws. The Clayton Act, for instance, was interpreted in a very narrow fashion by the Supreme Court, thereby nullifying any effect it might have had on the merger movement. Managers and entrepreneurs, therefore, took this opportunity to increase their market share and stabilize their industry, like the steel industry twenty years earlier, without opposition from the antitrust authorities.

Section 7 of the Clayton Act outlawed the purchase of competitors' stock when doing so would lessen competition. The intent of the law was at least partially to impede the development of monopolies. Four Supreme Court cases were heard in the 1920s which tested this law. Three of the cases involved firms that had purchased the assets and then stock of other firms. One of the cases was against a firm that had purchased the stock first and then the assets. In all four cases the Supreme Court decided for the purchasing firms even though there was evidence the mergers would have anticompetitive effects. Their defense had been that the Clayton Act forbade purchase of stock not assets and therefore the mergers were perfectly legal. When stock was purchased first, but assets were acquired subsequently, the Supreme Court decided there was no case. On the basis of this interpretation of the Clayton Act, any attempts at slowing the merger movement through litigation were eliminated.

The manufacturing solution to competition was successful but placed limits on growth because it was a defensive tactic. In economic downturns, vertically integrated firms faced rapidly declining markets. Since collusion was disallowed, those firms with large investments in fixed capital stock were still vulnerable. The largest firms continued their efforts to control competition through the 1920s and expanded them during the 1930s. Their managers and owners favored some form of legalized price fixing before the Depression.

The National Industrial Recovery Act gave firms the right to set reasonable prices and workers the right to unionize. The philosophy of the act was to increase profits by increasing prices, thereby expanding business. Unions would guarantee higher wages and job security and workers would have more money, thereby increasing consumption. The effect of the act, however, was to raise prices but not production and consumption. It failed to produce industrial recovery as promised and would have disappeared had it not been declared unconstitutional in 1935. The Roosevelt Administration's economic policy drifted for the next several years, trying only government spending to stimulate consumption. In 1937, Roosevelt shifted his policy to vigorous enforcement of the antitrust laws.

At the same time, the sales and marketing conception was emerging in organizational fields where oligopolies did not exist and rules of competition of the manufacturing conception had not yet triumphed. These firms tended to be in consumer product industries such as food, drugs, chemicals, automobiles, and other durables. The marketing revolution had begun during the 1920s when managers and entrepreneurs realized that products had life cycles. This meant that firms needed to have a mix of products, some new and some mature, to insure continued growth in the firm.

As firms began to produce related products, a shift occurred in the organizational fields of the large firms. Managers and entrepreneurs began to define their fields in broader terms. They participated in many markets with different competitors depending on the product. Marketing departments gained power because they knew how to sell the products and how to find new markets. The sales and marketing conception began when one firm in an industry pursued product diversification and spread when others followed.

This new conception of the firm required a new structure. The multidivisional form became the accepted organizational structure for the large corporation between 1920 and 1970, with the greatest diffusion after World War II. For many of the firms the marketing function within each division became quite powerful by dictating the schedules, innovation, and introduction of products. The central office monitored their progress and overall contribution to the firm's growth and profits, and also approved large-scale development projects.

During the Depression diversified firms outperformed nondiversified firms. When most of the vertically integrated firms were seeking government aid in raising prices, sales and marketing-oriented firms introduced new products at a high rate, indeed higher than during the 1920s. Managers and entrepreneurs realized they needed to sell products to survive, and if traditional markets declined then the firm had to enter new markets.

Because the government had a narrow definition of monopoly, diversification did not seem threatening at this time. Consequently by 1950 it was the primary strategy of big business in America. Several events between 1940 and 1960 reinforced this trend. One was increased antitrust activity in the 1940s. Beginning in 1937, Roosevelt encouraged Thurman Arnold, head of the Antitrust Division, to make creative use of the antitrust laws. After World War II, antitrust prosecution reached an all-time peak. The largest firms were constantly being threatened by the federal government and by 1950 about half of the 100 largest firms had an antitrust suit pending against them.

In the late 1930s several people throughout the federal government wanted to use the antitrust laws to increase competition in the American economy. Thurman Arnold headed the Antitrust Division, a modern, professional corps of lawyers who worked toward that end. In the Congress, Senator Joseph O'Mahoney and Representatives Estes Kefauver and Emmanuel Celler became interested in the issue. The federal trade commissioners also became more active in studying and prosecuting violations of the antitrust laws. These people were brought together by the formation of the Temporary National Economic Commission (TNEC) in 1937. The commission concluded that the central problem in the economy was the existence of large firms which tended to create monopolies or oligopolies in key markets. While the commission had little immediate legislative or policy impact, it set the stage for more vigorous antitrust enforcement in the postwar era.

The TNEC recommended altering Section 7 of the Clayton Act to outlaw anticompetitive mergers through the purchase of assets, thereby closing the loophole in the act. The antitrust community, with the FTC in the lead, began to push for that legislation after World War II because they argued that mergers were increasing. Kefauver and Celler guided the legislation through Congress. They introduced bills to amend the Clayton Act in every session of Congress from 1945 on. The final bill passed in 1950 when Democrats controlled both the House and the Senate.

The Celler-Kefauver Act was intended to slow the growth of monopoly by preventing firms from increasing their product concentration. While the act was also intended to prevent mergers among firms that were producing related or unrelated products, it rarely succeeded. The Celler-Kefauver Act was most often applied to horizontal and vertical mergers. The dominant theory of antitrust at the time was that concentration within product lines restricted competition. The unintended consequence of the Celler-Kefauver Act was that it set up the preconditions for the third large merger movement. But the mergers of the late 1950s and 1960s did not produce monopolies or oligopolies. Instead they produced conglomerates and the large modern diversified multinational firm.

The finance, and most recent, conception of the firm developed for two reasons. In order to grow, large firms needed to diversify. The sales and marketing conception had continued to prove profitable, but lacked a way to direct diversification. Those who controlled the firm lacked the expertise to evaluate new products on their own merits. As a result, investments began to be made only on a financial basis. The implementation of financial controls and advanced accounting systems, therefore, shifted power in the large firms to those who could judge whether a product made money. Firms then paid more attention to short-run objectives. Instead of building a new plant which might take years to show a profit, it was easier to buy an existing company.

The second impetus for the finance conception was the antitrust environment, which was hostile toward large firms in general and horizontal and vertical mergers in particular. The first Supreme Court decisions after the passing of the Celler-Kefauver Act made mergers illegal between relatively small firms with moderate market shares. The large firms quickly responded and stopped merging for market share. Instead, they turned their attention to product related and unrelated mergers as a strategy for growth.

From 1945 to 1969 the largest firms rapidly diversified mostly through mergers. The business community had one important example of the pure financial strategy: the acquisitive conglomerate. The acquisitive conglomerates were built by people on the edges of the American corporate sector, often outside New York, where most of the large firms were located. Many of the original conglomerates had been in declining industries and then their founders removed them from their established organizational fields. Using financial ploys, these executives parlayed the smaller firms into larger firms through mergers and the floating of debt. By 1955 the conglomerate strategy of buying disparate firms and creating a large highly diversified corporation was already well known. The emergence of Textron, Ling-Temco-Vought (LTV), International Telephone and Telegraph (ITT), Litton Industries, and Gulf and Western in the early 1960s, encouraged other firms to try instant growth through mergers.

The finance conception remade the organizational fields of the largest firms. Managers saw that the acquisitive conglomerates merged their way into the ranks of the largest industrial enterprises in a short period of time. This caused managers in otherwise stable organizational fields that were defined by industry to shift their attention from their position in the industry to their position in the hierarchy of large American corporations. While the acquisitive conglomerate garnered much attention, the most important phenomenon in the economy was the spread of product-related diversification strategies to firms such as Rockwell International, W.R. Grace, Thompson-Ramo-Wooldridge (TRW), and Minnesota Mining and Manufacturing (3M). It eventually also spread to firms in the staid oil and steel industries. The finance conception rose to prominence and today still dominates the actions of the largest U.S. firms.

The merger movement of the 1960s, however, ended for two reasons. First, when the stock market crashed in 1969, money for mergers got tighter. Equally important was the antitrust policy of the Nixon Administration. John Mitchell, then attorney general, announced in 1969 that all mergers of large corporations would be pursued under the amended Clayton Act. Richard McLaren, the head of the Justice Department Antitrust Division, prepared highly publicized cases against ITT, LTV, and other acquisitive conglomerates. Soon thereafter mergers slowed considerably.

The Mitchell-McLaren antitrust policy was abandoned in 1972. The Supreme Court no longer accepted the government's arguments regarding Section 7 of the Clayton Act. Antitrust cases had been built mostly on the potential, not the actual, anticompetitive effects of increased product concentration. In order to apply those laws to product related and unrelated mergers, those arguments had to extend to show how those mergers were potentially anticompetitive. Consequently some scholars and people in the private antitrust community began to question whether or not mergers in fact restricted competition. Most thought that mergers were probably creating more efficient organizations. The core of their counterargument was that the government's cases needed to concentrate not only on the structural effects of mergers on an industry, but on the performance of firms in that industry.

The Nixon appointees to the Supreme Court were more sympathetic to their perspective. In 1973 and 1974 the Supreme Court limited the use of the Celler-Kefauver Act for product related and unrelated mergers and even limited its applicability in horizontal and vertical mergers. The Antitrust Division under Ronald Reagan basically abandoned its enforcement and mergers have greatly accelerated in recent years initiating the fourth large merger movement.

By 1979 finance presidents were the single largest group of presidents of the 100 largest firms. Finance-oriented executives are not committed to any given industry and no longer identify their firms in market terms. Instead, the population of the largest firms is now the reference group for these managers. Nonetheless, because many of the firms are in one or two major industries, they must continue to monitor competition in those industries.

The current vogue is to argue that the economy should be left alone. Investment decisions, merger decisions, and industrial policy should be placed in the hands of the largest firms who are most influential in the marketplace. But this argument ignores the fact that over time firms have operated under different conceptions which resulted from the dynamic interaction of the economic environment, the political environment, and the internal organization of the firm. The structures that are in place now are not the products of some pure process of competition. Nor has competition been weakened by the actions of government. Instead, what has come into existence is the result of a social and political process that defines and redefines markets. If left to their own devices, the managers of the largest firms would continue to do what they are doing. Eliminating government regulation and antitrust enforcement will not automatically produce a more competitive corporate world. The finance conception remains in effect and the incentives that produced it continue.

To view the economy and its development outside of the current conceptions of the actors dominating major institutions means one will not understand the actions of those institutions. One is also not likely to be able to anticipate what any political action oriented toward the economy is going to have. To argue that current conceptions somehow reflect the best of all possible worlds is neither historically informed nor scientific, but ideological. Instead, what has emerged is the product of large-scale social organization over a substantial period of time.

2

Direct Control, the State, and the Large Firm

Between the Civil War and the turn of the twentieth century, the American economy shifted from a bazaar economy to one based on production markets. At the beginning of this period, there were few corporations and those had highly limited charters that strictly controlled their actions. Production was small scale, product quality uneven, markets were local, and selling often was direct between the maker of the goods and the consumer. Individual producers made independent decisions on price, product, and quality. Often, local firms enjoyed near monopolies. The rules governing this form of trade were simple and the problems of overproduction were relatively minor.

In the years that followed rapidly growing capital-intensive organizations emerged which created many new markets, so-called production markets. This type of market is "a self-reproducing social structure among specific cliques of firms and other actors who evolve roles from observations of each other's behavior" (White, 1981, p. 518). The key feature of such markets is that their actors choose a course of action depending on what their competitors do. This makes the development of a shared-market schedule of production quite difficult. In other words, these markets were often unstable: competition was severe, overproduction endemic, and business tactics were brutal. There were no accepted practices, no dominating conception of control, and no well-defined organizational fields.

The conception of direct control developed from 1865 to 1904 to deal with this lack of stability. Newly formed large-scale organizations needed rules to govern their interaction. The state and federal governments were mainly reactive and did little to stabilize competitive relations. Therefore, for the individual manager or entrepreneur, the only way to ensure the survival of their organization was to attempt to directly control the actions of others. Three strategies were used by the largest firms: predatory trade practices, cartelization, and mergers.

Predatory trade practices were the most common form of direct control. Their major purpose was aggressive: destroy your competitors. Managers and entrepreneurs consciously undercut their competitors' prices; undertook to deny direct access to raw materials, essential technologies, and customers; secretly purchased their competitors' stock; and, in the extreme, engaged in illegal disruption of production and sales. The problem with this form of competition was that even after a firm destroyed its most important adversaries, it often had to face opposition from new ones. Further, one could as easily be the victim of these practices as the victor. In all, direct control using predatory strategies did not offer much stability to the managers and owners of large firms. Still, when all else failed, firms continuously resorted to these survival tactics precisely because there were few alternatives.

The costs of predatory competition were high to all participants, which encouraged managers and entrepreneurs to try to directly control competition through cooperation. Cartels, one form of product-based cooperation, were organized in a number of ways. Often trade associations were formed to divide markets, set prices, and regulate production. When the number of corporate actors was small, they made explicit agreements to control competition. The railroads, for example, came together to set prices for various classes of freight. Cartelization failed, however, because contracts to control prices and production were illegal and therefore unenforceable. When they failed, there were often periods of intensified competition, followed by renewed attempts at cartelization.

The various levels of government and the courts generally supported corporations, but in this one area consistently ruled against the interests of large firms. The issue was simple: actions by firms to control prices were anticompetitive and, hence, illegal. These restraints of trade tended to benefit one segment of the community over others as they undermined the power of market forces to determine prices. The government was not swayed even as the largest firms were threatened by competition.

The final strategy of direct control was the horizontal merger. Its aim was to control a sufficient quantity of the assets in an industry and thereby stabilize production and price. The logic of this approach was to avoid the difficulty of maintaining cartels by uniting the owners of firms into a single firm. After the depression of the early 1890s, a merger movement began which created large corporations in the form of holding companies. The role of the law in this movement was complex. While cartels were illegal, the conventional wisdom at the time was that tight combinations— mergers that created monopolies or near monopolies—were not illegal, even if they were intended to restrain trade.

Creating rules by which the system of firms would be governed was always a complicated issue for the various levels of government. The Constitution provided the states with a great deal of control within their borders, but specified that the federal government held sway over interstate commerce. The rights of private property often came into conflict with the rights of the states and federal government. The growth of corporations and their role in interstate trade led to difficult problems for a political and legal system built to regulate an agrarian economy. The courts often had to decide cases that revolved around such issues.

In the nineteenth century politicians were still dependent on the votes of a rural population. Further, voters in the cities had working-class interests. So the state and federal governments were confronted by interest groups who were unhappy with industrialization. Farmers, workers, and merchants claimed to suffer from capitalist development, emphasizing the railroads and other emerging large firms. In response, the government tried to walk carefully between the contending groups.

Early nineteenth-century law did not recognize the corporation as an actor with rights and privileges. Indeed, it was late in that century that a corporation was defined and rules to govern it were established. Government agencies had to answer central questions. Who would charter and control corporations? What rights did corporations have? How would the various groups in society relate to rapid economic development? The political and legal solutions attempted to blend the interests of the various groups in terms of the dominant economic and legal theories of the time. They were worked out in the following way.

After the Civil War, the federal government and the federal courts tended to favor corporations for promoting interstate trade, which often hampered the states' ability to regulate trade. The establishment of corporations as entities with rights, like individuals, led to greater and greater freedom for corporations. States felt that local economic development was aided by foreign, that is, out-of-state, corporations and severe regulation could undermine internal development, as well as tax revenues.

Nonetheless, federal courts attempted to leave the regulation of business within a state to that state. Incorporation and the rules of corporations were left up to the states. The courts maintained a states-rights ideology unless disputes involved interstate commerce. Then as interstate commerce expanded, the role of the federal courts increased in spite of their desire to honor states' rights. They began to protect the rights of corporations over those of individual states under the guise of protecting interstate commerce and private property.

Antitrust law helped bring order to this complex nexus of interactions. Looking at formation and implementation of the Sherman Act from 1888 to 1904 is one way to examine the important political and economic debates of the late nineteenth century. The effect of this law was that by 1895 the horizontal merger, not coercion or cooperation, was the organizational tactic most actors employed to control their collective fates.

The terms *loose* and *tight* combination in this discussion refer to the interorganizational links between firms when the goal was cooperation. Loose combinations meant that the bonds were fewer and the identities of the individual organizations were maintained. The tighter cooperation became, the more bonds existed and the more the identities of the participants became merged. The purpose of moving from loose to tighter combinations was to gain more direct control of competition. My argument suggests that what propelled firms toward tighter forms of cooperation was the failure of predatory trade practices and loose combinations to solve the problems of competition. The only strategy of direct control that seemed to promise stability, and was legal was tight combination, or the merger of firms.

The loosest combinations were those of firms who came together to form a cartel or pool in order to control prices or production. Trusts were legal loose combinations of firms that gave their stock to a central trust, which was then controlled by a committee of the owners of each individual firm. Decisions about production and price were made collectively, with the larger units having more say. The trust was a tighter combination organizationally than a cartel because firms operated within a legal framework, but maintained their separate identities. The next tighter combination in the continuum was the holding company. A main office held the stock of all the constituent parts, thus, ownership and decision making were combined, but the identities of separate units were still somewhat intact. The tightest combination occurred when the individual firms actually lost their identities by becoming one integrated firm under a unitary or functional structure.

The conception of direct control and its strategies dominated American business into the twentieth century. This conception failed primarily because the tactics it constructed from loose forms of control to tight ones became illegal.

The Economic Background of the Late Nineteenth Century

After the Civil War America experienced a great expansion of its economic base in terms of geography, technology, organization, and product. Manufacturing activity increased four-fold from 1870 to 1900, while employment tripled. In 1869 the petroleum, chemical, steel, and machine-making industries were all in their infancy. The two largest industries were food and textiles. While they grew continuously during the period, both were overtaken by the rapidly growing petroleum, steel, and machine making industries. The railroads also grew phenomenally. In 1870 there were about 60,000 miles of track. By 1900, when investments in railroads reached $10 billion, there were 258,784 miles (U.S. Bureau of the Census, 1960, p. 409).

Between 1860 and 1900 the importance of agriculture in the economy decreased and manufacturing and mining increased substantially. Within the mining sector, the most rapid increases were in the coal, petroleum, and cement industries. The greatest growth in metal production was in copper, iron, gold, and lead. By 1875 the United States exported more raw materials and foodstuffs than it imported. By 1900 the country also tipped the balance of trade in finished manufactured goods (U.S. Bureau of the Census, 1960, pp. 540–541).

Three severe economic downturns also occurred during this

period—1873 to 1877, 1885 to 1887, and 1893 to 1897—and the last was the most severe (Hoffman, 1970, p. 4). The major cause of all three was a general crisis of overproduction. Firms extended themselves so far that when the markets for their products failed to materialize, those deepest in debt went bankrupt. This often set off a chain reaction of further economic decline and more bankruptcies.

At the same time, prices for all major commodities fell because of more efficient production and increasing competition. The entire economy experienced booms and busts as activity would lurch forward and then suddenly decline when prices dropped too far with the increased production.

The Cartel Strategy

Andrew Carnegie, writing in the *North American Review* in 1889 (pp. 141–142), summed up the economic situation:

> Goods will not be produced at less than cost. This was true when Adam Smith wrote, but it is not quite true today. When an article was produced by a small manufacturer, employing, probably at his own home, two or three journeymen and an apprentice or two, it was an easy matter for him to stop production. As manufacturing is carried on today, in enormous establishments with five or ten millions of dollars of invested capital and with thousands of workers, it costs the manufacturer much less to run at a loss per ton or per yard than to check his production. While continuing to produce may be costly, the manufacturer knows too well that stoppage would be ruin. His brother manufacturers are, of course, in the same situation. They see the savings of years, as well, perhaps as the capital they have succeeded in borrowing, becoming less and less, with no hope of change in the situation. It is in soil thus prepared that anything promising relief is gladly welcomed. Combinations, syndicates, trusts—they will try anything.

Forms of direct competition during good times tended not to threaten the existence of all firms. When rapid growth slowed and competition intensified, profit margins were threatened and managers and owners of firms would undertake to organize their industries. Table 2.1 presents a list of fifty-eight product lines where some form of pooling or cartels existed between 1865 and

1898. This list is based on a reading of turn of the century sources and probably understates the amount of cartelization. Generally, the term cartel or pool is used to indicate any attempts by the members of an industry to formally control production or prices. Many different kinds of schemes were tried over the years.

There are two points to examine in order to understand the cartel strategy. First, cartels were undertaken to directly control competition through cooperation. In almost every case, actors in the firms were not trying to collect monopoly rents, but instead were trying to guarantee themselves an adequate profit and continued existence. The purpose was to stabilize the organizational fields, defined in product terms, and guarantee market share, price stability, and a profit for all of the firms in the agreement. Second, cartels emerged in those industries which were creating the first production markets, markets characterized by a high level of capital investment.

One case of cartelization was the railroad companies. Because all suffered in a prolonged rate war, railroads were constantly trying to control their markets by forming pools or cartels to quell competition. Despite all efforts to control rate wars, railroad rates still decreased from 2.5 cents per ton mile in 1878 to .7 cents in 1901 (Ripley, 1913, p. 413). The most severe rate wars occurred over the lines that connected New York City and Chicago. This link was the busiest in the United States and railroad rates in the rest of the country generally followed the rates between those two cities (Gilchrist, 1960). In 1874 there were four major lines that connected the two cities. One of the lines, the Baltimore and Ohio, was then denied access to the New York market. It retaliated by cutting rates and diverting traffic from New York City to Baltimore and Philadelphia. All of the lines later joined in the rate cutting. Finally, in 1877, under pressure from investors in New York and Europe, the four railroads agreed to create the Trunk Line pool (Benson, 1955, pp. 46–49; Kolko, 1965, pp. 17–28). The first head of the Trunk Line pool was Albert Fink. Fink had been a railroad executive with the Louisville and Nashville Railroad and had organized a large and successful pool in the South in 1875.

The pools, however, were unstable. Albert Fink, in testimony for the Cullom Committee (U.S. Senate, 1886, p. 10), which was considering legislation to regulate railroads, said in reference to the instability of pools:

Table 2.1 Product lines that experienced some cartelization between 1865
and 1898

Product	Source for information[a]
Sugar	U.S.I.C.,[b] Stevens (1913), Ripley (1905)
Whiskey	U.S.I.C., Jenks (1889)
Oil	U.S.I.C., Clark (1928)
Pipelines	U.S.I.C., Clark (1928)
Railroads	U.S.I.C., Ripley (1913)
Tin plate	U.S.I.C., Clark (1928)
Steel plate	Clark (1928)
Rails	Jenks (1900), Clark (1928)
Silverware	U.S.I.C.
Glucose	U.S.I.C.
Corn flour	U.S.I.C.
Corn oil	U.S.I.C.
Steel wire	Clark (1928)
Steel hoop	Clark (1928)
Shears	Clark (1928)
Nails	Clark (1928), Edgerton (1897)
Salt	Jenks (1888)
Iron and steel	U.S.I.C.
Merchant marine	U.S.I.C., Ripley (1905)
Asphalt	U.S.I.C.
Shipbuilding	U.S.I.C.
Meatpacking	Jeans (1894)
Cottonseed oil	Jeans (1894)
Beer	Jeans (1894)
Milk	Jeans (1894)
Coal (anthracite)	Jeans (1894)
Envelopes	Stevens (1913)
Tobacco	Stevens (1913)
Table and oilcloth	Stevens (1913)
Wallpaper	Stevens (1913)
Rubber	Stevens (1913)
Plumbing supplies	Stevens (1917)
Explosives	Stevens (1912)
Aluminum	Stevens (1917)
Leather	Dewing (1914)
Rope	Dewing (1914)
Light electrical goods	Dewing (1914)
Malt	Dewing (1914)
Cotton goods	Dewing (1914)
Baking powder	Haney (1914)
Cotton bagging	Jones (1921)
Agricultural implements	Jones (1921)

Table 2.1 (continued)

Product	Source for information[a]
Pipe	Clark (1928)
Freight cars	Clark (1928)
Locomotives	Clark (1928)
Stoves	Clark (1928)
Thread	Clark (1928)
Shoe machinery	Clark (1928)
Paper	Clark (1928)
Straw board	Clark (1928)
Brick	Clark (1928)
Pottery	Clark (1928)
Glass	Clark (1928)
Fertilizer	Clark (1928)
Woolens	Lamoreaux (1985)
Bicycles	Lamoreaux (1985)
Sandpaper	Stevens (1913)
Felt	Stevens (1913)

a. Many industries had multiple citations. Generally, the most complete source is listed.

b. U.S.I.C. = U.S. Industrial Commission Report (1900).

Why are the tariffs [rates for various classes of freight] not enforced? Each railroad company is at liberty to deviate from the established tariff whenever it pleases, although it may have given voluntarily consent to it, and agreed to maintain it; yet, in the hope it may secure some advantage over its competitors, any one of the companies may enter into secret arrangements with shippers, and reduces the rates, in the hope of procuring a larger amount of business than it could otherwise attain . . . I venture to say that every complaint which may have been made against the railroads can be traced directly or indirectly, to the cause that I have just assigned, namely the strife between the railroads and other transportation companies to secure business for themselves and to take it away from others.

In spite of their constant failure, railroad pools became common after 1875 and by 1886 railroads in nearly all of the country participated in one pool or another (Ripley, 1913, p. 446). The southern pool was in place by 1875 and the Trunk Line agreement was made in 1877. In the west, pools emerged in New Mexico and Colorado. In 1875 the Texas Traffic Association was formed and in 1881 this agreement was reinforced in the division of the Texas railroads by Jay Gould and Colis Huntington. By 1886, all competitive traffic north and west of Chicago was pooled.

The Trans-Missouri Freight Association was an example of a typical pool. Its purpose was the "mutual protection of the railroad companies which were parties thereto, by establishing and maintaining reasonable rebates, rules, and regulations on all freight traffic."[1] It operated by dividing freight by regions and setting prices for classes of freight. In 1897 the Supreme Court ruled the association in violation of the Sherman Act. A similar pool was formed in the East called the Joint Traffic Association. Its purposes were identical to those of the Trans-Missouri Freight Association.[2] In 1898 the Supreme Court decided that it was also in violation of the Sherman Act.

None of the railroad pools survived for long. The central difficulty was that they could not be enforced by law and, therefore, it was impossible for railroads to control the behavior of their competitors. The repeated attempts to pool and their continuous failure only convinced railroad executives that until the practice was made legal, railroads would remain unstable (Benson, 1955, pp. 233–240; Gilchrist, 1960; Kolko, 1965, pp. 46–47). Again at the Cullom Committee hearings, Fink argued:

> The difficulty has not been in agreeing upon the proper tariffs [railroad rates for freight], but in carrying them into effect. The necessary means and machinery for that purpose have not been adopted, and there is no authority to enforce such agreements. The managers of railroads meet in convention, and make agreements which are broken as they disperse . . . I express it as my opinion, the result of the most careful consideration, that the only legislation required to accomplish the object which the most zealous advocate of the public interests can desire to accomplish, is to legalize, and even to enforce the cooperative system of the railroad companies. (U.S. Senate, 1886, pp. 18, 24)

Fink's admonitions to legalize pooling were not heeded. The result was that during the depression of the 1890s there was an enormous consolidation of the railroads (Campbell, 1938, pp. 30–62).

The salt industry also expanded greatly in the post–Civil War era. The first agreement to control salt production was made in

1868. This association ended when one of the largest members left in 1871. When the price of salt dropped in 1875, J.E. Shaw organized a meeting of the salt manufacturers with the following proposal:

> That the organization [of salt manufacturers] has remained inactive, is attributable to the fact that it could not secure control of a sufficiently large percentage of the state product to warrant aggressive action. And what was the result? Salt has depreciated in value, dropped steadily down. The oldest manufacturers of the Syracuse, Kanawha, and Ohio districts tell us that their experience has always been this: "Organized we have prospered. Unorganized we have not." This is the experience which we have been paying dearly for. The other salt districts of the United States are now organized and are ready to deal with us relative to fixing and maintaining prices, dividing the territory, and making other arrangements. But first we must be organized. (Jenks, 1888, p. 81)

The motives of the organizers of the association should be clear. In order to prevent the price of salt from declining, the manufacturers joined an association to pool their production. Under Shaw's leadership, the Michigan Salt Association was formed in 1876 to control the production of salt in that state (Jenks, 1888, p. 98). At that time the association controlled 85 percent of the Michigan production and 40 percent of the industry total.

The association operated by giving shares to each producer based on its capacity. Each year contracts were renewed with manufacturers whereby they agreed to deliver all of their products to the association and, in return, they received payment plus a 7 percent semiannual dividend. If members sold their salt outside the association, they agreed to pay the association 10 cents a barrel for every barrel sold. Jenks (1888, p. 100) argued that generally the manufacturers secured an average rate of return and stabilized the radical price swings in the industry. But the other salt pools, notably those in New York and Ohio, were less successful.

The whiskey pools reflected similar motives. After 1880 U.S. distilleries were capable of producing four times what the market could absorb. The president of their first pool, H. B. Miller, argued, "Some said: let this go on and let the fittest survive. Our experience was that a distiller would keep on going until all his own money and all he could borrow was gone, and then when he was used up, there was another man ready to step into his shoes" (Jenks, 1889, p. 100).

From 1880 on, whiskey pools were organized on a yearly basis, which sometimes worked and sometimes failed. The key issue was organization: how to divide and monitor production. Usually the plan was for each distillery to agree to production limits and then allow the firms to market on their own. But sometimes the group would have to subsidize members to get them to comply. The members also contributed to a special fund for underwriting the cost of exporting surplus production. In this way, whiskey shipped overseas at a lower price supported the artificially high domestic price.

Problems arose in pools around how to monitor the members. Jenks (1889, p. 102) noted that "provisions were also made for the examination of the government books of each distiller by the officers of the pool, in order to prevent deception and cutting of rates on the part of any distiller; but in spite of the high prices they were able to maintain in the pool, it was found that the temptations to secure sales by the cutting of prices were so great that members would violate the terms of agreement."

In response to these problems, the head of the whiskey pool addressed the association in 1886, leaving no question as to the motives of the organizers:

> That we shall over-produce for the holidays we all know. That we have already overproduced, figures will show . . . As long as we have funds to export the surplus, there will be no difficulty in maintaining prices. When goods accumulate without any outlet, then this is the time when the cutting commences. I am well convinced that there is cutting going on secretly now and unless some provision is made at once to arrest it, it will be done openly, until there is nothing left to the market. This is the problem for you to solve right here. You can fly in the face of providence if you see fit, but it will bring its own punishment with it. (Jenks, 1889, p. 103)

The whiskey pool was somewhat successful in its manipulation of prices. Indeed, it was the subject of two congressional inquiries in the late 1880s and early 1890s.[3] In 1887, the whiskey pool formalized its desire to control prices and production and formed the whiskey trust.

The iron and steel industry attempted to pool numerous times, beginning in the early 1860s. The great growth in the steel industry after the Civil War from expanded railroads and the building trades led to some of the earliest attempts to control markets. Charles Schwab, the president of U.S. Steel at its formation, testified that pools existed "in all lines of business, not only in steel, but in everything else. There were similar agreements, known as joint agreements, to maintain prices. They have existed in all lines of the business as long as I can remember" (U.S. Industrial Commission, 1900, vol. 13, p. 474).

The first attempt to organize the steel industry and restrict subsequent entry occurred in 1875 when the Bessemer Steel Association was formed to share by quota system the market for steel rails. The effort was unsuccessful as prices were low during that period because of the depression. In October 1877 the association was renewed. The manufacturers who utilized the Bessemer process restricted entry into the steel business by not allowing other firms access to the Bessemer patents. Even though they held a virtual monopoly on the production of steel rails, prices for rails did not increase appreciably as the demand for rails was relatively low (Clark, 1928, pp. 331–336).

In 1887 the steel rail pool was formed once again. The goal of the association was to control prices by restricting production: "We the before named companies and corporations, manufacturers of steel rails, hereby mutually agree one with the other, that we restrict our sales and the production of steel rails of 50 pounds to the yard and upward, and we respectively bind ourselves not to sell in excess of our current allotments without first obtaining the consent of the Board of Control" (U.S. Commissioner of Corporations, 1911, p. 69).

In spite of continuous attempts to control the price of steel rails, the Bessemer Association was not very successful. The price of rails was influenced much more by the expansion and contraction of the railroad lines (Clark, 1928, pp. 333–335; Temin, 1964, pp. 182–189). In the depression of the 1890s, the railroads were struck first and hardest and as a consequence the steel companies suffered too. The price of steel rails fell from $31.75 in 1890 to $17.62 in 1898 (Temin, 1964, p. 284). Prices for all other iron and steel products fell commensurately.

The Addyston Pipe Association was established to pool the

markets for iron and steel pipe in the South. "Whereas the system now in operation in this association of having a 'fixed bonus on the several states' has not in its operation resulted in the advancement of the prices of pipe as was anticipated, except in reserved cities, and some further action is imperatively necessary in order to accomplish the ends for which this association is intended" (Whitney, 1905, p. 90).

Testimony given at the antitrust trial from key members of the association also reveals its purpose. Mr. Bowron of the South Pittsburg Company said it was "to restrain competition as among defendants and allow each a profitable division of work according to its relative capacity, and thereby maintain fair prices to all."[4] Mr. Callahan, of Dennis Long and Co. said the purpose was "to maintain fair prices, regulate credits, and accomplish equitable distributions of such orders by regulating to a certain extent the competition among the defendants only."[5]

In practice, the determination of fair prices and territory was generally decided in committee. A typical example can be seen in a letter written by Mr. Nichols of the Bessemer Company to the other companies on January 24, 1896. "I prefer that if any of you find it necessary to put in a bid without going to St. Louis, please bid not less than $27.00 for the pipe, and 2¾ cents per pound for the specials. I would also like to know as to which of you would find it convenient to have a representative at the letting. It will be necessary to have two outside bidders."[6] This pool proved successful and ended only after the Supreme Court decided the association acted in violation of the Sherman Act.

The nail industry experienced a boom in the late 1880s and early 1890s. By 1895 the industry produced over market capacity and prices were low (Edgerton, 1897, p. 250). That same year John Parks began organizing a pool of nail producers. Parks had previously been involved in tack and bolt pools. *Iron Age,* the leading publication of the industry, announced on May 2, 1895, that the wire nail association was being formed: "With a view to securing a better condition of things and correcting influences which hitherto have tended toward irregularity in prices and unsettling of the market, the manufacturers have been conferring to a concerted action in this direction. The manufacturers directly concerned in the movement disclaim any intention of advancing prices unreasonably, their purpose being to market their goods at a reasonable profit" (p.1). Prices and output were fixed at monthly intervals and an inspector, hired by the association, was placed at each mill.

For a year the association was able to prevent competitors from entering the industry by making it difficult to buy new machines. With these tactics, the price of nails doubled for a short time. Parks believed the pool was a success because the price was so high. "As a matter of fact, we had hardly any new competition in the first year. The new competition came mostly after the second year. Then men began to say 'Those fellows have kept together twelve months and they will probably do it a while longer. They are making a lot of money. I will try and get a slice of it' " (Edgerton, 1897, p. 252). In late 1896 the pool collapsed as new firms entered the market.

By 1871 the oil industry had changed from an industry of many small producers to one where large producers began to dominate. These producers had started to integrate their production vertically and were engaged in cooperative buying and selling arrangements. But in the early 1870s a depression hit the oil business. Refinery production was too great and the price for kerosene, the major product, dropped rapidly.

In the face of this depression, two alternatives were possible: firms could try to undercut their competition or they could form some kind of association of producers and refiners. The processors of petroleum in the New York area and in western Pennsylvania opted for the former strategy while John D. Rockefeller and his associates for the latter (Hidy and Hidy, 1955, pp. 14–23; Williamson and Daum, 1959, pp. 343–370). Rockefeller initially felt that the best solution was a unified ownership of all facilities. He and his group began to buy their competitors and by 1872 had purchased the largest refinery in the area and numerous other plants. But before Standard Oil came to control most of the oil industry, a number of other cooperative schemes were tried to restrict competition.

The South Improvement Company was formed in 1872 to facilitate the cooperative buying of crude oil and even out transport rates. The company was to secure oil business for the Pennsylvania, New York Central, and Erie railroads by offering substantial rebates to refiners. Before the company began operation, however, there was tremendous opposition from competitors and the Pennsylvania legislature repealed the charter of the company.

In 1872 the Petroleum Producer's Association attempted to get its members to reduce production. This attempt failed because there were no legal means to enforce the lower quotas. In August 1872 the Petroleum Refiner's Association, led by John Rockefeller, was formed. This group tried to negotiate exclusive contracts with the production association. The effort had not succeeded by early 1873 (Williamson and Daum, 1959, pp. 346–358). Then, in 1875, the refiners in all areas came together to form the Central Association. The group, again headed by Rockefeller, attempted to delegate authority for buying and selling crude oil and refined products and negotiating transportation contracts to the association. Within a year it failed.

Because attempts at cooperation had failed, the leaders of Standard Oil began to pursue a strategy of mergers oriented toward vertical and horizontal integration. Through the late 1870s, the Standard Group continued to gain dominance in refining by controlling the transportation of crude oil and buying out competing refineries. In 1877 Standard began to construct its own oil pipeline from the oil fields to its refineries. By 1880 the company was already the largest in the country. In order to centralize administrative authority and coordinate far-flung production, the leaders of Standard Oil decided to reorganize their company and the Standard Oil Trust was formed in 1882. The company controlled 90 percent of the oil industry at its peak.

Glucose production began in this country in 1860. The product was mainly used for candy, jellies, artificial syrups, and honey. By 1885 growing competition prompted the manufacturers to form a pool (Dewing, 1914, p. 75). The members of the pool gathered once a year to determine the amount of glucose they could sell profitably and each manufacturer was allotted production in proportion to its capacity. This system was enforced by a special examiner who audited the books of all members in the pool. The pool lasted until 1890 when the Chicago Sugar Refining Company refused to continue the agreement.

Predictably, the price of glucose then dropped as competition increased and the industry was struck by the depression of the 1890s. By 1896 only a dozen producers of any size were left. Joseph Greenhut got the major producers to agree to consolidate and in 1897 the American Sugar Refining Company was formed with 85 percent of the glucose production capacity in the United States.

The cordage industry produced rope of all varieties and first began pooling as far back as 1861 (Clark, 1895, p. 6). These agreements relied on major producers meeting weekly to exchange information. In 1874 a more formal agreement was made and the "manufacturers pledged themselves, as men of honor and integrity, to the true and faithful observance of the rules" (Clark, 1895, p. 8). Unfortunately, the rules were disobeyed and a new pool was established in 1878.

J. M. Waterbury, the president of the National Cordage Company, formed in 1887, described the failure of the pools and the subsequent rise of the trust. "I think that they [the pools] lasted about three years, and they were broken up by other new competition starting or by some men not willing to act up to the agreement . . . The failure of the pools had some effect on the formation of the National Cordage Company. I know the pool made the business profitable, and induced me, for one, to favor a closer alliance with the manufacturers" (U.S. Industrial Commission 1900, vol. 13, p. 126).

In April 1872 representatives of DuPont and seven other firms began the first gunpowder pool. This and other pooling attempts failed and a more elaborate agreement was signed in 1886. "Whereas, it is therefore desired by all parties hereto to enter into the agreement hereinafter set forth . . . for the purpose of avoiding unnecessary loss in the sale and disposition of such powder by ill regulated or unauthorized competition and underbidding by the agents of the parties hereto, and for the purpose of protecting consumers and the public from unjust fluctuations in prices and unjust discriminations."[7]

This agreement and a subsequent agreement signed in 1889 held sway in the industry. The 1889 agreement, known as the "Fundamental Agreement," contained a potent enforcement clause: "As for instance the reduction of a price at a place, in treatment of a local disturbance of trade, the firm should be compensated for the loss sustained by the payment of money by the offending firm."[8] This agreement covered 95 percent of the industry and was able to maintain prices and division of the market through the 1890s.

The gunpowder association often took concerted action against a potential rival. In the early 1890s, three new concerns appeared in the industry. Eugene DuPont instructed F. J. Waddell, then president of DuPont, "to put the Chattanooga Powder Company out of business by selling at lower prices" (Stevens, 1912, p. 455). In 1895 the company was sold. Members of the combination also attacked the two other new firms and by 1896 had bought their assets.

The association operated so effectively that it even came to an agreement with European manufacturers about dividing the world market.

> As to black powder, both parties binds themselves to erect no factories, the Americans in Europe, the Europeans in the United States.
>
> For the sale of high explosives the world was divided into four districts. All of the United States, its territories and possessions, present and future, Mexico, Guatemala, Honduras, Nicaragua, Costa Rica, Colombia, and Venezuela were to be the exclusive American territory. All other countries in South America and the islands of the Carribean Sea, not Spanish possessions, were to be common territory and designated as "syndicated territory." The Dominion of Canada and the Spanish possessions in the Carribean were to be a free market unaffected by terms of the agreement. The rest of the world was to be exclusively the territory of the European factories.
>
> A chairman and vice-chairman were to be appointed by each party to the agreement . . . They were to establish a selling price for each market to be regarded as the convention price below which no sales were to be effected. (Stevens, 1912, pp. 466–467)

The gunpowder combination eventually gained control of the U.S. dynamite business through the joint ownership of a number of plants and dynamite producers. Beginning in 1902, DuPont, now a holding company, began to purchase shares of the other companies involved in gunpowder and dynamite production. By 1907 a substantial share of the industry was concentrated under DuPont's control.

While the motives for cartels seem somewhat self-evident, the actual ability to mount a cartel effort is more problematic. Only a few firms were successful at doing so. To assess the spread of cartel strategies among manufacturing industries I used the detailed

1900 census manufacturing categories. Given the fifty-eight product lines listed in Table 2.1, it was possible to map 46 industries out of 272 that made attempts at cartelization (about 17 percent). The census industry categories often placed several products in the same industry. For instance, steel wire and steel hoops were both products of the steel industry. The measure used here indexes only whether or not there is evidence that producers in that industry attempt to form a cartel anytime during the period 1870–1896. It is not a measure of success, or the extent of cartelization in an industry.

Cartels might appear in industries with the same four conditions: high levels of capital investment, low growth, low profits, and few firms. High capital investment gave owners and managers a great deal of incentive to engage in price and production agreements. It also characterized new industries in need of solving competition problems. Industries with high growth, indicating success, were less likely to form cartels than those struggling with low growth. Because competition is indexed by the level of profits, those industries with high profitability, meaning less competition, did not need cartelization. In industries with low profitability, firms competed intensely and hence were more likely to engage in cartels or pools. Finally, the number of establishments in an industry made it more or less difficult to form a cartel. The more firms, the more difficult it was to collectively organize and reach an agreement.

Appendix A contains a detailed discussion of the attempt to assess which industries were most likely to engage in cartel behavior. The results of that multivariate analysis demonstrate that the strongest predictors of a cartel were the high levels of capital investment in an industry and the low levels of profitability. Growth and number of establishments were not statistically significant predictors of the presence of a cartel.

From this perspective, the existence of production markets, which are characterized by high levels of capital investment, was a precondition for cartels. The leading edge of American economic development was also the site of the construction of a conception of control that would stabilize relations between firms. Production markets were new, so they had no rules. Consequently, strategies of directly controlling one's competitors through cooperation were tried when crises of overproduction squeezed profits. These conditions led actors to enter into agreements to restrain production and fix prices. Direct control through cooperation was favored by those with the most to lose and with the fewest rules to protect them from competition.

The Law, Politics, and the Corporations

During the first half of the nineteenth century, states gave U.S. corporations their charters. If corporations overstepped the strict definitions of their charters, then state governments could revoke them. States, therefore, held great control over corporations until economic activity increased and the firms expanded beyond their boundaries.

Two problems limited the power of states. First, different states could have different laws regarding incorporation. Therefore, if one state had a law that was more favorable to corporate development, other states were threatened with a loss of business activity. Second, as markets grew from local to regional and national, firms produced in the more favorable states and shipped goods to the less favorable ones. Since firms were then engaged in interstate commerce, state laws no longer applied to their activities. Their actions could only be regulated by the federal government. But the federal government and the courts did not want to undermine the power of the states, nor abridge the rights of private property. Thus, they did little to check the power of corporations.

There were three variants of political economy that dominated nineteenth century discourse. The farmers and the emerging working class often subscribed to conspiracy theories of economics. From their point of view, the government, railroads, merchants, and manufacturers worked to their disadvantage and to the advantage of the capitalist groups. There was ample evidence to support their opinion. At the time, it was a radical one.

Farmers and workers made a number of criticisms of the status quo. They thought the gold standard was a tool of the bankers to control the money supply by keeping interest rates high and prices low. Tariffs raised the prices of necessary commodities and benefitted only the manufacturers, who made higher profits. Merchants and railroads charged high prices for their goods and services and paid low prices for the goods farmers and workers produced. Popular movements of the day saw the problem as one of greed and powerful entrenched interests who could do what they wanted. Further, these interests controlled the government and conspired to take the public lands. (Clark, 1931, p. 33; Thorelli, 1955, pp. 54–71; Letwin, 1965, pp. 54–71; Galambos, 1975, pp. 79–116). This point of view was espoused most successively by the Populist movement.

Others held that the government should do as little as possible in the economy and allow the market to rule. This extreme laissez-faire position viewed the emergence of the large firm as a natural development of capitalism. A large market and infrastructure called forth the most efficient organization of production, the large firm. The trusts were not problems, so regulation was not required (Thorelli, 1955, pp. 166–169; Letwin, 1965, pp. 77–85). In the nineteenth century, this was a liberal view which was favored by some progressive capitalist elements and the newly emerging economics profession. It did not come to be important in the debate on the trusts until the early twentieth century and indeed played no part in the discussions of antitrust legislation in the 1880s and 1890s.

Finally, the dominant conservative ideology held that free competition needed to be preserved at all costs. From this perspective, individuals were to be able to dispose of property any way they chose. The market maximized the good of all by encouraging individuals to invest to increase their wealth. They had the freedom to enter or exit markets. Unreasonable restraints of trade were therefore illegal because they interfered with individual or corporate rights to participate in market transactions. This conservative point of view dominated legislative and judicial discourse and was at the heart of the Republican Party.

Nineteenth-century state and federal governments were deeply involved in the functioning of the economy (Scheiber, 1975, pp. 58–59). They encouraged economic development by underwriting the expansion of transportation systems, selling cheaply large blocks of land, and setting up tax incentives, zoning, and rules of corporate governance. Intervention changed after 1887 with the advent of the Interstate Commerce Commission (ICC). New policies emerged at all levels of government as the size and scale of business increased. The legitimacy of the government was at stake, but more important, the emergence of a national economy implied that only the federal government could create rules for corporations. One could argue that the Populists put the issue of the trusts on the political agenda. But once legislative action was taken, it was consistent with the promarket ideology of the Republican Party.

The owners and managers of corporations generally got what they wanted from state legislatures and federal courts. The great changes in the rules governing corporations occurred mostly through the courts, although the issues regarding corporate charters were left to the individual states (Hurst, 1956, 1970; Friedman, 1973, pt. 3, chs. 2, 8; Cornish, 1979, p. 281; Keller, 1981; Lamoreaux, 1986, p. 179). Willard Hurst argues that between 1820 and 1860, the corporate charter shifted from being viewed as a special privilege granted to groups serving the interest of the state to a general charter which was available to many firms.

Originally, state governments wrote extremely explicit charters defining all activities in which firms could engage. Often they granted charters for exclusive privileges or franchises and specified a time limit for how long the corporation could exist. Most of the charters were for corporations in banking, insurance, or transportation. For example, of the 2,333 corporate charters granted in Pennsylvania between 1790 and 1860, less than two hundred were for manufacturing (Hartz, 1948, p. 38).

As time passed, the corporate form appealed more and more to potential entrepreneurs for at least three reasons. First, corporations allowed individuals to combine resources for a specified purpose and detail by share who owned what proportion of the firm. This meant that larger agglomerations of capital could be used to increase economic gain. Second, the corporation could exist independent of any particular actors. Individuals could sell or bequeath their shares to others. Third, a corporate charter limited the liability of the shareholders to the value of their investment in the firm. In other words, they could not be held liable for the debts of the corporation beyond what the corporation was worth (Hurst, 1970, pp. 18–28).

The pressure on state legislatures to grant corporate charters increased over time. This pressure came mostly from manufacturing enterprises. Since every charter had to be passed by the legislature, little time was left for other business. In state after state, therefore, the rules regarding incorporation were relaxed and by 1870 almost all of them had general incorporation rules.

By the 1840s the courts upheld the right of corporations to hold property outside of the state in which they were chartered. Contracts entered across state lines were legal and corporations could sue or be sued in other states. Limited liability of corporations was also settled (Dodd, 1954, pp. 46–57).

Whole areas of corporate law were murky because the principles of interstate commerce remained somewhat undefined until after the Civil War. Gibbon v. Ogden (1824) seemed to give corporations the right to do business in states in which they were not chartered. But Bank of Augusta v. Earle (1839) appeared to permit states to prevent out-of-state corporations from operating. States also resisted the interpretation of Swift v. Tyson (1842) which asserted federal jurisdiction over disputes between corporations chartered in different states (Dodd, 1954, p. 93).

In the post–Civil War era, the tendency to increase the rights of corporations continued and many of the previous conflicts were resolved. The major tools used by the federal courts were the power to control interstate commerce granted by the Constitution and the Fourteenth Amendment to protect the rights of corporations from undue governmental regulation. The Supreme Court consistently ruled that states could not discriminate against foreign corporations through taxation or interfere with interstate trade in other ways. The Fourteenth Amendment was used to extend the principle of due process to corporations. Hence, corporations could not be deprived of their ability to dispose of their wealth by any state law (Scheiber, 1975, p. 85). By 1890 the corporate form had assumed its modern guise. The managers and owners of corporations along with the actors in the courts, states, and federal government had helped develop sufficient law and precedence to protect the corporation from almost any attack.

There remained two areas of contention: the role of the federal versus state authorities in the regulation of corporations and the issue of competition. The first issue stayed on the political agenda until 1910 (Scheiber, 1975, pp. 104–105). The problem was that states had different laws regarding restrictions on incorporation. Eventually, the states allowed corporations more and more freedom, including the ability to own other corporations, that is, holding companies. This meant they were unable to regulate the corporations collectively because firms would reorganize in states that had more favorable laws. The Supreme Court's actions to support corporations over the states' objections only reinforced this practice.

In the second area, competition, both the legislatures and courts acted against the interest of large firms. The development of common and statute laws protected competition. In the beginning of the nineteenth century, states regularly gave exclusive franchise privileges in order to encourage investment in transportation infrastructure. But as time went on, the courts began to realize that the state no longer needed monopolies to achieve economic development. Instead, it became apparent that anything done to lessen competition might harm economic development (Horwitz, 1977, pp. 127–139).

From 1850 on, a body of decisions in the American common law attempted to protect competition by disallowing combinations or conspiracies in restraint of trade. As Hans Thorelli (1955, p. 39) put it: "The common law doctrine primarily applied to collective arrangements to restrict competition, at least since the middle of the 19th century . . . the application of the doctrine in the latter nation [United States] tended to be such as to place considerable limitations on the freedom of contract in instances where that freedom had been used to restrict the freedom of trade and competition."

A well-known and often-cited decision, Central Ohio Salt Co. v. Guthrie, summarized the central idea of this law. The case concerned a salt pool that had attempted to restrict production. The decision was that "public policy, unquestionably favors competition in trade, to the end that its commodities may be afforded to the consumer as cheap as possible, and is opposed to monopolies, which tend to advance market prices, to the injury of the general public. The clear tendency of this agreement is to establish a monopoly, and destroy competition in trade and for that reason, on the grounds of public policy, the courts will not aid in its enforcement."[9] These principles were later extended to the trust form (Thorelli, 1955, pp. 48–49).

The law and government, which had done so much to promote the accumulation of private wealth, worked hard to preserve the competitive market, in spite of the hardships that the market presented for those who owned that wealth. The judges and politicians accepted that the market was where wealth was created. Protecting the market and competition went hand in hand with protecting property rights against the intrusion of the state. The owners and managers of corporations won on every issue in the nineteenth century, except the issue of restraints of trade. While they were free to do what they wanted with their capital, they could not act to undermine the operation of the free market, even if that market threatened their survival. By 1890 the owners and managers of the largest firms were looking for another way to control their markets and protect their investments. Direct control of competitors through cartels was unstable and illegal. To solve the problem of ruinous competition, the owners and managers of corporations considered another solution: mergers.

In the 1880s there had not yet existed a legal form of corporation to bring together the stock of many disparate companies. The first tactic to bring firms together had been the trust, which was conceived by S. C. T. Dodd, the legal counsel for Standard Oil. His basic idea was that individual companies would exchange their stock for trust certificates. The stock would then be held by a board of trustees, who would then control the affairs of the individual companies. Those who had brought a larger firm into the trust would have greater control by virtue of their amount of trust certificates.

In spite of all the rhetoric surrounding trusts, the form was quite short lived. Indeed, Alfred Chandler (1977, ch. 2) could identify only eight industries that actually utilized the trust form: cattle, cordage, cottonseed oil, lead, oil, sugar, whiskey, and linseed oil. The trusts came under attack by state governments immediately upon their formation on the grounds they violated common law principles and state incorporation laws. Trust agreements restrained trade and, hence, violated corporate charters. Firms that remained in trusts would lose their charters and forfeit the right to do business.

In 1887 the state of Louisiana moved against the Cottonseed Oil Trust and won its suit because the trust was conducting business in Louisiana without a corporate charter. In 1888 New York state brought suit against one of the members of the Sugar Trust and won the case claiming that the constituent company had renounced its independent power and hence violated its corporate charter. The Sugar Trust was charged with a similar violation in California in 1889. In 1890 the states of Nebraska and Illinois voided the membership of one of the companies in the Whiskey

Trust for the same reason. The most important antitrust suit was filed against Standard Oil in the state of Ohio in 1890. The result was Standard Oil of Ohio had to leave the trust in 1892 (Thorelli, 1955, pp. 79–82).

These suits made it obvious to companies that the trust was not an adequate way to reorganize the production of an industry. What was needed was an incorporation law that would allow firms to expand their operations. With the encouragement of Dodd and other executives, the state of New Jersey in 1889 passed the most lax incorporation law in the country. This law allowed firms to hold the stock of other firms and conduct business in any state or industry they chose. Delaware and New York followed with similar laws. The trusts were all reorganized in a short time as holding companies.

The outcry against the large firms that were emerging in the 1880s was directed toward the trusts, holding companies, and pooling agreements. While some have doubted the strength of the growing push for a federal antimonopoly act, it is clear that there was a great impetus to pass one (Thorelli, 1955, pp. 108–159; Galambos, 1975, ch. 3). Evidence of this effort is that by 1890 a dozen states had enacted legislation against trusts and other restraints of trade and by 1900 an additional fifteen states had passed similar laws (U.S. Industrial Commission, 1900, vol. 2).

The federal government reiterated their stand against restraints of trade and passed the Sherman Act, making a federal statute of the common law. The Sherman Act stated, "Every contract, combination in the form of trust or otherwise, or conspiracy, in restraint of trade or commerce, is illegal." One critical problem of judicial interpretation was how to distinguish such a restraint. The second section of the act contained similar language. "Every person who shall monopolize, or attempt to monopolize, or combine or conspire with any other person or persons, to monopolize any part of the trade or commerce among the several states, or with foreign nations, shall be deemed guilty of a misdemeanor." Another important part of this act concerned clarifying the terms "trade or commerce." The courts also needed to decide the jurisdiction of the act and the extent of their ability to regulate corporations.

The Merger Movement, 1895–1905

The first significant merger movement lasted from 1895 to 1905, with the peak years being 1898–1902. Ralph Nelson (1959, ch. 1) estimated that 3,012 firms disappeared due to mergers and the resulting consolidations totaled $6.913 billion. The industries affected most were primary metals, food products, transportation equipment, machinery, tobacco, and chemicals. The only large-scale industry relatively untouched by the merger movement was the petroleum industry, which was already dominated by Standard Oil.

The merger movement was a function of three major causes. First, the severe depression of the early 1890s, which showed that the problems of competition could not be easily resolved. Second, the desire of owners and managers to directly control competition. The merger movement represented an alternative strategy to cartels to gain that control and aid the survival of the newly created production-oriented corporation. Third, by 1896 the only legal strategy actors in firms could pursue to directly control competition was through merger. The Sherman Act and the cases decided in the 1890s are crucial to understanding the merger movement. There were only sixteen cases filed between 1890 and 1899 and only eight of those had been decided by 1898 (Posner, 1970, p. 366; U.S. Attorney General, 1955, pp. 29–35). Some have argued on this basis that the Sherman Act could not have affected the course of the merger movement, however, I disagree (Nelson, 1959, pp. 134–136).

The decisions of the 1890s were important in two ways. First, the Sherman Act was a constitutional tool to prevent restraints of trade. Second, the cases confirmed that the holding company was legal and cartels, trusts, and pooling were illegal. The logic of these decisions shows clearly the dilemmas of nineteenth-century thought and politics. The legal and educated communities were quite aware of these decisions and the implications for corporations. While the Sherman Act was not the cause of the merger movement, it certainly contributed to defining what were legal and illegal ways to lessen competition. And mergers were determined to be legal.

The leaders of the new large firms generally saw cutthroat competition as their worse problem. They felt that competition had gone beyond reasonable market processes. Almost all of the witnesses in the various hearings on the subject agreed that the central cause of consolidation was such strong competition that it threatened everyone's livelihood. Economists have generally discounted the role of competition, but I will show that leaders in the merger movement at the turn of the century were quite cognizant of that motive.[10]

In order to create a stable organizational field, it was necessary for the leaders of firms to smooth out the effects of competition. This required an analysis of their situation and a course of action that would stabilize prices and production. Given their testimony, most of the executives questioned did not believe their goal was to create monopolies. Indeed, many of them felt that any attempt to raise prices too high would bring in new competitors (U.S. Industrial Commission, 1900, vol. 13). Instead, the purpose of the large horizontal (same-product) mergers was to reduce the number of plants and, hence, control production enough to insure a reasonable rate of profit. Mergers would allow a newly created large firm to produce full-time in its most efficient plants, and thereby maintain prices, production, and profits.

H. O. Havemeyer, the president of the American Sugar Refining Company (the reorganized Sugar Trust), is most frequently quoted for his view that tariffs were the chief cause of the trust, an earlier form of consolidation. But in his testimony concerning the rise of his company, he said: "There were about 25 firms or corporations in the sugar business. I think the evidence is that for a period of 5 or 6 years before the formation of the trust, 18 of them failed or went out of business. It occurred to some to consolidate the others. Question: When these 18 different companies failed, business was in such a condition, as a whole, that it was considered unprofitable? Answer: Very unprofitable—ruinous." Havemeyer went on to conclude that "the greatest advantage to consolidation is in working the refinery full and uninterruptedly . . . by buying up all of the refineries, burning those that were not efficient, and concentrating the meltings in four refineries, and working them full, you work at a minimum cost" (U.S. Industrial Commission, 1900, vol. 1, pp. 109–110).

C. R. Flint was an organizer of the National Starch Company, the American Caramel Company, the U.S. Rubber Company, and the Sloss-Sheffield Company, a steel producer. When asked the motives of the managers and owners who made the various agreements, he replied: "The inducement on the part of many people to enter combinations has been that, owing to the war of prices which has existed, such wars being the death instead of the life of trade, they have felt forced to enter into combinations in order to avoid failure or serious depreciation of their interest" (U.S. Industrial Commission, 1900, vol. 1, p. 33).

E. R. Chapman was an investment banker and broker of a number of major mergers. In his discussion of the motives for the creation of the American Smelting and Refining Corporation (ASARCO), he argued:

> The evils of competition having been borne for years by the various smelting interests of the country had convinced the proprietors of those interests that some such combination should be effected with a view to reducing expenses and eliminating such competition. These interests had been in frequent consultation, but no satisfactory arrangement had ever been made for any combined operation that eliminated the competition complained of. Finally, it was universally conceded that the only course open was a consolidation of the various interests. (U.S. Industrial Commission, 1900, vol. 1, p. 93)

The Pittsburgh Plate Glass Company (now known as PPG) was another of the large firms produced during the merger movement. John Pitcairn, the president of the firm, gave this account of its genesis. "For several years large profits were made, which stimulated the erection of 7 new factories, resulting in a production largely in excess of the requirements of the country and a consequent depression of prices. The industry became unprofitable. One factory was sold by the sheriff, and several others were on the verge of bankruptcy. This condition lasted several years, when an effort was made to consolidate the largest factories" (U.S. Industrial Commission, 1900, vol. 1, p. 227). When it was formed, the company controlled 80 percent of the glass market.

A. S. White, the president of the National Salt Company, gave a similar explanation for the development of his company: "Economic conditions demanded the formation of the organization. It was organized by salt manufacturers for their self-preservation. The competition was severe, not only as to prices, but also to quality" (U.S. Industrial Commission, 1900, vol. 1, p. 253).

The formation of the U.S. Steel Corporation in 1901 was precipitated by a complex series of events. The steel industry had
been a participant in the merger movement from the beginning.
By 1901 there were about a dozen large steel producers who were
somewhat vertically integrated. This meant that firms controlled
iron ore, coal, transportation systems, coke plants, and steel mills
to varying degrees. The potential for competition between these
giants remained. John Gates was president of the American Steel
and Wire Company, which was one of the companies that entered
the U.S. Steel Corporation. In testimony, he gave this account of
the role of competition in the formation of the company:

> *Chairman:* What was the trouble with the situation?
> *Mr. Gates:* The trouble was that Carnegie had threatened to build
> the tube mill at Ashtabula and a railroad to haul his own ore down.
> *Chairman:* He was going to build a railroad to come into competi-
> tion with the existing railroads?
> *Mr. Gates:* Yes; and a tube plant to tear the National Tube, that
> [J. P.] Morgan had just put together, all to pieces.
> *Chairman:* He was going to give Morgan trouble, both in his manu-
> facturing industry and with his common carrier?
> *Mr. Gates:* It looked that way.
> *Chairman:* And it was to obviate this anticipated competition that
> this tentative plan was drawn up that afterwards became the
> United States Steel Corporation?
> *Mr. Gates:* Yes, sir.   (U.S. Senate, 1912, p. 40)

Charles Schwab, the first president of the U.S. Steel Corporation,
confirmed this version of the story in testimony before the same
Congressional Committee (U.S. Senate, 1912, p. 1312). During
the same hearings, Andrew Carnegie was read the following passage and asked to comment: "Thus, there was suddenly revealed
to the industry what the trade press at the time called 'the
impending struggle of the giants,' a contest between great concerns who under the circumstances, might be forced to work out
in rigorous competition the survival of the fittest. Such were the
conditions in the steel industry in 1900. The spark that lighted the
train was the threat of the Carnegie Co. to erect a great tube plant
near Cleveland, thus invading the field of finished manufacture."
Carnegie said that the account was substantially accurate (U.S.
Senate, 1912, pp. 2508–13).

International Harvester was formed in 1902 when the five

largest companies in the industry merged and then controlled 85 percent of the world harvester market. In testimony given to the Commissioner of Corporations in 1913, the president of the firm argued that competition had been severe and prices unstable. Mr. Glessner, the president of one of the five merged companies, said, "In the harvester business there was a competition never known in other business before" (U.S. Commissioner of Corporations, 1913, p. 60). The commissioner who heard the testimony remarked that the competition was "active, persistent, strenuous, and fierce" (p. 61). The final report concluded: "There is no doubt that the principal motive for the formation of International Harvester Co. was to eliminate competition and to secure a dominant position in the trade" (p. 70).

The American Thread Company was formed in 1899 when fifteen firms merged. Lyman Hopkins, the president of the firm, discussed the motives behind the combination in the following exchange:

Question: Will you tell us what was the condition of the business at the time that it was proposed to organize the American Thread Company?
Answer: Well, there was quite a rivalry between the different companies with reference to the disposition of goods. Some were cutting prices in all kinds of ways to get the trade, and the consequence was that the business was down to a very low profit, if any at all. This was true of the many concerns that went into the organization.
Question: So, that you would give as one of the chief reasons for coming together, the desire to avoid ruinous competition?
Answer: Yes.   (U.S. Industrial Commission, 1900, vol. 13, p. 346)

Hugh Chisholm, the president of International Paper, echoed these sentiments concerning business conditions in the paper industry before the merger which produced his firm in 1898.

There was more paper manufactured than the consuming power of the nation could take. As a result of reckless competition for business and unbusiness-like methods in vogue, the forms of contracts and the conditions under which paper was sold to the consumer, and the whole question as to what price the manufacturer was to receive for his paper, had practically passed out of his hands into those of the middlemen and the consumer. The net results were such as to make no adequate returns upon the invested capital in the manufacturing of newspaper. (U.S. Industrial Commission, 1900, vol. 13, p. 431)

When the new firm was organized, the corporation closed the least efficient plants and ran only the largest and newest plants. The corporation then controlled 75 percent of the paper market. Previous to its formation, the price of newspaper was 1.6 cents per pound and two years later, the price was 2.75 cents per pound. When asked about this Chisolm replied, "Before the consolidation the paper had been sold at a less price than the individual mills could possibly make it, and bankruptcy was staring them all in the face. The product of a plant that cost $2,000,000 we will say, did not give adequate return nor anything approaching it . . . I fail to understand the criticism upon the policy of selling at a price that produces a fair return for it only" (U.S. Industrial Commission, 1900, vol. 13, p. 435).

These are only a few examples of the large consolidations of the first merger movement. To summarize, I quote from the Industrial Commission's final report. "It is clearly the opinion of most of those associated with industrial combinations that the chief cause of their formation has been excessive competition. Naturally, all business men desire to make profits, and they find their profits falling off, first through the pressuring of lower prices of their competitors. The desire to lessen too vigorous competition naturally brings them together (U.S. Industrial Commission, 1900, vol. 13, p. v.).

It is important to explore more systematically the motive of merging to reduce competition. Theoretically, all owners or managers who experienced severe downturns wanted to control competition. But as I have shown, cartels were attempted first in new industries and where the stakes were the highest, that is, in capital-intensive industries where profits were squeezed. Here, the conclusion is that the motive for cartels and the one for mergers were identical. If this is so, then where cartels failed, firms would merge in order to achieve some control over production and price. This explanation accounts for the move from loose associations to pools to trusts, and finally to holding companies formed by mergers.

Lamoreaux (1985) has presented one variant of this argument. From her perspective, the motive for monopoly was that firms had large investments in fixed capital and in order to protect that investment they decided to merge. She presents several models that support this explanation. The industries in which mergers dominated were those that had grown the most rapidly and had high levels of fixed capital investment.

Table 2.2 presents cross-tabulation of industries where cartels occurred with industries that engaged in the merger movement. Of the thirty-eight industries where cartels were present, thirty-six of them were participants in the merger movement. The chi-square test shows clearly that there was a high statistically significant relation between an industry's propensity to merge and its propensity to engage in a cartel.

In order to test this hypothesis more formally, a multivariate data analysis was performed and appears in Tables A.3 and A.4. Generally, Lamoreaux's results were reproduced. The minor differences are discussed in Appendix A. When a variable indicating whether or not an industry experienced cartelization is added to the equation predicting whether or not consolidation occurred in an industry, it becomes the only statistical significant effect in the model.

These results imply two things. First, the strongest predictor of whether or not an industry participated in the merger movement was whether or not its member firms participated in cartels. Second, the central factors in the formation of cartels had been high levels of capital investment and low levels of profit. These conditions characterized the high-investment production markets

Table 2.2 Cross-tabulation of cartelization by participation in the 1895–1904 merger movement for 240 industries (numbers in parentheses are percentages)

	Cartelization	
	No	Yes
Mergers		
No	186 (89.4)	2 (5.3)
Yes	16 (10.6)	36 (94.7)
Total	202	38

Note: $\chi^2 = 140.0$; 1 d.f.; $p < .0001$; Pearson's $r = .77$.
See Appendix A for definitions of variables.

where the competition was heaviest. This evidence suggests that any explanation of the merger movement that does not identify the central motivation as the desire to control prices and output in single-product organizational fields is substantially wrong. The merger strategy was a form of direct control.

The Sherman Act was used in the 1890s against pools and cartels. These forms of collusion were clearly illegal, and the act did not seem to apply to holding companies. Consequently, Sherman Act cases stimulated the merger movement by suggesting to owners and managers that the only legal strategy to control competition was to merge.[11]

It was difficult to enforce the Sherman Act. The most serious problem was administrative. The Justice Department had few resources to carry on serious investigations of large firms in the 1890s. Most of the cases, therefore, were brought by the U.S. district attorneys around the country. Attorney General William Miller advised the district attorneys to try to enforce the law after its passage, but he took no direct action himself. The Republican Harrison administration moved cautiously.

The first case was against a group of coal dealers in Nashville, Tennessee, who had formed an agreement and raised the price of coal (Letwin, 1965, p. 106). The Jellico Coal case was quickly decided against the defendants. After this victory, the government attempted to prosecute other coal merchants. These attempts never materialized. The law was as yet untried against the holding companies. Miller thought the law could be used against the whiskey trust. But the district attorney in Chicago, where the headquarters of the firm were located, felt that because it was operated as a single company, the Sherman Act could not be used against it (Letwin, 1965, pp. 107–109).

There were further attempts to pursue the whiskey trust, but the cases were dismissed. In 1892 a suit was filed against the sugar trust which had been reorganized as a holding company. It took three years to reach a decision. By that time there was a new president, Grover Cleveland, and a new attorney general, Richard Olney. Olney was not a strong supporter of the Sherman Act (Letwin, 1965, pp. 117–119). In order to prove that it was inappropriate to use against the holding companies, Olney chose to pursue the sugar case. The decision of U.S. v. E. C. Knight confirmed Olney's view. This made mergers legal and suggested that tight combinations were not covered by the Sherman Act. After the Knight case, the Sherman Act was directed mainly against pools and cartels and was not used against tight combinations until 1904.

One of the peculiarities of the Knight case was that all of the merged sugar refineries were in Pennsylvania. Since one state produced for the entire country, one of the central questions to be decided was who was to have jurisdiction over the regulation of the company: the federal government or the state of Pennsylvania. McCurdy (1979) has provided a reinterpretation of the Knight decision taking this fact into account. His argument is that the case must be examined in the context of state / federal relations and the desire of federal judges to preserve the power of states whenever possible. Since all of the sugar refineries involved were in Pennsylvania, that state had jurisdiction. The following excerpt from the Supreme Court decision is relevant.

No distinction is more popular to the common mind or more clearly expressed in economic and political literature than that between manufacture and commerce. Manufacture is transformation . . . The buying and selling and the transportation incidental thereto constitute commerce . . . If it be held that the term (commerce) includes regulation of all such manufactures as are intended to be the subject of commercial transactions in the future, it is impossible to deny that it would also include all productive industries that contemplate the same thing. The result would be that Congress would be invested, to the exclusion of the states, with the power to regulate not only manufacturing, but every branch of human industry. (U.S. Attorney General, 1899, p. 23)

Based on this reading of the division of power between the states and the Congress, Chief Justice Fuller concluded:

Congress did not attempt thereby to assert the power to deal with monopoly directly as such, or to limit and restrict the rights of corporations created by the states or the citizens of the states in the acquisition and control, or disposition of property, or to regulate or prescribe the price or prices at which property or the products thereof should be sold, or to make criminal the acts of persons in the acquisition and control of property which the states of their residence created or sanctioned or permitted . . . the law [Sherman Act] struck at combinations, contracts, and conspiracies to monopolize trade and commerce among the several states or with foreign countries; but the contracts and acts of the defendants related exclusively to the acquisitions of the Philadelphia refineries and the business of sugar refining in Pennsylvania, and bore no direct relation to commerce between the states or foreign nations. The object was manifestly gain in the manufacture of the commodity, but not through the control of interstate or foreign commerce.   (U.S. Attorney General, 1899, p. 24)

Fuller goes on to argue that the states had ample power "to deal with the monopoly directly as such."[12] The state of Pennsylvania controlled the charters of the companies that entered into the holding company, and could invalidate the agreement itself.

The result of this suit was that the Sherman Act applied only to cases that focused on the interstate commerce aspect of monopolization. In order to use the Sherman Act, one would have to prove collusive actions to restrain interstate commerce. The consolidation of assets in holding companies did not appear to come under this definition. Indeed, Fuller seemed to hold that such matters were rightly in the province of state governments to control.

If the power to regulate firms was so great, why didn't the states set up rules to prevent out-of-state corporations from buying local corporations or restrict the ability of local corporations to sell out to out-of-state interests? There are two answers. First, the individual states did not want to threaten potential business activity within their boundaries and, rather than fight the holding company, they chose to embrace it (McCurdy, 1975, pp. 336–340). Second, even if states would have tried to regulate the selling of assets, businesses would have sued them on the grounds that they were being prevented from disposing of their property as they saw fit. These types of suits were likely to make the regulation of mergers impossible, given that the right to dispose of property was consistently upheld by the courts (McCurdy, 1979, pp. 330–335).

Other important suits prompted by the Sherman Act were directed at cartels. The decision of U.S. v. Trans-Missouri was against a railroad pool in 1897. This was followed by U.S. v. Joint Traffic and U.S. v. Addyston Pipe in 1898. The Joint Traffic case was against a railroad pool and the Addyston Pipe case against a price fixing cartel of pipe manufacturers. They involved explicit collusive attempts to control interstate commerce and were decided in favor of the government.

In order to show that the Sherman Act and subsequent cases had some effect on the merger movement, it is important to have a sense of what kind of advice the legal community was giving its clients. If lawyers were telling their clients that mergers were legal and cartels or pools problematic, this would give my argument more credence. It is, of course, difficult to establish exactly what advice clients were receiving. But we can see that the legal community was aware of the decisions of the Supreme Court and their implications for the organization of corporations.

Once the Knight decision was announced, Attorney General Olney said, "Combinations and monopolies, therefore, although they may unlawfully control production and prices of articles in general use, can not be reached under this law merely because they are combinations, nor because they may engage in interstate commerce as one incidence of their business" (U.S. Attorney General, 1895, p. 13). In order to violate the Sherman Act, firms had to directly engage in collusive behavior to control interstate commerce. The holding company did not constitute a direct attempt to restrain trade. Olney went so far as to say to the business community: "Give yourselves no anxiety as far as the federal government is concerned. So long as you do not do your manufacturing on railway trains on their way across borders I will not be superofficious" (Public Opinion, April 30, 1896, p. 391).

The next attorney general, Judson Harmon, suggested that the law had failed to control monopolies because of the Knight decision. He suggested that the act be modified to allow prosecution of firms wherever monopolization was evident even if the specific object was not the control of interstate commerce. He said, "The limitation of the present law allows those engaged in such attempts to escape from both state and federal governments, the former having no authority over interstate commerce, and the latter having authority over nothing else" (U.S. Attorney General, 1896, pp. 3–4).

Attorney General John Griggs wrote an open letter in reference to the firms involved in the merger movement: "As a matter of fact, all the companies which you refer to as now organizing for the purpose of securing complete or partial monopoly of different branches of manufacturing are similar to the sugar combination, and are not in the jurisdiction of the courts" (Public Opinion, March 30, 1899, p. 252).

Philander Knox, Theodore Roosevelt's first attorney general, proposed to Congress a suggestion similar to Harmon's. He argued that the Sherman Act should be extended to manufacturing firms which operate in single states, but participate in interstate commerce. He also proposed to establish a corporation commission that would study corporate actions and recommend legislation (U.S. Attorney General, 1903, pp. 15–21).

The various attorneys general, thus, held that the Sherman Act in its present form did not apply to holding companies that had formed to control a large share of productive capacity. Presumably other lawyers interested in antitrust issues took their pronouncements quite seriously.

In a well-known law casebook of the time, A. Eddy discussed the issues surrounding restraints of trade quite thoroughly (1901, ch. 8). His conclusion was like that of the attorneys general. The act did not touch upon combinations in restraint of trade that did not directly attempt to control interstate commerce. In another law book on the topic by A. J. Hirschl, similar conclusions were drawn (1896, pp. 66–82).

Commentators of the day agreed. In an editorial about the Knight decision, the *American Law Review* (1896, p. 305) argued: "But the appalling fact left by this decision is that if it is to stand, the people of the United States are absolutely remedyless against the great combinations like the one in question, unless the particular state (New Jersey), in which such combinations are organized as corporations chooses to act in defending itself and the other states of the Union against them." J. S. Auerbach (1899, p. 393) argued in the *North American Review* that the states could not prevent the entry of foreign firms or the merger of domestic firms because of the Fourteenth Amendment. There were great limitations on "state legislation against those corporations, nearly all of which are engaged in interstate trade or commerce. Corporations, therefore, domiciled in New Jersey and trading elsewhere have nothing to fear and no favors to ask of any hostile state." Frank Goodnow (1897, p. 243) concluded in an article in the *Political Science Quarterly* that "the court was so nearly unanimous in its decision as to justify the belief that the decision itself will not be reversed in the immediate future. Any attempt at efficient regulation must come from the national government."

In September 1897 the governors and state attorneys general met in St. Louis to discuss the issue. They recommended new state laws that would standardize the charters of corporations, restrict the ability of firms to operate out of their home state, outlaw trusts and holding companies, and vigorously enforce the antitrust laws. The basic argument was that the federal antitrust law—the Sherman Act—had failed and that the trust problem could only be solved by concerted action on the part of the various states (*American Law Review*, 1897, pp. 905–907).

Five prominent attorneys authored a report to the American Bar Association Committee on Jurisprudence and Law Reform in 1897 on the federal antitrust law and its judicial construction. Their report reviewed the Sherman Act cases and concentrated on two issues: the distinction made between manufacture and commerce in U.S. v. E. C. Knight and the question of what constituted a restraint of trade. "We presume it may be considered settled that the purchase of sugar refineries in different states of the country, or the purchase of stock in the companies operating such establishments, in such a way as to largely control manufacturing, does not essentially involve a monopoly or restraint of interstate or international commerce within the meaning of the statute now under consideration" (*American Law Review*, 1897, p. 726). The major concern of the rest of the report was whether the law was unconstitutional because it outlawed all restraints of trade, reasonable and unreasonable. This issue became the central question in the cases decided after U.S. v. E. C. Knight until U.S. v. Standard Oil (1911).

Edward Keasbey (1899, p. 379), a prominent lawyer, wrote an article in the Reports of the American Bar Association concerning the effects of the New Jersey law on the merger movement. "In many of the leading industries of the country, manufacturers have abandoned the struggle of competition and have united their interest in a large corporation to which they have surrendered all their property and business to be operated under a common head and for a common purpose." He goes on to say in regard to the effect of the antitrust laws on the merger movement that "the remedies devised against the combinations in the form of agreements and trusts, seem to be inapplicable to the combinations that consist in the actual merger of existing corporations, or in the formation of companies which merely exercise the common right of the purchase of various properties and the good will of many business enterprises" (1899, p. 380). The rest of the article describes how the New Jersey holding company act was created and how the largest firms that were being created were chartered in New Jersey. Keasbey points out that "it is difficult to treat the existence of a corporation lawfully formed as an agreement in restraint of trade or to hold the ownership of all the flour mills that can be purchased to be an indictable conspiracy" (1899, p. 402).

One purpose of the U.S. Industrial Commission hearings was to evaluate the effectiveness of the antitrust laws and to consider the causes of the merger movement. The goal was to recommend to Congress potential courses of action to remedy problems created by the merger movement. The commission recommended a number of specific pieces of legislation including the protection of shareholders from overcapitalized corporate stock offerings, the federal regulation of incorporation, the standardization of state rules regarding incorporation, and strengthening federal control over interstate commerce. The commission wanted to use the antitrust laws carefully and not destroy the "positive" effects of combination, mostly those associated with increased efficiency. The concern was not to confuse the positive effects with the "negative," mostly those associated with monopolization and overcapitalization (U.S. Industrial Commission, 1900, vol. 1, pp. 5–36).

By the end of the nineteenth century, lawyers, politicians, judges, and academics concurred that the Sherman Act was problematic in use against manufacturing combinations that were not formed for direct control of interstate commerce.[13] While the Supreme Court decisions against pools and cartels and for holding companies were not the direct cause of the merger movement, it is certain that they influenced what strategies actors in the large firms chose. Because it was determined that the holding company

Table 2.3   Mergers by types, 1895–1904

Type of merger	Number of mergers	Percentage
Horizontal	170	78.3
Vertical	26	12.0
Horizontal and vertical	21	9.7
Total	217	100.0

Source: Ralph Nelson, original coding sheets (1959).

was not a restraint of trade, even though it was organized to diminish competition, the direct control of competitors through mergers appeared to be a good solution to the problem.

One explanation that I have not yet mentioned is that recent organization theory and research has found that organizations tend to mimic each other's behavior. The merger movement seems to reflect imitative behavior. That is, firms were quite aware that other firms merged in order to control competition. They then adopted the strategy for the same reason. This explanation helps us understand the extent and duration of the merger movement. The financial community, which promoted the largest mergers, certainly aided in spreading the tactic, as they had much to gain in doing so.

There are three competing explanations of the merger movement. First, the development of capital markets gave firms the incentive to merge (Stigler, 1966, p. 101). Two problems with this view are: The market had existed for a number of years and therefore could not be considered a proximate cause; and the existence of a market for securities is a necessary but insufficient condition for large-scale mergers. The market continued to exist after the merger movement ended rather abruptly in 1904.

A more sophisticated version of this argument is that the fluctuation of stock prices is related to mergers (Nelson, 1959, pp. 116–120). In other words, as stock prices rise, mergers occur more frequently. The problem with this view is that the actual causal mechanism is left somewhat unspecified. Are stock prices causing mergers, or are the possibilities for mergers causing the increase in stock prices? Neither stock market view provides an adequate explanation of the timing or depth of the merger wave.

A second view stresses that the merger movement was intent on creating more efficient organizations. The most important proponent of this view currently is Alfred Chandler (1977, ch. 1). The central point he makes is that the large modern corporation arose as a vertically integrated firm that produced efficiently because it controlled its product line from raw materials to ultimate sales. I have difficulties with this view for two reasons. First, as Lamoreaux (1985, pp. 90–94) has shown, the degree of vertical integration had no effect on the propensity for mergers to occur in an industry. Second, evidence also shows that 78.3 percent of the mergers were clearly horizontal and not vertical. (See Table 2.3.)

Only 12 percent of the mergers were undertaken for vertical integration.

The third point of view is that horizontal mergers created large enough firms so that economies of scale were possible. This argument was made by a number of the participants in the hearings of the U.S. Industrial Commission (1900, vol. 13, pp. vi–viii). About 60 percent of the mergers failed, however, and that suggests that the new large firms were not efficient. Indeed, this implies that instead of creating economies of scale, mergers created diseconomies of scale.

3

The Manufacturing Conception of Control

All of the strategies of direct control of competitors were unsuccessful. The merger movement at the turn of the century proved to be as ineffective at controlling competition as cartels and predatory trade practices. These tactics failed because they ultimately could not legally prevent the entry or existence of firms in similar product lines. From 1900 to 1914, the federal government intensified its regulation of the trade practices of large firms, which clarified what kinds of behaviors were to be sanctioned. The Justice Department won lawsuits against some of the largest firms. The managers and entrepreneurs who controlled them were still haunted by problems of overcompetition. They needed to find a new way to protect themselves without overt collusion or engaging in unreasonable restraints of trade. The stakes were enormous and the rewards potentially high for someone to construct a conception of control that would preserve the large firm.

The manufacturing conception of control is fundamentally a defensive conception oriented toward discouraging competitors from directly competing by making the costs high and the probability of success low. It proposed an entirely new mechanism of control. Instead of confronting one's competitors, the manufacturing conception relied on the size, integration, and relative effectiveness of the large firm as a potential threat to competitors. By controlling the input of raw materials and the sales output, managers and entrepreneurs could lower their vulnerability to the threats of their competitors or the vagaries of their markets. Integration of production, both backward to control suppliers and forward to control customers, led to tighter control which increased the relative effectiveness of the organization and helped eliminate bottlenecks. Large size meant the more control over the production process, the lower the cost of production. It also produced a greater market share and gave the firm more leverage to maintain its price in the market and threaten price cutters.

Manufacturing control required that dominant firms form and head an organizational field. This meant that leading firms needed to identify their major competitors and what prices were being charged. It also meant that leading firms wanted their competitors to know their production capabilities and average costs. If competitors did not clearly know the intentions of the dominant firms, then the possibility for stability was compromised. In this way, the first stable organizational fields based on the recognition and interdependence of firms came into existence. These fields were organized on mutual respect, respect built on the power of the largest firms to cause havoc for their competitors. Smaller competitors still had the power to lower the profits for all, but if they cut prices and took too much market share from the dominant firms, they were likely to suffer the consequences of a price war with the larger firms.

Since the larger firm had deeper pockets, lower costs, and the ability to cut off access to supplies, there was a great incentive for the smaller firms to go along. Nonetheless, they were also tempted to mimic the defensive tactics of the largest firms. They integrated in both backward and forward directions and attempted to raise their market share to threaten their competitors. The overall effect was the creation of product-line organizational fields that became oligopolies.

Both the manufacturing and direct forms of control set lessening competition as their goal. The fundamental difference between them was the mechanism by which each tried to achieve this end. The manufacturing conception focused on the internal structure of the organization and the ability to produce goods reliably and cheaply and in great quantities. Rather than directly confronting competitors, firms using this conception tried to control competition by becoming formidable. The emergence of this new conception required some managers and entrepreneurs to pioneer new tactics to stabilize prices. The oil and steel industries were the leaders in this effort.

The failure of direct-control tactics stemmed mainly from the increased enforcement and expansion of the antitrust laws. Between 1900 and 1916 the federal government asserted control over the trade practices of the largest firms and defined legal and illegal trade practices. Once in force, these rules guided the actions of the largest firms. Their desire to resolve problems of competition, however, did not diminish.

While the economy drifted in and out of recession until World War I, the struggle to achieve price stability did not subside. It was at this time that the manufacturing conception of control began to develop. In a small number of important industries, defensive tactics of vertical integration and concentration of production began to produce stable interactions between firms. Firms respected one another's capacities and publicly announced price changes. The important symbolic victory of the rise of the manufacturing conception of control came when U.S. Steel won its antitrust suit. The Supreme Court ruled that the company's tactic of acting as a price setter for the industry, which it was able to do because of its large market share, was not an illegal restraint of trade.

Evidence demonstrates that the firms that emerged during the merger movement at the turn of the century and survived engaged in tactics of integration and acquiring large market shares. Manufacturing personnel came to dominate the largest firms and as managers they chose to reorganize their firms from holding companies to functional/unitary structures. Finally, vertically integrated firms grew more rapidly during the period of the 1920s than nonintegrated firms. The conception of control based on size and relative efficiency paid off.

The 1920s was the decade of triumph for the manufacturing conception of control. The accepted wisdom at the time was that forming oligopolies of vertically inegrated firms was the way to price stability and guaranteed growth and profits for large firms. The second great merger wave, which occurred during this time, was driven by managers and entrepreneurs who sought to make their firms sufficiently large and integrated to prevent competitors from directly attacking them. The effect of that wave was to create oligopolies across many organizational fields. The merger wave was buoyed by continuous economic expansion through the decade.

The federal government, in general, and the antitrust authorities, in particular, did little to prevent the mergers from occurring. The Clayton Act, which appeared to outlaw mergers that potentially effected competition, was narrowly interpreted in a number of cases, and its effect was nullified. The Republican administrations of the 1920s still opposed price fixing arrangements. But they encouraged executives to try to stabilize competition by publicizing prices and forming trade associations to disseminate information and professionalize business. They did not oppose mergers that created oligopolistic pricing. The manufacturing conception of control, therefore, triumphed with the blessing of the federal government.

Why did the federal government, including Democratic and Republican administrations and the Supreme Court, not view the manufacturing conception of control as a restraint of trade, albeit a more passive one? The dominant ideology reflected in the Sherman and Clayton acts, as well as the decisions made by the courts, suggested that an illegal trade practice was characterized by two conditions. First, someone had to pursue their competitors aggressively in order to restrain trade. In other words, there must be an intent to restrain trade. Second, it was important to establish that the restraint was unreasonable. Firms had to pursue restraints of trade directly, persistently, and aggressively with the goal of destroying one's competition. The manufacturing conception of control did not constitute an active or unreasonable restraint of trade. Also, public attitudes toward the large corporations shifted during and after World War I. Even the Democrats softened toward the large firms as a result of their participation in the war effort. The Republicans were quite friendly toward big business and did little to control its activities so long as they appeared nonpredatory and noncollusive.

Direct Control and Strategies of Survival, 1900–1916

The basic problem of excessive competition remained after the turn of the century merger movement. Only 45.7 percent of the large firms that were formed in the turn of the century merger movement survived until 1919 (see Appendix B). In 1909, 45 of the 100 largest manufacturing firms were products of the merger movement; this decreased to 27 by 1919. It is not surprising that the leaders of large corporations continued their search for strategies to increase their odds of survival in the twentieth century.

One of the most common tactics was the renewal of cartels or pools in spite of the illegality and instability of such arrangements. Indeed, of the 212 cases brought under the Sherman Act between

1901 and 1920, almost 40 percent concerned pools or cartels (see Table 3.1). Table 3.2 presents a list of the companies and industries against which these cases were filed. This list shows that pools were common devices in a large number of industries, particularly food products.

The meat-packing industry, for example, almost continuously made attempts at pooling. Seven firms formed a pool in 1893 that lasted in various forms until 1902. The pool divided the entire U.S. market and maintained market share by creating penalties for firms that oversold in a particular market (U.S. Federal Trade Commission, 1919, pt. II, p. 14). In 1902 the Justice Department filed suit against the members of the pool and on April 18, 1903, the combination was declared illegal (U.S. Attorney General, 1938, p. 90).

As a result of the suit, the five largest firms entered negotiations to merge into one firm. This attempt failed when Jacob Schiff, the investment banker who was trying to arrange the merger, decided not to make the loan because of unstable financial conditions produced by the panic of 1903 (U.S. Federal Trade Commission, 1919, pt. II, p. 21). The leading group continued to try to control the market for fresh beef through renewed pooling. In December 1902 the three largest producers, Armour, Swift, and Morris, formed the National Packing Company from the properties they

Table 3.1 Types of case brought under the Sherman Act, 1901–1920

Type[a]	Number	Percentage
Pools or cartels	84	39.6
Mergers	28	13.2
Unfair practices	74	34.9
Railroad cases	15	7.1
Labor unions	11	5.2
Total	212	100.0

Source: The Federal Antitrust Laws. Washington, D.C.: U.S. Government Printing Office, 1938.

a. Pools or cartels = cases where multiple firms colluded to control prices or production; mergers = cases where firms or groups of firms merged with the intent of restraining trade; unfair practices = cases where a single firm engaged in practices to control prices or production by using unfair trade practices; railroads = cases involved with railroad pools; labor unions = cases where Sherman Act was used against labor unions.

Table 3.2 Companies and industries that engaged in cartels or pools and were taken to court under the Sherman Act, 1901–1920 (partial list)

Industry	Companies
Railroads	Various
Meat packing	Various
Salt	National Salt, Federal Salt
Wholesale grocers	Various
Paper	Various
Retail grocers	Various
Lumber	Various
Fertilizer	Virginia-Carolina
Ice	Various
Furniture	Various
Anthracite coal	Various
Plumbing supplies	Various
Window glass	Various
Bathroom fixtures	Various
Electric lights	General Electric and others
Copper wire	Various
Cable	Various
Bituminous coal	Various
Brakes	Various
Steamships	Various
Motion pictures	Various
Thread	American Thread and others
Fish	Various
Cantaloupes	Various
Potatoes	Various
Cement	Various
Milk	Various
Onions	Various
Butter and eggs	Various
Bread	Various
Farm equipment	Various

had been going to merge. This company acted as the clearinghouse for information by which prices for beef were fixed (U.S. Federal Trade Commission, 1919, pt. II, p. 25). A second antitrust suit was filed against the meat packers in 1911 and a third in 1912. The last lawsuit required the dissolution of the National Packing Company.

In 1913 a new division of the market operated in a subtle

fashion (U.S. Federal Trade Commission, 1919, pt. I, p. 58). Each firm was granted a share of live animals at the various stockyards. The price paid for the animals was decided by collusion. At the end of each week, the five largest companies exchanged information on purchases. If one firm was buying too much, the others would bring it into line by threatening to purchase more at higher prices. From 1913 to 1929 the market shares of the five largest meat-packing firms maintained enormous stability.[1] The industry was stable because the five largest firms controlled the majority of the stockyards, often through joint ownership, as well as the packing plants (U.S. Federal Trade Commission, 1919, pt. I, chart 1). This made it difficult for any new firm to enter the market as the supply of cattle was controlled.

A feel for how matters were handled by the pool can be gleaned from a memorandum written by Germon Sulzburger, the president of one of the five largest firms.

> Armour seemed very discouraged with the general situation and prospects. I explained this was due, a good deal, to his own foolish tactics in New York; that the situation there had been completely demoralized by his action and that this was a very sensitive situation. He admitted that he thought they had made a mistake there, but that the rest of the situation did not make him anxious to change his attitude. I explained to him that he was injuring us more than anyone else as we had a larger proportionate interest. He said he had no intent to work against us and said that he would arrange now to do the following: reduce N.Y. 10% this week. 10% next week.   (U.S. Federal Trade Commission, 1919, pt. I, p. 59)

Market sharing extended both to the international scene and to other products. Minutes of a meeting held by the major meat packers on June 4, 1914, show the following division of the international market.

> Mutton: No one thought this item of any particular importance or interest, as they found the business unprofitable, excepting at a certain particular season of the year.
> Beef: They also stated percentages which had been allotted us on beef for England as follows: up to one-half to Sansinema [a foreign meat packing firm] contributed equally by everyone; difference up to one-half contributed by La Blanca (controlled by Swift).
> Sheep and Lambs: The understanding had been that these were to

remain as in the old pool previous to 1913. (U.S. Federal Trade Commission, 1919, pt. I, p. 61)

A pool was formed in the bathroom fixture industry in 1909 and included 85 percent of the industry's capacity.[2] This pool fixed prices by agreeing to allow its members to use the patents covering the products. The agreement specified that "for each violation of the price regulations of the license agreement we agree to forfeit a sum equal to the amount of the shipment in question, and such other penalties as may be agreed upon" and that the selling prices to the jobbers were "to be established through the licensor by a price committee appointed by the various manufacturers."[3] The pool was enforced in a somewhat ingenious fashion. The patents were given over to E. L. Weyman who acted as the licensor and head of the price committee. Each firm paid royalties to the licensor that were held in case the firm undercut prices. Weyman and the price committee enforced prices by getting the jobbers who sold the products to agree to prices in given districts.[4] This pool was broken up by the federal government under the Sherman Act.

The window glass industry began efforts to control prices in 1913. There were two parts of the industry: one using a labor-intensive glass blowing process and the other using a mechanical process. The mechanical process was not efficient enough to put the glass blowers out of business. The independents, who employed glass blowers, sold through a single agent and this facilitated the ease of controlling prices and production. There were annual meetings of the National Association of Window Glass Manufacturers to decide the wage scale and production limits for the following year. Production was restricted by agreeing to operate factories for only a certain portion of the year (Watkins, 1927, pp. 156–159). The president of the association remarked in 1915 that "the window glass industry during the past year has operated at 50 per cent capacity. Most producers have recognized the fundamental law of supply and demand and demonstrated a willingness to exact his share and be satisfied" (Watkins, 1927, p. 158).

The General Electric Company organized what was a cross between a pool and a holding company. In the 1890s, there existed a pool of fifteen electrical goods producers including General Electric and Westinghouse. In May 1901 the National Electric Company was formed as a holding company for all of the members of this pool except General Electric and Westinghouse. But the combination was actually controlled by General Electric.[5] The National Electric Company proceeded to absorb thirteen additional firms in the next eight years. The National Electric Company also acted as an organizer of price fixing between the remaining companies.[6] Eventually, the entire combination was broken up in an antitrust suit.

A number of firms engaged in a variety of tactics that one might term cutthroat competition. These included selective pricecutting, tying agreements that would force customers to consume only one firm's products, threats and coercion against competitors and customers, attempts to cut off supplies from competitors, and dummy corporations to hold stock secretly and thereby control competitors. Table 3.1 shows that the second largest category of antitrust cases is labeled "conspiracies." This catch-all category includes all of the cutthroat tactics to restrain trade. If the Justice Department prosecuted such acts as a sample of all illegal acts, the large number of suits suggests that these practices were widespread.

Selective pricecutting was used by many firms in local markets. One firm that systematically used this tactic was the Standard Oil Company. In one of many antitrust suits brought against the firm, the following testimony was given by E. M. Wilhoit, an executive in the Standard Oil Company in Missouri, who said that the company based "their prices in a locality on their nearest competitor, or upon the presence or absence of competition" (Stevens, 1917, p. 11). It was also revealed that local pricecutting was the dominant way of competition.[7] In Albuquerque, New Mexico, for instance, where there was little competition, the firm averaged 6.48 cents per gallon profit on illuminating oil. In Los Angeles, where there was more serious competition, the firm was losing over 3 cents a gallon.[8]

DuPont and its allies in the powder trust undercut their competitors too. The Chattanooga Powder Company was undercut when F. J. Waddell, acting for the DuPont Company, paid a railroad agent for a weekly statement of Chattanooga's powder shipments. Waddell then approached its customers and offered them powder at below cost. Chattanooga sold out after one year.[9]

The National Cash Register Company used the same tactics. In the antitrust suit against the firm, a company memorandum outlined this policy:

> This circle represents the earth. The small crosses represent the several offices of the National Cash Register Company in every civilized country. Suppose competition springs up in territory pointed out by arrow no. 1. The National Cash Register Company can afford to do business here at a loss if necessary to meet the competition, because the profit made at the office marked arrow no. 2 will make up for the loss, while all the other offices of the Company all over the civilized globe will make a profit and keep up the income of the company.[10]

The firm had a "Competition Department" whose function was to destroy the competition. Its employees were known as "knockout men" and their special duty was to interfere with competitors' sales contracts. They did so by obtaining lists of the other firms' clients and by hiring competitors' personnel to gain more information from them.[11]

Tying agreements forced customers to consume extraneous products in order to buy a desired product. Often the desired product was protected by patents, so customers had little choice but to purchase the entire package of goods if they wanted access to the patented item.

The most striking use of this tactic was by the United Shoe Machinery Company. The company produced almost all of the equipment used to make shoes because of its control of patents. Charles Jones, a witness at the 1912 hearings to consider the patent laws, explained the basic motivation for tying agreements.

> In 1900, at the time of the original controversy over these leases, most of the machines were protected by valid patents, and we were advised by our counsel that if we desired to use their patented machines we should probably have to do so on whatever terms they saw fit to impose; but these important patents were nearing the day of their expiration, and at the present time a very large proportion of the important basic patents have expired, and but for the restrictions imposed upon us by their leasing system we should today be exercising our undoubted right to use, without royalty, a large part of the machinery employed. (U.S. House of Representatives, 1912, p. 65)

The Motion Picture Patents Company took a similar advantage of tying agreements. In order to use their film, which was patented, companies had to buy their projectors, which were not. The license agreement signed by all of their customers contained the following clause: "The licensor hereby grants to the licensee the right and license to manufacture, print, and produce positive motion pictures upon condition that they be used solely in exhibiting or projecting machines containing the inventions, or some of them of said letters patent and licenses by the licensor."[12]

The General Electric Company and National Electric Company obtained their patents for tantalum and tungsten filament lamps between 1906 and 1910. The patents on carbon filament lamps had expired in the 1890s and the three types of lamps were in competition. General Electric forced wholesalers who wanted to purchase tantalum or tungsten lamps to purchase their carbon lamps as well. This meant that any firm wanting to produce carbon lamps could not easily find outlets for their products.[13]

The use of dummy corporations to hold stock secretly in the competition or the actual creation of corporations, illusory competitors, was somewhat common. The competitors of the American Tobacco Company advertised their goods based on not being part of that company which had a reputation as an "evil" trust that was anti-union. From 1903 to 1904, the American Tobacco Company secretly bought the stock of twenty-one of their competitors. The firms continued to be run by the same management, but they stopped competing with the American Tobacco Company (U.S. Commissioner of Corporations, 1912, pt. I, pp. 20–21). This tactic was one of the central issues in the antitrust suit that eventually resulted in the dissolution of the company.

DuPont used companies it controlled to help undercut competition. These companies had the appearance of independence, but would pricecut a common rival. In this way DuPont appeared to be uninvolved. In testimony during the antitrust suit against DuPont, F. J. Waddell described how this strategy worked.

During the conversation with T. C. DuPont, the president, in which he was endeavoring to explain to me the objects of the trust, he told me that no one man could sell all the powder, or any other article, in any particular territory, and it was necessary for him, therefore, just like a little boy to have a dog, to which he could call and whistle . . . He termed it a "yellow dog" and he explained to me that after I had exhausted all of my resources, and those of the travelling men under my office, that if I was

> unable to regain the trade, that I was to whistle by writing a
> letter, and they would send on a little yellow dog, which, at the
> time, in the high explosives business was known as the Climax
> Manufacturing Co. and the New York Powder Co. . . . If we met
> the prices that meant the lowering of our prices on our brands;
> but the little yellow dog would come in, and we could say that we
> didn't recognize them at all, that their goods were of no account,
> and were of low grade, and all that kind of thing; so we didn't
> have to lower our prices to the adjoining trade; but the yellow
> dog got the business.[14]

Standard Oil frequently did business the same way. In its antitrust
suit, the government alleged that Standard had operated over
sixty firms at various times as independent companies in different
parts of the country.[15]

After 1905 mergers occasionally created new, large firms: Singer
Manufacturing (1906), National Lead (1906), General Motors
(1908), International Business Machines (1911), John Deere
(1911), B. F. Goodrich (1912), Continental Can (1913), Union
Carbide (1917), and Allied Chemical (1920) (Nelson, 1959, table
C.1, pp. 154–156). Three motives underlay these consolidations:
the desire for monopoly, oligopoly, or vertical integration. General Motors was founded in an attempt to create a monopoly in
the manufacture of automobiles, although at the last moment
Henry Ford decided to remain outside of the merged company
(U.S. Federal Trade Commission, 1939, pp. 627–633). Chemical
firms often merged with firms that produced goods with similar
chemical processes. A number of mergers in the petroleum
industry were defensive in nature. Firms found it desirable to
become totally integrated so that Standard Oil could not cut off
supplies or customers.

One strategy of firms interested in controlling their markets was
to get the federal government to regulate prices in the industry.
Only a few industries were successful using this strategy: railroads,
public utilities, banks, airlines, trucking, and communications.
Many of these industries have been called "natural monopolies"—the services they provide are essential to the infrastructure
of the country—and therefore should be exempt from competitive
pressures.

The problem of regulating industries concerned whose interests
would be benefitted. The railroads and their principal customers,

large shippers of raw materials and finished manufactured goods, had different interests in the regulation of railroad freight rates. The shippers wanted low, stable rates and to prevent the railroads from charging different rates for short and long hauls. The railroads wanted to control competition, prevent rebates on rates, and guarantee themselves a fair rate of return.

The ICC attempted to regulate railroad rates with both constituencies in mind. By 1900 the commissioners, the railroads, and the shippers agreed that the commission did not have the power to solve the problems of all groups. In 1899 legislation had been introduced into Congress to allow the ICC to determine minimum and maximum rates on freight (Kolko, 1965, pp. 87–90). This legislation, known as the Cullom Bill, was not supported by the railroads because they wanted pooling to be legalized. The bill failed to pass.

In 1900 Senator Stephen Elkins took over leadership of the Senate Committee on Interstate Commerce. Elkins was a wealthy man who controlled coal mines, timber, and a railroad in West Virginia. He came to be closely allied with railroad interests. The first major piece of railroad legislation subsequent to the ICC Act was the Elkins Anti-Rebating Bill passed in 1903. This act, which was written by the Pennsylvania Railroad, made it illegal for a railroad to offer rebates to customers and imposed stiff fines both on the offending companies and those customers who accepted the rebates (Kolko, 1965, pp. 87–90). The law also allowed railroads to announce joint rates for certain routes and have that rate approved by the ICC. The passage of this law seemed to imply that there was no longer a need for one to legalize pooling.

But after two years it was apparent that the law did not work because it was difficult to enforce. In 1906 the Hepburn Bill was passed to tighten the Elkins Bill and provide the ICC with enough power to set maximum rates. The Hepburn Bill has been given pro- and antirailroad interpretations by historians. The classical view is that the bill was written to control the railroads by giving the ICC the power to prevent unjustified rate hikes. Alternatively, Gabriel Kolko has argued that the railroads generally supported the legislation and even helped write certain of its key provisions.[16] Given what occurred after its passage, the Hepburn Act reflected a piece of compromise legislation that could have been used to raise or lower rates.

The major problem with the legislation was that, while it gave the ICC power to set "just, fair, and reasonable rates," it gave it no guidelines for how such rates could be calculated. Both shippers and railroads were in the position to argue for or against any rate changes. In the years just after the passage of the Hepburn Act, the ICC tended to side with the shippers against the interests of the railroads (Martin, 1971, ch. 7; Kolko, 1965, pp. 175–192).

The Mann-Elkins Act, passed in 1910, added an important procedure to making rate decisions. A special court was created called the Commerce Court. This court was given the power to rule on the legality of ICC decisions in regard to rates. The railroads supported the legislation. They thought the court would serve as a weapon against the commission when it would not allow rate increases. Consequently, the court was controlled by people who were friendly to the railroad industry (Kolko, 1965, pp. 179–203). In its three years of operation, it decided most frequently for the railroads. In 1913 one of the judges on the court was indicted for accepting favors from railroads. The same year Congress abolished the Court amidst this scandal and the general perception that the court worked only for the interests of the railroads.

The railroads continued to argue that their rates of profit were too low, given their need for capital investment. After being denied general rate increases for eight years, the railroads finally turned the tables in 1914. The ICC with the support of Woodrow Wilson, decided that a rate hike for the major northeastern railroads was appropriate. Thereafter, the railroads called upon Wilson whenever they felt they had a valid case and he generally was sympathetic (Kolko, 1965, pp. 208–230). But the ICC occasionally ruled against the railroads, especially in rate cases involving western grain and raw material shipments. In 1920 the Esch-Cummins Bill was passed to allow the ICC to take into account the profitability of the railroads and their need to reinvest capital in its decisions on rate hikes (Kerr, 1968, ch. 9). The shippers generally supported this legislation as it forced the railroads to justify their rate increases and contained a number of other sections that favored their interests. More important, the railroads had finally secured a way to guarantee their profits.

The manufacturing conception of the corporation proposed a break with all tactics of direct control of competitors. It had two components: the goal of a more efficient organization and the use of price leadership to control competition. The first involved the integration of production and the second depended on the announcement of prices by the largest firm for important commodities and the subsequent adoption of those prices by the rest of the industry.

This discussion brings us to two major conclusions. First, problems of competition persisted in the emerging industrial economy during the first twenty years of the twentieth century. Second, the organizational fields of the largest firms continued to be unstable. There were no accepted rules to define how firms could avoid destructive competition, so they attempted to control their markets through various aggressive trade tactics, continued mergers, cartels, getting the federal government to guarantee profitability, or by utilizing the manufacturing conception of the corporation. The federal government and courts closed off the opportunity for firms to continue these unfair trade practices and restraints of trade by defining legal and illegal courses of action in markets, and directed them to the manufacturing conception as the best legal tactic for survival.

The Federal Government, the Courts, and the Large Firms, 1900–1916

There were two key issues in the debate over the regulation of the large modern corporation: who would control the incorporation of large firms and how could the law be used to maintain competition. The merger movement at the turn of the century demonstrated that the existing law was not sufficient to solve those problems and, indeed, encouraged consolidations. Roosevelt, Taft, and Wilson did not set out to destroy the large corporation. Instead, each attempted to protect the legitimacy of the system by using existing law against the worst offenders or proposing new laws to change the rules of the system.

The state, in a capitalist society like America's, must promote the economic environment so that it insures firms' profitability as well as maintains the existing social order. The first goal is achieved by manipulating macroeconomic conditions and aiding individual firms or industries. The second is attained by appealing to the democratic character of our political institutions and focusing on the promotion of individual rights. These two purposes of the state can produce complementary or contradictory policies.

The legislation of the Progressive era (1900–1916) makes the most sense when viewed through this theoretical lense. Some legislation was oriented toward making capitalism more profitable for only certain sectors of the economy, in particular the Elkins Act (for railroads) and the Federal Reserve Act (for banks). Legislation like the Hepburn Act and the Esch-Cummins Act appeared to compromise differing interests. Two other pieces of legislation of concern here, the Federal Trade Commission Act and the Clayton Act, were more clearly efforts to maintain the legitimacy of the capitalist system. These acts attempted to define acceptable competition and preserve the ability of other firms to enter markets. In the context of twentieth century political struggles, they tried to make the economic system fairer for everyone.

Similarly, the state is made up of different organizations, each with its own interests and these interests are founded in complex ideologies. In the early twentieth century, the House and the executive branch were the most concerned with controlling the large corporations. The Senate, which was more conservative, often blocked the revision of antitrust statutes. The ideology of state's rights continually came into conflict with antitrust sentiments. Roosevelt wanted to shift incorporation laws to the federal jurisdiction and even considered a constitutional amendment that would have given the federal government more power over the large firms. Neither of these proposals ever became law as the various branches of government never agreed. Finally, the courts, particularly the Supreme Court, worked toward a consistent interpretation of the Sherman Act.

The backdrop of progressivism was two-fold. First, the economy experienced rapid swings of expansion and contraction. At the political level, there was a rise in working-class consciousness and more working-class political activity. The Socialist Party, the various factions of the union movement, and other political groups constantly pressured the system. The Progressives were responding not only to what they perceived as injustices of the industrial order but also to the emerging working-class movement and its threats to society. Any reforms, therefore, still had to legitimate capitalism while they amended the alleged abuses of the system.

The debate over what should be done about the new large firms occurred in the legislatures, the courts, and the press. It was necessary for each of these groups to define exactly what the problem was in order to propose a solution. Not surprisingly, the debate was almost entirely conducted in the vocabulary I discussed earlier. The issue was to separate legal and illegal behavior of large firms and thereby protect markets from unfair trade practices.

It is useful to consider how widespread this concern was. Table 3.3 presents the number of congressional hearings held each session on antitrust issues and the number of distinct pieces of legislation that were proposed. There was some activity on these issues before 1895, including, of course, the passage of the Sherman Act. The late 1890s was a period of disinterest in the topic, but beginning in 1900 discussion of antitrust questions increased and peaked following the presidential election of 1912.

The table suggests how the issue rose in importance for Congress, but it does not specify the topics of the hearings or bills. The earliest hearings were held to consider the problems of trusts in

Table 3.3 Hearings and bills dealing with antitrust issues, 1880–1917, by congressional session

Date of Session	Hearings	Bills
1888–89	3	0
1890–91	0	1
1892–93	1	0
1894–95	2	0
1896–97	0	0
1898–99	0	0
1900–01	1	2
1902–03	1	4
1904–05	3	0
1906–07	1	2
1908–09	4	2
1910–11	13	4
1912–13	24	7
1914–15	4	3
1916–17	3	3

Sources: hearings: U.S. Congressional Hearing Index, pt. 1. Washington, D.C.: Congressional Information Service, Inc., 1985; bills: "Congress and the Monopoly Problem," H. doc. 240, 80th Congress. Washington, D.C.: U.S. Government Printing Office, 1957.

the whiskey, cotton bagging, oil, sugar, meat-packing, and coal industries. After 1900 interest shifted toward investigating the laws and the large firm as an economic phenomenon in order to formulate new regulation. Twenty-eight of the fifty-four hearings held from 1900 to 1917 were concerned with these more general issues while the rest concentrated on conditions in one industry or firm. The first hearing to consider creating a Federal Trade Commission was held in 1908. In 1912 alone there were nine hearings on possible antitrust legislation.

Theodore Roosevelt's position on the issue is noteworthy.

> One of the great troubles, I am inclined to think much the greatest trouble, in any immediate handling of the question of trusts comes from our system of government. When this government was founded, there were no great individual or corporate fortunes, and commerce and industry were carried on very much as they had been carried on in the days when Ninevah and Babylon stood in the Mesopotamian valley. There was no particular need at that time of bothering as to whether the Nation or the State had control of corporations. They were easy to control. Now, however, the exact reverse is the case . . . I do not believe that you can get any action by any state, I do not believe it practicable to get action by all the states, that will give us satisfactory control of the trusts, of big corporations; and the result is at present that we have a great powerful artificial creation which has no creator to which it is responsible. (*The Outlook,* Sept. 13, 1902, pp. 118–119)

Roosevelt went on to outline was he saw as the following solutions to the problem:

> The first thing we want is publicity; and I do not mean publicity as a favor by some corporations. I mean it as a right from all corporations affected by the law. I want publicity as to the essential facts in which the public has an interest. I want the knowledge given to the accredited representatives of the people of facts upon which those representatives can, if they see fit, base their later actions . . . As far as the antitrust laws go, they will be enforced . . . I cannot say I am sure, but I believe that it is possible to frame National legislation which shall give us more power than we now have, at any rate, over corporations doing an inter-state business. (p. 119)

In order to secure his first goal, Roosevelt formed a corporation bureau in the newly founded Department of Commerce and

Labor (U.S. Commissioner of Corporations, 1904, p. 12). The bureau was in charge of procuring information for the Congress and the executive branch on matters dealing with interstate commerce. Its first responsibility was to review state and territorial corporation laws in order to determine their substance and the possibility of a federal incorporation law (U.S. Commissioner of Corporations, 1904, pp. 37–48; 1906, p. 6; 1908, pp. 4–8). The second goal was to investigate industry or company practices in order to publicize potential restraints of trade. By the time the bureau was transformed into the FTC in 1914, it had investigated the beef, petroleum, cotton, steel, lumber, tobacco, and water transportation industries. It published reports on U.S. Steel, American Tobacco, Standard Oil, and International Harvester and provided the basic evidence used in the antitrust suits against each of these firms.

The Justice Department, under Roosevelt's urgings, stepped up its antitrust activities following the merger movement. The number of suits rose from six between 1895 and 1899, to thirty-nine between 1900 and 1904, to ninety-one between 1905 and 1909. The Justice Department won slightly less than 25 percent of the cases in the 1900–1905 period which increased to about 44 percent between 1905 and 1909 (Posner, 1970, table 1, p. 366; table 5, p. 375). Philander Knox, Roosevelt's first attorney general, expressed his attitude in testimony before the Senate Judiciary Committee in 1903: "The end desired by the overwhelming majority of the people of all sections of the country is that combinations of capital should be regulated and not destroyed, and that measures should be taken to correct the tendency toward monopolization of the industrial business of the country" (p. 19). Knox also suggested several concrete ways this could be achieved, stressing the importance of the Bureau of Corporations and antitrust suits.

It is worthwhile to explore the nature of the increasing number of suits and the types of arguments that motivated them. Most of the contemporary commentaries focus narrowly on judgments running from U.S. v. E. C. Knight (1895) through U.S. v. Northern Securities (1904), to U.S. v. Standard Oil (1911) (Thorelli, 1955, pp. 561–562; Letwin, 1965, pp. 253–270). While the issues they raised were fundamental, most of the Sherman Act cases were not against the firms resulting from large-scale mergers, but instead were directed against unfair trade practices and restraints of trade. Table 3.1 demonstrates that the vast majority of cases concerned firms involved in pools or unfair trade practices.

The reason for this is quite simple. The language of the Sherman Act caused the Justice Department to focus on *conspiracies* in restraint of trade. Thus, actions that took place between firms were much easier to prosecute than actions involving only one firm. Mergers proved to be the most difficult because the Justice Department needed to prove the intent to restrain interstate trade. Indeed, most of the lawsuits against Standard Oil, DuPont, and U.S. Steel turned on evidence of their behavior toward competitors and not their attempts to use vertical or horizontal integration to expand their power.

Table 3.4 presents a list of the firms formed in the merger movement that were capitalized at more than $40 million and had greater than a 60 percent market share. Seven of the fourteen firms were prosecuted by the Justice Department. Those that were not tended to be either in declining industries or facing renewed competition.

American Tobacco was convicted on the basis of their use of unfair trade practices, such as secretly controlling competitors, engaging in discriminatory pricecutting, and generally aggressively pursuing a monopoly. The lawsuit against Standard Oil, the largest case in history, focused on that firm's unfair efforts to restrain trade and not on the mergers it undertook or its market share.[17]

International Harvester was convicted of conspiring with other

Table 3.4   Companies formed in the merger movement with greater than $40 million in capitalization and more than 60% market share

*American Tobacco	*American Can
*U.S. Steel	American Locomotive
International Paper	*International Harvester
National Biscuit	*American Sugar Refining
American Car and Foundry	*DuPont
American Smelting and Refining	*General Electric
Distilling Company of America	Pullman

Source: Ralph Nelson, original coding sheets (1959).
Note: An asterisk indicates that an antitrust case was brought against the firm in the period 1904–1920.

firms in its industry to fix prices and market shares. The case against American Sugar Refining concerned its attempt to control the Pennsylvania Sugar Refining Company through the secret purchase of that firm's stock. DuPont was sued on the grounds that it had conspired to control the gun powder trade through merger, collusion, and the use of unfair trade practices. As a result, the gun powder association was dissolved and eventually DuPont was forced to spin off two of its constituent companies. The General Electric lawsuit centered on that firm's use of bogus independent firms and tying contracts.[18]

The U.S. Steel and American Can cases were the only antitrust suits of the seven that involved mergers to any degree and the government lost both of them. The Justice Department argued that U.S. Steel should be broken up because of its size and attempts to fix prices. The company won because it did not engage in explicit price fixing and the Supreme Court ruled that size per se was not an offense. A similar suit charged American Can with forming a monopoly by merging 90 percent of the can business. The Supreme Court ruled against the Justice Department on the grounds that subsequent competition demonstrated that the firm had not engaged in illegal trade practices to attain its position.

During the Roosevelt presidency (1901–1909) and the Progressive period antitrust enforcement was stepped up substantially. Roosevelt also proposed new legislation. The House was concerned with passage of various pieces of antitrust legislation throughout the period, but the Republican-dominated Senate Judiciary Committee blocked these efforts continuously. A number of bills were introduced that would have strengthened the Sherman Act and extended its provisions. Roosevelt chose to take a more conservative tack and opted to support four pieces of legislation that fit his political program. First, the Bureau of Corporations was added onto the bill founding the Department of Commerce and Labor. Then, Roosevelt supported the Elkins Anti-Rebating Bill as a way to deal with railroad rate discrimination (Thorelli, 1955, pp. 555–556).

In order to add to the administrative tools available to the Justice Department, two pieces of legislation were passed. First, the Justice Department was authorized to appoint an assistant attorney general whose major task was to pursue antitrust. The Antitrust Division in the Justice Department was given $500,000 to operate, which at the time, was more than the entire budget of the Justice Department (Thorelli, 1955, pp. 534–537). Attorney General Knox, with the aid of Roosevelt, also got the Congress to pass a bill that allowed antitrust suits to be expedited by providing immunity to witnesses and allowing suits decided in district courts to move immediately to the Supreme Court. Knox wanted this legislation in order to bring the Northern Securities case to a rapid conclusion (Letwin, 1965, p. 216; Thorelli, 1955, pp. 537–538).

During Roosevelt's administration, there was one major attempt to produce a federal incorporation law, which has been chronicled by a number of scholars (Kolko, 1963, pp. 61–88, 113–138; Letwin, 1965, pp. 195–207, 247–250; Lamoreaux, 1986, pp. 170–173). Basically, the legislation failed because, as it evolved, it was controlled by business interests and appeared to compromise the effectiveness of the Sherman Act. The various groups who supported the legislation were unable to hold together and the possibility of federal incorporation disappeared.

Toward the end of his term in office Roosevelt began to favor the formation of an interstate trade commission along the lines of the ICC. He argued that "the law should make its prohibitions and permissions as clear and definite as possible, leaving the least possible room for arbitrary action, or allegation of such action, on the part of the Executive, or of divergent interpretations by the courts" (1926, pp. 420–421). To do this Roosevelt proposed to set up a trade commission. This agency would have the power to rule on fair and unfair trade practices and would specify to businesses what would constitute such practices.

President Woodrow Wilson set up the FTC and supported passage of the Clayton Act. The FTC had the power to investigate trade practices, issue cease and desist orders, and make these orders subject to judicial review. The Clayton Act explicitly outlawed certain trade practices. The act including prescriptions against discriminatory pricing practices, tying contracts, interlocking directorates, and the secret holding of stock of competitors; exemptions for labor unions from the antitrust laws; and an antimerger rule that outlawed holding companies.

The last issue to take up is how the Supreme Court's view of the Sherman Act was altered after U.S. v. E. C. Knight (1895). As I have argued, this case reflected the problem of who was to regulate corporations, the states or the federal government. In 1900 holding companies were effectively protected from prosecution under the Sherman Act on the grounds that tight combinations were not a direct restraint of trade. But after the Knight decision, the Supreme Court began to backpedal. In U.S. v. Addyston Pipe (1898), the Court refused to accept the Knight case as a precedent. The issue, as it was framed then, was whether or not the Addyston contract was an illegal restraint of trade.[19]

The U.S. v. Trans-Missouri and U.S. v. Addyston Pipe decisions were viewed by Roosevelt and Knox as evidence that the Sherman Act could potentially be used against tight combinations (Letwin, 1965, pp. 195–207). For this reason they chose to pursue the Northern Securities Company, a holding company formed to control the Northern Pacific and Great Northern Railroads. The government won the suit, which was important for two reasons. First, it established that the form of the restraint of trade, be it pool, cartel, unfair trade practice, or holding company was irrelevant. What was important, was that the organizers of the group intended to restrain trade. Second, it interpreted the Sherman Act to mean literally that all restraints of trade whether reasonable or unreasonable were illegal. In other words, any merger or act of competition that might damage a competitor could be construed as a restraint of trade and would constitute a violation of the Sherman Act.

The "rule of reason" was elucidated in the Standard Oil case to circumscribe this problem (Thorelli, 1955, pp. 31–34; Letwin, 1965, pp. 174–178). This meant that one needed to prove that firms acted unreasonably in their attempts to restrain trade. The Standard Oil Company violated the Sherman Act, from this point of view, because the firm sought a monopoly in an unreasonable fashion. In the U.S. Steel decision the Court ruled that the company had not acted in restraint of trade because they did not try and destroy all other steel companies in order to establish a monopoly.[20]

While these cases established that holding companies or merged firms could be prosecuted under the Sherman Act, the fact remains that not many of them were. The main reason was that to prove a violation of the Sherman Act, the government needed to show that the merger was undertaken *primarily* to restrain trade. As one might imagine, this was somewhat difficult to do. The government needed to establish not only this intent but also that the merger actually constituted an unreasonable restraint of trade. In the face of these difficulties, it is not surprising that most suits were brought against unreasonable restraints of trade that appeared obvious, that is, pools or unfair trade practices.

Because the government and courts would not sanction behavior that preserved monopoly power or tended to restrain the acts of competitors, the owners and managers of the large firms had to adjust their strategies. This meant that all forms of direct control were now illegal and a new conception of control needed to be constructed. The antitrust community never threatened to outlaw or destroy the large firms. Instead, it supported those that worked within the rules and challenged only those who threatened the existence of markets. In this way, the free market and competition were protected. While the owners and managers of the largest firms would have preferred to keep the government out of their affairs entirely, the government intervened to guard the capitalist order by guaranteeing that the largest firms could dominate only if they competed in a reasonable fashion.

Contemporary scholars of antitrust history and economics choose to ignore this fundamental fact. Antitrust legislation and the debates they engendered seem like anachronisms today, precisely because they were effective. The practices they outlawed have generally been nonexistent in the business community since the 1920s. Firms had to develop alternative strategies for growth and profit, ones that did not constitute unfair trade practices nor restraints of trade.

The Rise of the Manufacturing Conception of Control

There were two major ways managers and entrepreneurs who adopted the manufacturing conception of control formed new organizational fields. First, a leading firm that controlled a large portion of the output of a given organizational field operated as a price setter. To set prices, the actors in that firm had to control their suppliers and marketing in order to increase their own efficiency and have the potential to cut off other firms from supplies or customers. If one firm was to have the power to make rules for the entire organizational field, it had to have the ability to back it up. The leading firm also had to communicate to its competitors that it could set prices and make sure that they knew what it intended to charge. In this situation, actors in other firms responded by following the price leader and integrating to retain some control of both suppliers and marketing. Integration, for these firms, was a defensive tactic to prevent the larger firm in the field from completely controlling them. This pattern appeared in the steel, oil, paper, and agricultural equipment industries.

The second way in which new organizational fields emerged occurred when there was a small number of large firms in a field. In this case, the firms would cooperate to set prices. Their power was based on similar size and organization. Similarly efficient producers were more likely to watch one another closely and jockey for market share than to engage in all out price wars. Communication and mutual respect would again require detailed knowledge of the others' actions. In this situation all of the firms would tend to integrate vertically as a defensive measure. Where equality reigned, stability might follow. This pattern could be construed as an oligopoly and the meat-packing industry fit it most neatly. Close communication between the meat-packing firms had evolved from the late nineteenth century as the industry engaged in collusion. But a shift toward the manufacturing conception implied they would need to abandon direct restraints of trade and adopt more indirect tactics.

Standard Oil's dominance in the industry was built on its control of transportation facilities, refining capacity, and aggressive marketing. The central feature of this control was the ownership of pipelines from the oil fields. Oil producers that were not owned by the company had little choice but to accept the prices that Standard offered because there was no one else to whom to sell the oil. With the opening of new fields in the Gulf of Mexico, the Midwest, California, and Illinois, Standard Oil was unable to prevent other firms from entering the pipeline business and controlling a portion of the industry. This began to undermine the company's lead position.

Standard Oil and later the group that formed when the company was split up tended to be price leaders. When others would try to undercut Standard in certain markets or products, Standard would generally meet their price (U.S. Federal Trade Commission, 1928, pp. 99–136). The basic strategy for preserving large firms in the oil industry was price leadership. But the oil business was growing so quickly at the time that making profits was not a problem (U.S. Federal Trade Commission, 1928, pp. 266–285).

Competitors who rose against Standard Oil concentrated in all phases of the industry. The largest of these competitors began to adopt the strategy of vertical integration. In order to protect themselves from Standard Oil, large firms needed to have a guaranteed production, transportation, refining, and marketing capacity. Even smaller firms adopted the integrated form (Williamson and Daum, 1959, vol. 2, pp. 65–110). William Mellon, the president of Gulf Oil, summed up the situation. "I concluded that the best way to compete was to develop an integrated business which would first of all produce oil. Production, I saw, had to be the foundation of the business. That was clearly the only way for a company which proposed to operate without saying 'by your leave' to anyone" (Williamson and Daum, 1959, vol. 2, p. 82).

The companies that spun off in the breakup of Standard Oil tended not to be integrated companies. Standard had operated as a holding company and each of the constituent firms engaged in one particular phase of the business. In fact only Standard New Jersey and Standard California were involved in all phases of the oil industry. The FTC found that by 1926 most of the firms formed in the breakup had become vertically integrated producers and all of the largest ones were producing, shipping, and refining oil except Standard Oil of New York (1928, p. 78). Many of these firms merged to achieve integration.

The oil industry illustrates the creation of the manufacturing conception of control for defensive purposes. Vertical integration, mainly through mergers, ensured that any given company would not have its oil supply threatened or be unable to ship its products to market. Managers were obsessed with this threat and most of their actions were taken to avoid it. At the same time the industry used price leadership to guarantee all firms a certain level of profit. This leadership could stabilize prices in the short run, but tended to encourage the formation of new firms in the long run.

Integration in the steel industry began in the 1890s when Andrew Carnegie formed the Carnegie Steel Company, which combined many plants into the largest steel firm. In 1898 the Federal Steel Company, under the leadership of Elbert Gary with the aid of J. P. Morgan, merged the Illinois Steel Company, the Lorain Steel Company, the Minnesota Iron Company, and the Elgin,

Joliet, and Eastern Railroad. The purpose of this merger was to integrate successive stages of production in order to capture profits at all stages and protect the firm from loss of raw materials due to shortages or control by other firms (U.S. Commissioner of Corporations, 1911, vol. 1, p. 2). These companies were run as companions to the Federal Steel Company and their integration was more formal than substantive. The firm produced semifinished steel for the trade and heavy steel products such as rails and beams.

This consolidation was followed by a series of consolidations in other parts of the business, which were also somewhat integrated. These consolidations produced the American Steel and Wire Company of New Jersey, the American Bridge Company, the National Tube Company, the Shelby Tube Company, the National Steel Company, the American Tin Plate Company, the American Sheet Metal Company, and the American Steel Hoop Company (Hogan, 1971, ch. 14). The U.S. Steel Company was formed to avoid competition between the already large firms in the industry. The company then had operations in all parts of the industry from the mining of ore and coal, to the production of coke, pig iron, steel, and finished products such as wire, tin plate, and other structural products. One little known fact is that U.S. Steel controlled 75 percent of the iron ore reserves in 1910 (U.S. Commissioner of Corporations, 1911, vol. 1, pp. 380–381). The other firms in the industry needed to protect themselves from U.S. Steel in two ways. First, they had to avoid direct competition, because with its integrated operations and control over iron ore, U.S. Steel could be a formidable competitor in every line of the business. Second, they had to secure access to raw materials.

Bethlehem Steel was formed in 1903 from an earlier firm that produced mainly steel plates for ships. Over the next seventeen years, the firm expanded through merger and internally to become an integrated unit. Its purchases included the Philadelphia, Bethlehem, and New England Railroad, the Tofo Iron mines (located in Chile), the Forge River Shipbuilding Company, the Titusville Forge Company, the Pennsylvania Steel Company (at the time one of the eight largest steel companies), and several other companies (Hogan, 1971, pp. 537–558). A similar process of integration took place at National Steel, Jones and Laughlin Steel, Inland Steel, Armco, and Youngstown Steel (Hogan, 1971, pp. 559–664).

As a result of these mergers and U.S. Steel's attempt to maintain prices, U.S. Steel's market share drifted slowly downward and by 1920 the company controlled only about 40 percent of the market. As I noted earlier, steel prices remained stable for much of this period and rose only under the impetus of World War I. The company's role in this price stability, however, was pivotal. Because of its leadership, the U.S. Steel Company was able to keep the price of steel rails at $28 a ton from 1901 to 1916. This is remarkable when one considers that there were three recessions during this period.

The mechanism for exercising price leadership was the so-called "Gary dinner." Between 1901 and 1911 Elbert Gary, the president of U.S. Steel, held dinners with the presidents of the other large steel companies. At these meetings Gary would try to prevent, "not by agreement, but by exhortation, the wide and sudden fluctuation of prices which would be injurious to everyone interested in the business of iron and steel manufacturers."[21] Since the steel industry required large amounts of fixed capital, there was great inducement to follow the lead of U.S. Steel so that all firms could profit.

The strategy worked extremely well. When other firms began to lower prices in bad times, Gary would threaten to undercut them (Burns, 1936, pp. 109–117). The ultimate goal of price leadership was not to maximize prices, but instead to make them stable. When times were bad, prices were stabilized at higher than average levels. When times were good, they were lower than average. As the demand for steel increased, the overall effect of price stability was to make the industry more attractive to prospective competitors. The constant erosion of market share for U.S. Steel demonstrates that while there were considerable barriers to entry in the industry, firms overcame them and were able to earn profits. It was also the case that, when times were good, customers were willing to pay premiums for steel above the posted prices. Since U.S. Steel generally honored the posted price, they did not benefit from these bonuses during upswings. In downturns, competitors also maintained market share and price (Burns, 1936, pp. 205–215; Kolko, 1963, pp. 35–39).

The price leadership of U.S. Steel was based on its ability to control the supply of iron ore and its sheer size in every product market. The rest of the steel industry became vertically integrated as a defensive measure against the possible cutoff of ore and the desire to control the input of iron and unfinished steel. Since the capital expenditures needed to run steel plants were high, firms attempted to control the entire production process to prevent needless shutdowns. During the early 1920s, there was a significant depression in the steel industry. As a result a large number of mergers occurred that influenced the basic structure of the industry until the late 1960s. Both vertical and horizontal integration left U.S. Steel with powerful competitors who controlled all aspects of the business (Hogan, 1971, pp. 877–892).

International Harvester was accepted as the price leader in the agricultural implements field during the same period. It produced more efficiently than its competitors and priced its products high enough to guarantee an above-industry rate of return (Burns, 1936, pp. 109–117). International Harvester was vertically integrated and produced its own steel. When the firm was formed it controlled 85 percent of the market and the five leading brand names in farm implements as well as an extensive network of distributors. (U.S. Commissioner of Corporations, 1913, vol. 1, pp. 10–23). Any competitors in the business needed to reproduce the firm's dominance in all phases of the industry. The firm practiced price moderation and did not directly attack its competitors. Over the years a number of highly integrated firms followed in its wake, notably John Deere and Company.

The International Paper Company determined the price for paper in much of the country. Only on the West Coast was there a rival. Long-term contracts were written specifying prices tied to those of International Paper. The three largest producers accounted for 50 percent of the production. The industry consistently operated under its capacity and profits were generally high (Burns, 1936, p. 132). International Paper maintained its power by being highly integrated. It owned timberlands, electric power plants, and paper mills that produced all grades of paper. Other firms, such as Weyerhaeuser and Georgia-Pacific, that emerged in the industry followed its practice of securing sources of raw materials.

The meat-packing industry showed the effects of both concentration and price leadership through market sharing. The Commissioner of Corporations Report (1907, vol. 3, p. 85) concluded that "so long as the big packers retain their present control over stockyards, and enjoy the present advantages from the ownership and operation of private car lines and branch houses, there is little promise that additional live-stock marketing centers will develop unless the big packers themselves own and develop them."

All of the large packing firms were involved in every stage of the market from the purchase of the animals to the sale of the meat. Their sharing of markets began with joint ownership of stockyards and extended to the division of marketing territory (U.S. Commissioner of Corporations, 1907, vol. 3, pp. 126–132). The effect of these arrangements was a division of the market that remained almost constant for fifteen years for the five largest firms (U.S. Federal Trade Commission, 1918, vol. 1, p. 56).

The automobile industry seems to offer a counterexample to the general issues raised here. One could argue that because Henry Ford pioneered the methods of modern manufacturing, by producing the largest number of standardized cars for the lowest cost, he proved that the strategy of concentrating on efficient production motivated the most successful managers. But this view of Ford ignores a number of important issues. First, Ford took many of his ideas about mass production from the steel and meat-packing industries. The relative efficiency of those industries was his model. Second, in the first twenty years of this century, the structure of the automobile industry more closely resembled the oil industry of 1870 than the relatively stable oil industry of 1920. Since Ford was instrumental in creating the market for automobiles in the first place, it would have made little sense to engage in cartel or monopoly behavior (U.S. Federal Trade Commission, 1939, pp. 627–633). When the industry matured, a stable oligopolistic organizational field emerged which stressed competitive division of the market and not direct confrontation. This arrangement lasted until the 1970s.

Even Ford was not above considering a monopoly, however. In 1908 William Durant created General Motors in an attempt to gain control over the motor vehicle industry. Ford participated in the negotiations. In 1909 Durant tried to buy the Ford company for $8 million, but Ford wanted cash and Durant was unable to raise that much (U.S. Federal Trade Commission, 1939, p. 638). Ford also recognized the importance of vertical integration for control of production in the automobile industry. To lower costs Ford opted to standardize parts and output. He began to integrate the various parts suppliers into the firm and eventually purchased a steel mill.

The Effectiveness of the Manufacturing Conception

Once the manufacturing conception proved to be legal and relatively successful, it spread across the population of the largest firms and led to the development of many new organizational fields. The merger movement of the 1920s was a direct result of the belief that this conception of control would aid the survival of these large firms. The goal of managers and entrepreneurs in firms with a large market share was to stabilize prices. I will demonstrate that this was achieved through the concentration of assets and integration of production.

By the 1920s the unitary and functional forms came to replace the holding company as the preferred form of organization. These structures integrated production and allowed mangers and entrepreneurs to control their organizations more effectively. Once the manufacturing conception of control succeeded in a few organizational fields, manufacturing executives began to be made presidents of the largest corporations. The strongest predictor of the presence of a manufacturing president was the percentage of firms in a particular organizational field that already had a manufacturing president. Individuals with manufacturing backgrounds claimed the power in the largest firms on the basis of their intimate knowledge of the production process, knowledge that was essential to the formation of stable organizational fields. Finally, the vertically integrated firms outperformed their unintegrated competitors during the 1919–1929 period. The ultimate marker of success for the manufacturing conception of control was a firm's growth.

After the industrial recovery that began in 1898, prices began to rise slowly until 1915. One wholesale commodity index rose from 56.1 in 1900 to 69.5 in 1915; the norm price was 100 in 1926 (U.S. Bureau of the Census, 1960, pp. 113–114). While the overall commodity index rose, the changes in prices across various industries were mixed. The value of farm products, food products, and hides and leather products increased in step with the overall index. But textiles, fuel, building materials, and house furnishing goods lagged behind. In metals and metal products, prices were at

Table 3.5 Comparison of changes of prices for 36 commodities in industries characterized by high and low degrees of concentration

Year	Low concentration[b]		High concentration[c]	
	$\overline{X}$[a]	Variance	$\overline{X}$[a]	Variance
1897	99.32	0.67	103.71	15.29
1898	101.43	8.44	105.32	1.82
1899	114.32	53.18	115.98	40.13
1900	127.79	41.74	130.73	3.74
1901	119.63	5.41	128.23	2.84
1902	126.95	3.48	127.82	5.44
1903	129.15	3.79	125.32	2.24
1904	127.04	14.80	122.28	7.23
1905	128.10	16.06	121.98	0.99
1906	135.65	15.70	125.52	3.45
1907	147.73	16.84	131.96	2.63
1908	134.82	18.41	130.75	0.67
1909	136.72	12.46	130.28	5.22
1910	139.59	11.14	135.83	7.00
Grand mean	126.30	15.86	123.98	7.04

Source: Data are from Meade (1912).

Note: t-test: $\overline{X}_{NT} - \overline{X}_T$; $t = 1.34$, $p = 0.20$, 13 d.f.;
$\overline{V}_{NT} - \overline{V}_T$; $t = 2.79$, $p = 0.015$, 13 d.f.,
where $\overline{X}$ = grand mean, $\overline{V}$ = grand mean of variance, T = trust, NT = non-trust.

a. Means are based on monthly averages. Numbers are computed by forming an index for 18 products where 100 = price of product in January 1897 and changes reflect percentage increases or decreases in products on a monthly basis. Changes in product prices are summed across products each month. The means are the average across each year. Hence, prices in 1897 for low-concentrated items decreased 0.68 percent over the year.

b. Products with low concentration are manila rope, bituminous coal, molasses, pig iron, bleached sheetings, corn meal, yellow pine, plain white oak, print cloth, glass tumblers, vici kid shoes, zinc, flour, cotton, bare copper wire, wilton carpet, earthenware plates, bleached shirtings.

c. Products with high concentration are anthracite coal, cement, refined petroleum, cottonseed oil, glucose, newspaper, proof spirits, leather, wire nails, steel rails, raw linseed oil, lead, salt, plug tobacco, sulphuric acid, granulated sugar, cotton thread, matches.

a much higher level than the rest of the index at the beginning of the period and were slightly down at the end. Prices for chemical products increased substantially over the period (U.S. Bureau of the Census, 1960, pp. 113–114).

A formal test of the effect of consolidations on prices is presented in Table 3.5. This table contains indices of monthly prices for eighteen commodities controlled by firms with large market shares and eighteen produced in competitive markets. From 1897 to 1902 commodities dominated by firms with a large market share were priced at a higher level, while the pattern is reversed between 1903 and 1910. This suggests that the large firms were not able to produce or sustain higher than average price increases. There is no statistical difference between these mean price levels, however, the variation is statistically significantly lower for commodities dominated by larger firms. The leading firm strategy, therefore, was to sustain prices at a certain level so that all firms could be profitable. The goal was not to raise prices to monopoly levels.

This evidence shows only that firms with the greater market share were able to control the variations of the prices received for their commodities. It does not explicitly link the concentration of production with the integration of production, as my argument concerning the manufacuring conception of control suggests. Table 3.6 presents the relation between integration and concentration for the firms involved in the merger movement at the turn of the century. One can conclude that there is a strong, statistically significant relationship between concentration and integration of

Table 3.6 Cross-tabulation of level of concentration by presence of vertical integration for firms involved in the 1895-1904 merger movement

	Integration[a]	
	No	Yes
Concentration <40[b]	75	64
	(88.2)[c]	(59.8)
	(46.0)	(54.0)
Concentration >40	10	43
	(11.8)	(40.2)
	(18.9)	(81.2)

Note: $\chi^2 = 17.75$, 1 d.f., $p < .000$; Pearson's $r = 0.32$, $p < .000$.

a. Defined as presence or absence of a sales and marketing unit.

b. Industry concentration ratio dichotomized as greater than or equal to 40% of the industry market share.

c. Column percentage, followed by row percentage.

the sales function in a large firm. In other words, the managers and entrepreneurs who consolidated a large part of their industry's production simultaneously integrated that production.

To carry this argument a step further, if the manufacturing conception of control improved the large firm's chances of survival, one should be able to demonstrate that success with a statistical model. I will consider all the firms valued at more than $1 million that were formed in the merger movement to test this hypothesis. (See Appendix B for a description of the data discussed in this section including sources, coding, and statistical analysis.) There have been two major studies of the success of these large consolidations, both dating from the 1920s and 1930s (Dewing, 1922; Livermore, 1936). Livermore found that many of the large consolidations had been successful. Dewing studied a similar group of firms and their performance in subsequent years. On the basis of the same data, he concluded that the large firms were generally not successful. Whether the movement was a success or failure depends on one's judgment of how much success is enough. Instead of accepting another's judgment, my intention is to test why some of the largest firms survived and others did not.[22]

Of the 317 consolidations resulting from the merger movement, 145 (45.7 percent) still existed in 1919. The rest of the firms were lost in other mergers or bankruptcy. Because these firms were large by the standards of their time, this appears to be a substantial failure rate. The average consolidation was capitalized at $53.6 million and involved 10.9 firms. A total of 3,460 firms disappeared into these large consolidations between 1895 and 1904.

The manufacturing conception of control suggests that survival was related to controlling a significant level of the product line as well as being an integrated firm. If a firm was able to absorb a sufficient amount of its competition, it could stabilize prices and survive. But the ability to enforce the price also depended on the integration of production (Chandler, 1977, pp. 337–339).

The alternative explanations of their success revolve around the size of the firms and the various qualities of industries in which they operated. One might expect that larger firms would be able to control more resources and have access to more capital, thereby increasing their likelihood of survival. There are at least three kinds of factors that might characterize the industries in which firms survived. First, the size and growth of an industry could have had a positive effect. In industries that were large and getting larger, firms perhaps held on to their market share more easily than in industries that were stagnant or contracting. Second, the capital intensiveness of an industry could have aided success. If it was costly to begin production in an industry, then other firms would have been less likely to build plants in that industry (Bain, 1956, pp. 53–113). Third, unique factors in an industry, its technology, for instance, could also have provided barriers to entry.

When these alternative explanations are tested in an appropriate statistical model we see the following results. First, the size of a firm did not affect its odds of survival. Second, neither the size and growth of industries nor their capital intensiveness contributed to firm survival. The only two factors that help explain the survival are the level of concentration in the industry and whether or not a firm was integrated. In essence, the firms that survived were those that practiced strategies of the manufacturing conception of control.

The product mix and structure of the 100 largest corporations are considered in Table 3.7. Most of the firms were operating predominantly in one product line in 1919 and this changed little

Table 3.7   Strategies, structures, and subunit backgrounds of the 100 largest firms, 1919–1929

	Number of firms	
	1919	1929
Strategy		
Dominant	89	85
Related	11	15
Structure		
Holding company	31	25
Unitary/functional	69	73
Multidivisional	0	2
Subunit background		
Manufacturing	23	34
Sales and marketing	6	9
Finance	8	7
Entrepreneur	28	24
Other	35	26

Note: See Appendix C for data definitions and sources.

between 1919 and 1929. The functional/unitary structure implies a firm was internally integrated with separate departments for the firm's different activities, such as raw material purchasing, manufacturing, marketing, and finance. The holding company was an unintegrated firm of separate companies that operated somewhat independently. In 1919 only 31 of the 100 largest corporations were run as holding companies while 69 were organized as functional structures. By 1929 holding companies had declined to 25 and unitary/functional forms had increased to 73. The overwhelming majority of the largest firms had become integrated by 1919.

Additional evidence on the product mix of vertically integrated firms is available from a study done by Willard Thorp. His study of 4,813 firms concluded that only 18.8 percent of them utilized backward integration (1924, p. 238). He defined a vertically integrated firm as one with two separate manufacturing facilities that were successively related in a production process. Since this excludes individual plants that produced a number of products feeding into the next stage of production, his is probably a conservative estimate of the extent of vertical integration. Nonetheless, the bulk of these firms were located in the iron and steel, lumber, paper, chemical, stone, glass, clay, other metalmaking, and petroleum industries. These industries also had the highest concentration. This evidence corroborates the evidence in Table 3.6.

Another indicator of the rise of the manufacturing conception concerns who controlled the largest firms. Internal to every firm is a power struggle over the strategy and structure of the organization. At the turn of the century, most of the largest firms were run by the entrepreneurs who founded them. But by 1919 professional managers began to dominate the largest firms. These managers had to have an interpretation of their environment that would justify their firm's actions and structure. They also needed a power base in the organization to legitimate those actions.

These factors are operationalized by considering the functional backgrounds of the presidents of the largest firms (Fligstein, 1987, pp. 44–58; also see Appendix C). Presumably the entrepreneurs' power rested on their ownership. Presidents with manufacturing, marketing, and finance backgrounds rested their claims to power on a coherent vision of their organization and the importance of their subunit in that organization. Manufacturing presidents viewed the problems of the firm as production based, while marketing presidents focused on sales and product mix, and finance presidents on capital allocation.

Because the manufacturing conception provided the most successful strategies at the time, one would expect that presidents with a manufacturing background would have been on the rise. They knew how to produce goods cheaply so that they could fight off threats from competitors and achieve price stability and vertical integration. By 1929 manufacturing presidents were indeed the largest group of presidents (see Table 3.7).

Table D.5 presents the conditions under which manufacturing presidents came to power. The major one is that if they predominated in an industry, then other firms in that industry were also likely to select a manufacturing president. One interpretation of this tendency is that these presidents were defined as reasonable heirs to power in their organizational fields. As the manufacturing conception of control spread and organizational fields emerged, manufacturing personnel came to dominate the firms in those fields.

The final evidence to consider concerning the success of the manufacturing conception, is the effect of that conception on the growth of the large firms. Table D.2 contains a model for the growth in assets, sales, and profits for the 100 largest firms from 1919 to 1929. Three types of factors are included as predictors of growth: the change in growth in a firm's main industry; measures of strategies for growth including product mix, vertical integration, mergers, and multinational presence; and the functional background of the president. Details on these factors, the statistical model, and the framework informing the model are presented in Appendix D. For my purposes, the only coefficient of interest is the effect of vertical integration on growth. During the period, vertically integrated firms outperformed their nonintegrated competitors on growth in sales, assets, and profits.

The quantitative evidence supports my assertions in the historical discussion. The manufacturing conception of the large corporation, which focused on the integration of production and the simultaneous control of a large market share, produced the most successful tactics for stabilizing the large firm and setting up stable organizational fields. Firms that engaged in manufacturing controls were able to stabilize prices, promote their own survival, and enhance their growth during the 1920s. The success of this conception in producing firms that operated legally meant that the largest firms began to emulate their competitors who engaged in this conception. The holding company declined in importance and the unitary/functional form rose. Manufacturing presidents who were able to control the production process came to dominate as presidents of the largest firms.

The First World War and the Merger Movement

The most important force that preserved capitalism in the first twenty years of the century was World War I. To coordinate the war effort President Wilson formed the War Industries Board, which was headed by Bernard Baruch.[23] The board allocated resources throughout the economy in order to maximize war-related output. The government was ensured resources because the system gave defense needs first priority. The board also engaged in price fixing to control profiteering.

The administrative mechanism to implement these policies was a system of committees, each concerned with the production of certain commodities (Baruch, 1941, pp. 47–61, 102–108). These committees were run by executives of firms in an industry with the cooperation of the government and the rest of the firms in that industry. The experiences of the war changed both Baruch's and Wilson's attitude toward the large firm. Following the war their antifirm rhetoric was replaced with praise for the large firms' patriotism and contribution to progress (Baruch, 1941, pp. 109–116). One indication of this, is that antitrust suits decreased after the war and many were against smaller firms (Posner, 1970, p. 366).

When the war ended all commodity prices dropped, but they never reached their prewar level. Using 1926 as a base year (100), commodity prices stood at 68.1 in 1914. They rose to 161.3 in 1920 and dropped quickly to 102.4 in 1922. While prices more than doubled during the war, they were only 50 percent higher after the war. The war had a similar effect on wages. In 1914 the average hourly wage was 23 cents and by 1919 had risen to 48 cents. Wages never dropped following the war and rose to 49 cents in 1922 (U.S. Bureau of the Census, 1960, pp. 93–94, 119–120).

One obvious cause of the postwar boom in the United States

was the ability to maintain higher commodity prices, which increased profits, and the ability of individuals to obtain income to purchase goods as consumers, which increased sales. This was, of course, an unintended consequence of the war. The threat of Socialism was also eliminated during the war (Weinstein, 1968, p. 137). With the destruction of the political left and the conversion of the Democrats to the side of big business, large firms enjoyed prosperity in the 1920s. High incomes and high prices drove the economy for nine good years.

The government generally supported business. For instance, the Supreme Court accepted an extremely narrow view of the Clayton Act's antimerger clause, which basically made that part of the act unenforceable. It also held that U.S. Steel was not in violation of the antitrust law because the company had not engaged in any unreasonable acts to restrain trade. The court continued to rule against other restraints of trade, however. The most important of these decisions was directed against "open-price" trade associations. These associations involved firms that exchanged extremely detailed information about one another's business transactions. This exchange was viewed as a restraint of trade because it led to price fixing.[24] Antitrust enforcement continued to reinforce the definition of illegal behaviors as restraints of trade and unfair trade practices. Where these motives or tactics were absent, firms generally escaped antitrust litigation.

The Republican administrations of the 1920s also adopted a more benign attitude toward the large firms. While they consistently opposed price fixing or cartel arrangements, they did not oppose cooperation between firms to stabilize competition or eliminate unfair trade practices. One of the primary ways firms cooperated was through trade associations. As long as the associations were not used as organizations to exchange detailed information on prices or to control prices or production, the antitrust authorities approved them (Himmelberg, 1976, pp. 1–4).

Indeed, the Republican administrations encouraged the use of trade associations to stabilize business relations. Herbert Hoover was one of the leading advocates of what was called "associationalism" or "corporatism" (Hawley, 1981, pp. 95–123). Hoover recognized the problems of competition and felt that the solution was a set of cooperative associations within each industry that would establish standards and, in times of industrial crisis, control prices and production (Hawley, 1981, pp. 99–101). He felt that these associations should be independent of the federal government's regulatory powers and that they would help stabilize the economy.

The Coolidge Administration, with Hoover as Secretary of Commerce, undertook a number of steps to put such a system in place. Both the Antitrust Division and the FTC began to approve trade association agreements to regulate industries. In 1925 William Donovan, the head of the Antitrust Division of the Justice Department, began to hold meetings with representatives of trade associations to consider their plans for information sharing. At those meetings he ruled whether the agreements constituted violations of antitrust law (Himmelberg, 1976, pp. 54–62). Donovan remained adamantly opposed to price fixing agreements and prosecuted firms or associations engaged in such acts.

Coolidge appointed William Humphrey, a former U.S. Representative and lobbyist for West Coast lumber interests, head of the FTC in 1925. Humphrey initiated a policy similar to Donovan's. Business groups could call a conference under the auspices of the FTC to construct governing rules for an industry. The FTC would then consider the results and decide which of the rules were unfair merthods of competition and which were legal. Between July 1, 1927, and November 15, 1929, sixty-one conferences were held (Johnson, 1985, pp. 172–176). These actions strengthened the trade association movement.

All of the Republican officials remained committed to antitrust laws to the extent they outlawed overt price fixing or cartelization. Indeed in the early years of the Depression, Hoover, who was then president, began to enforce the antitrust laws more rigorously in response to a call from business for relaxation of those laws (Himmelberg, 1976, pp. 88–101). Given that the attitude toward business had been generally positive, it is not surprising that the merger movement of the 1920s, which resulted in oligopolies at the core of the economy, was not opposed by the FTC or the Justice Department. The antitrust authorities supported the attempts to create stable organizational fields where fair competition and product standards were maintained.

The manufacturing conception of control was, by 1920, the most effective tactic to escape price competition and ensure firm survival. All other tactics were illegal or unstable. The new merger movement reflected the recognition of the manufacturing strategy of control as the leading strategy to promote firm survival. In the most thorough study of that movement, Carl Eis (1978, pp. 79–81) concluded that 39.6 percent of the total value of mergers from 1926 to 1930 were horizontal, 28.8 percent vertical, and 30.9 percent product related or unrelated (the rest were unclassifiable). The industries which were most involved in the movement were primary metal, petroleum, food, chemical, and transportation equipment.

After extensive analysis Eis concluded, "In certain industries, merger activity by firms of the second rank helped transform an industry dominated by a single large firm into some form of oligopoly, in others they strengthened an existing oligopoly structure, while in others, they replaced many-firm markets by oligopoly" (1978, p. 132).

Eis (1978, p. 131) tended to downplay the role of vertical mergers in the movement. He failed to note that many of the mergers that strengthened or created oligopoly occurred in industries where vertical integration was the central tactic of the dominant firms and those oligopolies were attained because of vertical and horizontal integration. Given that the metal-making and oil industries accounted for the largest share of mergers and given their highly integrated and concentrated character, I can only conclude that those firms were pursuing manufacturing conception of control. Similar patterns emerged in the transportation equipment industry (Eis, 1978, pp. 152–153). Oligopoly is too narrow a description of what occurred. While firms were seeking to secure their market position, they did so by pursuing integration of production as well as market share. It was equally important to create organizational fields that defined product lines and appropriate courses of action around the vertical and horizontal control of production. The merger movement of the 1920s, therefore, reflected the triumph of the manufacturing conception of the firm.

4

The Sales and Marketing Conception of Control

The manufacturing conception of control operated to stabilize prices for some organizational fields during the 1920s. These fields were characterized by a small number of vertically integrated large firms who made their prices public and encouraged competitors to do the same. The market power of these large firms was backed up by relatively efficient production and large capacity. This power meant that other firms had little incentive to confront the price leaders and great incentive to go along.

But this conception of control created a number of problems. The dominant firms often lost their market share over time as they clung to set prices. This opened the door for competitors to enter the field and lessen the potential clout of the market leaders. The very problem that the manufacturing strategies had set out to control—competition—could instead eventually undermine an organizational field. This occurred in the steel and petroleum industries.

The development of stable organizational fields implies that managers and entrepreneurs within fields thought alike. Key actors shaped the view of what constituted appropriate behavior and managers in other firms conformed. The analysis of and solution to the problems of these fields was sought collectively and the terms of these considerations were quite narrow. Within the manufacturing conception of control, managers and entrepreneurs tended to resist technological and organizational innovations and embrace tactics to promote price stability. The manufacturing personnel who led these firms viewed stable pricing as attainable through attention to the production process. This caused them to focus only on what they could control as a counterthreat: the flow of goods through the production process. In this way, given stable or declining markets, controlling the sources of raw materials and the distribution of goods became more important than product demand or the need to introduce new products.

Ultimately, weaknesses were most pronounced in an economic downturn. Since the central purpose of organizational fields was to maintain prices, the only way to do so in a recession or depression was to scale back production. This caused havoc in the firms, particularly in those with a large plant investment and vertical integration of production. Once a downturn began, organizational fields dominated by the manufacturing conception of control were likely to reduce production until prices could be stabilized. Indeed, from a manufacturing point of view, this was the *only* choice.

The Depression of the 1930s proved catastrophic for the large firms dominated by the manufacturing conception of control. They sought relief from the federal government. They wanted to return to direct control of competitors by allowing cartels to set prices. The Roosevelt Administration went along with this view and through the National Recovery Administration (NRA) suspended the antitrust laws and allowed cartels to set prices for various commodities in order to stabilize them. But this attempt failed to increase production and, more important, was declared unconstitutional less than eighteen months after being put in place. Subsequently Roosevelt felt that the managers and entrepreneurs who controlled the large firms had not worked hard enough to bring the country out of the Depression. He began to pursue an aggressive antitrust program that broke up cartels and efforts to restrain trade.

My perspective offers a novel view as to why the Depression was as long and severe as it was. The leaders of the large firms dominated by the manufacturing conception saw the key problem as low prices. This meant that they were intent on controlling prices by cutting production. But once prices were stabilized, they were cautious about increasing production for fear that prices would once again collapse. Since their competitors had roughly equal production capacities and costs, all would lose by too rapid an increase in production. Indeed, the main effect of the National Industrial Recovery Act (NIRA) was exactly that: prices increased, but production did not.

The sales and marketing conception of control began with an entirely new premise. Instead of price stability, managers and entrepreneurs began to focus on selling goods. Firm survival no longer depended on threatening one's competitors directly. Instead, firms sought outlets for their goods where no other firms were selling. This was done in a number of ways. Firms differentiated their products from their competitors' and appealed to buyers with price differences based on quality. An extension of this tactic was to establish brand names and build consumer loyalty through advertising. Firms also sought new markets for their goods either nationally or multinationally. Finally, if one product line faltered, firms ensured their survival by making new products, products for which markets did not yet exist or for which demand was high. The important feature of all these courses of action is that managers and entrepreneurs turned from directly confronting their competitors to finding unique markets for their products. While competition continued to exist, prospects for firm survival were greatly increased by selecting noncompetitive market niches for products.

The structure and functioning of organizational fields began to change once firms no longer tried to influence one another's prices directly, but instead rapidly tried to differentiate their products. Firms in similar organizational fields watched one another in order to occupy different places in their products' markets. This meant that competition was more indirect and less confrontational. It also meant that managers and entrepreneurs tried to learn from their competitors how to differentiate their products as well as how to locate rapidly growing markets. As this differentiation led to diversification of products, organizational fields were defined more in terms of entire industries rather than in single-product terms. Organizational fields operated more as reference groups to provide information about markets and successful products than as centers of power in which a leading firm used fear of competition to control pricing. The sales and marketing conception of control was a complete break with the manufacturing and direct conceptions of control.

This new conception of control was the product of the sales and marketing revolution of the 1920s. A number of firms pioneered the tactics and provided the basis for a new way of stabilizing the large firm. But the proof of the success of the sales and marketing conception came during the Depression. Firms and organizational fields dominated by the manufacturing conception of control did poorly. But firms whose managers and entrepreneurs concentrated on finding markets for goods, any market for any goods, were successful. The story of these successes spread across the population of the largest firms and soon after World War II became the new conventional wisdom guiding the actions of large firms.

The Depression and the Failure of the NRA

While the manufacturing conception offered some stability for large firms, it was less useful in an economic downturn. The leaders of American industry, including those most dominated by the manufacturing conception of control—paper, rubber, steel, and oil—favored more explicit forms of cooperation during the early years of the Depression. These opinions were eventually translated into legislation.

The origins of the NIRA and the subsequent failure of the NRA have been thoroughly explored (Hawley, 1966; Belush, 1975; Himmelberg, 1976; McCraw, 1981; Freese and Judd, 1985). The pressure to relax the antitrust laws dated from the relative prosperity of the late 1920s and came from firms in older, lower-profit industries (Himmelberg, 1976, pp. 76–77). The representatives of these industries, who were owners and managers of relatively small- and medium-size firms, felt that they were not sharing in the prosperity of the 1920s and that to guarantee themselves an adequate profit they needed a more cartelized economy. From their perspective, the trade association agreements did not go far enough in promoting stable prices or profits.

Their cause was taken up by the National Civic Federation (NCF) which led the movement to relax the antitrust laws and promote cartelization between 1928 and 1931. As the Depression deepened, larger firms began to share this view because manufacturing strategies failed to control prices. By 1931 the Chamber of Commerce and the National Association of Manufacturers began to put pressure on the federal government to allow cartels (Himmelberg, 1976, ch. 7). Robert Himmelberg prepared a series of tables that illustrate which firms and industries supported revision of the antitrust laws, based on who supported the NCF's proposals. His conclusion is worth citing.

> The movement for antitrust revision during the Depression depended for its cutting edge upon the industries which were

relatively depressed for a long period of time. Almost entirely absent were the fabled industries which played so great a role in remaking the American economy during the 1920s, the automobile and electrical equipment industries. Other booming industries which enjoyed a new prominence during the twenties thanks to the emergence of modern advertising methods and to the availability of higher disposable income were toiletries, patent medicines, newspapers and periodicals, cleansing preparations, packaged goods, toys, and confectionary. Heavily represented, on the other hand, are older more heavily concentrated undifferentiated, product industries, such as lumber, paper, rubber, factory machinery, oil refining and extraction, iron and steel, textiles, grain milling, and builder's supplies. (1976, p. 124)

Even though they did not initiate the movement, firms in industries guided by the manufacturing conception became its leaders.

The leading business organizations held a series of meetings in 1931 to debate antitrust policies and consider what could be done to end the worst effects of the Depression. They were cautious in their actions and recommendations. They were afraid to call for too radical a revision of the antitrust laws or for laws allowing cartels where firms had to comply with set prices and production quotas. It was thought that such proposals might encourage the government to intervene more in the economy. Instead, those organizations supported a relaxation of antitrust laws through decreased enforcement of the laws (Himmelberg, 1976, pp. 145–146).

A series of bills was introduced in Congress in 1931 and 1932 that contained a number of provisions to suspend the antitrust laws as well as to legalize voluntary price cooperation. None of the measures passed. Hoover was against these attempts while Roosevelt was in favor of them. While big business did not desert Hoover during the 1932 election campaign, the electorate did. Roosevelt entered the presidency with a promise to take action.

The NIRA was an enabling piece of legislation rather than a plan for economic recovery. It reflected a mixture of bills with different purposes and interests, including business and labor. The act created a new government agency, the NRA, to approve industry-wide codes of business behavior. The content of these codes was not specified, which gave firms great latitude to control production and price. The codes suspended the antitrust laws and allowed collusion between firms (Hawley, 1966, pp. 31–32). Business in return had to recognize the right of labor to organize and bargain. Each code was to contain provisions for maximum hours, minimum wages, and regulation of working conditions (Hawley, 1966, p. 32). The codes were to be written by representatives of business, labor, and consumers. But in fact, business controlled the writing of codes. There were two other features of the NRA. The first of these contained a public works program with a budget of $3.3 billion that was intended to stimulate the economy and create jobs. The other was a tax provision for public works. Most of the taxes were to be levied on corporate stockholders and the profits of firms (Hawley, 1966, p. 31).

The ideas behind the NIRA reflected a number of views regarding the causes of the Depression. Business executives argued that the key problem was that commodity prices were not high enough. This view reflected the manufacturing conception's focus on the stabilization of prices for industrial goods. The inability to control prices in an organizational field resulted from overproduction. The solution was to support prices by controlling production, that is, to cartellize. The NIRA was a victory for the forces that had failed to stabilize fields in the economic downturn by using the manufacturing conception. From labor's point of view, overproduction meant that jobs were lost and wages were cut. Labor wanted the right to organize and the guarantee of a living wage. Roosevelt's advisors felt that the general problem was to support prices, raise wages, and increase aggregate demand by employing workers in public works.

The NRA failed for two major reasons. First, and most important, the effect of the NRA codes was to raise prices and sustain low wages, but not increase demand. Firms were successful at raising prices in their organizational field, but they did so by restraining production. Thus, the central goal of the legislation, to stimulate demand and put people back to work, was never realized (Lyon et al., 1935, ch. 23–28; Hawley, 1966, p. 62). By the fall of 1933 protests were coming from labor, consumers, and the small business sectors because prices were rising and employment and wages were decreasing. The codes were written mainly by the largest firms in each industry. Consequently, although workers' rights were written into the bill, it was still difficult for labor to organize. The public works program was slow to emerge and the positive effects came late.

By the time the NIRA was declared unconstitutional in 1935, its supporters and critics had deemed it a failure. Even if the act had not been declared unconstitutional, it is unlikely that it would have been renewed in Congress (Hawley, 1966, p. 130). Ellis Hawley argues that there were three ideological positions on what should be done. The first was a cartellized economy controlled by business. The second was a collectivist democracy where the state would aid in planning the economy to the benefit of all. The third was the competitive ideal, where the pursuit of individual self-interest would result in the greatest good for the greatest number (pp. 35–36).

The NIRA was the embodiment of the cartellized approach. The firms in each industry organized with the blessing of the NRA. A government-directed economy was the goal of socialist planners, a goal that was never actually on the Roosevelt political agenda. In the competitive ideal the state served as the regulator and protector of competition. Antitrust enforcement was viewed as the key to economic recovery. Both of the last two ideologies were skeptical of business's ability to govern itself without hurting labor or consumers. The experience of the NRA showed this view was not without merit.

The recession of 1937 precipitated a shift in the direction of New Deal economic policy. Roosevelt and his advisors began to blame the owners and managers of large firms for the recession. They argued that the concentration of the economy gave too much power to large firms and that they refused to respond to the measures taken to stimulate production and consumption (Hawley, 1966, ch. 20). As a result Roosevelt instituted two new policies: a vigorous antitrust campaign and hearings held by the TNEC to investigate the role of monopoly in the economy (see Chapter 5).

Two conceptions of control helped stabilize large firms in the 1920s: the manufacturing and the sales and marketing conceptions. For those firms who did not or could not employ strategies from either conception, the 1920s were not prosperous. The manufacturing conception had failed economically and politically during the economic crisis of the 1930s. But the sales and marketing conception introduced in the 1920s proved more viable during the Depression. It is to the origins of this conception that we now turn.

The Rise of the Sales and Marketing Conception of Control

The sales and marketing conception of control required a radical break with previous views on the nature of markets, competition, and what courses of action would ensure firm survival. Markets under manufacturing control were arenas where powerful firms tried to maintain prices. Markets under sales and marketing control became segmented. If potential competitors were producing in one segment of the market, they differentiated their product to avoid direct price competition. The competitive process under manufacturing control was held in check by the threatening power of the largest firms. Those who cut prices might start price wars that could end in the ruin of all. The competitive process under the sales and marketing conception of control became more indirect. The emphasis was on producing brand loyalty, expanding market share, and finding new markets for existing and new products, rather than on direct price competition. This meant that the organizational fields that adopted this new conception were reorganized. Firms no longer produced a narrow line of products, but began to produce full lines that spanned entire industries. Organizational fields were no longer systems of power oriented toward controlling price and production levels. Instead, they were places to observe what competitors were doing in order to avoid direct competition and find new opportunities to increase sales.

The emergence of this conception of control began with the marketing revolution of the 1920s when it was recognized that the ultimate goal of business was selling, not controlling prices. Once managers and entrepreneurs realized that selling was the key it was possible to devise multiple sales strategies. The internal organization of the firm and its goals shifted to allow large firms to act in a new way. The marketing perspective justified certain courses of action during the 1920s, which included advertising, differentiating products in both quality and price dimensions, and diversification into new products. The rise of modern marketing began with the following recognition:

> But genuine marketing practice is not only coordination of sales and advertising; it is something more. All the operations of a factory enter into, and constitute marketing. This is imperfectly understood even now in American business; finance and production monopolize to too great an extent the administrative

capacity of industrial captains, instead of being regarded as merely functions, or departments, of business, another name for which is marketing; because, essentially speaking, a factory does not exist for production, but for marketing the goods produced; goods have no value whatever unless there is a market for them and unless they can be sold to that market, and sold economically and effectively. (Sullivan, 1924, p. 116)

The importance of product differentiation was stressed by a number of executives. William Childs, the president of the Barrett Company, a producer of consumer goods, argued that "any product which has a reason for being sold can be lifted out of the run of products and made into a highly individualized, non-competitive product—which is the easiest way to go ahead when others are standing still" (System, June 1921, p. 785). Advertising and aggressive sales were the major tactics in this effort and as a result advertising expenditures increased from about $500 million in 1921 to $1.5 billion in 1927 (Copeland, 1929, p. 402).

The analysis of market possibilities led sales executives to new solutions to the sales challenge. The effect of cyclical sales of various product lines, for instance, were tempered by producing complementary products. Alternatively, new markets were found for old products. Finally, expansion into new products aided overall firm growth and made firms less dependent on one market. Diversification and differentiation both stressed the significance of growth through the increase of sales.

Mass production now exists, and will only exist as a result of constructive and accurate sales planning. It is not and will not be a primary cause of sales volume and industrial prosperity. In the skill of consumer market analysis and in the ability to make a product which will appeal to that market are the keys of business success . . . The problem of increased selling has, for example, developed a new type of consolidation. Under this form, groups of noncompeting products selling to the same general market or subject to the same kind of management have been brought together under one ownership. The Postum Company, the General Motors Company, and the Radio Corporation are examples. This type offers to the constituent member of the group either the economy of selling or increased power in the sales market. (Review of Reviews, June 1928, p. 631)

The marketing revolution recognized the need of large firms to find markets for their products. In a review of marketing trends in the 1920s, Melvin Copeland, a professor at the Harvard Business School, noted:

> A characteristic of many U.S. industries during the nineteenth century and the early twentieth century was mass production of more or less standardized articles, a system which reached its zenith in the Ford plant. That method of operation permitted the economic utilization of labor and resulted in great economies of production. Since 1920, however, a different set of conditions has been apparent, as indicated by the new tempo of demand, the rapidity of style changes, and the receptivity of consumers to new varieties of and types of products . . . These changes in demand can be attributed to the ingenuity of manufacturers in applying to ordinary uses new ideas, materials, and machinery which were developed during the war period, and to the devising of new products which rapidly attained popularity. The spread of the demand for many of these products was stimulated by the utilization of aggressive methods of marketing and promotion. (1929, pp. 329–330)

Once mass production was employed by large firms, the next problem was how to dispose of those goods. There have been various theories in the business community concerning the appropriate strategies for success. Scientific management was popular in the 1910s and, in the early 1920s, market analysis came to the fore (*System*, August 1924, pp. 147-149). Market analysis was defined as research to discover ways to sell one's product more effectively and widely, and was thought to be the extension of Frederick Taylor's principles of production. Indeed, its introduction was debated at meetings of the Taylor Society (*Bulletin of the Taylor Society*, October 1920; February 1926; December 1927). The solutions to marketing problems ranged from finding new markets, increasing advertising, and changing product mix to completely reorganizing the sales and marketing function.

Sales departments in large firms began to become differentiated because of distribution problems. Solutions were typically organizing a sales force, engaging in market research, and designing an advertising strategy (Doubman, 1924, pp. 174–176; Denison, 1929, pp. 531–533). Finding new markets and products were often integrated into the function of the sales and marketing department. Before 1920 the creation of new products was somewhat chaotic. It became evident later that bringing sales and production together in a new function called merchandising was advantageous. In some firms research and development departments were set up to coordinate the production and selling of new products; knowledge of consumer demands was combined with knowledge of the production process (Denison, 1929, pp. 535–536).

In 1921 the American Management Association established a sales executives division that began to hold yearly meetings. The members of the executive board included the sales managers of Burroughs, Swift, Proctor and Gamble, American Radiator, Atlantic Refining, DuPont, Goodyear, Ralston Purina, and National Cash Register, among others (American Management Association, 1924, p. 1). The organization very much reflected trends in the largest firms.

This group held annual meetings and published a series of papers on sales issues and their relation to business organization for the next eight years. The association published discussions written by academic experts most frequently from the Harvard or University of Chicago business schools or by sales managers reporting their own experiences.

In a publication about how firms stabilized their markets, the vice-president of sales for the American Radiator Company said that they discovered from market analysis that their business peaked in the spring and fell off in the fall. To compensate they dropped their prices in the fall. In another article the head of the Paint Makers Association stressed the role of advertising for increased sales.

The vice-president of a large window frame manufacturer described the following solution:

> Usually for about eight months we would be oversold and in the dull season not have sufficient work to hold our organization. A complete revision of products and broad development of sales organization was necessary to secure the stabilization of production and sales necessary to the maintenance of the organization and satisfactory return on capital invested. Development of casements, double hung windows, continuous sash, tension operators, steel partition, shelving and factory equipment in addition to broader distribution of pivoted sash, has, to large extent equalized peaks and valleys of both sale and production. (American Management Association, 1926, p. 40)

In the same publication (p. 44) appeared the results of a questionnaire to members asking, "What steps have you taken to stabilize sales either from year to year or season to season by adopting new marketing policies or sales methods?" The three most frequent answers were: diversification, attempts to find new markets for goods by using market analysis, and continuous advertising.

The sales perspective became a somewhat common point of view in the 1920s. C. H. Hobbs, the president of a steel tube company, wrote:

> Whether he be the head of a retail establishment, president of a distributing organization, or a manufacturer, the business executive of this period of commercial history must look at his business from the standpoint of its ultimate aim—the sale of a product. I would in no way minimize the importance of the production role. Nor would I gainsay the necessity for sound purchasing. But these and every other movement of business seem to me and to this business so dependent on the several basic functions of sales that I believe a sales bringing-up is the best foundation for business leadership, whether it be manufacturing or selling. (*System*, January 1927, p. 32)

Arthur Burns, a leading economist, devoted an entire chapter to the rise of marketing in the 1920s in his review of the decline of competition in American industry. Burns focused on the role of advertising, sales forces, and quality and style differences between products. He noted that such differences had increased and aided in the reduction of overall competition (Burns, 1936, ch. 8).

Given this concern with marketing it is not surprising that 30.4 percent of the mergers in the 1920s contained a substantial amount of product-related diversification. By 1929 diversification was an accepted if not dominant part of American business. "More than one shrewd observer of current happenings in industry has suggested that one of the impressive changes now going on in business is the tendency to spread out, not to form a monopoly of a single product, but to bring into the management of a single group of men a group of kindred industries. Business seems to grow by accretion, either through this kind of merger of kindred companies or by adding complementary lines" (*Review of Reviews*, October 1928, p. 112). Another observer noted, "Diversification has became a settled policy with many companies. The object is the same as that which brought about diversification in agriculture; that is, the insuring of continuity in earnings. Some companies, however, have been obliged to enlarge their interests to find employment for their capital where their own particular operations have already expanded to the maximum" (*Literary Digest*, December 1929, p. 64).

In 1937 *Business Week* published an article reviewing the link between sales and diversification. The major reasons for diversification were by this time well established: to employ excess plant capacity, to eliminate seasonal humps, to guard against dependency on one industry, to enter new expanding industries, to supplement existing product lines, to use old products to create new products, and to secure a larger share of business in general (May 29, 1937, p. 37).

The Automobile Industry

The history of the automobile industry is well known—the story of the rise of General Motors and the decline of Ford has been told many times.[1] Indeed, it is the primary test case for product differentiation and diversification as successful tactics for growth (Chandler, 1964, pp. xi–xii). I will recount the story with an emphasis on two factors: the role of key actors in creating and transforming their organizational fields and the success and failure of two distinct strategies of growth.

The automobile industry was a latecomer to the industrial scene. In 1900 it ranked 150th largest in the country, but by 1920 it was number one (Thomas, 1977, p. 1). While there were hundreds of attempts to found automobile companies from the 1890s on, the first major success was in 1908 with the introduction of the Model T. Since the industry was not well established, setting prices through collusion or other tactics of market control were untenable. Although some tried to monopolize the auto market before 1908, their efforts failed (Thomas, 1977, pp. 95–106). The greater challenge was to create a market for the product in the first place.

Ford Motor Company is generally remembered for its innovative mass production assembly line. But this is a limited view if we do not examine the marketing conception behind this strategy. Before 1908 Ford argued:

A motor car was still regarded as a luxury. The manufacturers did a good deal to spread this idea. Some clever persons invented the name "pleasure car" and the advertising emphasized the pleasure features. The sales people had ground for their objections and particularly when I made the following announcement: I will build a motor car for the great multitude. It will be large enough for the family but small enough for the individual to run and care for. It will be constructed of the best materials, by the best men to be hired, after the simplest designs that modern engineering can devise. But it will be so low in price that no man making a good salary will be unable to own one. (1922, pp. 73–74)

Ford's strategy of producing only one model in only one color seems archaic to modern marketing. But his logic turned on what he felt people wanted.

Ask a hundred people how they want a particular article made. About eighty will not know; they will leave it to you. Fifteen will think they must say something, while five will have preferences and reasons. The ninety-five, made up of those who do not know and admit it and the fifteen who do not know but do not admit it, constitute the real market for any product. The five who want something special may or may not be able to pay the price for special work. The majority will consider quality and buy the biggest dollar's amount of quality. If, therefore, you discover what will give this 95 percent of the people the best all-around service and then arrange to manufacture at the very highest quality and sell at the very lowest price, you will be meeting a demand which is so large that it may be called universal.   (1922, pp. 47–48)

Ford was also convinced that the creation of a mass market for automobiles depended on service.

A manufacturer is not through with his customer when a sale is completed. He has only then started with his customer. In the case of the automobile the sale of the machine is only something in the nature of an introduction. If the machine does not give service, then it is better for the manufacturer if he never had the introduction, for he will have the worst of all possible advertisements—a dissatisfied customer . . . And it is right on this point that we later made the largest selling argument for the Ford. The price and quality of the car would have undoubtedly have made a market, and a large market. We went beyond that. A man who bought one of our cars was in my opinion entitled to continuous use of that car, and therefore if he had a breakdown of any kind it was our duty to see that his machine was put into shape again at the earliest possible moment.   (1922, p. 41)

Ford saw that once he had framed the marketing strategy for the automobile, then the solution to the manufacturing problem followed. "The only further step required is to throw overboard the idea of picking on what the traffic will bear and instead go to the common sense basis of pricing on what it costs to manufacture and then reducing the cost of manufacture. If the design of the product has been sufficiently studied, then changes in manufacturing will come very rapidly and wholly naturally. That has been our experience in everything we have undertaken" (1922, p. 50).

Ford's greatest concern was balancing quality and service while lowering costs. While his implementation of the assembly line is well known, certain of his other organizational tactics are not. Because he was afraid of becoming too dependent on other firms for materials, he moved toward vertical integration of production. In the 1920s Ford went so far as to buy coal and iron ore mines and he built a steel mill. He also purchased a railroad line in order to speed the movement of cars and parts to market (Katz, 1977, pp. 120–141). In this way he followed a manufacturing conception of control. His strategy of vertical integration worked dramatically to organize production. Ford was able to produce a large quantity of cars for a very low price. By the early 1920s he controlled 60 percent of the automobile market.

When the industry was young, Ford thought that the basic goal was to produce a car cheap enough to attract first-time buyers. His view proved to be correct. He recognized that the established organizational field was pursuing a strategy that was not taking advantage of the potential market. He permanently altered that field by producing a car for a mass consumer market. He also created an organization that embodied the marketing strategy that he perceived would operate most successfully.

His strategy was based on the opinion that price was the most important issue to consumers. When price considerations ceased to be the central issue, Ford's strategy began to fail. Between 1924 and 1929 Ford continued to produce at lower prices. By 1928 it is estimated he was making only a five dollar profit per car (Katz, 1977, p. 129). He made the vast majority of his profit through the sale of parts. When the Depression hit, the automobile market was decimated. This situation and Ford's investment in fixed capital stock, such as a steel mill, almost drove the company to bankruptcy. In spite of the contrary evidence, however, Ford never abandoned his conception of the automobile industry.

William Durant, a brilliant salesman, had great faith in the auto industry's potential. In 1908 he formed General Motors through the merger of several car companies (Crabb, 1969, pp. 234–247; Cray, 1980, pp. 70–97). By 1921 General Motors was producing ten distinct lines of cars (Sloan, 1964, p. 59). Unfortunately Durant was an ineffective manager. The company was never integrated and almost went out of business twice under his leadership. In 1917 the DuPonts became interested in General Motors as an investment. In 1920 when Durant almost brought the company down for the second time, the DuPonts bought Durant's shares of the firm and installed Pierre DuPont as president (Sloan, 1964, pp. 32–40; Crabb, 1969, pp. 381–391). DuPont wisely made Alfred Sloan his principal assistant.

Sloan had entered the automobile business through his co-ownership of a ball bearing firm. His primary responsibility in that firm was sales and through his business contacts he eventually got to know the major figures in the auto industry (Sloan, 1964, pp. 17–25). In 1916 Durant bought Sloan's company and merged it with others to create United Motors, who supplied various parts to General Motors and other automobile companies. As president of this new firm, Sloan learned the nuts and bolts of the auto industry as well as how to manage companies engaged in disparate activities. He came to accept diversification and realized the importance of marketing in the industry (Sloan, 1964, p. 25). In 1918 Durant absorbed United Motors into General Motors and Sloan became a high-level executive in General Motors. Sloan almost left the firm in 1920 because he disagreed with Durant's style of leadership and inattention to management issues.

Sloan described General Motors' problems as organizational: the product line lacked focus and the firm's organizational structure could not monitor the production process (Sloan, 1964, pp. 26–28).

> Nevertheless, there was then (1921) in General Motors no established policy for the car lines as a whole. We had no position in the low price area, Chevrolet at that time being competitive with

Ford in neither price nor quality. The fact that we were producers of middle- and high-price cars, so far as I know, was not a
deliberate policy. It just happened that no one had figured out
how to compete with the Ford, which had then more than half
the total market in units. Not only were we not competitive with
Ford in the low-price field—where the big volume and substantial future growth lay—but in the middle, where we were concentrated with duplication, we did not know what we were trying to
do except sell cars which, in a sense took volume from one
another. Some kind of rational policy was called for. Each division, in the absence of a corporation policy, operated independently, making its own price and production policies, which
landed some cars in identical price positions without relationship to the interest of the enterprise as a whole. (1964, pp.
58–60)

At the time, only the Cadillac and Buick divisions of the company were making any money. Sloan's solution was:

It was clear that we needed an idea for penetrating the low-price
field, and for the deployment of the cars through the line as a
whole; and we needed a research and development policy, a sales
policy, and the like, to support whatever we did . . . We said first
that the corporation should produce a line of cars in each price
area, from the lowest price up to one for a strictly high grade
quantity production car, but we would not get into the fancy
price field with small production; second, that the price steps
should not be great enough to keep their number within reason,
so that the greatest advantage of quantity production could be
secured; and third, that there should be no duplication by the
corporation in the price fields or steps. (1964, pp. 62, 65)

The firm undertook a marketing policy to price their products at
the upper end of any given price category. They justified such
prices by offering extra amenities in the car. They induced customers in a particular range to buy up slightly and thereby receive
additional quality (Sloan, 1964, pp. 68–69).

In the same decade the automobile industry employed another
marketing strategy: new models every year. "General Motors in
fact had annual model changes in the twenties, every year after
1923, and has had them ever since, but . . . we had not in 1925
formulated the concept in the way it is known today. When we did
formulate it I cannot say. It was a matter of evolution. Eventually
the fact that we made yearly changes, and the recognition of the

necessity of change, forced us into regularizing change. When change became regularized, some time in the 1930s, we began to speak of annual models" (Sloan, 1964, p. 167).

In order to implement the marketing plan, the firm needed to be reorganized. Sloan had written such a plan for General Motors in 1919 and this plan was set in place in 1921. It contained two components: a decentralized administrative structure because the firm made multiple products and financial controls that allowed the performance of each division to be monitored by the central office.

Alfred Chandler has argued that General Motors took the idea for a multidivisional structure from DuPont. Sloan makes a persuasive case to show that the problems of General Motors were exactly the opposite of DuPont's. "The DuPont Company then was evolving from a centralized type of organization, common in the early days of American industry, while General Motors was emerging from almost total decentralization. General Motors needed to find a principle of coordination without losing the advantages of decentralization" (1964, p. 46).

Sloan explained his organizational plan as the result of two basic principles: "1. The responsibility attached to the chief executive of each operation shall in no way be limited. Each such organization headed by its chief executive shall be complete in every necessary function and enabled to exercise its full initiative and logical development. 2. Certain central organization functions are absolutely essential to the logical development and proper control of the Corporation's activities" (1964, p. 53).

The elaborate financial controls of the central office took three forms. First, there was a centralized control of cash, inventory, appropriations, and production. Large projects needed to be approved by high-level committees and the firm could tell, at any given moment, how much inventory was on hand, how much cash it had, and how well sales were going. Second, each division was responsible for reporting its own finances and profitability. The central office then monitored divisional performance by examining costs, price, volume, and rate of return on a monthly basis. These reports formed the foundation of business decisions. Third, Sloan implemented a system of pricing for transfers within General Motors. If one division of General Motors produced output for another, it was allowed to charge the second division the cost of production plus a fixed profit. In this way, managers could compare the costs of products from internal divisions to those from outside. The effect of these controls was that managers of internal units that did not produce as efficiently as potential suppliers might find themselves out of work (Sloan, 1964, pp. 48–50, ch. 8).

In an important sense, Alfred Sloan created modern management practices. The large firm was no longer limited by size or product constraints. It could grow limitlessly through the addition of new divisions and extensive financial controls maintained by central offices. The critical function for the large firm became marketing. Once many different products could be managed under one corporate roof, modern marketing practices concentrated on selling the products to consumers. General Motors was an innovator of these practices and between 1929 and 1950 the company introduced a large number of new products through its decentralized structure (Gort, 1962, pp. 164, 168, 172).

Because Sloan was a hired manager his exercise of power within General Motors is interesting to consider. General Motors was being run as a holding company when Sloan implemented his plan for reorganization. In other words, any division within the firm could have opposed measures to centralize authority. As Sloan put it, "Some of them [the executives of each division] had no broad outlook, and used their membership on the Executive Committee mainly to advance the interests of their respective divisions" (1964, p. 49). The strong point of the divisional plan was that it recognized the interests of each separate division and preserved the power of each top executive. At the same time, the financial controls allowed the executive and finance committees to assess the contributions of each division to the whole. The question remains as to why the divisions would allow those controls. Sloan argued that financial controls aided the divisions. "It increases the morale of the organization by placing each operation on its own foundation, making it feel that it is a part of the corporation, assuming its own responsibility and contributing its share to the final result" (1964, p. 50).

In the contest between firms, Sloan's sales and marketing strategy of producing multiple products worked for two reasons. First, as the auto market matured, General Motors was positioned to sell people more expensive cars. Ford stuck to its strategy of producing only for the low-price end of the market, which eventually dwindled. Second, when the Depression came the consumers of Ford products were the most hard hit and his investment in a vertically integrated plant structure created severe financial problems for the firm. Ford lost money and customers during the Depression and the firm never fully recovered. Meanwhile, the diverse General Motors products sold so well that the firm lost money in only one year of the Depression and experienced significant growth in sales and profits after 1932 (U.S. Federal Trade Commission, 1939, pp. 525–526, 649).

The role of important actors in the auto industry must be kept in perspective. Both Alfred Sloan and Henry Ford interpreted their own companies and organizational fields based on their previous experiences. On the one hand, Ford devised a strategy that worked magnificently. Unfortunately, many others copied his factory innovations and he quickly lost any price edge he might have had. Furthermore, when the market became differentiated Ford did not adjust. His point of view brought him much success under one set of circumstances, but under another, it almost drove him to bankruptcy.

Sloan, on the other hand, dealt with a standing organization and what he perceived its problems were. He was truly innovative, but in the context of an already existing structure, the General Motors that William Durant had built. His strategies for growth, diversification and annual product changes, and his strategy for organization, the multidivisional form, resulted in the creation of the largest and most successful organization of its time. General Motors came out of the 1930s as the premier example of what the large-scale modern firm could be.

Others followed suit. Chrysler, for instance, was built along General Motors lines. After Henry Ford was forced to retire, his son saved Ford by implementing the General Motors' sales and marketing strategy of diversification. Today, Chrysler, Ford, and General Motors have similar structures and product lines because they have mimicked General Motors' pioneering conception. Firms in other industries as well have followed General Motors' lead.

The Steel Industry

In contrast to the auto industry, the steel industry was quite mature by 1920. The dominant strategy in the steel industry was vertical integration of production and the industry was most concerned with price stability. In 1920 the Supreme Court decided that U.S. Steel had not violated the Sherman Act and the company's price leadership tactics continued to control the field (Hogan, 1971, pp. 1015–95). The auto industry bought 10 percent of the steel produced in 1920; this increased to 18 percent by 1929. The railroads decreased their demand for steel over the decade while the petroleum and construction industries greatly increased theirs. Markets for consumer goods such as refrigerators and tin cans were opening up and steel became an important component of these industries' growth (Hogan, 1971, p. 1000). The steel industry did not meet new demand with new products as one might expect from its manufacturing conception of control. The industry implemented, instead, new technology to produce steel that met the specifications of its expanding market (Hogan, 1971, p. 831–860).

The structure of the industry underwent some dramatic changes. The merger movement of the 1920s was concentrated in the primary metal industry and, within this category, the steel industry accounted for about 75 percent of the activity (Eis, 1969, p. 52). U.S. Steel's market share dropped from 39.9 percent in 1920 to 37.2 percent in 1930 despite two small mergers. Bethlehem, Republic, and Youngstown, the next three largest steel companies, engaged in extensive mergers and were able to increase their market shares. Almost half of Bethlehem's growth, and nearly three-quarters of Republic's and Youngstown's, were due to mergers (Eis, 1969, p. 103). Of the next four largest firms, two, Wheeling Steel and National Steel, were formed during the decade.

The steel companies lost money continuously during the Depression. The industry only began to recover with the increase in demand for steel products brought on by World War II. The manufacturing conception of control with its concentration on vertical integration and price stability meant that even in the face of the decreased demand and mounting losses for their products, none of the firms diversified.

The U.S. Steel Company reorganized following the death of Elbert Gary, its longtime president, in 1927. Previously, the company had been run as a holding company. Myron Taylor, the new president, reorganized the company into a functional structure where individual departments were responsible for purchasing, mining, shipping, production, and sales. The company still operated some parts of the firms as subsidiaries (Hogan, 1971, pp. 1203–04). U.S. Steel centralized control through the use of functional departments and, in terms of strategy and structure, it was moving in the opposite direction of General Motors and the large chemical companies.

The other steel companies were also functionally organized (Chandler, 1962, pp. 331–337). The steel industry had constructed an organizational structure that controlled the flow of resources through the organization's successive stages of production. The leadership of the industry consisted of manufacturing personnel who had direct experience with the production process. Their solution to organizational problems was the coordination of production. Their solution to marketing problems was to absorb the market share of competitors through mergers and integrate suppliers into a functional structure. The small number of large producers perpetuated the possibility for price leadership. The industry tended to be highly vulnerable to the overall demands of the economy. When times were good, the steel companies prospered. In a recession, the firms could do no more than close down plants. Given the large amount of capital involved, this entailed huge losses. New technology could only be supported in times of prosperity. This vulnerability ultimately led to the downturn of the industry in the 1960s.

I have discussed the problems of the steel industry in a structural framework. Vertical integration leads to control by persons who are mostly interested in manufacturing. Then when problems of marketing arise, the organization cannot respond to shifts in the product market because management is too attached to strategies for achieving price stability. Over time, the tendency is to reinvest capital only when necessary and to use horizontal and vertical integration to control markets, suppliers, and competitors.

The Chemical Industry

When the organizational field of chemical companies formed in the 1920s, it was led by firms who produced multiple products. Their paths to diversification were numerous. DuPont began as an explosives company and diversified as protection against the cyclical nature of the business (Chandler, 1962, pp. 78–80; Taylor and Sudnik, 1984, pp. 75–90). Dow Chemical was founded by Herbert Dow, an inventor who created chemical products as a by-product of his experiments with salt brine. The company grew as uses were found for the various chemicals (Whitehead, 1968, pp. 1–14). The intent of the founders of Allied Chemical was to create a diversified enterprise to compete with the large European drug and chemical producers of the twenties (Hennessey, 1984, pp. 6–14). Monsanto Chemical was a relatively small firm during this period but rose to prominence after the war because of its use of organic chemistry. Celanese, Merck, and Union Carbide were all diversified by the mid-1930s (Haber, 1971, pp. 310–318).

The chemical industry was one of the first truly multinational industries. By 1900 the German and British companies led the world in the production of organic and inorganic chemicals and the U.S. industry trailed. By the mid-1930s, U.S. firms were rivaled only by the Germans' (Haber, 1971, pp. 9–29; Taylor and Sudnik, 1984, pp. 1–17). The Germans pioneered links between the academic research world and the practical world of the large firms. Initially both U.S. and British chemical firms bought German patents and produced goods using their methods. The U.S. industry before World War I was quite fragmented and most producers manufactured only a small number of products. The only chemical firm of any size was DuPont, which was primarily an explosives manufacturer, the General Chemical Company (which was later involved in the merger that formed Allied Chemical), and various producers of fertilizer. The competition from already established European firms prevented U.S. firms from successfully producing important products such as dyes and alkalis.

The United States was cut off from important sources of chemicals when World War I started. American firms immediately began producing the necessary chemicals. After the war they convinced the government that the industry needed protection from foreign competition. Tariffs levied against foreign products aided the growth and diversification of American firms (Haber, 1971, pp. 222–246). The other major source of growth was the auto industry which relied on the chemical companies to produce gasoline additives, car finishes, and fabric. The chemical firms experienced growth during the Depression because the industry was highly diversified and continued to introduce new products and find new markets even in the worst of times.

The history of DuPont is well known (Chandler and Salsbury, 1971; Taylor and Sudnik, 1984). Initially it was not a pioneer, but relied on expertise obtained by purchasing patents or through a merger (Haber, 1971, p. 312). Dupont was the major U.S. producer of explosives and at the turn of the century was following the same strategy of cartelization and monopolization as much of American industry. In 1902 DuPont consolidated its hold on that industry by merging approximately 80 percent of plant capacity. The leader of this new firm was Alfred DuPont who along with Pierre and Coleman DuPont engineered DuPont's rise to leadership as a diversified chemical enterprise.

Unlike many of the other firms that evolved from mergers, DuPont underwent a lasting reorganization that created a centralized administrative structure and included active, aggressive sales and marketing (Chandler, 1962, pp. 57–62; Taylor and Sudnik, 1984, p. 22). In 1911 the Supreme Court decided that DuPont was guilty of violating the Sherman Act and forced DuPont to sell some of its gunpowder assets. The firm had already been looking for new products in 1908 because, as Alfred DuPont said, the gunpowder business was cyclical; it would move from boom to bust and back again in very short order. The firm searched for related products and after rejecting a number of them finally began to produce artificial leather (Chandler, 1962, p. 81).

World War I was critical for DuPont. It became out of necessity a highly diversified producer, supplying itself with the various chemicals required to produce other goods (Haber, 1971, pp. 184–246). Diversification continued throughout the 1920s and 1930s, mainly through the purchase of patents and the execution of mergers. In 1917 DuPont bought Harrison Brothers and Company, a large producer of paint and sulphuric acid, and Grasseli and Company, a diversified producer of various industrial chemicals, in 1928. DuPont purchased other firms in order to aid its entry into the electrochemical and arms industries. It bought patents for the production of film, industrial alcohol, and synthetic fibers. In 1917 DuPont began to purchase shares in General Motors when it could no longer find profitable investments in the chemical industry. Eventually it held 23 percent of General Motors stock (Haber, 1971, pp. 311–312).

Chandler has shown how this diversification led to problems of coordination at DuPont (Chandler, 1962, pp. 74–96). The firm recognized that numerous product lines could not be controlled in a tightly centralized functional structure after years of struggling with organizational issues. The recession of 1921 presented the firm with a crisis; it could not respond quickly enough to changing market conditions. This situation precipitated the implementation of a new organizational structure, one that took into account that because the firm was highly diversified it was impossible for top management to spend time analyzing the performance of each of the many products. To solve these problems, DuPont pioneered the multidivisional form in 1921 (Chandler, 1962, pp. 112–113). By creating divisions to handle the production of the diverse products, the central office could turn to analysis of overall strategy.

The Allied Chemical Company was formed in 1920 out of: General Chemical Company, National Aniline, Solvay Process Company, Semet-Solvay Company, and the Barret Company (Hennessey, 1984, p. 6). These five firms produced a wide variety of chemicals (each was already moderately diversified) and together formed one of the largest industrial enterprises of its time. The founders of the firm self-consciously viewed their creation as an attempt to maintain America's chemical industry in the postwar era (Haber, 1971, p. 314). Orlando Weber was Allied's first president. He thought that the firm was already sufficiently diversified and that it would be best to concentrate on the existing products. His background was in manufacturing so he worked on perfecting the chemical processes utilized by the firm (Hennessey, 1984, p. 11).

Henry Atherton and Fred Emmerich were presidents after Weber. Both began to alter Weber's strategy and by the end of World War II Allied Chemical was diversifying quite rapidly. Emmerich, who came up through the ranks with a finance background, oversaw the firm's diversification, which was primarily based on products produced by the corporation's research division. This shift in strategy was in line with what was occurring in the rest of the industry. By the 1930s all of the major chemical firms had constructed laboratories and were researching new products.

Dow Chemical was the prototype of a firm driven by research

and development. DuPont was prompted to diversify by the boom and bust of its central business, gunpowder. Allied was created, like General Motors, as a diversified firm. They were neither one innovators. Herbert Dow, however, began his company in 1897 with a new product, bleach extracted from chlorine in brine wells (Whitehead, 1968, pp. 3–4). It was used in a variety of manufacturing processes including papermaking. The company produced chemicals from raw materials in commercial quantities and then sought a use for the chemicals. In this way, Dow diversified through innovation.

The second important product that Dow manufactured was bromides. At the beginning of World War I Dow grew rapidly from the sales of this product. Dow also began to produce dyes during this period. When Herbert Dow saw the need for a number of chemicals during the war he pioneered commercial processes for manufacturing magnesium and chlorine. After the war Dow lobbied for tariffs on chemical products in order to protect the growing chemical industry (Whitehead, 1968, p. 90). The company continued to research and produce chemicals for which there were no known commercial uses. Herbert Dow believed that eventually someone would discover ways to use them and he would be ready. Dow Chemical was mainly producing for other firms' consumption in the 1920s and 1930s.

One of the biggest opportunities for expansion came in 1924. A central problem for automobiles was the quality of gasoline. General Motor's chemists had discovered that one way to end engine knocking was to add lead to the gasoline. Unfortunately, this fouled the pistons. Herbert Dow proposed to use ethylene dibromide as a gasoline additive to solve this problem. This worked quite well but there was little of the additive being manufactured. Dow perfected a process to mass produce the chemical and by the late 1920s ethylene dibromide was one of the firm's mainstay products (Whitehead, 1968, pp. 93–104).

In 1939 Herbert Dow died and his son Willard took over the company. Willard formalized the company's dependence on new products by expanding the research function and ensured that the firm's product lines would be determined by Dow's own laboratory work (Whitehead, 1968, p. 127). The company was one of the first to produce petrochemicals and plastics. Dow pioneered the production of artificial rubber and produced great quantities of magnesium during World War II and was one of the largest chemical companies by the end of the war. Its success was based entirely on the production and marketing of new products.

The other major chemical firms that emerged from the 1920s on generally followed Dow's lead. Monsanto, Union Carbide, and American Cyanamid expanded during the Depression by introducing new products based on the chemical research of the day (Haber, 1971, pp. 317–318). Diversification was motivated by two forces: the creation of new products and markets and the need to spread risks across product lines in order to promote growth and prevent collapse in bad times. One could argue that the technology of the industry lent itself to diversification. The problem with this perspective is that a chemical firm might be established to produce just one group of chemicals and might not adopt diversification strategies. A more adequate view suggests that the organizational field of the chemical companies came into existence with a sales and marketing conception of control, one that stressed growth through the research and development of new products.

The Petroleum Industry

The oil industry was dominated by the manufacturing conception of control between 1920 and 1950. All of the large firms tended toward the horizontal and vertical integration of production and consequently introduced few new products during that time (Gort, 1962, tables B-4, B-5, B-6, pp. 164–169). During the 1920s merger movement the oil company mergers numbered second in volume to those of the steel companies (Eis, 1969, p. 53). Mergers allowed oil firms to enter into new aspects of their business. They absorbed suppliers which helped secure their market share and protect their fixed capital investment. Manufacturing personnel tended to dominate in the large oil companies.

The modern structure of the industry emerged in the 1920s (De Chazeau and Kahn, 1959, p. 94). All of the major oil companies strategized to secure their access to petroleum supplies, pipelines and other forms of distribution, and refinery capacity and to lessen their dependence on the Standard Oil group of firms. Within the original group of companies left after the breakup of the monopoly, many used mergers to guarantee their supply of crude oil, means of transportation, or marketing capacity (De Chazeau and Kahn, 1959, p. 94). Even with these mergers the Standard Oil firms were not able to sustain the regional monopolies that they previously enjoyed. By 1938 the regional market shares of the successor firms had dropped to between 11.8 and 31.4 percent from their near-monopoly levels before 1911. Nowhere did any of the Standard companies achieve anything near a monopoly (U.S. Temporary National Economic Commission, 1941, monograph no. 39, p. 27).

New independent companies emerged because the Standard Oil group lost the ability to control the new oil fields and the transportation facilities of the industry. As the product markets expanded for fuel oil and gasoline, the Standard group was also unable to meet all the demand. While oil firms grew during the prosperity of the 1920s, the Standard group could not maintain any price or product advantage. Large integrated firms emerged including Marland, Shell, Phillips, Doherty, Sinclair, Skelly, Gulf, Texaco, Tide Water, Pure Oil, and Union Oil.

The supply of crude oil became critical as the demand for petroleum products increased. Once an oil field was discovered it was fully exploited. Anyone could sink a well there so the finder of the pool had a huge incentive to pump the field dry before a competitor did. Fields were often underutilized because the oil was pumped inefficiently. One estimate is that only 20 percent of the oil in any given field was being pumped (Williamson and Daum, 1959, p. 319). In the early 1920s it was not clear that petroleum reserves were sufficient to provide oil to the industries that needed it.

In addition to the supply problems the petroleum industry was slow to implement new technologies to increase yield and reduce wasted petroleum and natural gas in refining practices (Williamson and Daum, 1959, p. 313). The oil industry was dominated by managers who believed that the solution to their problems was to drill for more oil, not to use what they had more effectively. This practice reflected a fear of the potential cutoff of petroleum as the worst threat a firm had to face. It is not surprising that all of the large firms quickly bought the existing fields and engaged in large-scale exploration. This fear was indicative of the manufacturing conception of control which then dominated the oil industry.

The concern with securing supply in order to maintain a high level of refinery capacity meant that the industry was not introducing new products. Instead it was content to grow at the same pace as the demand for the small number of petroleum products, especially gasoline, heating oil, and fuel oil. Few of the large firms maintained large-scale research facilities. The petrochemical industry was pioneered by the chemical industry, not the petroleum companies. The oil firms entered that business only after they realized in the postwar era that a large part of their production was being used by the chemical companies. The most common tactic for the oil companies was to acquire through merger the expertise needed to enter the chemical business.

The supply of crude oil finally outpaced consumption and the price dropped dramatically. Oil companies then turned to government controls and international cartels to suppress the overabundance and control the price (Williamson and Daum, 1959, pp. 506, 545–560). In 1928 Standard Oil of New Jersey entered into an agreement to share the international market with the Anglo-Persian Oil Company and Royal Dutch Shell (Williamson and Daum, 1959, p. 530). This agreement was kept until 1950 (Blair, 1976, pp. 54–76). The agreement set in place a structure that divided the world market permanently and led to national and international cooperation in the petroleum industry subsequent to that date (Blair, 1976, p. 76). During the Depression both the state and federal governments attempted to control the supply of oil by limiting the amounts that could be pumped from any given field. The results were price and production quotas for the major companies.

The oil industry during the 1920s and 1930s was dominated by the manufacturing conception of control. The early experiences of the industry with the Standard Oil Company encouraged producers to integrate vertically and protect themselves from being cut off from supplies. When overproduction threatened the industry, instead of diversification, firms engaged in government-sanctioned price controls.

Product Differentiation and Diversification, 1919–1948

My examples show that the sales and manufacturing conception of control was unevenly spread across American Industry and pioneered by key firms. The manufacturing conception continued to dominate industries, in both good and bad economic times, where it was already strongly established. In industries where some firms innovated the sales and marketing conception with success, other firms followed. While these examples show some of the paths to sales and marketing differentiation and diversification, and what sometimes prevented those strategies, they do not present systematic evidence regarding the spread or extent of those tactics. I will now explore, therefore, the dispersion of various product differentiation strategies in order to determine how, where, and why they spread.

The four major sources of my data are studies done by Thorp, Crowder, and Gort, and the statistics discussed in Appendixes C and D (Thorp, 1924; Thorp and Crowder, 1941; Gort, 1962). There are a number of reasons I use different data sets. First, data sets contain different measures of relevant facts and cover different time periods. Second, the data sets were gathered independently and contain slightly different sampling schemes. This gives us a chance to triangulate results to see if conclusions from one study hold up in other studies. The original work on product diversification was done by Thorp using 1920 census data. A similar study was done by Thorp and Crowder using data from the 1937 census of manufacturing and a sample of the fifty largest firms prepared for the TNEC in the late 1930s. Gort's data were based on a sample of 111 large firms between 1929 and 1954. While the samples are not entirely comparable, it is important to note that the authors generally reach similar conclusions.

The first set of data to consider is the data described in Appendix C. These data contain information on the 100 largest corporations at each ten-year interval from 1919 to 1979. Table 4.1 presents data on the various strategies pursued by the largest

Table 4.1   Strategies of the 100 largest firms, 1919–1979 (in percentages)

Strategy	1919-29 (N = 102)	1929-39 (N = 104)	1939-48 (N = 102)	1948-59 (N =104)	1959-69 (N = 102)	1969-79 (N = 104)
Vertical	.51	.69	.79	.82	.73	.68
Related	.13	.14	.20	.34	.54	.51
Unrelated	.00	.00	.00	.08	.11	.21
Multinational	.40	.52	.61	.62	.75	.88

Note: The sample is defined in Appendix C; strategies are defined in Appendix D. Numbers are percentages of firms using given strategies.

firms during that period. The first measure to consider is the evidence of vertical integration of production. This measure was coded as a dummy variable indicating whether or not a firm controlled some aspect of raw material production. It is a crude indicator that does not take into account the amount of vertical integration that may have been present. Fifty-one percent of the firms had some form of integration in 1919. This trend increased continuously until 1948 when it began to decline.

The measures indexing whether a firm had a product dominant, related, or unrelated strategy are also coded in the table. If firms produced more than 70 percent in one product line, then they are defined as product dominant. If they produced less than 70 percent in one product line, but the different products are in similar industries, then they are called product related. If they produced in product lines that are substantially unrelated, they are called conglomerates. Note that a firm can contain elements of vertical integration and have a product mix that is either related or unrelated. This measure may understate the amount of diversification because it requires firms to be producing across major industry groups in order to be classified as diversified.

Until 1948 there were no conglomerates and only 8 percent existed that year. In the postwar era diversification increased rapidly and by 1979 the product-dominant category was the smallest (see Appendix C). These numbers show that the largest firms diversified during the period and that that trend accelerated after 1929, which is consistent with my earlier discussion.

I include data collected by Thorp and Crowder in order to explain the spread of these strategies over a large sample of firms. In 1919 there were 290,105 establishments in American manufacturing and 5,838 central offices controlled 21,464 of these establishments (Thorp, 1924, p. 13). If one assumes that all of the large firms were multiplant firms by 1919, these 5,838 firms were the largest firms of their time. While these establishments comprised only 7.8 percent of the total number of firms, they employed about one-third of the manufacturing labor force and produced one-third of the total output (Thorp, 1924, p. 267).

A more interesting point in this context is the level of diversification of these firms. Table 4.2 presents data on this issue. The first item to consider is the differentiation between simple and complex central office structures. Simple central offices were those that had multiple plants producing the same products while com-

Table 4.2 Central office relations to branch plants, 1919 and 1937

| | 1919 | | 1937 | |
	Number	%	Number	%
Simple central office	3,029	62.8	3,574	63.5
Complex central office	1,784	37.2	2,051	36.5
Complex central offices by function:				
Divergent	706	31.8	781	31.2
Convergent	561	25.3	1,058	42.3
Successive	903	40.7	565	22.6
Unrelated	47	3.2	95	3.9

plex central offices had plants producing different products. The vast majority of central offices were simple.

Complex functions are categorized in four ways. Divergent functions imply that firms started out with a particular product and turned it into multiple products, for example, a steel company that made steel girders for buildings and tin plate for cans. Convergent functions mean diversification that led to making related products. An example is a musical instrument company that produced violins and saxophones. This type of diversification is of the greatest interest because it reflects the entry of firms into markets that were not directly related. Successive functions mean producing a product in order to produce another one, that is, an oil company that drills, ships, and refines oil. Unrelated functions are conglomerate in character. The data in Table 4.2 concerning the number of complex functions include instances in which central offices had plants in each of the categories. Hence, one central office was counted many times if it had plants in different functions.

Vertical integration involved 40.7 percent of the complex central offices and another 31.8 percent produced multiple products out of the same raw materials. Only 25.3 percent of the complex central offices produced related products and only 3.2 percent produced unrelated products. In 1919 the largest firms were producing multiple products, but they most likely did so either as inputs for later processes or as a result of finding different end uses for a commodity.

The data gathered for 1937 can be compared to the 1919 data, however the universe of firms in the sample was different. Only firms with more than $5000 of production were included (Thorp and Crowder, 1941, pp. 105–110). Comparisons should therefore be made cautiously. Of the 166,794 manufacturing plants in existence in 1937, 25,699 were controlled by 5,625 central offices. Hence, 15.4 percent of the establishments were controlled by the largest firms. These firms were the largest in the economy because they employed 51.1 percent of the total wage earners and produced 61.1 percent of the total value of products (Thorp and Crowder, 1941, p. 111). In 1919 the average number of plants per firm was 3.8, while in 1937 the average number was 4.6. Both the relative size of firms and plants increased during the period.

Table 4.2 shows that 63.5 percent of the central office structures were simple in 1937 and over the eighteen-year period the percentage of simple central office organizations remained stable. The complex central offices in 1937 show a marked change from those in 1919. The number of complexes engaged in vertical integration of production decreased substantially to only 22.6 percent in 1937, while the number of central office structures that oversaw the production of related products (defined as convergent) increased to 42.3 percent in 1937. The number of central offices producing diverse products from the same raw material and producing unrelated products remained stable. Table 4.2 shows that the production of related products was becoming the major strategy of diversification by 1937.

Gort's data pertain to the period from 1929 to 1954 and contain evidence on the experiences of 111 large firms. These firms were drawn from a list of the 200 largest firms in 1954. The sample was selected to represent the major manufacturing industries. Firms also had to exist during the entire period and have data available on product diversification in order to be chosen. Gort concluded that by 1929 the 111 large firms were already quite diversified (Gort, 1962, pp. 1–11). His study addressed two questions. First, how much diversification took place over the period and, second, why did firms diversify.

His answer to the first question was based on the data concerning product introductions over the period (see Table 4.3). From 1929 to 1939 many new products were introduced in spite of the Depression. The 1939–1950 period had a lower rate of product introductions, and between 1950 and 1954 there was a great increase. In other words, firms continued to innovate, especially during the Depression, in order to maximize capacity and stay in business. The rapid increase of new products after 1950 is also quite impressive. Although new products in a firm's main industry was 40.9 percent in the earliest period and dropped to 31.7 percent by 1954. This fact indicates that the largest firms were rapidly diversifying into other industries.

Table 4.3 also presents a summary of data concerning the number of new products that were introduced before the Depression. Thorp and Crowder studied only sixteen firms (all of which were among the fifty largest firms in 1937) over a substantial period of time. Because of the small sample size, one must be cautious in drawing conclusions, however it is clear that the Depression prompted more new product introduction than during the prosperous 1920s.

All four data sets provide evidence that diversification was on the increase over the period. The most interesting results are that the Depression (1929–1939) was a period of significant product innovation for the largest firms and their overall level of diversification also increased more then than from 1919 to 1929. The most cogent interpretation of this development is that the uncertainty of the Depression encouraged firms to create new product lines. Innovation was a response to bad economic times. Managers reacted to stagnant or decreasing revenues by finding new opportunities for their businesses. While diversification began in the marketing revolution of the 1920s, the business conditions of

Table 4.3 Comparison of the rate of introduction of new products, 1910–1954

Thorp and Crowder[a]			Gort[b]			
Year	New products	Average per year	Year	New products	Average per year	% in main industry[c]
1910–19	15	1.5	1929–39	484	44.0	40.9
1920–29	31	3.1	1939–50	474	39.5	35.0
1930–39	43	4.3	1950–54	431	86.5	31.7

a. Thorp and Crowder's sample includes 16 of the 50 largest firms in 1937. Data are from Thorp and Crowder (1941), table 31, p. 661.

b. Gort's sample refers to 111 of the 200 largest firms in 1954. Data are from Gort (1962), pp. 44–48.

c. Main industry refers to two-digit SIC scores.

Table 4.4 Distribution of the 50 largest companies in 1937 according to the number of products required to account for 25, 50, and 75 percent of the total value of products of each company

Number of products	25 percent of the total value of products		50 percent of the total value of products		75 percent of the total value of products	
	Number of companies (cumulative)	Percent (cumulative)	Number of companies (cumulative)	Percent (cumulative)	Number of companies (cumulative)	Percent (cumulative)
Fewer than 2	28	56.0	11	22.0	4	8.0
Fewer than 3	41	82.0	20	40.0	5	10.0
Fewer than 4	47	94.0	30	60.0	13	26.0
Fewer than 5	49	98.0	33	66.0	18	36.0
Fewer than 6	49	98.0	35	70.0	20	40.0
Fewer than 7	50	100.0	39	78.0	23	46.0
Fewer than 8			44	88.0	27	54.0
Fewer than 9			47	94.0	29	58.0
Fewer than 10			47	94.0	29	58.0
Fewer than 11			47	94.0	30	60.0
Fewer than 12			48	96.0	31	62.0
Fewer than 13			48	96.0	31	62.0
Fewer than 14			48	96.0	35	70.0
Fewer than 15			49	98.0	38	76.0
Fewer than 16			49	98.0	40	80.0
Fewer than 17			49	98.0	42	84.0
Fewer than 18			49	98.0	43	86.0
Fewer than 19			50	100.0	44	88.0
Fewer than 20					45	90.0
Fewer than 22					46	92.0
Fewer than 24					47	94.0
Fewer than 38					48	96.0
Fewer than 41					49	98.0
Fewer than 55					50	100.0

Source: U.S. Temporary National Economic Commission (1941), monograph no. 37, The Structure of Industry, table 13, p. 608.

the Depression provided the stimulus for many additional firms to diversify.

It is useful to establish how important diversification was to the largest firms and to get a sense of the industry and firm dispersion of this strategy. One would expect that a small number of products accounted for the bulk of the activity of the largest firms given that the overall level of diversification among them was not high in 1929. Table 4.4 contains evidence regarding the importance of product diversification for the fifty largest firms. In all of those firms five products made up at least 25 percent of total production. Indeed for 78 percent of the firms five products accounted for 50 percent of production. One can conclude that while many of the largest firms were producing multiple products by 1937 a few products in one industry still accounted for the bulk of their production. Gort (1962, p. 32) confirms this view in his data (see also Table 4.1). Thus, while diversification was becoming more important, the major industry of a firm still accounted for a substantial percentage of its revenues.

The industrial dispersal of diversification was uneven. The number of new products introduced by each major industry between 1929 and 1954 is presented in Table 4.5. The leading

Table 4.5   Primary industries by number of industries entered, 1929–1954

Industry	Number of companies	Number of industries entered	Average number entered
Food	12	54	4.50
Tobacco	5	2	0.40
Textiles	4	11	2.75
Paper	8	26	3.25
Chemicals	14	62	4.43
Petroleum	10	8	0.80
Rubber	5	32	6.40
Stone, clay, and glass	7	25	3.57
Primary metals	10	24	2.40
Fabricated metals	5	22	4.40
Machinery	13	23	1.77
Electrical machinery	5	41	8.20
Transportation equipment	13	46	3.54
Total	111	376	

Source: Gort (1962), table 55, p. 131.

industries in diversification were electrical machinery, rubber, chemicals, food, and fabricated metals. The tobacco and petroleum industries were the least likely to diversify, which reflected their vertical integration of production and high levels of concentration. The primary metals industry, which includes the steel industry, was also not diversifying at a high rate. The industry differences reflect the dominance of different conceptions of control in the organizational fields of each industry.

Within industries there was a great difference in the level of innovation, an indication of which important firms had leaders who pioneered the sales and marketing conception of control. Table 4.6 presents a list of firms from Gort's study that introduced ten or more new products during each of the intervals 1929–1939 and 1939–1950. General Foods, Union Carbide, Dow Chemical, U.S. Rubber, General Electric, Westinghouse, General Motors,

Table 4.6   Firms that introduced 10 or more products in the periods 1929–1939 and 1939–1950

1929–1939	1939–1950
Swift & Co.	General Foods
General Foods	Borden
Armstrong Cork	United Merchants
International Paper	3M
DuPont	Union Carbide
Union Carbide	Dow Chemical
Dow Chemical	Koppers
Goodyear Tire	Food Machinery & Chemical
U.S. Rubber	Standard Oil, Indiana
PP&G	U.S. Rubber
U.S. Gypsum	Firestone
Republic Steel	B. F. Goodrich
General Electric	General Tire
Westinghouse	Alcoa
RCA	A. O. Smith Corp.
Electric Autolite	General Electric
General Motors	Westinghouse
Bendix Aviation	Sylvania
Borg Warner	General Motors
	Chrysler
	Bendix Aviation
	Pullman, Inc.

Source: Data taken from Gort (1962), tables B-4, B-5, B-6.

Table 4.7   Firms that produced no new products in the periods 1929–39 and 1939–50

1929–1939	1939–1950
Coca-Cola	Seagram's
American Tobacco	Cannon Mills
P. Lorillard	Sherwin-Williams
Cannon Mills	Republic Steel
Celanese Corp.	Youngstown Sheet & Tube
Merck & Co.	American Can
American Can	Babcock & Wilcox
Ford Motor	National Cash Register
Boeing Airplane	Crane Co.
Lockheed Aircraft	

Source: Data taken from Gort (1962), tables B-4, B-5.

and Bendix Aviation were leading innovators throughout the entire period. Table 4.7 lists the firms with no new products during the two intervals. Only two companies studied by Gort introduced nothing new in neither period: Cannon Mills and American Can. There were eleven firms that introduced only one product between 1929 and 1939 and seven firms only one product between 1930 and 1950 (Gort, 1962, pp. 162–173).

Perhaps the most interesting issue that can be explored using these two data sets is the motive for diversification. Both Gort and Thorp and Crowder drew similar conclusions, although with different methodologies (Thorp and Crowder, 1941, pp. 658–659; Gort, 1962, pp. 103–110). Crowder's conclusions were based on interviews with executives involved in product diversification in twenty-six of the fifty largest firms in 1937. They named seven major causes of diversification: new products developed by research and development units, the need to carry a full line of certain products, the need to utilize existing plant capacity, less demand for stable products, vertical or horizontal integration, new products requested by customers or the government, and products suggested by the flow of raw materials. Gort concluded that diversification was more likely to occur in firms in industries with stable growth and into industries that were rapidly growing. Firms that diversified the most frequently tended to be in technologically based industries such as chemicals, electronics, and machine making (Gort, 1962, pp. 103–110).

The Depression, Diversification, and the Largest Firms

Gort's and Crowder's arguments, however, are ahistorical. The motive to expand into other industry, at least theoretically, was probably always present for the large firm. One interpretation of both researchers' results is that firms in stable industries had to seek ways to promote growth if they were to survive. But the sales and marketing strategies of differentiation and diversification had just come into existence in the 1920s and spread during the Depression. Once in place the sales and marketing conception reorganized the organizational fields of some of the large firms and by the end of World War II dominated the population of the largest firms.

Chandler (1962, pp. 3–10) has argued that diversification was dictated by the market. If the market was so omnipotent, then one must ask why its influence was uneven amidst industries and firms. To find an explanation for the innovation of the sales and marketing conception, one must first acknowledge that the key actors in large firms could invent and initiate new corporate behavior. These actors had to invent new markets, not just react to a vague sense of consumer demand. This required them to alter completely their notions of what the large corporation was. These managers tended to be sales and marketing personnel who, if successful, would then operate as role models for others. One must also acknowledge that in organizational fields where the manufacturing conception was so deeply imbedded, alternative conceptions were difficult to pursue. Even in hard economic times, the actors who controlled large firms in these fields stuck to their tactics.

From my perspective, the tendency for diversification to occur in the technologically advanced fields is not due to the technology itself. Instead, I argue that it was the timing of the emergence of these fields that produced this tactic. Managers pursued a science-based diversification strategy only when the sales and marketing conception opened up that possibility in the 1920s. (See Appendix D.)

The key issue is where the new sales and marketing conception came from. The largest firms were operating in somewhat stable organizational fields in 1919. These fields were characterized by well-defined production strategies based mainly on the size and relative efficiency of the largest firms and their ability to enforce prices. For new strategies to develop in these fields, one of three things had to happen. First, the economic or political conditions in the field or in nearby fields had to be substantially altered so that managers would be motivated to change their courses of action. Second, some firms could enter the field and disrupt it, thereby forcing other firms to adopt their strategies in order to prosper. Third, actors in the field had to perceive the crisis and have the power to promote diversification. In fields that were not well established, the possibility for new firms to create a new set of rules existed. The post–World War I chemical industry was created by actors in firms who pursued the sales and marketing strategy of diversification. Since their field did not exist prior to the war, it seems logical that it came into existence embodying the most progressive business conception.

All of these forces were at work. The environmental shock that pushed diversification from a tactic employed by a small number of firms to the central tactic used by almost all of the largest firms was the Depression. To explore this assertion more systematically, see Table D.2. There, the results of a regression analysis are presented where the dependent variables are changes in the assets, sales, and profits of the 100 largest firms over the decades 1919–1929 and 1929–1939.

Between 1919 and 1929 vertical integration successfully predicted growth. Firms that engaged in mergers, product-related strategies, and operated in a number of countries also achieved growth. Thus, firms following the sales and marketing conception were growing faster than the other firms in their organizational field. It should be remembered that only 13 percent of the 100 largest firms in 1919 were sufficiently diversified to be called product related. The achievements of these diversified firms were even more striking during the Depression. Sales and profit growth were predicted only by the product-related strategy. Firms wedded to one product line during the Depression faced disaster as the demand for their single products dropped substantially.

Although the Depression shocked the largest firms, it was not enough to get firms to change their tactics, even when there was clear evidence in their immediate environment that firms with diversified strategies were performing better than their nondiversified counterparts. Let us keep in mind that organizational fields provide actors with a model of how to act and the support for a particular world view. The fields emerge as the result of competition between firms, hence, the collective field is evidence of the power of certain firms to set the agenda for others. The conception of control guiding the strategy and structure of a given firm results from the role that the firm plays in the field and the resolution of its internal power struggle over how to play that role. This means that powerful firms have a great incentive to maintain the status quo. More concretely, when firms were vertically integrated and leaders of those firms were committed to a manufacturing conception, the only alternative was to close plants and maintain some level of prices. This tactic dominated the petroleum and steel industries in the Depression.

Table 4.8 supports this point with the cross tabulation of vertical integration by product-related strategies. The presence of vertical integration in a firm is taken as an indication that the manufacturing strategy dominated the organizational field. If firms were vertically integrated, there should be a negative relationship to the emergence of diversification, an indicator of the sales and marketing conception. In all three periods, firms that pursued a product-related strategy were less likely to be vertically integrated. This suggests that in fields where the manufacturing conception held sway, the sales and marketing product-related strategies were less likely to be employed. Even during the Depression when sales were difficult firms in certain organizational fields were less likely to diversify because the actors in those fields were committed to the manufacturing conception.

The question of where diversification came from still has not been answered. There seem to be two possible sources. First, diversification could have been introduced by new firms, those that entered stable organizational fields and upset their rules. In such a situation, actors in other firms in the field would see the example of the new successful firm and attempt to follow suit. Second, actors in firms in a given field could choose to alter their organization's strategies, a change that would require considerable vision and power. There is evidence that both processes were involved.

Table D.3 relates the shift in strategies with the change in the identity of the 100 largest firms. Between 1919 and 1929 most of

Table 4.8   Cross-tabulation of vertical integration by product-related
strategies for the 100 largest firms in the decades 1919–1929,
1929–1939, 1939–1948

1919–1929

	Related strategy	
	No	Yes
Vertical integration		
No	56 (48.7)	13 (81.3)
Yes	59 (51.3)	3 (18.8)

$\chi^2 = 5.97$, 1 d.f., $p < .05$

1929–1939

	Related strategy	
	No	Yes
Vertical integration		
No	26 (27.7)	13 (56.5)
Yes	68 (72.3)	10 (43.5)

$\chi^2 = 6.92$, 1 d.f., $p < .01$

1939–1948

	Related strategy	
	No	Yes
Vertical integration		
No	12 (16.0)	14 (35.9)
Yes	63 (84.0)	25 (64.1)

$\chi^2 = 5.80$, 1 d.f., $p < .05$

Note: Data and coding are defined in Appendix D. Numbers in parentheses are percentages.

the firms that were continuously in this group did not switch strategies. The increase in the percentage of the largest firms with a product-related strategy came mainly from those firms who were new to the group. Five of the six firms that joined the group with a product-dominant strategy in that decade, however, shifted to that strategy by the end of the decade. The cause of their growth and entry to the list of the 100 largest corporations was, therefore, their strategy of diversification. This pattern continued during the

Depression, which is evidence that, initially, firms that entered an organizational field with a new strategy grew with that strategy.

During the next decade, however, the pattern began to change. Many of the firms that remained among the largest had begun to adopt strategies of diversification. The example of the Depression was not lost on some managers in organizational fields where firms had entered with diversified product structures, so between 1939 and 1948 many of them self-consciously shifted strategies.

It is useful to model this process in a more systematic fashion. Table D.4 presents the results of a logistic regression where the goal is to predict a firm's strategy at the second time point as a function of three factors: the original strategy, the percentage of firms in the firm's major industry that had already shifted to a new strategy, and the background of the president within the organization.

As one would expect, the strongest predictor of the later strategy was the strategy at the beginning. Organizations are set up to operate in a certain way and the managers' interests are linked to that strategy. Therefore strategies usually remain stable. We can also see the effects of the organizational field on a firm's decision to diversify. If firms in the industry diversified, then a nondiversified firm was more likely to switch strategies. As new firms entered the organizational field with successful diversification strategies, others in the field were also more likely to diversify.

The role of a sales and marketing president influenced the decision to diversify as well. Earlier, I argued that an actor or actors had to have both the vision and power to lead an organization toward a new course of action. Since diversification was one aspect of a sales and marketing conception, one would expect that presidents with a sales and marketing background—those most concerned with increasing growth in the organization—would pursue a diversification strategy. The evidence bears this out. The presence of a sales and marketing president in 1919 or 1929 increased the likelihood of a firm switching to a product-related strategy by 1929 or 1939 respectively.

Once the diversification strategy caught on in a given organizational field, one would expect that sales and marketing presidents would be able to increase their power in those fields by claiming to be able to solve a firm's problems. Table D.5 confirms this hypothesis. In firms that had a product-related strategy, sales and marketing managers were more likely to become president of the firm. Also, in the 1939–1959 period, in industries with more sales and marketing presidents, new sales and marketing presidents were more likely to come to power. Overall, after 1929 manufacturing presidents began to decline as a proportion of presidents of the 100 largest corporations and sales and marketing presidents began to increase.

It is useful to consider one additional important change. Throughout this chapter, I have focused on the changes in the conception of control and the strategies that implied. But the sales and marketing conception also caused a change in the structure of large firms. In order to coordinate the production of multiple products, the multidivisional form was invented. Table D.6 documents the causes of the implementation of this structure. The model shows that a product-related strategy at the beginning is positively related to the implementation of the form within a decade. It also shows that if some firms in an industry adopted the form, others were more likely to do so. Finally, firms with sales and marketing presidents were more likely to adopt the form regardless of whether or not they were product related. This last result demonstrates the importance of key actors in the innovation and diffusion of the multidivisional form.

The change in the population of largest firms came about for two reasons. First, firms entered organizational fields with new growth strategies based on the sales and marketing conception, which stressed the differentiation and diversification of products. Second, once these new strategies proved to be effective managers in other firms had to adopt them or cease growing. The Depression was a crucial test of diversification for the largest firms. The role of sales and marketing executives in guiding their firms toward product diversification and the multidivisional form cannot be overestimated. These actors had a new conception of the possibilities for growth in their firms and, once they gained power, they implemented strategies based on that conception.

It is interesting to speculate about the effect of the spread of the sales and marketing conception on the overall health of the economy. If the manufacturing conception tended to prolong the Depression of the 1930s, one could argue that the sales and marketing conception would dampen industrial declines. When recessions hit, firms with the sales and marketing conception would respond by stimulating sales and expanding production into new markets. In this way, the largest firms operating under the sales and marketing conception of growth, may act collectively to limit the severity of economic downturns. The lack of a repeat of the 1930s Depression is prima facie evidence for such a view.

5

The Emergence of the
Celler-Kefauver Act, 1938–1950

The sales and marketing conception of control dominated the tactics of the largest firms from the Depression until the mid-1950s. From an economic point of view, this conception produced higher growth rates and evened out the effects of production and business cycles for individual firms more effectively than the manufacturing conception of control. The sales and marketing conception was being inadvertently reinforced by political events as well. The antitrust authorities began to prosecute the largest firms more strenuously in 1938. While most of this enforcement focused on restraints of trade, the political discussion centered on the economic and political clout of the largest firms. World War II diverted this debate, but the campaign was stepped up in two ways when it ended. The antitrust authorities renewed their pursuit of the largest firms under existing antitrust law. They also pushed for increased antitrust legislation and eventually passed the Celler-Kefauver Act in 1950.

I will discuss the antitrust enforcement of the Roosevelt and Truman administrations to show how its theory and practice changed and how the antitrust community pushed for the passage of the Celler-Kefauver Act as an expression of that change. The new antitrust policy brought together a group of individuals from various governmental agencies who began to analyze the problems of the American economy in a very similar way. These individuals continuously occupied important positions in the FTC, the Antitrust Division of the Justice Department, and the House and Senate.

The antitrust environment, together with the relative success of the sales and marketing conception of control encouraged the leaders of the largest firms to increase their levels of diversification markedly. In spite of much of the anti–big business rhetoric of the antitrust community, the law targeted restraints of trade within lines of business. One obvious strategy to avoid antitrust prosecution was to expand one's business by entering new businesses. But this tactic began to undermine the sales and marketing conception of control which promoted actions to increase the market share of a product line as well as expansion into related product lines. Firms needed to be wary of gaining too much market share through advertising or other marketing ploys. The antitrust authorities would bring a lawsuit even though high concentration might have been achieved through legitimate means.

The antitrust climate encouraged a new conception of control to emerge in the 1950s, the finance conception. If firms were prosecuted for concentration in one industry, a problem sales and marketing strategies compounded, then diversification became the only legal strategy for expansion. Managers responded by increasing their reliance on mergers to enter industries producing related and unrelated products. The acquisitive conglomerate represented the logical endpoint of this new conception of control and led to the rise of finance personnel leadership in large firms. These managers began to make all of their decisions on the basis of financial criteria; products and divisions were judged, bought, and sold on their short-run financial performance. The finance conception of control came to replace the sales and marketing conception of control and continues to dominate today.

When the NIRA failed to solve the problems of the economy during the early 1930s, the Roosevelt Administration began to adopt an alternative perspective toward the Depression. The largest firms were viewed as the obstacle to renewed economic growth. Two actions were implemented as a result of this shift in perspective. First, the Antitrust Division of the Justice Department, under the leadership of Thurman Arnold, began a vigorous prosecution of firms that lasted until the war broke out. Second, the Roosevelt Administration undertook an investigation of the economy in 1938 with the goal of promoting competition. While this investigation had no immediate effect on policy, it created an antitrust community. The members saw the central problem of the economy as a lack of competition caused by the concentration of production in the largest firms. Their solution was to attack this problem by strictly enforcing the antitrust laws as well as working for new antitrust laws to prevent increased concentration.

The overall effect of this shift in perspective culminated in the Truman Administration's significant antitrust campaign after the war. This new antitrust concern led to the amendment of the Clayton Act by the Celler-Kefauver Act which made horizontal and vertical mergers illegal. The antitrust rhetoric and enforcement of the 1940s and 1950s were decidedly antimonopoly and anti–large firm. The rhetoric was that increased concentration within product lines decreased competition and that large size tended to be associated with monopoly. The enforcement of antitrust policy meant that large American firms could not grow by increasing market share.

The Celler-Kefauver Act was a most unlikely piece of legislation. Consider the era. Tensions were rising throughout the world as the Cold War began. In the United States the economy had barely shifted from defense to civilian production and there was a constant danger of the economy dipping into depression. Finally, the political environment was turning conservative. The House Unamerican Activities Committee (HUAC) was beginning its witchhunt to uncover communist subversion within important American institutions. In the context of all of this turmoil, passing a piece of antitrust legislation that was and continues to be the most significant such act since the Clayton Act seems an anomaly. The impetus to the Celler-Kefauver Act was distinctly populist, anti–big business, and more consistent with New Deal liberalism than the conservative rhetoric of the era. Three groups were most responsible for the passage of the bill: the FTC, supporters in the House and Senate, and the Truman Administration.

The FTC was instrumental in gaining congressional support and interest in the act as well as involving President Truman. The commissioners were both ideological and self-interested. The FTC was searching to justify its existence (Skocpol, 1985). Closing the loophole to the Clayton Act would do just that. The FTC commissioners also sincerely believed that the intent of the Clayton Act had been subverted so they were quite anxious to restore the law that they believed had been undermined by the narrowly legalistic interpretation of the Clayton Act by the Supreme Court. The people who played important roles at the FTC included Robert Freer, Ewen Davis, William Kelley, Walter Wooden, and John Blair.

There were also members of Congress who were committed to

New Deal values. Many of them had been involved in measures regarding industrial concentration for many years. Senator Joseph O'Mahoney of Wyoming, Senator Estes Kefauver of Tennessee, Representative Emmanual Celler of New York, and Senator Herbert O'Conor of Maryland played instrumental roles in the Celler-Kefauver Act. They knew one another, shared the same values, and worked together to pass this legislation.

Harry Truman became interested in antitrust as a campaign issue in the 1948 presidential election. He was concerned about the increases in prices in the postwar era and felt that antitrust was one weapon to use against the largest firms. Without Truman's support, the FTC and the Congress would never have passed the act. Further, Truman's victory coincided with a Democratic majority in both the House and Senate. Democrats tended to be more in sympathy with controlling monopoly than the Republicans who favored a hands-off policy toward the largest corporations.

The Celler-Kefauver Act was presented to Congress in rhetoric that reflected the emerging Cold War liberalism of the Democrats. This ideology was extremely anticommunist and internationalist, but at the same time was liberal regarding domestic programs. The Celler-Kefauver Act was seen as a measure of prevention against fascism or communism taking over the country. The argument was made time and again that the largest firms were too dominant in American economic life. The fear was that continued growth of large firms would develop into fascism—large firms united with the state to control society—or communism—firms so large the state would have to take them over. The impact of this ideology turned what seems like legislation distinctly out of time and place into a piece of legislation whose time had come.

The Temporary National Economic Commission

By the time the NIRA was declared unconstitutional in 1935, its supporters and critics had already deemed it a failure. It was not until the recession of 1937 that New Deal economic policy began to propose alternative solutions to the problems of the Depression. Roosevelt and his advisors blamed the owners and managers of large firms for the recession. They argued that the concentration of the economy gave too much power to the large firms which refused to respond to the government measures to stimulate production and consumption (Hawley, 1966, ch. 20). As a result, Roosevelt pursued two new strategies: a vigorous antitrust campaign and the TNEC hearings to investigate the role of monopoly in the economy. The most important countercyclical measure taken by Roosevelt was to stimulate the economy by increased government spending.

In 1937 the TNEC was formed to investigate why the economy had not rebounded from the Depression. This commission, headed by Senator O'Mahoney with participants including members of the FTC's Board of Commissioners, published forty-one volumes of investigations in 1941 with a set of recommendations to strengthen the economy. One of the most important of these recommendations was to close the so-called loophole in the Clayton Act—purchase of another corporation's assets that might limit competition was not prohibited, but the purchase of stock was.

The final report of the TNEC (1941, p. 38) is worth citing at length.

> No person who with an open mind reviews the materials gathered by this committee can fail to conclude that the rise of political centralism is largely the product of economic centralism. People have not wanted to surrender local government, but the very basis of local government has been undermined because economic life in the modern world has broken down all geographical boundaries. Chambers of commerce, mayors of great cities and governors of great states have beaten a path to Washington begging the Federal Government to undertake Federal enterprises in the local communities to solve local problems of unemployment and failing business, because before they turned to Washington, the control of even local economic activity had been removed from within the borders of their respective communities.

The report goes on to argue:

> So great a proportion of all national savings and all national wealth have fallen under the control of a few organized enterprises that the opportunity of those individuals who will constitute the next generation will be completely foreclosed unless, by common consent of leadership in business and government, we undertake to reverse the trends responsible for the present crisis.

We know that most of the wealth and income of the country is owned by a few large corporations, that these corporations in turn are owned by an infinitesimally small number of people and that the profits from the operation of these corporations go to a very small group with the result that the new opportunities for new enterprise, whether corporate or individual, are constantly being restricted. The committee therefore recommends the vigorous and vigilant enforcement of the antitrust laws, confident that an awakening business conscience will realize the necessity of complete cooperation in the elimination of monopolistic practice.   (p. 39)

The central argument expressed by the TNEC was that large firms controlled the economy to such an extent that they threatened the basic democratic institutions in American society. The analysis showed that the existence of large firms had numerous negative consequences. The Depression was prolonged because the large firms refused to respond to the policies of the Roosevelt Administration. Further, opportunities for individuals were foreclosed by the large firms' dominance of the economy. Concentration of the nation's wealth increased the need for government regulations. Finally, the greatest fear was that continued concentration would lead to complete state control or the destruction of the free enterprise system.

The economic theory underlying these assertions was relatively primitive. Economists frequently distinguish between the concentration of production and its centralization. Concentration refers to the amount a product line is controlled by a small number of firms. Centralization refers to the absolute size of firms. While the two are somewhat correlated, they point to quite different problems. Economists generally do not see that size alone is a problem. It can in fact index economies of scale. Concentration, however, can be a problem if too few firms control too much production within a product line and they conspire to lower production or raise the cost of the finished goods. The TNEC rhetoric did not recognize this distinction. The issue of concentration and centralization is also confounded in a way that ignores restraints of trade. The focus of the TNEC and the Celler-Kefauver Act, therefore, was the size of business and the alleged abuses that result from size, mostly the concentration of economic power and its effects on the aggregate economy.

The TNEC was important for two reasons. First, the commission put the blame for problems in the economy on the largest firms. Its rhetoric played the forces of the large firms against the individual. It supported antitrust actions against the largest firms and the extension of antitrust laws. By the late 1940s the issue of "bigness" was firmly on the political agenda. Second, the TNEC created an antitrust community. Members of the commission continued to play key roles in administrative agencies such as the Justice Department and the FTC as well as in Congress. In 1941 this group did not have the power to impose their view of the economy on the country. But by 1950 their view prevailed in the administration and Congress.

Antitrust Enforcement in the New Deal and the 1940s

Thurman Arnold began his antitrust campaign in March 1938 with Roosevelt's support. Arnold faced a number of obstacles that had to be surmounted before he could make the antitrust laws more effective. First, the Antitrust Division had neither the staff nor budget to engage in serious antitrust enforcement. Second, Arnold felt that the program needed public and business support and that required a new set of tactics.[1]

Table 5.1 presents the number of cases and the expenditures for the Antitrust Division. Antitrust enforcement during the Depression was lower than during the 1920s. The budget remained at $400,000 from 1935 to 1938. In 1939 Arnold got an additional $200,000 to hire lawyers and by 1939 employed ninety-seven attorneys. He argued that the major reason for the failure of the antitrust laws was the lack of money to support lawyers and staff. His antitrust campaign was successful and popular with Congress. His highest budget was $2 million in 1942. The number of cases increased between 1938 and 1941 from 13 to 105. Suzanne Weaver (1977, ch. 1), in her history of the Antitrust Division, argues that Arnold was the first head of the division to set up a professional staff. Even though the case load and budget declined during the war, both picked up afterward.

Arnold's strategy for breaking up trusts had both a substantive and public relations thrust. In terms of the latter, Arnold explained why every antitrust action was taken so that other businesses could avoid a similar fate.

Table 5.1 Cases and expenditures on antitrust enforcement

Year	Antitrust Division Number	Antitrust Division % won	Expenditures (in millions of dollars)	FTC cases	Expenditures
1920	11	63.6	.1	18	1.2
1921	26	46.1	.1	26	1.0
1922	22	72.7	.2	32	1.0
1923	10	10.0	.2	50	1.0
1924	16	56.3	.2	51	1.0
1925	14	71.4	.2	21	1.0
1926	11	100.0	.2	4	1.0
1927	14	100.0	.2	8	1.0
1928	21	61.9	.2	10	1.0
1929	11	81.8	.2	17	1.2
1930	10	80.0	.1	12	1.5
1931	3	100.0	.2	4	2.0
1932	5	60.0	.2	3	1.8
1933	11	63.6	.1	4	1.5
1934	9	55.5	.2	14	1.3
1935	4	50.0	.4	30	2.1
1936	9	66.6	.4	33	2.0
1937	8	62.5	.4	18	2.0
1938	13	46.2	.4	28	2.0
1939	38	68.4	.8	31	2.2
1940	82	79.3	1.4	33	2.3
1941	105	86.7	1.4	32	2.2
1942	74	73.0	2.0	16	2.3
1943	38	63.2	1.5	14	2.1
1944	25	80.0	1.4	8	2.0
1945	25	84.0	1.5	6	2.0
1946	43	86.0	1.9	9	2.1
1947	33	69.7	2.1	11	2.9
1948	56	67.9	2.4	11	3.6
1949	35	82.8	3.6	10	3.7
1950	60	70.0	3.9	5	3.8
1951	44	70.5	3.6	18	4.3
1952	32	53.1	3.4	16	4.2

Sources: Antitrust Division: *Congress and the Monopoly Problem*, Select Committee on Small Business, House of Representatives, 84th Congress, Washington, D.C.: U.S. Government Printing Office, 1957, table 2, pp. 659–660; expenditures: *Congress and the Monopoly Problem*, table 1a, p. 657; FTC cases: R. Posner (1970), table 2, p. 369; expenditures: *Congress and the Monopoly Problem*, table 1b, p. 658.

Competition is a kind of game which requires a referee. Without a referee it is a contest in which the men who form gangs will win. Often antitrust offenses involve no moral turpitude. Sometimes they are protective measures taken in order to survive against the aggressive tactics of others. Where one business turns buccaneer, others must follow suit. It is important to recognize that antitrust enforcement is not a moral problem. It is the problem of continuous direction of economic traffic. It requires an adequate organization to penalize those who are reckless or in too much of a hurry.[2]

Arnold was devoted to enforcing the restraint of trade clause of the Sherman Act. Most of his big cases were against price fixing conspiracies, such as those which appeared in the electrical goods, milk, oil, cement, and steel industries. He basically argued that the rule of reason was to be followed in choosing which offenses to prosecute. In a published address, he stated that he would not pursue large firms because of their size nor because they had violated the laws in the distant past. He also used the cases to educate executives about what constituted antitrust violations.[3] From Table 5.1 it is evident that he had great success in convincing the courts to go along with him.

When World War II started Arnold intended to continue his antitrust campaign. The War Department tried to get Arnold to relax his prosecution of various defense-related companies. Arnold's resistance led, in the end, to his leaving the Antitrust Division in March 1943, when he was appointed a federal judge (*Fortune*, Aug. 1943, p. 139). He was replaced by Wendell Berge. The war brought a slowdown in antitrust activity as suits dropped from a prewar high of 105 in 1941 to 25 in 1945.

Berge was already planning to increase antitrust activity in 1944 (*Business Week*, Oct. 21, 1944, p. 15). At the end of the war, mergers began to pick up and the agitation to do something about them resurged. In 1946 a number of senators and representatives proposed bills to strengthen the antitrust laws. This renewal included one version of the bill that eventually was passed as the Celler-Kefauver Act (*New Republic*, Aug. 5, 1946, pp. 120–121). The Justice Department began to step up its prosecution of cases and its budget was increased. In 1947 John Sonnett became head of the Antitrust Division and he was succeeded by Henry Bergson in 1948. The postwar peak in cases filed for the Justice Department was between 1948 and 1950.

The election of 1948 proved to be a turning point for antitrust enforcement. The postwar era brought a rapid increase in prices. Renewed antitrust enforcement was viewed as one mechanism by which prices could be maintained (*New Republic*, Aug. 5, 1946, p. 120, Sept. 7, 1947, p. 8; *Time*, Sept. 1, 1947, p. 74). As the election approached, antitrust became part of the campaign. Truman directed the Justice Department to file suits against the four largest meat-packing companies, Alcoa Aluminum, DuPont, and U.S. Rubber. Attorney General Tom Clark said that by December 1948, 45 to 50 percent of the 100 largest firms had some action pending against them (*U.S. News and World Report*, Dec. 17, 1948, p. 36). Bergson remarked, "We will out trustbust Teddy Roosevelt. We have a lot more cases in the mill than they had" (*Time*, Oct. 4, 1948, p. 86).

The FTC was the other antitrust agency. During the Republican administrations of the 1920s, it had become moribund. The major cause of this was the number of its members who were friendly with business. Roosevelt in fact chose not to locate the NRA in the FTC because he was afraid of how the program might be administered (Johnson, 1985, pp. 167–170, 179–180). Roosevelt then got a chance to remake the commission by appointing Robert Freer, Ewen Davis, and William Ayres to the FTC. All three saw that their job was to police business, not promote it. The FTC became more active in the mid-1930s and began to investigate numerous industries including the textile, milk, chain store, steel, and automobile industries (U.S. Federal Trade Commission, 1935–1939; *Business Week*, April 13, 1946, pp. 90–92). The FTC was also deeply involved in the TNEC hearings.

Table 5.1 presents evidence on the prosecution of antitrust cases by the FTC. The probusiness attitude of Humphrey's FTC can be seen as cases dropped substantially from 1925 to 1933. Cases rose subsequently and then declined during the war. The FTC appropriations remained throughout the 1930s between about $1 million and $2 million, the level until the late 1940s. The FTC was in charge of enforcing both the FTC and the Clayton acts. It did so by investigating alleged violations of these acts and general trade practices in many different industries.

In the mid- and late 1940s, the FTC turned toward studying the problems of competition in the economy as a whole. The goal was to amend the Clayton Act so that mergers by asset acquisition, which tended to diminish competition, would be outlawed. The FTC could not push too hard on Congress during the war years, but in October 1944 it began to lobby for that legislation.[4]

Joseph O'Mahoney introduced such a bill in the Senate on February 26, 1945. At the same time, Estes Kefauver introduced similar legislation in the House of Representatives.[5] On March 1, 1945, Commissioner Barnes argued that the FTC ought to examine the pattern of mergers of the largest firms in the recent past to justify such legislation. The FTC agreed to have their chief economist instigate such a study.[6] In May 1945 Kefauver held hearings on the House bill (U.S. House, 1945). The invited witnesses included Kefauver and O'Mahoney, as well as Ewen Davis, William Kelley, Roger Barnes, and Everette MacIntrye, all of the FTC. These hearings were reconvened in September 1945 and additional testimony was taken from FTC representatives and other parties. The only negative views were presented through letters from business groups.

In July 1945 the FTC proposed a $1 million project to study mergers in the following fiscal year.[7] The FTC passed a resolution outlining their support of such an investigation on September 5, 1945.[8] The FTC argued that when World War I ended, a merger movement had followed, and it was concerned about a recurrence because the merger pace had picked up. How real were these concerns? The Depression was an era of low merger rates. The annual average was around twenty-five. The early war years also had relatively few mergers, particularly by historic standards. Mergers increased from 1943 to January 1945, and then declined sharply the first six months of 1945. While this rate picked up in the last six months of that year, and remained relatively high through the first half of 1947, the danger the FTC saw was clearly overexaggerated.[9]

It is important to attempt to understand the FTC's motives, given there was no merger problem. Federal agencies try to convince Congress and the president that they are useful institutions serving the public interest. The FTC apparently decided that an antimerger campaign would justify its postwar existence. So in 1944 it recommended for the eighteenth straight year the closing of the loophole in the Clayton Act (U.S. Federal Trade Commission, 1944, pp. 7–8). When O'Mahoney and Kefauver introduced their legislation, the FTC seized the opportunity by offering data and assistance for the passage of the antimerger act. I do not mean to suggest that the commissioners were acting in a purely self-interested way. It is clear that they took the issue of industrial concentration quite seriously. Yet it was necessary to get Congress to pass legislation that would aid the FTC in their attempts at controlling incipient monopoly. The small merger movement between 1944 and 1947 provided the justification for action that the FTC sought. The FTC requested an additional $1 million from Congress to study mergers, but the monies were not immediately forthcoming. The report of the FTC meeting on November 14, 1945, shows that the budget for 1946 had been cut from $3.7 to $2.753 million indicating that the additional funds for the merger study were deleted from the appropriations bill.[10]

Following this cut a series of exchanges between Robert Freer, the head of the FTC, and President Truman took place. Truman began the correspondence by asking for information on the size and profits of General Motors and a report on General Motor's participation in the war effort. What followed concerned U.S. Steel, TNEC recommendations about the antimerger amendment, Bethlehem Steel, and the other auto companies. Truman, in the postwar era, became quite interested in the monopoly problem and the structure of the economy. In a letter to Truman dated April 14, 1946, Freer suggested that Truman use the FTC as a source of information. He added that Roosevelt had called on the FTC quite frequently in the 1930s when he needed information on anything to do with industry or trade.[11] President Truman took Freer's advice and on November 19, 1946, he gave the FTC an additional $1 million to study the merger movement.[12] Truman's motives are not hard to discern. The antitrust issue was a natural one for the Democrats. The Seventy-eighth and Seventy-ninth Congresses were both controlled by the Republicans, who were definitely against any new antitrust legislation.

In spite of the fact that Congress refused to appropriate the money in 1945, the FTC began the merger study in September of 1945. John Blair was responsible for coordinating and authoring the study. In December 1946 he issued a preliminary report to the commissioners entitled "The Merger Movement."[13] They thought that one graph was so persuasive they voted to include it in their annual report to Congress. This graph was then followed by a continued plea for the antimerger amendment to the Clayton Act. The final report, issued on March 3, 1947, was called "The Present Trend of Corporate Mergers and Acquisitions." It vigorously argued to close the loophole in the Clayton Act in order to prevent further damage to the economy from more mergers. The small postwar merger movement became the vehicle by which the FTC promoted the antimerger legislation.

Copies of the completed report were first transmitted to Senator O'Mahoney and Representative Kefauver.[14] They were sent to the president of the Senate, Speaker of the House, and chair of the judiciary committees in both branches of the Congress a few weeks later. This early access to documentation suggests that the links between the FTC and its major congressional allies were quite strong.

During May 1947 the FTC accepted a new responsibility. In a series of letters the FTC asked the Department of Commerce if it could begin to keep track of all mergers in the economy. The acting Secretary of Commerce, William Foster, replied that as long as it made the merger data generally available, it was acceptable for the FTC to take on that function.[15] The merger information that the FTC has subsequently collected is the best documented data on large U.S. mergers. No previous data are as detailed or complete.

The Campaign against Bigness

From 1948 to 1950, the Justice Department, the FTC, and the Congress campaigned against the largest firms. While there was a variety of opinions about the exact problem with those firms, it is clear that they were under political and legal attack. The increased antitrust enforcement and the push by the FTC to make the merger movement a political issue are only part of the story. The emerging antitrust community from diverse political organizations embodied the philosophy of the TNEC.

The FTC report on mergers is worth exploring more fully. "If nothing is done to check the growth of concentration, either the giant corporations will ultimately take over the country, or the government will be impelled to impose some form of direct regulation in the public interest. Either this country is going down the road to collectivism or it must stand and fight for competition as the protector of all that is embodied in free enterprise" (*Newsweek*, Aug. 9, 1948, p. 54). When the report was released, *Business Week* ran a story entitled "FTC Wants Bigness Stopped" (July 31, 1948, p. 24).

Walter Wooden, the general counsel for the FTC, made a number of arguments about why the large firm was problematic.

> If there is any validity to the economic theory of price determination in free competitive markets and of the relation between monopolistic pricing methods and inflation, the present state of affairs is a classic example. Unless the Commission and the Supreme Court both are wrong, it would appear that some substantial part of the inflated prices and profits of some basic industries today is the reflection of a pricing method that frustrates competition in price and creates a monopolistic structure. (*Vital Speeches*, Dec. 15, 1948, pp. 133–134)

He went on to explain:

> The future relations between the Commission and American business may depend in the last analysis on whether business itself wants to preserve the competitive system as the Commission and courts have defined it or whether they would prefer an increasing amount of government regulation. As I see it, we have developing here under our very eyes what is essentially a dynamic conflict between what very powerful business interests regard as good business economics and what the statutes which define our public policy define as discrimination, unfair or collusive. (p. 137)

Robert Freer echoed many of these sentiments when he said, "My concern is that if there continues much longer the present trend of concentration of power in fewer and fewer hands and the present trend of sniping at the antitrust laws and seeking by every means to avoid competition, the power of choice between all out government regulation and a free competitive system will have been removed" (*Vital Speeches*, Jan. 7, 1949, p. 210).

But the problems of size and monopoly were difficult for the antitrust authorities and the courts. The problem stemmed from the development of the "rule of reason" approach to antitrust. From this perspective it was necessary to show that people intentionally engaged in unreasonable acts to restrain competition. The

U.S. Steel case, decided in 1920, suggested that large size was no violation of the law. The oligopolistic market structure that embodied the manufacturing conception was not illegal. *U.S. News and World Report* summarized, "In cases where prices are set by leading producers and where competitors follow along, no clear antitrust violation takes place. The Department of Justice recognizes this condition and intends to limit criminal charges to fields where outright conspiracies are suspected. Businessmen who steer away from outright price deals with competitors would appear to be safe from prosecution" (Nov. 17, 1947, p. 24).

When the 1948 election took place, the philosophy had changed. U.S. v. Alcoa (1945) and U.S. v. American Tobacco (1946) seemed to reflect a softening of position by the Supreme Court. The government's cases were not based on alleged conspiracies, but on the size and concentration within the industries. The Columbia Steel case illustrated the polar positions regarding size. The case involved the purchase of the largest West Coast steel producer by U.S. Steel. The majority opinion was that "U.S. Steel is large, but the steel industry is also of impressive size and the welcome westward extension of that industry requires that existing companies go into production there or abandon that market to other organizations." The minority argued, "U.S. Steel has over 51% of the rolled steel capacity of the Pacific Coast area. This acquisition gives it unquestioned domination there and protects it against growth of the independents in developing that region . . . The least I can say is that a company that has that much leverage on our economy is big enough" (*Newsweek*, June 21, 1948, p. 68). The Supreme Court's ambivalent attitude eventually swung to the latter position. One interesting aspect of this discussion is that the Court began to accept statistical arguments on size and concentration.

Others began to question, with a much more hostile attitude toward the largest firms, whether or not bigger meant better. Emmanuel Celler articulated this position in its most extreme form. "Bigness, if unchecked, comes to a point where initiative becomes deadened—it gets too heavy handed. I deprecate the idea that efficiency and lower prices only come with bigness. We know that in many lines the middle sized concerns are either more efficient than the big ones, or else there is no difference. I think that bigness in business brings bigness in labor unions concomitantly. Big business and big labor unions bring about big govern-ment too." Celler went so far as to suggest the following amendment to the Clayton Act: "Any corporation whose size and power are such as to substantially to lessen competition or to create a monopoly in any line of commerce in any section of the country shall be dissolved into a number of independent enter-prises sufficient to restore competition in such a line of com-merce" (*U.S. News and World Report*, Sept. 23, 1949, p. 30).

Senator O'Mahoney took a slightly different tack, one that stressed how the assault on big business was part of the struggle against fascism and communism.

> We say we don't like big government. But isn't it true that what we most detest about government is its adoption of techniques of many of our business organizations? And isn't it likely that one good way to prevent public regimentation by big government is to prevent private regimentation by big business? We reject the aims of the collectivists—fascists, communists, and socialists—to destroy competition through vast state-run monopolies. But isn't it evident that their aims are more readily achieved where competition is already weakened and the economy increasingly controlled by vast privately run monopolies? Let's not fool our-selves. If collectivism carries the day it will not be because of plots hatched in the Kremlin. It will be because of what—by our own shortsightedness and delay—we have allowed to happen in the U.S.A.   (*Reader's Digest*, April 1949, p. 45)

Truman's victory in the 1948 election and the Democrats' coming to power in the House and Senate made the problems caused by big business part of the political agenda. *Business Week* announced, "Here's the nub of Administration philosophy—if you can call it that: bigness, of itself, is bad. Put in work-a-day terms, this simply means batting down the giants, shoring up small outfits" (Nov. 12, 1949, p. 26). The campaign took three actions: antitrust lawsuits, legislative proposals, and continued investigations of the economy. The Justice Department began to pursue cases to break up large firms that controlled an inordinate share of the market. In August 1949, Henry Bergson, the head of the Antitrust Division, said, "Today the major antitrust problem is the unlawful concentration of economic power in industries controlled by a few large companies—the big threes and the big fours—following policies that avoid any real competition among themselves and that, at the same time, enable them to maintain dominant positions. It is against these concentrations of monopoly power that the Antitrust Division is now directing its main enforcement activities" (*Fortune*, pp. 123–124).

In July 1949 Emmanual Celler began a large-scale investigation of monopolies with the blessing and help of the Truman Administration. The purpose of the hearings was to prepare new antitrust legislation. Their focus was size and monopoly. Attorney General Tom Clark remarked, "Bigness, in itself, may not be unlawful, but there is no hope of preventing the evils directly attributable to monopoly unless our efforts are redoubled to cope with the gigantic agglomerations of capital which have become so dominant in our economic life" (*Business Week*, July 23, 1949, p. 46). John Blair of the FTC argued at the same hearings that bigness was at the core of the antitrust problems. The FTC continued its high-profile investigative activities by promoting its merger report and publishing a report on industrial concentration (*Business Week*, Sept. 24, 1949, p. 23). It was also involved in the Celler hearings and various antitrust cases.

The Emergence of the Celler-Kefauver Act

The most important legislation to come out of this activity was the Celler-Kefauver Act, which is also known as the Antimerger Act of 1950 and the 1950 Amendment to the Clayton Act. From 1927 on, the FTC had asked for the legislation and the TNEC had also recommended its passage. During the 1940s, no fewer than twenty-one versions of the final act were introduced. The actual Celler-Kefauver Act was finally passed during the high point of the antitrust campaign. Its passage was dependent on the antitrust community and the control of Congress by the Democrats.

The Celler-Kefauver Act was set up to address a deceptively simple issue. Section 7 of the Clayton Act was referred to as the Holding Company Act, the first paragraph of which originally read: "That no corporation engaged in commerce shall acquire, directly or indirectly, the whole or any part of the stock or other share capital of another corporation engaged in commerce where the effect of such acquisition may be to substantially lessen competition between the corporation whose stock is so acquired and the corporation making the acquisition, or to restrain such competition in any section or community, or tend to create monopoly of any line of commerce." The implication of the act was that holding the stock of a competitor was illegal if the effect was to diminish competition between corporations. The basic evil the law was supposed to mitigate, as summarized by one of its proponents, Senator Cummins, was, "Whenever the law permits the sale of a business then it ought to be open and public, and a corporation ought not to acquire control of a business simply through the purchase of the stock of a company which continues under its own name and, so far as the public knows, is independent in its management. That is what I think this section is intended in the main to prevent."[16]

The definition becomes ambiguous when one considers that the holding of stock is only one way to eliminate competition between two firms. The outright consolidation of two competing firms also limits competition. From the debates, we can see that both sides recognized this problem. The opponents of the bill thought that firms who sought to eliminate competition would do so by merging assets, not stock. The proponents of the bill thought that this outcome was acceptable because the purpose of the bill was to prevent the secret holding of stock (Martin, 1959, pp. 53–56).

Between 1918 and 1926 the FTC issued thirty-eight complaints under Section 7 of the Clayton Act (U.S. Federal Trade Commission, 1918–1926). Apparently the FTC did not interpret the law as narrowly as the Congress intended, however. As Martin argues:

> In deciding to order divestment of assets acquired after and as a result of stock acquisition, the commission interpreted Section 7 to mean that Congress had intended to prevent the lessening of competition, as if it were a general prohibition qualified merely by the provision that it must have resulted from a stock acquisition. The legislative history of Section 7, however, indicates that Congress intended, instead, to prohibit the creation of a holding company with the qualifications that the holding company must be such as to lessen competition.   (1959, p. 100)

The FTC's approach was to prosecute cases of mergers, through either stock or asset acquisition, that it thought lessened competition.

In 1926 the Supreme Court ruled on three cases, FTC v. Western Meat, FTC v. Thatcher Manufacturing, and FTC v. Swift and Company. In all three, stock purchases were followed by purchase of assets. The Supreme Court decided against the FTC because the law did not allow it to force divestiture of assets made after stock purchases. When assets alone were purchased, for example, FTC v. Eastman Kodak, 1925, the Supreme Court ruled that the FTC did not have legal authority to void the merger. The case that made the usefulness of Section 7 most suspect was FTC v. Arrow-Hart and Hegeman Electric Company, 1934. In this case the stock purchase became an asset acquisition after the FTC filed suit. The Supreme Court ruled that the FTC could not force the divestiture of assets, even though the merger took place after the suit was filed.

The Supreme Court's decisions made the law useless against mergers. If a firm merged, even intending to lessen competition, it could avoid prosecution by purchasing the assets outright. Given the original purpose of the Clayton Act, this action was perfectly legitimate. But it meant that the act was an insufficient tool against incipient monopoly that might arise from mergers. At the TNEC hearings the FTC argued, "By judicial interpretation many limitations other than those inherent to Section 7 have been imposed upon the Commission's authority to act thereunder; in fact, it is believed that the effectiveness of this section has been completely emasculated as the result of the Court's decisions" (1941, pt. 5a, p. 2379). In the postwar era, the FTC joined forces with allies in Congress to alter the Clayton Act and provide themselves with a legal tool to prevent mergers, independent of their form of acquisition.

There were three key proponents in Congress: Senator O'Mahoney, Representative (soon to be Senator) Kefauver, and Representative Celler. O'Mahoney was a liberal New Deal Senator from Wyoming who promoted a greater role for government in the economy and social affairs. He was one of the first champions of a full employment act. He also thought that large firms had narrow interests which they attempted to pass off as national interests. Business, therefore, needed regulations in order to act in ways that really did reflect the interest of all Americans.

World War II prevented any implementation of legislation favored by the TNEC. In 1941 O'Mahoney made a statement that later became the ideological basis of the antimerger act: "The termination of the war effort, putting to an end, as it may very suddenly, the industrial activity now gaining tremendous momentum, will bring with it problems more critical and more fraught with danger than those which followed the collapse of 1929. The unsolved problems of postwar depression will be heaped upon the unsolved problems of prewar depression and it is difficult to see how, in these circumstances, democracy can survive unless democracy prepares for peace now" (U.S. Temporary National Economic Commission, 1941, p. 48). O'Mahoney introduced legislation embodying the recommendations of the TNEC in every Congress from 1944 on.

Kefauver was a liberal Representative from Chattanooga, Tennessee, who began his political career as the finance and taxation commissioner for the state (Fontenay, 1980, ch. 2). He had extensive contacts in Tennessee unions and consistently supported the role of government in business, the existence of labor unions, and civil rights (Fontenay, 1980, ch. 6; Gorman, 1971, ch. 2). Once in Congress, he became a staunch supporter of the Tennessee Valley Authority. He began his career in the House by arguing for reforms of legislative and committee practices. Although few of them were implemented, he quickly gained prominence as an activist legislator.

Kefauver became interested in the Clayton Act around 1940 (Fontenay, 1980, p. 110). By 1942 he was in favor of amending the act. In 1945, when Kefauver met John Blair of the FTC, Blair remarked, "There was a quick recognition that we were intellectually, ideologically, and idealistically, simpatico" (Fontenay, 1980, p. 112). Kefauver was an articulate advocate for the view that the largest firms dominated the economy in too many ways. In 1946 he claimed, "The present trend toward concentration of production and distribution of goods into the hands of fewer and larger corporations constitutes one of the gravest issues of our times" (Gorman, 1971, p. 28).

Wright Patman, John Blair, and Emmanual Celler influenced Kefauver the most in his views about monopoly (Fontenay, 1980, p. 102). In 1943 Kefauver and Celler sat together on the House Judiciary Committee and in 1947 they were on the same subcommittee to consider the antimerger bill. Celler became a close friend. Kefauver pursued the antimerger legislation through four sessions of Congress and when he left the House for the Senate, Emmanual Celler took up the bill.

Celler was a liberal from New York City who came to the House of Representatives in 1922. He was an activist for various causes including curbing monopoly power, the formation of Israel, and civil rights. He was the second-ranking member of the House Judiciary Committee by 1945 and in 1948 became its chair. Celler's interest in antitrust went back to at least 1933.[17] Once he took over as chair of the House Judiciary Committee, he often used that forum to express his views on monopoly. The Celler-Kefauver Act was a by-product of the 1949–1951 hearings on monopoly. Celler was the most instrumental actor in bringing the antimerger bill to a final vote in the House.

Celler was also one of the strongest advocates of an anti–big business position in Congress. At one hearing in 1950, he proposed a bill to prevent firms from growing beyond a certain size limit (U.S. House, 1950). He wrote numerous articles and gave interviews that also showed he thought size should be limited by legislation. In *U.S. News and World Report*, Celler argued that size itself could be a criterion for breaking up a firm (Sept. 23, 1949, pp. 28–32).

Twenty-one different bills were proposed during the 1940s to amend the Clayton Act. They entailed not only formal changes, but reflected a shift in the direction of antitrust law as well. The bills took three different approaches. First, some followed the TNEC recommendations requiring large firms to seek approval for stock or asset acquisition. The final act did not include such language because it was thought that the courts were the appropriate place to decide if a violation of law had occurred.

The second type of bill only changed Section 7 of the Clayton Act to include prohibitions against purchasing assets as well as stocks. The third type included this change, but also altered the definition of lessening competition. The original Clayton Act specified the relevant lessening of competition as occurring between the acquired and acquiring corporations. This standard is problematic because any merger decreases competition between the acquired and acquiring firms. The third type of bill recognized this limitation and proposed a requirement to show a lessening of competition in the product market.

All of the bills generally included a change in Section 11 of the Clayton Act that would allow the courts to order firms that had illegally merged to divest not just stock, but assets. This change was in response to the Arrow-Hart and Hegeman case, in which the Supreme Court agreed that the purchase of stock was illegal. But the Court had said the FTC could not order divestiture of assets because, according to Section 11 of the Clayton Act, its only available remedy was the divestiture of stock.

In spring of 1945 Kefauver held hearings on H.R. 2357, a bill that reflected the final recommendations of the TNEC. It gave the FTC the administrative authority to approve any merger before it was consummated. It also made illegal the purchase of assets that might lead to a substantial lessening of competition and proposed to amend Section 11 of the Clayton Act to force divestiture of assets as well as stock. The hearings were dominated by the FTC (U.S. House, 1945, sec. 1). William Kelley, the general counsel for the FTC, was in fact one of the bill's principal authors (U.S. House, 1945, p. 45).

The central arguments in support of the bill were many of the ones I have already discussed. Kefauver began by stating that the intent of the Clayton Act was to prevent the acquisition of assets as well as stock and claimed the omission of the assets clause was an oversight in the original bill. He then argued that the Supreme Court had too narrowly interpreted the law and thereby rendered it ineffective (U.S. House, 1945, pp. 4–5).

O'Mahoney followed with a long speech about the level of concentration in the economy (U.S. House, 1945, pp. 5–15). He argued that the largest firms controlled much of the economy and had taken the greatest share of the defense contracts during the war. He also asserted that the large firms were choking off opportunity for small firms and that the result would be the growth and intervention of the state into the economy. Finally, democracy and liberty would decline. O'Mahoney concluded that mergers were the major cause of this increasing concentration. The antimerger act would prevent any continued concentration by preventing firms from increasing their ability to control markets through mergers.

Ewen Davis, an FTC commissioner, reiterated Kefauver's argument (U.S. House, 1945, pp. 39–47). His position was that the intent of Congress had been subverted by the Supreme Court and the antimerger bill was merely closing the loophole left open by the authors of the Clayton Act. Davis also argued that the future of the entire free enterprise system was at stake. Without closing the loophole, competition would continue to decline and result in increasingly concentrated markets. William Kelley followed Davis with essentially the same arguments (U.S. House, 1945, pp. 48–65). He gave a legal history of the cases decided by the Supreme Court and then presented a table showing how most mergers since the decisions in the 1920s were made through the purchase of assets, not stock. A close reading of the table shows that while 60 percent of the mergers were consummated by asset purchase, 40 percent were still stock buyouts. Although the majority of mergers were by asset purchase, the implication that the asset method had come into existence only after the Supreme Court decisions was not true (Martin, 1959, pp. 52–54).

After the hearings H.R. 2357 passed out of committee to the entire Judiciary Committee. The bill was amended twice and sent to the House Rules Committee.[18] The House Rules Committee, headed by Howard Smith, a Representative from Virginia, controlled the flow of legislation to the House floor. Smith objected to the part of the bill that gave the FTC the right to prior approval of all mergers. Smith, and others, were suspicious of granting such power to a federal agency, so the bill was blocked. Kefauver took the bill back to the Judiciary Committee and reintroduced the measure as H.R. 5535. This bill did not authorize the FTC to make a prior judgment as to the legality of the proposed merger, however, the House session ended before it could be considered.

When the Eightieth Congress convened, Kefauver introduced H.R. 515 and O'Mahoney introduced S. 104. Both bills were substantially the same as H.R. 5535 (U.S. House, 1947). The Senate was controlled by the Republicans and generally more conservative than the House. Hearings were held on S. 104, but were never published. According to House Report 1191 (Eighty-first Congress), S. 104 was in subcommittee, but never made it to the Senate floor. In March 1947 the House Judiciary Subcommittee again held hearings on H.R. 515. Harry Truman, in his annual economic address, mentioned the problem of monopoly and personally supported the measure to close the assets loophole in the Clayton Act (U.S. House, 1947, p. 6). With this auspicious beginning, there was a chance that the antimerger legislation would go forward. Unfortunately for Kefauver, the subcommittee hearings did not go as smoothly as they had previously because of a number of effective, hostile witnesses.

The most important witness was Gilbert Montague, an antitrust attorney from New York (U.S. House, 1947, pp. 125–223). Montague made several important arguments against the passage of the antimerger act. His first point was that the current antitrust laws were sufficient to handle the problems of anticompetitive mergers. He pointed to U.S. v. Aluminum Company of America and U.S. v. American Tobacco, which were successfully prosecuted under the Sherman Act in the mid-1940s. He argued that the Justice Department had successfully prevented Columbia Steel from merging with three competitors by blocking their attempt with a restraining order. He said that because there were new Supreme Court justices, the FTC ought to retry the cases and see if it could get a reversal on the earlier interpretations of the Clayton Act. He felt the FTC should not be allowed to lead in antimerger action because it was often very slow at issuing injunctions and pressing cases.

Montague believed that it was not the intent of Congress in 1914 to pass an antimerger bill of the sort H.R. 515 represented. He had been in Washington at the time and was a protégé of Louis Brandeis, who had supported antitrust legislation such as the Clayton and FTC acts. He claimed that the original Section 7 was meant to stop the formation of holding companies. This intent was reflected in the debate and the actual title of the bill, the Holding Company Act. He countered the arguments of the FTC by saying that asset acquisition was quite common in those days and that the legislators were well aware of the fact that the Clayton Act did not outlaw the practice. The act was intended to prevent instead the particular abuse of holding companies purchasing competitors' stock in order to control those competitors.

The most devastating criticism Montague made of the proposed legislation was a direct attack on the wording itself. Montague's own words are quite effective on this point.

This Kefauver bill, H.R. 4810 (which was a nearly identical piece of legislation to H.R. 515), began by amending sections 7 and 11 of the Clayton Act, so as to forbid any corporation to acquire any stock or assets of another corporation (no matter how small), if the latter corporation is at all engaged in interstate commerce (no matter in how small a degree), and if the effect of such acquisition may be to substantially lessen competition between the corporations involved (no matter how small such competition might have been) or if the effect of such acquisition may be to restrain such commerce in any section or community (no matter how small the section or community might be) or tend to create a monopoly of any line of commerce (no matter how small that line might be). (U.S. House, 1947, p. 144)

Montague argued that the act as written would generally prevent small firms from merging in order to compete with large firms and would have no effect on the continued existence of large firms and their concentration of assets.

Montague made a number of other powerful arguments. First, he said that the FTC had spent a great deal of time bemoaning the merger movement of the mid-1940s, but that they could not prove any increase in prices or decrease in production had resulted. The FTC felt that the Supreme Court limited its ability to force firms to divest assets that were acquired after illegal purchases of stock. But Montague argued that if that was the real problem, then only Section 11 of the Clayton Act should be amended.

The Chamber of Commerce reiterated Montague's arguments (U.S. House, 1947, pp. 272–278). The existing laws protected the public against monopolies or unfair trade practices. Anyone who wanted to sell or buy a business would be a potential candidate for prosecution under the antimerger bill. Further, the antimerger act would make it difficult or impossible for a firm that was going bankrupt to be sold to its competitors. The Chamber of Commerce said that the actual number of firms in the economy had increased and that the disappearance of 1800 firms over seven years due to merger was small when compared to the birth of new firms and the death of established firms.

Business Week essentially took the same position in an editorial arguing that the proprietor who needed to sell his small business for one reason or another would be the victim of the antimerger law (May 23, 1947, p. 128). The argument was that when a small firm needed an infusion of capital to grow and compete, it would be prevented from doing so by merger. Also, when an owner of a business retired or died without heirs, it would be difficult to turn the business over to someone else unless that person was already in the business. Selling one's business to one's competitor would be illegal.

By the time the hearings ended, a number of changes had taken place in the bill. Clifford Case, a Representative from New Jersey, had agreed with Montague that the act would prohibit the merger between any two firms. As the act was written, a merger of two firms' assets would by definition decrease competition between them. H.R. 515 became a new bill, H.R. 3736. The fundamental change was in the standard of illegality. The new standard was that "of another corporation engaged in commerce, where in any line of commerce in any section of the country, the effect of such an acquisition may be to substantially lessen competition" (U.S. House, 1947, p. 4).

House Report 596 presented the new bill to the House and attempted to counter the central arguments made by the bill's opponents. The report argued that the bill would not prevent bankrupt firms from selling because that right was already protected by legal precedent. In response to the objection that small firms were as likely to be prosecuted as large firms, the report said it was unlikely that small firms would control sufficient market share to attract the attention of antitrust agencies. The supporters of the bill said next that the bill would not give the FTC too much power because the offending prior approval clause had been removed. Finally, they objected to Montague's view that the Supreme Court should be used to reinterpret the law. Instead, they insisted that the recent Supreme Court decisions were not relevant to the proposed legislation and that it was better to rewrite the law than have the Court reinterpret it.

While the bill passed the House Judiciary Committee, there was substantial opposition. In fact, two sets of minority views were printed alongside the majority report. One of the minority reports emphasized that existing legislation was sufficient to prevent incipient monopolies, because the FTC could not identify any case that violated Section 7 by the purchase of assets that resulted in a monopoly to which the Sherman Act could be applied. The minority report also argued that the birth of firms far outweighed any decrease due to the mid-1940s merger movement. Further, the FTC could never show that any of these mergers actually resulted in anticompetitive effects. In essence, this report expressed Montague's arguments. The other minority report took up another of Montague's points. It concurred with the first report that the bill as it stood went too far, yet stated that new legislation was necessary. This report proposed that Section 11 of the Clayton Act be modified so that the FTC could force firms who avoided prosecution through Section 7 by purchasing assets to divest those assets. The bill once again went to the House Rules Committee where it was again held up by Representative Smith. The bill died in committee (Fontenay, 1980, p. 113).

The 1948 presidential election resulted in four important changes. First, President Truman was reelected and made the antimerger bill one of his legislative priorities (U.S. House, 1949, p. 17). Second, Emmanual Celler became chair of the House Judiciary Committee, an excellent position from which he could promote the antimerger act. Third, Estes Kefauver was elected to the Senate and he became active in promoting the antimerger bill there. The most important change was that the Eighty-first Congress was then controlled by the Democrats, which greatly increased the likelihood of passing an antimerger act.

In his annual address to Congress in January 1949, Truman again argued that the antimerger bill was essential to the economic well-being of the country. In the spring of 1949, Celler introduced the bill that would eventually become the law, H.R. 2734. In the same session, three other similar bills were introduced, H.R. 988, H.R. 1240, and H.R. 2734 (U.S. House, 1949, p. 1). At the same time Kefauver and O'Mahoney jointly introduced S. 56. While S. 56 did not get any consideration, H.R. 2734 progressed in the House.

On March 9, 1949, Emmanuel Celler invited a number of people to a meeting to discuss potential revision of all the antitrust laws.[19] Among those invited were John Clark, of the President's Council of Economic Advisors; Herbert Bergson, the chief of the Antitrust Division; John Stedman, an attorney for the Antitrust Division; and William Kelley and Walter Wooden of the FTC.

William Kelley was most interested in having Celler pursue the antimerger bill.[20] He argued that it was important for Celler's committee not to lose the opportunity to pass the amendment of the Clayton Act. The others agreed and also thought that a review of the other antitrust laws was in order. Herbert Bergson thought that the Sherman Act was still the most important piece of legislation and that it was quite workable.

Celler took his case to Truman. He wanted Truman's public support of hearings to review all of the antitrust statutes. Truman gave his approval and on July 8, 1949, he instructed the FTC and the Justice Department to give full cooperation to Celler's effort.[21] The Celler committee provided the most thorough review of antimonopoly matters since the TNEC. Celler and Kefauver proposed a new strategy of antitrust enforcement, one concerned with size itself. In an editorial *Business Week* (July 11, 1950, p. 125) argued that Celler and the Senate committee that took up H.R. 2734 were attacking the large firm for its size. *Fortune* made a similar argument (June 1950, pp. 142–145).

In a meeting held on August 23, 1949, Celler established the topics and witnesses for his monopoly hearings.[22] This meeting included the same people plus John Blair and Corwin Edwards, an economist who worked for the FTC. The primary purpose of the hearings for Celler was the issue of bigness. His key argument was that the existence of large firms would ultimately lead to fascism or socialism. "From an economic standpoint, all businesses reach a point where they begin to lose their efficiency because of their size."[23]

The discussion also centered on how to sell the hearings and any legislation to the rest of Congress. Two arguments were stressed. First, large firms represented a dangerous drift toward socialism as their control over the economy promoted more regulation. Second, large firms should have to prove that they were more efficient. Additional hearings grew out of this new antitrust philosophy. The business press was justifiably alarmed at this shift.

The Celler-Kefauver Act was just one of the bills being considered. While the earliest proponents of the antimerger act were in the FTC, Celler took control of the situation and was most responsible for its passage. With Truman's support, a Congress controlled by the Democrats, and an anti–big business rhetoric that stressed the antidemocratic tendencies of mergers, Celler was able to forge an alliance to pass the legislation.

Hearings on H.R. 988, H.R. 1240, H.R. 2006, and H.R. 2734 were held in the House Judiciary Committee on May 18, 1949. The list of witnesses was quite familiar. Kefauver, Celler, Bergson, Clark, Kelley, Montague, and Blair all spoke. The presence of Clark indicated that Truman himself was interested in the legislation enough to send one of his chief economic advisors to the House to testify. U.S. Representatives Mansfield and Jackson, the National Association of Manufacturers, and a number of representatives from other business and labor groups also testified.

Kefauver made his standard statement about how the Clayton Act's original intention had been subverted. Celler extended his remarks arguing that the purpose of the antimerger act was to aid small business in its struggle with big business. "The individual and small business man cannot flower amidst the weeds of monopoly" (U.S. House, 1949, p. 15). Then Celler named the industries in which the opportunity to compete was substantially reduced by the presence of large firms.

The people in favor of legislation to prohibit mergers shared an ideological commitment to reducing the power of large firms. The fact that their arguments were based on misinterpretations of the Clayton Act and an unclear reading of the Supreme Court decisions was not enough to sway their opinion. Further, the impact of the postwar merger movement was overstated. Their commitment pushed the antimerger act forward, not the strength of their arguments.

Herbert Bergson gave the most compelling testimony for the new antimerger act (U.S. House, 1949, p. 19). U.S. v. Columbia Steel, a subsidiary of U.S. Steel, concerned the purchase of assets of the largest steel manufacturer on the West Coast. The Justice Department tried to prevent the merger by arguing that it was a potential barrier to competition. The Supreme Court decided that the anticompetitive effects of the merger were not sufficient to prevent it. Bergson argued strongly that the only way that such incipient anticompetitive mergers could be fought was through additional legislation.

The subcommittee passed H.R. 2734 on June 17, 1949. It left the Judiciary Committee on August 4, when House Report 1191 was issued. Then the legislative struggle recommenced. Because the bill had been blocked in the House Rules Committee twice before, Celler decided to use a parliamentary maneuver to force a vote. On August 15 Celler asked that the House suspend its rules and allow H.R. 2734 to reach the floor.[24] This vote required a two-thirds majority, which Celler got. The bill moved to the floor, was debated, and passed by a vote of 223 to 92. It was then submitted to the Senate.[25]

The foes of the antimerger legislation tried to kill the bill in the Senate. A subcommittee of the Senate Judiciary Committee was formed in September 1949 and consisted of two Democrats, O'Conor and Kilgore, and one Republican, Donnell, who led the opposition. The Senate hearings contained much of the same information and arguments heard in the House. Generally, Donnell made the arguments that Montague had. He suggested that the merger movement that bothered the FTC was quite small and that its effects on aggregate concentration were low. He buttressed his position with an article prepared by two Harvard professors, John Lintner and J. Keith Butler. Donnell also claimed that the law would work against small firms as well as large, and because it was too vague it could make all mergers illegal. One of his examples was the merger of three gas stations in a neighborhood in Washington, D.C. He said that the law could be interpreted so that such a merger restrained trade in a narrowly defined section of the country (U.S. Senate, 1949–1950, p. 37).

Donnell continued the hearings into the second session of the Eighty-first Congress because many of the witnesses against the bill had not had a chance to testify. When the subcommittee reconvened in the spring, there were no additional witnesses, so he presented the Lintner and Butler article and a number of letters from various business groups who opposed the antimerger act. After the bill left the subcommittee and passed the whole committee on June 2, 1950, Senate Report 1775 was issued.

The Senate Report reiterated the arguments of the House Report. Donnell wrote a minority report and with his Republican counterparts kept H.R. 2734 off the Senate floor. Whenever the bill came up, an opponent objected to its consideration and the bill was passed over.[26] This happened three times and when Congress recessed before the 1950 elections, the bill had not yet been considered by the entire Senate. After the elections, the Senate reconvened for a lame duck session. On December 11, O'Conor brought H.R. 2734 to the Senate floor.[27] He also invited John Blair and Lawrence Stratton, an FTC commissioner, to the floor for the debate. Donnell led the fight against the bill arguing that it was unnecessary because the merger movement had not altered aggregate concentration substantially. Counterarguments were launched by Senators O'Conor, Kilgore, O'Mahoney, and Kefauver. The final vote on the measure was fifty-five for and twenty-two against.[28]

By December 14, 1950, the House and Senate had reconciled the differences between their bills and on December 29 Harry Truman signed Public Law 899, the Celler-Kefauver Act, into law.

6

The Impact of the Celler-Kefauver Act, 1948–1980

The finance conception of control is the product of two forces. First, the largest firms, already fairly diversified by the early postwar era, became more diversified in the late 1940s and early 1950s. They tended to operate in organizational fields characterized by major industry and to use the multidivisional form. Control within the large modern corporation, therefore, increasingly entailed a knowledge of financial controls and the ability to evaluate the performance of disparate product lines. Second, the antitrust activities of the Truman and Eisenhower administrations were directed toward preventing increased concentration within product lines.

But the finance conception of control not only concentrates on diversification, it conceives of the firm in purely financial terms. Each of the product divisions is evaluated on its short-term performance and ability to generate surplus revenue. Growth in the firm is produced by investing in products that provide a relatively high rate of return. When product lines do not perform, they are sold. The most important way to achieve instant growth and entrance into new product lines is to purchase a company active in that line. The financial conception of control emphasizes short-term gains and thereby discourages long-term investment.

The organizational field of the large financially driven firm cannot be defined in product terms because the firm is no longer committed to a single industry. While competition affects each division's performance, it does not determine the overall profitability of the firm. Performance is judged instead in terms of rates of return and stock prices relative to other large corporations. The reference group for firms dominated by the finance conception of control is most often the other large corporations operating across diverse industries. Indeed, divestment in an industry is undertaken precisely because the rate of return in that industry is too low relative to other industries. The actions of other large firms and their relative profitabilities are deemed most relevant in investment decisions. In this sense, only after the war did the largest corporations together form an organizational field. They were linked by a similar conception of what the firm should be, and that same conception dominates today.

Antitrust enforcement in the postwar era is directly linked to the emergence of the financial conception of control. The Antitrust Division and the FTC used the Celler-Kefauver Act to discourage vertical and horizontal mergers, which encouraged mergers for diversification. The corporate lawyers and leaders of the large firms who were interested in antitrust issues altered their behavior in accordance with the authorities. Executives with a finance conception of control were best able to interpret what the government was doing. They saw that the diversified merger was not only a quick way to grow, but a legal one as well. The government's policies made diversified mergers an attractive growth strategy from 1950 to 1969.

The largest firms were most subject to antitrust prosecution and understandably most attuned to the pronouncements of the Antitrust Division and FTC. Information on their activities appeared in the business press and the organizational links between the antitrust authorities and their legal counterparts in the private sector. The most important private source of this information was the Antitrust Section of the American Bar Association (ABA).

The importance of antitrust extends beyond the specific cases. Antitrust enforcement sets the tone for government-business relations and establishes limits for competitive behavior between firms. Leaders of firms are likely to take a hostile environment into account when they strategize. Therefore, the existence of antitrust lawsuits is less important than the perception of what is then legal and illegal behavior.

The Celler-Kefauver Act was written to forestall two problems. First, the act was supposed to prevent increases in market concentration by preventing certain mergers. Second, by generally discouraging mergers, its authors thought they could prevent the increasing centralization of economic activity among a relatively few corporations. The act indeed had the first effect. But, while market concentration in the postwar era has remained stable overall, aggregate concentration has increased dramatically

(Mueller, 1979). This great increase resulted from the longest continuous merger movement, 1954–1969, in the history of the United States. The complex interaction of three conditions led to its development: the continued spread of sales and marketing diversification strategies, the consistent use of the Celler-Kefauver Act to block horizontal mergers and force product related and unrelated mergers, and the emergence of a purely financial conception of control whereby firms chose to use mergers as a basic strategy for growth.

Antitrust violations are not pursued consistently. The degree to which lawsuits are filed depends on the president, the attorney general, the head of the Antitrust Division, the composition of the FTC, pressure from Congress, the receptivity of the Supreme Court, and the tactics of the largest firms at the time. Indeed, enforcement of the antitrust laws has been sporadic, and to some degree, idiosyncratic.

The commitment of participants in the antitrust community was strong from 1938 to 1950 and culminated in the passage of the Celler-Kefauver Act. The Eisenhower Administration prosecuted many firms under various antitrust statutes. When large-scale corporate mergers began to pick up in 1954, Eisenhower's antitrust agencies effectively employed the Celler-Kefauver Act. When the Kennedy and Johnson administrations continued antitrust prosecution, the courts, especially the Supreme Court led by Earl Warren, supported the government's position in case after case.

One important and interesting part of this story concerns the antitrust policy of the Nixon Administration. In 1969 Richard McLaren, the assistant attorney general in charge of the Antitrust Division, began to pursue aggressively firms that engaged in diversified mergers. Nixon's role in this was somewhat complex. While he initially knew of and appeared to approve of the antitrust suits, he later attempted to stop them. He was discouraged from doing so by his advisors and eventually the cases were settled out of court. They had a chilling effect, however, and contributed to the end of the merger movement.

The Nixon Administration began to shift its antitrust policy by 1971. A domestic policy group led by John Ehrlichman, one of Nixon's principal advisors, suggested a new approach to antitrust enforcement that focused on the behavior of firms after mergers in order to assess potential violations. The Burger Court, whose key justices were appointed by Nixon, began to decide in favor of firms. The Carter Administration continued the new antitrust philosophy which resulted in a diminished enforcement effort. The Reagan Administration, which generally took a positive view of corporate mergers, almost ended antitrust enforcement entirely. In essence, antitrust enforcement has come full circle since 1938.

The shift in merger policy reflected not only a somewhat politically motivated change but also a shift in antitrust theories. The dominant arguments in merger cases from 1950 to 1974 revolved around the level of concentration that mergers produced in an industry. In economic terms, the structure of the industry was supposed to determine its conduct and higher concentration implied the possibility for collusion and higher prices and profits. Cases were decided on the basis of increased concentration without regard to the actual effects of the mergers on prices or profits. In the mid-1960s and early 1970s antitrust scholars and lawyers argued that mergers could result in efficiencies and that concentration of production could lower costs for larger firms. From their perspective, the conduct and performance of firms after mergers was deemed more important than the structure of the industry. The most radical proponents of this theory claimed that mergers reflected the working of the market to produce efficient industrial organization. Any merger that did not produce a more efficient organization would fail so there was no reason to be concerned with mergers. A functioning market would choose the winners and losers.

This antitrust philosophy eventually came to the fore during the Carter Administration and extended into the Reagan Administration. Significantly, this shift in antitrust policy encouraged mergers and produced the fourth merger wave—1976 to the present. Because the current view is that all mergers enhance shareholder value, the Celler-Kefauver Act is no longer being enforced. Predictably, large horizontal and vertical mergers, which would have been illegal in the 1960s, occur now with some frequency.

Mergers and the Pattern of Enforcement

Table 6.1 presents the number and types of large mergers attempted from 1940 to 1977. It brings together the results of two studies, with the 1948–1953 panel overlapping the 1951–1955 panel. The 1940s was generally a period of low merger activity. The peak of the merger activity in this decade occurred between 1945 and 1948. By 1949 merger activity had subsided and continued to remain relatively low until 1954. Beginning in 1954, mergers increased until they peaked in 1968. They declined until 1976 when they began to increase again.

The causes of any merger movement are always a matter of great controversy. The characterization of merger movements, however, is less problematic. If the turn of the century merger movement was for monopoly and the 1920s merger movement created oligopoly, then the trend of mergers since 1950 has been toward diversification. Horizontal and vertical mergers formed the greatest number of mergers before 1950 and began to decline rapidly thereafter. By 1970 only 20 percent of the mergers were horizontal and vertical and the rest reflected product diversification. (See Table 6.1.)

Many analyses indicate that the major factor in this change was the Celler-Kefauver Act (Adelman, 1961; Stigler, 1966; Eis, 1978, p. 147; Mueller, 1979, pp. 20–21). In order to establish this causal relationship I will present evidence for three critical links. First, the antitrust record shows that the law was used against horizontal and vertical mergers and not mergers for diversification. Second, the business community was aware of the law and took it into account when firms engaged in mergers. Third, one can quantita-

Table 6.1 Number and percentage distribution of merger types over time

Type of merger	1940–47	1948–53	1951–55	1956–60	1961–65	1966–70	1971–77
Horizontal	62.0	37.9	38.0	32.0	24.0	12.0	27.0
Vertical	17.0	10.3	13.0	14.0	16.0	8.0	7.0
Related	21.0[a]	51.8[a]	36.0	38.0	44.0	51.0	33.0
Unrelated	—	—	13.0	16.0	16.0	29.0	33.0
Number of mergers	2,062	58	154	257	325	640	493

Sources: 1940–47 and 1948–53 data are from Eis (1969), p. 294 (these data include all mergers over $1 million); 1951–55, 1956–60, 1961–65, 1966–70, and 1971–77 data are from Mueller (1979), p. 20 (these data include all mergers over $10 million).

a. Eis combines related and unrelated mergers.

tively demonstrate that antitrust policy affected merger patterns.

An alternative perspective would suggest that firms were already turning away from horizontal and vertical integration and the manufacturing conception of control and toward the sales and marketing strategy of product diversification. From this point of view the Celler-Kefauver Act was less important and the timing of the act was perhaps only coincidental.

My position is that the Celler-Kefauver Act and the general antitrust environment convinced firms that horizontal and vertical mergers were illegal. Since the sales and marketing conception of control was already convincing firms to diversify, the Celler-Kefauver Act just encouraged them to pursue that strategy more systematically in order to avoid antitrust prosecution.

Evidence for my thesis is in Table 6.2, which presents the distribution of cases filed under the Celler-Kefauver Act by merger type. Enforcement began slowly in the early 1950s reflecting the small numbers of mergers. As they increased, the number of lawsuits increased and peaked between 1966 and 1970 during the height of the merger movement. From 1951 to 1955, 86 percent of the mergers that were challenged were vertical and horizontal, a fact that is all the more striking when one considers that these types accounted for 51 percent of all mergers. This pattern of enforcement continued from 1956 to 1977. From 1966 to 1970 horizontal and vertical mergers formed only 20 percent of all large mergers, but 81 percent of the challenged acquisitions were in these categories. Given these data the Celler-Kefauver Act was applied most successfully and nearly exclusively to horizontal and

Table 6.2   Distribution of lawsuits undertaken against large mergers using Celler-Kefauver Amendment by merger type (in percentages)

Type of merger	1951–55	1956–60	1961–65	1966–70	1971–77
Horizontal	53.0[2]	63.0	68.0	71.0	72.0
Vertical	33.0	30.0	19.0	10.0	7.0
Related	13.0	8.0	11.0	15.0	17.0
Unrelated	0.0	0.0	2.0	4.0	3.0
Number of lawsuits	15	40	47	52	46

Source: Mueller (1979), p. 16.

vertical mergers, even as those mergers decreased in importance. One can infer that their decline is not only a function of the decline of the manufacturing conception of control but also partially a function of antitrust enforcement.

The Antitrust Environment and the Pattern of Enforcement

In 1949 the Justice Department and the FTC continued their attack on big business. DuPont, the large meat packers, AT&T, A & P Grocery Stores, Alcoa Aluminum, the steel industry, the tire industry, and various firms in the oil industry were being assaulted with cases claiming that the largest firms in these industries had colluded to control their markets through monopolization, price fixing, or various forms of price discrimination (*Business Week*, Nov. 12, 1947, p. 26). In 1950 the Justice Department filed a suit against U.S. Steel. It also won a suit against the movie companies that forced producers to divest their theater ownership (*Business Week*, June 11, 1950, p. 83). Between 1945 and 1950 the Antitrust Division filed 341 suits, most of them against the largest firms.

The business press immediately took note when the Celler-Kefauver Act was passed in December 1950. In the months following articles appeared suggesting how to avoid prosecution and warned of impending actions (*Business Week*, Dec. 23, 1950, p. 26; Feb. 3, 1951, p. 40; *U.S. News and World Report*, Jan. 5, 1951, p. 43). A proposed merger between Minnesota Mining and Carborundum was called off due to fear of prosecution by the FTC (*Business Week*, Dec. 31, 1951, p. 40). Merger activity had declined after 1948 and by the early 1950s was at a low point by postwar standards. Certainly, the antitrust environment made large firms wary of mergers. The 1940s were generally years of aggressive antitrust enforcement and, even before Celler-Kefauver, firms had reason to avoid mergers or any behavior that might be considered anticompetitive.

In the early 1950s antitrust enforcement began to decrease for four reasons. First, just as World War II brought a halt to the activities of Thurman Arnold, the Korean War caused Truman to reduce antitrust enforcement. Second, Herbert Bergson resigned as head of the Antitrust Division and was followed by four antitrust chiefs within two years (Kovaleff, 1980, p. 51). The rapid turnover of personnel made pursuing a coherent policy difficult. Third, antitrust budgets were cut for both the Justice Department and the FTC (U.S. House, 1957, pp. 657–658). Finally, there was less concern with anticompetitive mergers. It was not until mergers increased that antitrust action utilizing Celler-Kefauver began.

Eisenhower's attorney general, Herbert Brownell, formed the Attorney General's National Committee to Study the Antitrust Laws. The committee was given the job of reviewing the entire body of antitrust laws and recommending how they could be better implemented (U.S. Attorney General, 1955, pp. iv–vi). The committee was co-chaired by Stanley Barnes, the first Eisenhower Antitrust Division head, and S. C. Chesterfield, a prominent law professor at the University of Michigan. The committee's report generally called for more stringent enforcement of the antitrust laws and proposed a number of procedures to streamline the process by which lawsuits were filed and pursued. It also provided a set of guidelines for executives based on principles of economics and law. Barnes wrote most of the report concerning the interpretation of the Celler-Kefauver Act. The arguments of the first Celler-Kefauver cases were based on his discussion. The intent of the legislation, was "to cope with monopolistic tendencies in their incipiency and well before they have attained such effects as would justify a Sherman Act proceeding" (U.S. Attorney General, 1955, p. 117). A violation of the Sherman Act was a conspiracy with the intent to monopolize or restrain trade. To prosecute one had to show intent as well as action to control prices or entry into a field.

The report argued that the Celler-Kefauver Act was intended to alter two kinds of criteria for anticompetitiveness in a merger. First, a violation of Celler-Kefauver did not turn on the intent of the firms involved. On this issue Congress was clear (and the report agreed): "thus, it would be unnecessary for the government to speculate as to what is in the 'back of the minds' of those who promote a merger; or to prove that the acquiring firm had engaged in actions which are considered to be unethical or predatory; or to show that as a result of a merger the acquiring firm had already obtained such a degree of control that it possessed the power to destroy or exclude competitors or fix prices" (U.S. House, 1949, p. 11).

Second, the act was intended to control incipient monopoly. That is, competition in a particular business could lessen over time. Hence, merger might not extensively alter the balance of power in an industry immediately, but a pattern of mergers might result in a substantial lessening of competition later. The report acknowledged this intent and concluded that "Section 7, unlike the Sherman Act, requires findings and conclusions, not of actual anticompetitive effects, but merely of a reasonable probability of a substantial lessening of competition or tendency toward monopoly" (1955, p. 118).

The report stressed a number of ways to make the law more effective. Every suspected merger needed to be analyzed in context. Four conditions were relevant for deciding whether a violation had occurred: "1) The character of the acquiring and the acquired company, 2) the characteristics of the markets affected, 3) immediate changes in the size and competitive range of the acquiring company and in the adjustments of other companies operating in the market directly affected, and 4) probable long range differences that the acquisition may make for companies actually or potentially operating in those markets" (U.S. Attorney General, 1955, p. 125).

Most of the report focused on vertical and horizontal mergers. The key questions involved the definition of relevant market in terms of product, geography, and function. Depending on the definition, an antitrust case was based on the pattern of mergers in the industry, the concentration already in the industry, the direction taken over time, and the possible long-run repercussions of the merger on the industry's structure. The report was careful not to mention exact figures for merger size and concentration.

This approach to mergers reflects a concern with the structure of an industry and not its performance. The assumption was that a concentrated structure tended to produce anticompetitive behavior. All of the antitrust cases decided in the Warren Court relied on these arguments and did not consider the issue of performance relevant, that is, firms could not argue that mergers produced more efficient firms. In fact, the Justice Department's merger guidelines spelled out that the structure of a market was the only relevant fact in considering the legality of a merger.[1]

The Celler-Kefauver Act was not intended to outlaw all mergers, nor was it intended to prevent mergers between small firms who might benefit from strengthening their competitive advantage (U.S. Attorney General, 1955, pp. 122–123). It was intended to be used against all types of mergers, including vertical and conglomerate mergers. The bill, as written, also provided clear criteria for pursuing horizontal mergers. It was useful in pursuing vertical mergers because those mergers could effect competition when a company controlled some product necessary to production downstream and would be able to control the production of the downstream product by withholding its product from potential competitors. Criteria for showing how mergers of related or unrelated products restricted competition proved more difficult to develop. If firms were in noncompeting lines how could one argue that competition was lessened. Indeed, by definition, conglomerate mergers imply noncompetition. The report was totally silent on this issue so, from the perspective of the Eisenhower Antitrust Division, the law could not be used against conglomerate mergers.

The Eisenhower Administration pursued a vigorous antitrust policy. The Antitrust Division engaged in 538 separate cases under the various statutes (Kovaleff, 1980, app. a). The FTC and the Antitrust Division began fifty-five lawsuits under the Celler-Kefauver Act and most of them were filed after 1955. Victor Hansen replaced Brownell as chief of the Antitrust Division in December 1956 and was subsequently succeeded by Robert Bicks in April 1959. The Republican administration embraced the antitrust laws as a way to protect the U.S. free market. What had started as a Democratic issue in the postwar era, quickly became a cornerstone of Republican policy.

The first two important cases filed under the Celler-Kefauver Act in the early 1950s were complaints against Pillsbury and its acquisition of Duff's Baking Mix and Ballard and Ballard Company and against Crown Zellerbach and its acquisition of St. Helen's Paper.[2] The complaint against Pillsbury alleged that its purchase of two competitors would increase concentration substantially in the prepared flour-base mixes in the Southeast. In that region Pillsbury ranked first in sales with 22.7 percent, Ballard was third with 12 percent, and Duff was fifth with 10.2 percent; together they controlled 44.9 percent of the market. After much legal maneuvering, the FTC ruled that there was prima facie evidence of a violation of the newly revised Section 7 of the Clayton Act.[3] Before the proceeding continued Pillsbury sold the

Duff assets. The case was important because the FTC established that the relevant market was defined by both region and product (U.S. Attorney General, 1955, pp. 120–124). In February 1954 the FTC alleged that the merger between Crown Zellerbach and St. Helen's Paper would give the combined firms 85 percent of the paper products market in the western United States. As a result of the hearings and the complaint, Crown Zellerbach agreed to divest itself of the St. Helen's properties in December 1957.[4]

In the early 1950s a number of other cases were brought by the Justice Department and the FTC. These included complaints against Curtis Publishing, Union Bag, Long Bell Lumber, Scott Paper, Brillo Manufacturing, Schenley Industries, General Shoe, Hilton Hotels, and Minute Maid. As mergers increased, enforcement increased. After 1955 cases were filed against many firms involved in the largest mergers, including American Radiator and Standard, Continental Can, Bethlehem Steel, Lever Brothers, Anheuser-Busch, Hertz, United Artists, and Kennecott Copper.[5] The attempt to merge Bethlehem Steel and Youngstown Steel was the largest merger stopped by the Justice Department.

Most of the judicial arguments contained the same elements. The mergers were almost all horizontal or vertical in nature. All of the cases were based on market shares of various firms in defined regions of the country before and after acquisitions occurred. Data on the trend of mergers and competition in the industry were allowed as evidence. It was not necessary to establish intent in order to show anticompetitive effects of mergers. The attorney general's report had established the guidelines for pursuing mergers under the Celler-Kefauver amendment.

The first antitrust chief in the Kennedy Administration was Lee Loevinger, who was a justice of the Minnesota Supreme Court when appointed. Loevinger continued a moderately high level of antitrust activity. The first merger case reached the Supreme Court during his term. U.S. v. Brown Shoe (1962) involved the 1955 merger between Kinney Shoe and Brown Shoe Company. The basic outlines for the case had been put together by the Eisenhower Antitrust Division. This case is considered a landmark decision; it contained all of the elements that would later be applied to scores of cases (Neale and Goyder, 1980, p. 186). The Brown Shoe Company was the fourth largest producer of shoes in the country, but had only a 4 percent market share. It was the third largest retailer with a market share of 6 percent. Kinney Shoe was the twelfth largest manufacturer with less than .5 percent market share and the eighth largest retailer with a 2 percent market share. On the face of it, the merger between the two firms did not appear to increase concentration greatly within the shoe industry.

The basis for the determination against Brown Shoe was presented in the opinion of Chief Justice Earl Warren.[6] He argued that the merger violated Section 7 of the Clayton Act for a number of reasons. First, the shoe industry had become more and more concentrated. The control of large firms extended both vertically and horizontally. Further, the combined merger of Brown Shoe would substantially increase the market share in certain geographic areas. Based on the statistical analysis and the tendency within the industry to increase concentration, the Supreme Court ruled to void the merger.

Loevinger, in a speech before the Antitrust Section of the ABA in August 1962, appraised the significance of the Brown Shoe decision:

> The Celler-Kefauver Amendment to Section 7 of the Clayton Act has now been made effective by judicial ratification. The Supreme Court has said that the Act means exactly what it says, and that it says what the Congress clearly intended to say when the Act was under consideration. To me Section 7 is definite and clear. It prohibits acquisitions, either of stock or assets, where competition in *any* line of commerce in *any* section of the country may be substantially lessened. The test as stated in the Senate Report on the bill is whether there is a reasonable probability that competition *may* be lessened. These are the words of Justice Clark in his concurring opinion and they express my own view as well as it can be stated.[7]

The antitrust authorities pursued mergers in the early and mid-1960s under the Celler-Kefauver Act and the limits of the Brown Shoe decision. From 1962 until 1970 the Supreme Court decided twenty-nine merger cases, of which the government won twenty-eight. In rapid-fire succession, the Court decisions made any large-scale mergers with vertical or horizontal elements potentially illegal. It is no surprise that firms moved quickly away from those types of mergers and toward mergers with firms that made related or unrelated products.

Willard Mueller (1977) showed that of the 2277 mergers involving firms of assets greater than $10 million that were attempted between 1951 and 1977, only 289 complaints were issued under the Celler-Kefauver Act. The probability of any merger attracting the attention of antitrust prosecution was small. The bulk of these complaints were issued against the largest firms, in fact, only 22 were issued against firms with less than $25 million in assets. Of the 136 firms with assets greater than $1 billion that attempted mergers, 127 were involved in antitrust suits because of one or more of their acquisitions (Mueller, 1977, p. 10).

Antitrust and Conglomerate Mergers

In spite of the threat of antitrust action, the 1960s witnessed an enormous merger movement. The character of this movement was an unprecedented purchase of corporate assets by the nation's largest firms. The FTC has estimated that between 1959 and 1969 the concentration of all manufacturing assets in the 500 largest firms rose 11 percent and was almost entirely due to the merger movement. Between 1965 and 1968 one-fifth of the companies that were larger than $10 million in assets were swallowed up by mergers. From 1967 to 1969 roughly $19 billion in assets were purchased. Most of these mergers were in the product-related and -unrelated categories. It is clear that while the Celler-Kefauver Act was used effectively against horizontal mergers, it did not prevent the large-scale mergers that were sweeping the American economy in the 1960s. Indeed, by foreclosing the possibility of vertical and horizontal mergers, the law encouraged diversified mergers.

For the antitrust authorities, the problem was not a lack of interest or will to do something about the situation. Indeed, two Democratic administrations pursued antitrust. Nor was the problem due to unfriendly courts. The Warren Court liberally applied the new Celler-Kefauver law to mergers. The problem was an insufficiently compelling argument for prosecuting the conglomerate mergers.

Antitrust matters were in the hands of the head of the Antitrust Division during the Kennedy and Johnson administrations. The four men who occupied this position from 1960 to 1968, Lee Loevinger, William Orrick, Donald Turner, and Edwin Zimmerman, paid the most attention to cases that were prosecutable under existing laws. Since the intent of the antitrust laws was to protect competition, any attacks on conglomerate mergers needed to be oriented toward their uncompetitive effects.

Turner was a Harvard law professor before assuming his position in the Antitrust Division. His academic work was in the area of antitrust and he wrote one of the seminal articles describing the relationship between the Celler-Kefauver Act and conglomerate mergers (1965, pp. 1313–95). In that article he suggested that the only way to proceed against conglomerate mergers, given the present law, was to show anticompetitive effects based on "reciprocity," "potential competition," and "decisive competitive advantage." In the mid-1960s the Justice Department was able to mount a number of lawsuits against conglomerate mergers on the basis of these arguments.

"Reciprocity" was the central issue in the case of the FTC v. Consolidated Foods (1965). Consolidated Foods, a large producer of processed foods, had purchased Gentry, a company that produced dehydrated onion and garlic. The merger was blocked on the grounds that Consolidated could force its own suppliers to buy from Gentry in order to secure Consolidated's business. This purchasing reciprocity would reduce competition in both lines of business by eliminating outside bids to either firm. This defense was also instrumental in blocking the merger of General Dynamics with Liquid Carbonic Company (Neale and Goyder, 1980, pp. 198–200).

The second effective argument against conglomerate mergers was elucidated in the FTC v. Procter and Gamble (1967). This case concerned the purchase of Clorox Bleach by Procter and Gamble, a large diversified soap and detergent company, and was decided partially on the grounds of "potential competition." The theory was that entry of a new firm by merger eliminated a potential competitor in the industry. Since Procter and Gamble was likely to enter the bleach industry, its entry by merger as opposed to creating a new product reduced competition in the industry in two ways. First, Procter and Gamble could not act as a hedge to promote competition in the bleach market. If a firm like Clorox decided to raise prices substantially, it could do so without threat of Procter and Gamble, a potential entrant, forcing prices down. Second, by entering through merger, especially with the leading firm, Procter and Gamble substantially reduced the competitiveness of the industry. If it had entered with a new product instead, it would have increased the competition.

The third argument, and the strongest in the Procter and Gamble case, concerned "decisive competitive advantage" (Goolrick, 1978, p. 33). Since Clorox was the leading producer of bleach (its market share was 50 percent), it already had a commanding position in the bleach business. Its association with Procter and Gamble would probably strengthen its competitive position by giving it access to Procter and Gamble's resources. The Supreme Court noted that "the products of the acquired company are complementary to those of the acquiring company and may be produced with similar facilities, marketed through the same channels and in the same manner, and advertised by the same media."[8] This would likely give Procter and Gamble, and its new acquisition, Clorox, a decisive competitive advantage in the liquid bleach industry and possibly drive other competitors from the field.

While all three of these arguments could be used against product-related or -unrelated mergers, they would require special circumstances. For instance, in the Consolidated Foods case there was evidence that Consolidated had used Gentry to obtain reciprocity agreements. The Court allowed the potential competition argument only when potential entry could be proven. In the Procter and Gamble case there was evidence that the company was considering entering the bleach industry. Finally, the competitive advantage argument could be avoided by firms if they chose not to purchase the leading firm in an already concentrated industry. These arguments actually encouraged conglomerate mergers. The less a product line could be used in any anticompetitive fashion, the less likely the antitrust authorities were to prosecute.

Turner felt that the antitrust laws, as they were written, did not give prosecutors legal ground to pursue conglomerate mergers on the basis of size alone. He argued:

> One cannot support an attack of much greater breadth on conglomerates without trenching on significant economic and other values, and therefore without an unprecedented reliance on judgments of an essentially political nature. There are indeed many who will rousingly make those judgments. There are many who believe that "superconcentration"—further concentration of

assets in the hands of large conglomerate firms—is a very bad thing, even if devoid of any anticompetitive effects . . . I do not believe Congress has given the Courts and the FTC a mandate to campaign against "superconcentration" in the absence of any evidence of harm to competition. In the light of the bitterly disputed issues involved, I believe the Courts should demand of Congress that it translate any further directive into something more formidable than sonorous phrases in the pages of the Congressional Record.   (1965, p. 1394)

Turner's behavior toward conglomerate mergers was consistent with these views. As head of the Antitrust Division, he filed only five complaints against conglomerate mergers and none of these involved the twenty-five largest firms (Goolrick, 1978, p. 42). In late 1966 Ramsey Clark was named attorney general. Clark had a more activist view of how antitrust laws could be used against conglomerates. He and Turner clashed immediately over the purchase by International Telephone and Telegraph (ITT) of the American Broadcasting Company (ABC). Clark, as Turner's superior, won the controversy. For thirteen months Clark fought to have the merger overturned by the Federal Communications Commission (FCC). In January 1968 the matter was dropped because ITT canceled its merger plans (*Business Week*, Jan. 28, 1968, p. 38).

Clark was unable to get Turner or his successor, Edwin Zimmerman, to change their position on the issue of conglomerate mergers and Lyndon Johnson left office before any substantial action could take place. Meanwhile, 1968 proved to be the height of the merger movement and 1969 promised more of the same. Clark did convince President Johnson to commission a study of conglomerate mergers. This commission was chaired by Philip Neal, the dean of the University of Chicago Law School. Most of its members favored stricter antitrust enforcement. They agreed that there was potential danger to the economy from conglomerate mergers, but also thought that merger law, as written, provided no means to stop them. The commission recommended new legislation to prevent mergers involving firms of large size.[9]

When Richard Nixon came to office he appointed a more conservative commission headed by George Stigler, a University of Chicago economics professor. This commission saw no need for new laws and concluded that, by their very nature, conglomerate mergers could not have anticompetitive effects.[10] It rejected the call for more legislation until further study of the issue could be completed. It appeared as if the more conservative Nixon Administration was prepared to do little or nothing about antitrust issues. In fact, when Nixon's election had appeared certain, ITT began three large purchases in late 1968: the Canteen Company, the Grinnell Company, and the Hartford Insurance Company.

Nixon named John Mitchell as attorney general and Mitchell chose Richard McLaren to head the Antitrust Division. McLaren was a Chicago antitrust lawyer who had spent his career defending large firms from antitrust attacks and also had been head of the Antitrust Section of the ABA. McLaren told Mitchell and Richard Kleindienst, Mitchell's principal assistant, in his job interview that he intended to use the existing antitrust laws to attack the conglomerate mergers with great vigor.[11] Mitchell approved of this plan and later supported McLaren publicly. At his confirmation hearing McLaren said, "I believe that the antitrust laws and more particularly section 7 of the Clayton Act are able to reach conglomerate mergers. I recognize that Dr. Turner and Mr. Zimmerman who followed him, felt there was legislation needed in order to make section 7 applicable to conglomerates. Personally, I am not persuaded that such legislation is needed" (U.S. Senate, 1969, p. 36). Once in office McLaren began to formulate arguments against the conglomerates. He rejected those concerning relative efficiency and instead claimed that large size would promote complacency and not innovation. He thought that large size would also lead to large concentrations of power and possibly to political abuse (Goolrick, 1978, pp. 59–60).

McLaren realized, however, that he needed new arguments to prove that conglomerates were potentially anticompetitive. His theories about the problems created by higher levels of aggregate concentration were too speculative and not based on existing case law. He wanted to bring suit against a conglomerate merger and then have the case go to the Supreme Court. Because the Warren Court had consistently followed the government's lead, it seemed probable that such a case would be successful. McLaren's goal was clear: "Basically, what we were shooting for, from the beginning of 1969, was to stop this merger trend that was leading more and more toward economic concentration" (Goolrick, 1978, p. 63).

He proposed an extension of the reciprocity argument: Suppliers of merging firms would sell to the other parts of the newly formed firm in order to maintain good relations. Hence, competitors of the merging firms' suppliers would lose sales opportunities. This would eventually result in less competition overall in many different markets. It is a small step from this position to the view that sheer aggregate concentration generally leads to too much interdependence between firms and less competition throughout the economy.

In 1969 McLaren filed three suits against ITT, one against Ling-Temco-Vought (LTV), and one against Northwest Industries. All three of these firms were conglomerates that engaged in a large number of mergers. In a widely publicized speech given in June 1969, John Mitchell agreed with McLaren's argument concerning the effects of reciprocity. Mitchell extended this argument in a distinctly populist tone.

> Another danger posed by the current merger trend is what is known as a "community of interest." But it is not a formal agreement but merely the recognition of common goals by large diversified corporations. This situation derives as much from common sense as from economics. It posits that large diversified corporations have little interest in competing with each other in concentrated markets. For, if the food subsidiary of corporation A aggressively competes with the food subsidiary of corporation B, then the electrical subsidiary of corporation B may start a price war with the electrical subsidiary of corporation A. Thus, it would be in both A's and B's interest to maintain the status quo and not engage in the type of aggressive competition which we expect in a free market.

Mitchell concluded with a warning to the largest firms:

> The Department of Justice may very well oppose any merger by one of the top 200 manufacturing firms or firms of comparable size in other industries. The Department of Justice will probably oppose any merger by one of the top 200 manufacturing firms of any leading producer in any concentrated industry . . . Some may regard these probabilities as something of an expansion of the published antimerger guidelines of the Department. But, we believe, that under today's circumstances, these probabilities are clearly authorized by present antitrust law (*Vital Speeches*, June 6, 1969, pp. 593–594).

It is clear that Mitchell, Kleindienst, and McLaren intended to pursue antitrust enforcement seriously and they acted as though it was the administration's policy to do so. In a meeting with the lawyers representing ITT on April 17, 1969, Kleindienst said, "The policy of this administration is to cool off the merger movement and this policy has been of long standing. The recent policy of the President is to stop large mergers by the top 200 companies."[12] At the same meeting McLaren said, "Any large merger by ITT, or any other large and diversified company is necessarily going to have an adverse effect on competition. Takeovers must be stopped."[13]

Nixon's role in making this policy is interesting to consider. Antitrust was just one of many foreign policy and domestic issues with which the administration had to deal. When he took office in 1969, Nixon probably did not pay much attention to antitrust activities and was content to let Mitchell establish policy in the Justice Department. Then in a memo sent to Mitchell on March 25, 1969, Nixon commented on an article he had read in *Barron's*, which said: "Are the conglomerates serving as corporate scapegoats? The current hue and cry strikes us as both sadly misdirected and badly timed . . . The real villains happen to be the US trustbusters." Nixon's response was, "John (Mitchell)—This is right! I agree. Keep a close watch on them (the trustbusters). They tend, at times, to be anti business professionals."[14]

But his comment did not reflect a strong feeling about policy. Nixon was aware of the merger suits against ITT and in April 1969 asked the Council of Economic Advisors to prepare a statement on the use of antitrust laws against conglomerate mergers.[15] On May 11, 1969, there was a meeting at the White House to discuss antitrust policy and McLaren was present. At that meeting Nixon supported McLaren's actions. He argued repeatedly that the antitrust laws should protect the small firms from the large firms. He said at one point: "This is a tremendously potent political problem which doesn't mean we don't tackle it. Does it mean that Mom and Pop stores are on the way out—and supermarkets are all we'll have? There is a sociological problem here. We may be helping consumers, but we don't help the character of our people. This is an old fashioned attitude, Dick [McLaren], I know—but I would rather deal with an entrepreneur than a pipsqueak manager of a big store."[16]

Nixon's awareness of the lawsuits and his support for the policy were evident at that same meeting. "At the leadership meeting they took us on, they said the war on conglomerates was going too far. A couple of weeks ago at Camp David I discussed this with John Mitchell. If anybody is business oriented, it's him. He vigorously defended what the antitrust division was doing and he said the business community supported it. I accept that."[17]

One could argue that Nixon had no explicit antitrust policy and that he delegated that responsibility to those in the Justice Department. Since Republicans had embraced antitrust as a way to promote competition, Nixon went along with the Mitchell-McLaren policy. Goorlick (1978, p. 178) argues that the anti-conglomerate policy was formulated without Nixon's knowledge and against his will. Kleindienst, one of the participants, agrees.[18] But according to the White House documents, Nixon was aware of what was going on and accepted its legitimacy. Nixon probably deferred to Mitchell, as his close and trusted friend, about the need to slow down the merger movement.

In the fall of 1969 Nixon shifted his ground and decided that the Mitchell-McLaren antitrust policy was no longer sound. Nixon saw, in his news summary of September 20, 1969, a reference to an article by Robert Bork which called the conglomerate lawsuits "one of the bleakest, most disappointing developments in antitrust history."[19] Nixon agreed with Bork and requested that John Ehrlichman "ask McLaren, Mitchell, et al. to come up with a new approach."[20] Nixon changed his mind because he felt that the business community did not support McLaren's actions.

A number of people were asked to comment on the antitrust situation, including James Lynn, the general counsel for the Commerce Department, and Hendrik Houthakker, from the Council of Economic Advisors. Ehrlichman then held a meeting with McLaren on October 13, 1969.[21] At that meeting Ehrlichman tried to get McLaren to modify his position, particularly in regard to the ITT lawsuits. His attempt failed. The political machinations involving ITT and the Nixon White House are a matter of public record and have been summarized elsewhere (Sobel, 1974, pp. 127–154; Goolrick, 1978; Schoenberg, 1985). In brief, McLaren was able to carry out the lawsuits despite intermittent pressure from the White House. Fear of negative publicity prevented the White House from intervening more actively.

More important, the White House began a series of discussions about antitrust policy that continued on and off for the next two years. By April 1971 the Nixon Administration had officially shifted its position against vigorous pursuit of the antitrust laws. In a memorandum dated June 7, 1971, Peter Flanigan, one of Nixon's advisors on economic affairs, summarized this shift in attitude:

> On April 12, the President met with Secretary Stans and Under-secretary Lynn to receive from them a report on areas of government harassment of business. The President directed that action be taken to reduce any such harassment, apparent or real. As a result, I have met with Attorney General Mitchell and told him that a less antagonistic attitude towards business must be taken by the antitrust division. Mitchell has agreed in this area. More specifically, I have discussed with him several pending mergers and received his assurances that he will personally monitor any antitrust activity in their regard.[22]

But the attempts to reverse course were too late to save the merger movement. Merger activity began to diminish in 1969 and by 1971 had dropped to its lowest level in twelve years. Eventually, the ITT and LTV cases were settled out of court. Northwest Industries gave up its attempt to take over B. F. Goodrich. The Justice Department and the FTC succeeded in preventing a number of other mergers by filing suit to halt proceedings. The major reason large firms stopped merging was because of the increased prosecution of firms involved in product-related and -unrelated mergers. Most business executives were convinced that cases that went to the Supreme Court would be decided against them. ITT won its lawsuits all the way up to the Supreme Court, but declined to take the case to the high Court. Instead, it agreed to divest some of its units.

McLaren left the administration for a federal judgeship in 1971. His replacement, Thomas Kauper, decreased enforcement and backed away from McLaren's pursuit of conglomerates. In his four-year term, he filed only three suits involving conglomerate mergers, which were all within traditional bounds. Since the merger movement had ended, the number of lawsuits was decreasing anyway. Nixon also replaced an activist FTC with one that was less interested in stopping conglomerate merger activities.

The final blow to antimerger efforts was the change in Supreme Court justices. The Supreme Court, in the 1960s, had applied the Celler-Kefauver Act consistently to merger cases brought before it.

It had also accepted the extensions of Celler-Kefauver to cover some forms of conglomerate mergers. The Supreme Court continued to decide cases in favor of the government until 1973. But in 1974 the Supreme Court decided four of five cases for the defendants. The Nixon appointees, led by Chief Justice Burger, took a dim view of Celler-Kefauver.

The most significant of the five cases was U.S. v. Marine Bankcorporation. This case involved a merger between two banks, one located in western Washington and the other in the eastern part of the state.[23] The government had sued under Section 7 of the Clayton Act. It claimed the merger was problematic using the potential competition argument. The Supreme Court ruled against the government and did so in language strong enough to make prosecution of any conglomerate merger cases difficult. Subsequent decisions further narrowed the applicability of Celler-Kefauver.

Not surprisingly, in 1976 merger activity picked up and accelerated in the 1980s. In 1984 the FTC issued only two complaints, both against minor mergers. The current Supreme Court justices are not likely to interpret the antitrust laws severely. With little fear of prosecution, the largest firms continue to engage in mergers.

Business and the Private Antitrust Community

What the business community knew about antitrust and the subtle effect that knowledge had on business behavior is important to gauge. The primary sources of information about the antitrust agencies were the lawyers and scholars interested in the issue, and the business press. The Antitrust Section of the ABA was the most important private sector source. Relations between the Antitrust Section and the Antitrust Division have been cordial since the 1950s.

Corporate officials never implemented a merger without advice from legal counsel on its possible antitrust effects. If lawyers advised that there might be problems, firms often inquired of the FTC and Justice Department to determine their reactions (Stone, 1977, p. 63; Weaver, 1977, pp. 173–175). If a firm announced a merger and the antitrust agencies began to investigate, the acquiring firm occasionally revoked its offer to merge.

For business, the problem has usually been that the laws are too vague. This point of view is understandable since the antitrust laws do not specify what constitutes a tendency toward monopoly or an anticompetitive effect. The courts and antitrust officials have to interpret when a violation has occurred. This interpretation, in turn, depends on the composition of the FTC, the Antitrust Division of the Justice Department, and the Supreme Court. For firms, the environment has seemed inconsistent, ever changing, and contradictory. The Supreme Court in the 1960s, for example, took the view that almost any horizontal or vertical merger was anticompetitive. The Supreme Court of the 1970s decided the opposite. Current antitrust officials will probably not act except in the most extreme circumstances. Given this fluctuation, business can only expect that interpretation of the laws might change again. For these reasons, legal departments of large corporations try to anticipate what the government will do. One important barometer of Justice Department intentions is the annual meeting of the Antitrust Section of the ABA. At this meeting, members gather to hear a speech given by the attorney general or the head of the Antitrust Division on current policy regarding antitrust enforcement. The speech is reproduced and thousands of copies are requested every year. This event has occurred since the mid-1950s.[24]

The relationship between the Antitrust Section and the Justice Department involves not only the exchange of information, but also the exchange of personnel (Weaver, 1977, pp. 160–163). Often, lawyers leave the Antitrust Division for jobs in large law firms. The meetings of the Antitrust Section offer Justice Department officials a chance to explain their activities and corporate attorneys a chance to ask questions about enforcement patterns. By monitoring antitrust activities in this way, corporate legal departments attempt to keep up with current practices.

The Justice Department has tried recently to answer questions about what types of mergers probably violate antitrust statutes. These guidelines were first formalized in 1967, when Donald Turner was head of the Antitrust Division. They have subsequently been updated in 1982 and 1984.[25] The guidelines and the close link between the government and private antitrust lawyers are the surest conduit of information.

If there is such tight monitoring of Justice Department and

FTC behavior, however, why are antitrust suits ever filed? Since the application of the guidelines is always somewhat questionable, firms can think they are in the right even when the Justice Department disagrees. In the Brown Shoe case, the firm's attorneys did not expect the antitrust authorities to prosecute (*Business Week*, June 19, 1955, p. 21). Even when that case was clearly going to end up in the courts, Brown maintained that the market shares involved in the mergers were small and, furthermore, that the new larger firm would be more competitive and efficient.[26] Indeed, Brown Shoe appeared to be correct because all of the courts up to the Supreme Court agreed with the company's argument. The Supreme Court overturned all the lower court decisions.

The antitrust community extends beyond agencies and private practices into the academic world. Law schools and economics departments often have experts in this field who teach and write on antitrust issues. Scholars' opinions have often found their way into the law or the courts. The antitrust authorities' basic theory in the enforcement of the Celler-Kefauver Act stems from industrial economics. Turner formulated the reciprocity and potential competition arguments while teaching law at Harvard. The most important scholarly group at present is located at the University of Chicago. The Chicago school has been instrumental in providing arguments for a loose merger policy that breaks with the structural approach that relies on concentration ratios to evaluate anticompetitive effects.[27]

Many journals and publications deal routinely with antitrust issues. For the practitioners, various legal publications monitor the antitrust scene, from the Antitrust Section's journal to the *Antitrust Bulletin* and the *Antitrust and Trade Regulation Review*. On the academic side are the *Journal of Law and Economics* and the various law reviews, including the *Harvard Law Review*. The business press has also regularly covered antitrust issues.

These communities' arguments and actions need to be linked to corporate behavior. Executives were generally aware of antitrust actions and we can see from different types of data how they reacted. Data can be gleaned from the business press and from interviews, memoirs, and surveys.

Diversification was already a fact of corporate life by 1940 and use of this strategy accelerated in the postwar era. However, merger for its own sake was new. In the early 1950s a few executives began to experiment with creating a new kind of firm, one that was not tied to a particular industry and was, by its very nature, diversified. These firms were built entirely by merging. Royal Little (Textron), Tex Thornton (Litton Industries), Jim Ling (Ling-Temco-Vought), and others were the pioneers of a new financial conception of control: Firms were constructed with acquisitions and the relations between the parts were less important than the financial manipulations that brought about the whole. The acquisitive conglomerates were only a small part of the diversification movement. Because they provided a spectacular example of explosive firm growth, most of corporate America followed their lead (Rumelt, 1974; Fligstein, 1989).

The conglomerate form emerged as a function of three conditions. The economic environment of the postwar period was generally good and interest rates were low. A large number of firms already practiced diversification strategies. And merger strategies for growth were limited by the fear of antitrust enforcement. Because the largest firms were disproportionately prosecuted and the most closely scrutinized, the conglomerates emerged from small firms. The existing large firms did not take the lead in the development of the new conception.

Instead, this innovation came from actors who did not have to deal with interests entrenched in the firm that dictated its mission or with a hostile federal government. The new conglomerates were all firms that emerged in the postwar era. They did not attract the attention of the Justice Department precisely because they started out small and as they grew they chose their purchases carefully. Their strategy was to buy firms in industries that were unrelated— smaller firms in any industry. Antitrust officials were uninterested in those activities. Once their strategy for growth became apparent, other large firms began to implement similar strategies. All the firms involved in inventing the conglomerate form tried to maximize growth, using financial criteria as opposed to product criteria to evaluate potential merger candidates, and explicitly sought candidates that would not draw the attention of the FTC or the Justice Department.

The first conglomerator was Royal Little. He tried to make Textron one of the leading textile producers in the country. His initial strategy was to buy moribund properties at low prices and make them profitable. Textron was a success, but Little saw that the industry was too cyclical and in decline (Little, 1979). As a result, he began to pursue mergers in other industries. This strategy was recognized by the business press and as early as 1955 Little was being hailed as an entrepreneurial genius (*Business Week*, Dec. 10, 1955, p. 28; *Fortune*, April 1955, p. 171). Little's basic strategy was to buy small, preferably privately owned, companies that were already profitable, in growth markets, and were led by aggressive young managers. He gave these managers great autonomy—his skill was financial and not operational. Because he most often bought small firms, he rarely attracted the attention of antitrust officials. Little knew his strategy for growth would avoid antitrust prosecution and even stated one of his goals as: "Eliminate any Justice Department monopoly problems by avoiding acquisitions in related businesses" (Little, 1979, p. 120).

The other large firms began to take notice of this new growth strategy quite early. By the late 1950s the modern merger movement was under way and most of the largest firms participated. Once it was clear that antitrust laws would not be applied to conglomerate mergers, other large firms began to imitate the conglomerates. While none grew as spectacularly as the acquisitive conglomerates, many added substantially to their size by purchasing firms in related industries. Their growth was not due exclusively to unrelated products, but products related to their primary production. This reflected a hybrid strategy. The large firm was already diversified by 1950, and mostly through internal expansion (Weston and Ornstein, 1973). But the example of the acquisitive conglomerate showed that diversification by merger was easier.

Antitrust had a peculiar role in this process. It shut off the possibility of continued expansion into already concentrated markets. It also made vertical integration of production potentially illegal. The elimination of these channels caused the largest firms to look for other avenues of growth. The financial conception of control adopted by the acquisitive conglomerates provided a new way to grow for all firms. It provided the benefit of growth without the need to compete for already existing customers and did so in a way that avoided prosecution by antitrust authorities. It allowed firms to enter markets without enduring the start up costs of building plants and gaining expertise in some unknown production process. The new, expanded multidivisional firm was controlled with financial tools that allowed actors to evaluate the profitability of each product line.

It is useful to track the level of awareness in the business community of antitrust enforcement. The attorney general's report generated by the Eisenhower Administration was written by a committee of prominent scholars, lawyers, and administrators. Of the sixty-three members, forty-one were practicing lawyers, most of whom were antitrust specialists, ten were economics professors, and seven were law school professors (Kovaleff, 1980, pp. 35–41). The lawyers included members of the leading New York and Chicago law firms and also reflected both the membership and leadership of the ABA's Antitrust Section. The report formed the basis of antitrust enforcement for the next fifteen years and undoubtedly influenced what kind of advice leading lawyers gave their clients.

The business press in the 1950s continuously listed the avoidance of antitrust as one major cause of diversification. *Fortune* noted, "In the postwar years, there have been some special pressures and temptations to diversify. The trend of antitrust enforcement has made it difficult for many corporations to expand in their own industries. Others have been inspired by concerns that the original business had only routine prospects" (April 1954, p. 155). *Business Week* reported in a discussion of mergers that "whatever happens, it won't be because all recent mergers were entered into blindly. There's plenty of evidence that they have been made only on careful advice of counsel. Most of the current deals do not look as though monopoly had been their goal. Rather, they seem aimed at some legitimate aims such as diversification" (Dec. 1, 1951, p. 120). In trying to account for the rise of product-related and -unrelated mergers, *Business Week* noted, "Conglomerate marriages between companies in different industries are now the fad; horizontal mergers are less popular. Partly this is because the Justice Department has given most conglomerates the green light, partly it's because companies want to blend marketing expertise or distribution lines" (May 15, 1959, p. 59).

The Brown Shoe decision had a great impact on the corporate world. *Business Week* reported, "Private lawyers agree that the most important influence of the Brown decision will be on merger decisions that have been held in abeyance awaiting the court's ruling. Nobody will ever know how many merger proposals automatically died when the court issued its decisions" (July 7, 1962, p. 52). The *Antitrust and Trade Regulation Review* assessed the impact of the ruling in the following way: "Antitrust experts generally conclude from the Brown decision that the Court will sustain efforts to halt any merger with potential competitive effect of any substance" (June 26, 1962, p. 20). *Fortune* argued that the Brown decision meant that "businessmen need to be aware of the steady procession of Court decisions upholding ever broader powers of antitrust enforcement . . . The Court majority has held that the government now has the power to limit mergers with a *probable* anticompetitive effect" (Nov. 1962, p. 131).

Turner's ascendance to head of the Antitrust Division was well noted in the business and trade press. Turner had a clear academic record and immediately became known as being wary of vertical and horizontal mergers and lenient toward conglomerate mergers. *Business Week* reported that "the only thing Turner is trying to do is to channel the merger movement away from 'horizontals' (and, to a lesser extent, vertical mergers between customer and supplier) into the conglomerate stream. Private lawyers are well aware of this attitude and advise corporate clients, 'If you're thinking about conglomerate mergers, do it now.' To their mind the climate—at least in the Justice Department—will never be better" (March 12, 1966, p. 168).

After the Brown Shoe case and a set of other decisions, horizontal mergers involving any amount of assets appeared illegal. An article in *U.S. News and World Report* advised, "If you are planning to buy a company that sells the same product your company sells in the same geographic area, watch out. The Government is almost certain to attack such a merger under the Clayton Act. It is not the size of the companies that matter, but their position in the business" (July 25, 1966, p. 23).

In 1965 National Economic Research Associates (NERA), a consulting group, conducted a poll of executives from the 500 largest firms. The purpose was to assess the awareness in firms of the first six decisions under Celler-Kefauver and whether those decisions had affected subsequent merger plans.[28] The respondents indicated that 70 percent of their mergers in the previous five years had been for diversification. The poll showed that 88 percent of the executives knew of the Brown Shoe decision. Leaders of firms that were larger and more involved in mergers were more likely to follow the Justice Department activities closely. Of the firms that had abandoned merger plans, 54 percent did so as a result of these decisions. Nonetheless, 89 percent of the firms said the law had not prevented all mergers and the most active firms told the NERA that they would continue to use mergers as a strategy for growth. The NERA report concludes by stating that while there was a great deal of awareness of the Celler-Kefauver decisions, there was still much interest in pursuing mergers.

Fortune (Aug. 1967, p. 94) conducted a poll of presidents of small- and medium-sized companies in 1967 to ascertain how they felt about the government's role in mergers. The magazine interviewed 114 executives from manufacturing firms doing between $40 and $60 million of business a year. The purpose of the poll was to find out how executives who "should" have felt protected by the antitrust laws actually felt about them. Their level of awareness was quite high. Over 90 percent understood the issues and had an opinion, 74 percent felt that the government merger policy did not help them, and 68 percent felt that the policy had not promoted competition in their industry.

The day that Turner left office he published a set of merger guidelines, proposing numerical levels of concentration that would bring about an antitrust suit. In a highly concentrated industry, a firm with as little as 4 percent of the market that acquired another firm with an equal market share would be prosecuted. In an industry where the four largest firms accounted for less than 75 percent of the market, an acquiring firm with a 5 percent market share needed to acquire only an additional 5 percent. As the market share of firms increased, their ability to acquire a firm in the same market without fear of recrimination decreased. In a market where concentration had increased 7 percent in the past ten years, an acquisition of only 2 percent was enough to prompt an antitrust suit.[29]

The guidelines announced, "Unless there are exceptional circumstances, the Department will not accept as a justification for an acquisition normally subject to challenge under its horizontal merger standards the claim that the merger will produce economies [i.e., improvements in efficiency]."[30] For conglomerate mergers, the guidelines provided three conditions: "At the present, the Department regards two categories of conglomerate mergers as having sufficiently identifiable anticompetitive effects as to be the subject of relatively specific structural guidelines: mergers involving potential entrants and mergers creating a danger of reciprocal buying. Another important category of conglomerate mergers that will frequently be attacked—mergers which for one or several reasons threaten to entrench or enhance the market power of the acquired firm."[31]

The business press reported the guidelines and *Business Week* remarked, "Department officials admit the guides contain no sweeping changes, but do tell business what government lawyers have been doing" (June 8, 1968, p. 24). The *Antitrust and Trade Regulation Review* agreed: "Antitrust experts see little, if anything new in the general factors the Antitrust Division says it will take into account in enforcing section 7 of the Clayton Act. But the guidelines do make a significant contribution to what has come to be known as 'the numbers game'—the use of market share figures to show a merger's anticompetitive effect" (June 4, 1968, p. A-10).

The academic and professional communities mounted an intellectual counterattack in the mid-1960s. They were led by Robert Bork, Ward Bowman, Milton Handler, William Baxter, Thomas Kauper, and Yale Brozen. They argued that the merger guidelines concentrated too heavily on market structure and not enough on the conduct of firms and the procompetitive effects of mergers.

In 1963, after the Brown Shoe decision, Robert Bork, one of the Chicago school proponents, said, "Too few people understand that it is the essential mechanism of competition and its prime virtue that more efficient firms take business away from the less efficient" (*Fortune*, Sept. 1963, pp. 200–201). Bork's central thesis was that the Supreme Court, antitrust agencies, and Congress were attempting to protect competition by preserving small firms. But the problem was that small firms were often less efficient than large firms, hence, disallowing mergers was promoting inefficiency.

This thesis was elaborated by Handler and Robinson in 1965 following a string of Supreme Court decisions under the Celler-Kefauver Act. They asked, "What evidence is there that the fragmentation of industry would enhance our national security, promote research and development, elevate quality standards, improve conditions of employment, reduce prices, and enlarge our rate of growth? What proof is there that having eight companies instead of four, sixteen instead of eight, thirty-one instead of sixteen, will improve the nature and quality of competition?" (*Fortune*, Jan. 1965, p. 178).

When McLaren began his attacks on conglomerates, the counterarguments became louder. Baxter, who later became antitrust chief under Ronald Reagan, argued that mergers were positive for three reasons:

> 1) From the standpoint of those selling out, a merger represents a way of exiting from an industry—often it is the only practicable way. 2) Mergers permit companies to grow rapidly when that is necessary to achieve cost reductions that are obtainable only with great size. 3) Third, and probably most important in the present context, is that mergers permit removal of facilities of a company from the control of unimaginative or lazy or corrupt management. It is the only competitive threat that the managers of many large corporations face as individuals. (*New Republic*, Aug. 16, 1969, p. 14)

Bork continued his assault on the antitrust laws by suggesting: "Where economic theory tells us that certain business behavior is likely to result in monopoly profits and misallocation of resources, such behavior should be illegal. All other behavior should be lawful so far as antitrust is concerned, since, in relation to consumer welfare, it is either neutral or motivated by considerations of efficiency. Efficiency motivated mergers deserve the law's protection. The market will penalize those that do not in fact create efficiency" (*Fortune*, Sept. 1969, p. 104).

In the fall of 1969, the ABA held a symposium on McLaren's conglomerate policy. Harold Geneen and Jim Ling delivered speeches attacking McLaren for inconsistent use of the antitrust laws and for ignoring the possible efficiency gains of conglomerate mergers. Kenneth Dam, a University of Chicago law professor, condemned McLaren and the Nixon Administration for ignoring both the Neal and Stigler reports on the issue. There was generally no support in the private sector antitrust community for the McLaren policy (*Business Week*, Nov. 1, 1969, pp. 95–96). While the antitrust and corporate worlds were attacking the McLaren policy, Congress was considering legislation to ban any mergers for the 200 largest corporations. By 1970 the rate of mergers slowed.

In 1974 the Burger Court began to rule against the government in merger cases. A review of these decisions by a proponent of the efficiency view of mergers concluded:

> If we compare the antitrust performance of the Burger Court with that of the latter Warren Court, a clear pattern emerges. The Burger Court has distinguished itself not only by insisting that the antitrust laws contain an exclusively economic test of legality but also by rejecting its predecessors' assumptions about the functions and likely competitive impact of various types of business conduct the Court has been required to scrutinize. More affirmatively, the Burger Court has been more sensitive to the possible efficiencies such practices may yield, far more skeptical about the reliability of various rules and presumptions that had been previously employed to make competitive-impact predictions.   (Markovits, 1983, p. 97)

The Burger Court turned the tide on merger enforcement by applying different criteria to test the anticompetitive effects of mergers. The antitrust community realized this and began to advise the corporate world that mergers would no longer be challenged as effectively.

Turner's antitrust guidelines remained in place until 1982, although they were no longer enforced. In 1982 William Baxter, then Reagan's antitrust chief, rewrote the merger guidelines. The central points of these new guidelines were to raise the level of concentration necessary for horizontal or vertical mergers to cause the Justice Department concern and to accept efficiency as a justification for mergers.[32] The part of the antitrust community that favored a merger policy based on performance and not structure was now in control of the Antitrust Division.

Statistical Evidence

I have argued that the Celler-Kefauver Act had three effects. First, it greatly slowed the growth of horizontal and vertical mergers. An activist Justice Department and FTC, combined with a liberal Supreme Court, carried out a legal program that prohibited many of these mergers. The second and unintended consequence of the act was to encourage firms to merge into related or unrelated industries. Indeed, the law made it attractive to choose merger candidates in industries that were quite distant. The third effect was to actually slow the pace of mergers. The Nixon Administration's prosecutions in the late 1960s were a major factor in this regard. Once this policy changed and a more conservative Supreme Court took over, merger activity resumed. In this section I will discuss some regression analyses to demonstrate these results more formally. Appendix E contains a description of the data sources and presents an appropriate statistical analysis of the merger time series.

Table 6.3 presents data on the pattern of large mergers in the American economy from 1948 to 1980. The mergers began to increase in 1954 and peaked in 1968. From 1971 to 1975, larger mergers remained relatively few, but increased in 1976.

First, my goal is to explain the change in relative numbers of horizontal and vertical mergers compared with product-related and -unrelated mergers. Three significant variables are: the level of stock prices in the previous year, the average prime interest rate in the previous year, and a set of indicators that capture the effects of the Celler-Kefauver Act enforcement from 1962 to 1974. The first two variables measure conditions thought to be conducive to mergers. Historically, as the stock market rises, mergers become more prevalent. The interest rate is important because most mergers require borrowing huge sums of money. As interest rates rise, it becomes more costly to engage in mergers. The period 1962–1974 was the peak of Celler-Kefauver enforcement and a variable indexing those years captured how firms, the antitrust authorities, and the private antitrust community viewed what rules were being applied to mergers.

The regression analysis shows that the interest rate predicted changes in the mix and types of mergers. As interest rates increased, both types of mergers decreased. Interestingly, firms still undertook product-related and -unrelated mergers more frequently than horizontal or vertical mergers, possibly because they felt that such mergers were more profitable then. The stock market did not effect the relative mix of mergers. The variable measuring the enforcement of the Celler-Kefauver Act greatly affected the relative mix of mergers. Firms were much more likely to engage in product-related and -unrelated mergers during the period of Celler-Kefauver enforcement than before or after that period. These results also appear in the regressions where the number of mergers in each type is presented. In sum, the enforcement pattern of Celler-Kefauver decreased horizontal and vertical mergers

Table 6.3 Number and assets of large mergers, 1948–1980

Year	Number	Assets (millions of dollars)
1948	4	63.2
1949	6	89.0
1950	5	186.3
1951	9	201.5
1952	16	373.8
1953	23	779.1
1954	37	1,444.5
1955	67	2,165.7
1956	53	1,882.0
1957	47	1,202.3
1958	42	1,070.6
1959	49	1,431.1
1960	51	1,535.1
1961	46	2,003.3
1962	65	2,251.9
1963	54	2,535.8
1964	73	2,302.9
1965	64	3,253.7
1966	76	3,329.1
1967	138	8,258.5
1968	174	12,580.0
1969	138	11,043.2
1970	91	5,904.3
1971	59	2,459.9
1972	60	1,885.5
1973	64	3,148.8
1974	62	4,466.4
1975	59	4,950.5
1976	82	5,961.1
1977	101	—
1978	111	—
1979	97	—

Source: Federal Trade Commission, Statistical Report on Mergers (1980).

substantially and encouraged product-related and -unrelated mergers.

My second analysis determines why the level of all mergers changed. I assessed three variables: the average prime interest rate for the past year, the average stock prices for the past year, and a measure indexing the years of the Nixon antitrust policy.

According to conventional wisdom, the decline of stock prices and the increase of interest rates in 1969 ended the 1960s merger movement. If this explanation is correct, then the Nixon antitrust policy should not have affected the change in the level of mergers.

The regression results show that both interest rates and stock prices affected the change in the total number of mergers. But there is also a statistically significant effect of the Nixon Administration's antitrust policy on the total number of mergers. This is clear evidence that despite falling stock prices and increasing interest rates, the Mitchell-McLaren antitrust policy caused a steep decline in the number of mergers.

Taken together, these results reinforce my arguments. Antitrust enforcement played a significant role in the postwar era in discouraging vertical and horizontal mergers and encouraging mergers for diversification. When large-scale mergers reached what was perceived as a dangerously high level, the antitrust authorities used lawsuits to curb them. When that enforcement policy was altered and the Supreme Court began to accept that mergers were generally efficiency-based, mergers resumed.

7

The Finance Conception of Control

The sales and marketing conception of control came to dominate the largest firms after World War II. But even as managers concentrated on increasing sales through extensive marketing, expansion overseas, and diversification, a new conception of control began to take shape by the mid-1950s. The finance conception of control stressed the use of financial tools to evaluate product lines and divisions. The multidivisional form became the accepted organizational structure and control was achieved by decentralizing decision making while paying close attention to financial performance. Product lines or divisions that did not meet corporate expectations for growth or earnings were divested. Because financial performance was all that mattered, managers with the financial conception of control pursued growth in whatever industry there were opportunities. The largest firms became multiproduct, multiindustry by 1970. This diversification was achieved mainly through mergers. Merger candidates were evaluated on their growth and earnings potential.

This conception of the corporation reflected both an extension of existing tendencies in the organizational fields of the large corporations as well as a clean break with the past. The pioneers of this new strategy were trained in finance and accounting. Their views were not shaped by the necessities of production or the desire to sell more products. Instead, they focused on the corporation as a collection of assets that could and should be manipulated to increase short-run profits.

The spread of this point of view resulted from complex interactions within the organizational fields of the largest firms and the antitrust environment. These conditions provided the incentive for finance-oriented executives to experiment with a new conception of the corporation. Once that conception proved successful, that is, produced growth, it spread through the population of the largest firms. To understand the shift from a sales and marketing conception to a finance conception of control, we must consider which firms innovated the new conception and how it was passed to other firms until it dominated them all. Those who pioneered the finance conception of control often ran sizable enterprises, but most frequently were outsiders whose examples were copied by the largest firms.

A set of conditions made the finance conception of control possible. The diversification of American industry was well under way by the end of World War II. Actors in firms realized that in order to grow and be profitable, they needed to increase sales. The desire of managers to spread risks across product lines and to enter growing industries and leave stagnant ones was already firmly established. Indeed, the largest firms depended on new product lines for continued growth. Thus, diversification was already a tactic of managers in the largest firms.

The second condition for the new conception of control was an organizational structure that would allow a multiproduct firm to be controlled by a central office. The multidivisional form pioneered by General Motors and DuPont became the blueprint for the reorganization of other large firms. Once managers chose to venture into industries where they had little production or marketing expertise, the only way to evaluate products was through financial performance. The financial controls that supported the multidivisional form because the chief source of power in the large corporation over the past thirty years. They allowed managers who could skillfully apply them the ability to claim control over the organization and its goals.

The decision to grow through merger rather than through internal expansion required cash, stock, or the capacity to borrow large sums of money. The generally prosperous periods, 1946 to 1969 and the 1980s, left firms with money and rising stock prices. Where firms lacked money, innovative financial techniques such as the leveraged buyout were developed to borrow money for mergers. In this bullish economy high rates of growth through acquisitions were possible. Of course, to take advantage of these possibilities required people with a new view of the corporation.

The final condition for the emergence of the finance conception of control was the antitrust policy of the federal government. I have already shown that the enforcement of the Celler-Kefauver Act greatly influenced the types of mergers in the postwar era. It discouraged firms from pursuing mergers that tended to increase intraindustry concentration. By the 1960s, it was an accepted fact that diversified mergers were legal and horizontal and vertical mergers problematic.

These conditions allowed finance-oriented executives to create large organizations entirely through large-scale mergers. The relative success of their actions caused other firms to pay attention to these tactics and eventually adopt them.

Certain managers and economists worried that after the war the economy would sink back into economic depression. But they were still thinking in terms of fixed markets and low levels of consumer demand. The problem of postwar adjustment, from the then dominant sales and marketing point of view, was how to take advantage of the latent consumer demand. There were a number of barriers to increased sales. Large firms had to identify and please their customers. As consumers became more quality and price conscious, marketing considerations began to dictate production decisions. The ability to adjust to shifts in demand and analyze new markets was difficult in a centralized organizational structure that sold many products. The problem of giving product managers authority to take advantage of new opportunities and, at the same time, controlling such decisions was unresolved.

Many large firms faced additional problems. In industries where there was low or no growth, it was difficult to expand market share. The major firms in these industries had similar technologies and costs; hence, there was little advantage in price cutting to increase market share. Since a great number of the largest firms were already dominant in their industries, it was difficult to achieve growth by continued expansion. Other firms were in cyclical industries. For instance, defense contractors depended on an expanding military for growth. Managers of those firms had to seek product lines that would balance the ups and downs of their markets.

A manufacturing solution to these problems would have focused on centralizing control and stabilizing price in given markets. But a sales and marketing analysis offered different solutions. Managers decentralized control internally in order to respond more quickly to changes in consumer demand. Marketing played an increasing role in production decisions and price a much less important one. Managers in large firms also chose diversification strategies as the primary method of growth. But there were many ways to diversify. The most logical tactic was for research and development departments to create new products that were related to a firm's major industry. Many firms pursued this kind of diversification even though it required large amounts of capital, long lead times, and brought uncertain results. A much quicker and seemingly more certain way to enter into related or unrelated industries was through merger. Buying another company meant that one had instantaneous access to a new product and market. But it also meant risking whether the new company could be successfully integrated.

The new conception of control was invented by and relied on actors with finance backgrounds who were willing to merge firms with disparate product lines into one decentralized administrative structure. Financial criteria alone were used to evaluate the performance of products. The industry of a firm did not matter. Firms had product lines with different rates of return and growth. The executive's function, therefore, was to invest so that sales, assets, and profits would increase. If products or divisions did not meet expectations, they were divested and new ones purchased.

The pioneers of the finance conception and its strategy of diversification through mergers provided a new model of the corporation. Their spectacular growth rates could not be ignored by the managers of the other large firms. Many of them evaluated their strategies and opted to follow the finance conception. They reorganized their internal organization and adopted mergers as a growth strategy. Those who resisted the new conception of the firm often became merger targets.

The organizational fields of the largest firms were thus restructured. Once a firm adopted the finance conception of control, the industry in which it operated mattered far less than its short-run profitability. The stock market, stock prices, and the relative rates of return of firms in other industries became as important as the behavior of a firm's competitors. The largest firms for the first time formed an organizational field that served as a reference group for other large firms. Although all firms did not participate equally in this field, and many continued to define themselves industrially, much more attention was given to the collective behavior of large firms. The spread of these tactics has generally increased the power of finance executives. The result is the large, financially driven, multiproduct firm that dominates American business today.

Sales and Marketing Strategies in the Postwar Era

Thomas McCabe, the president of the Scott Paper Company, said before the close of World War II:

> It is obvious that industry's most important problem is marketing. We have mastered mass production, but we have not built up peacetime mass consumption to take the output of our industrial machine running at top speed. The solving of this problem will go far in solving the postwar problem of providing jobs . . . It will take tremendous sums of money invested in research and sales work and, especially, consumer advertising to repair the damage to markets and distribution caused by the war effort. It is obvious that sales executives staffs will have to be improved and enlarged, and that the chief official in charge of marketing will of necessity have to be a much broader gauge man than ever before. Marketing research should become as important as chemical or physical research and the right executives should be found to make it so. (*Vital Speeches*, October 15, 1943, pp. 190–192)

This sales and marketing outlook came to dominate the large firm in the postwar era. The problem was to increase sales and shift from military to civilian production. Managers pursued two strategies: bolstering sales through increased marketing, particularly advertising, and diversifying their product lines. In order to respond more quickly to market opportunities, many firms adopted a more decentralized administrative structure, the multidivisional form.

The general view of the postwar economy stressed the consumer. Disposable income had increased from $33 billion in 1940 to $90 billion in 1947. The population had grown substantially and there were shortages in housing, automobiles, and other consumer goods. Given the size of the potential market, business leaders agreed that the key problem was reaching the consumer.

> Basically, a people's standard of living consists of the use of goods and services made available through the channels of distri-

bution. But effective distribution expressing itself in higher and higher levels of consumption does even more to maintain an economy. It is a primary—or even the primary—factor in the production miracle called America. It was the development of extraordinarily large domestic consumer markets through intensive and, in a sense, costly distribution methods that created the sales volume so essential for the economies of mass production. (*Fortune*, November 1947, p. 138)

Another author put it similarly:

Today in the United States, as in no other country in the world, considerations of marketing and distribution saturate the thinking of American businessmen. At a recent conference of the American Management Association, to pick an example at random, one speaker said, "the consumer is the king who determines what and how much will be made, when it will be made, and how much he will pay for it." Another speaker called mass distribution and mass production the "Siamese twins" on which depend "this country's welfare, standard of living, and ability to defend the free world." (*Business Week*, May 5, 1956, p. 127)

Market research and advertising became big businesses after World War II. *Fortune* estimated that by 1947 $50 million was being spent annually on market research, up from less than $10 million before the war (November 1947, p. 242). The American Management Association (AMA) sponsored a poll of the members of the National Association of Manufacturers (NAM) in 1947 to determine how widespread market research practices were. The results were that 44.6 percent of the firms that did over $5 million in business had market research departments and another 27.9 percent of those firms had an executive in charge of market research. Over 72 percent of the firms of substantial size were already engaged in market research of some kind (Dooley et al., 1948, pp. 338–353).

Food, petroleum, chemical, automobile, and electrical machinery industries led in market research, while apparel, lumber, and rubber industries lagged (p. 342). The market research departments and executives most frequently forecasted sales of new products. Another indicator of the importance of market research was that over 78 percent of these departments reported directly to top management while the rest reported to the executive in charge of sales. In about half of the companies the market research director attended policy meetings to decide what direction the company should take. These findings suggest that the marketing function was viewed as critically important to the organization.

Advertising expenditures grew from about $3.2 billion in 1946 to $5.6 billion in 1950 and close to $10 billion in 1956 (*Business Week*, August 30, 1958, p. 64). Indeed, advertising expenditures outpaced growth in sales and personal income. As one observer interpreted this trend: "U.S. management plainly has taken a new attitude towards advertising. The notion that advertising was a sort of corporate luxury, to be indulged in when there are no demands left over, now seems archaic and quaint. Businessmen are increasingly inclined to view the appropriation as a true capital investment—as much so as a new plant" (*Fortune*, September 1956, p. 106). While advertising was increasing, however, advertising executives were generally subordinate to the new heads of marketing. In this way advertising became defined as one of the tools of marketing (*Fortune*, December 1956, pp. 123–127).

Diversification was another strategy of firms and was achieved through both internal expansion and merger. *Business Week* explained the postwar merger movement by noting:

> What most of the companies are trying to do is put themselves in shape to tackle the postwar problems of marketing that they see closing in on them . . . A quick way to revamp an organization is to combine it with another company that has the features you want. This saves the expense of building a new line, or training a staff, or putting over a brand name, from scratch. One of the commonest forms of merger just now involves the manufacturer or producer who wants to buy a ready made sales organization or use trade connections that another company has built up. Now that the lid is off production and the race for postwar markets is beginning, there is a scramble to get selling lines out, to patch up old selling organizations, and to acquire new ones.   (1945, p. 71)

Diversification was a strategy to increase a firm's sales. Sales-oriented executives saw that the ability to gain market share in a given industry was limited by the size and growth potential of the market. Any market was cyclical, so to insure that a firm's growth potential was achieved, it was useful to diversify into products that counterbalanced a firm's main markets. Let us consider some examples of firms that increased their sales by simultaneously pursuing the twin strategies of stimulating sales through aggressive marketing and diversifying product lines.

DuPont had been a major producer of chemicals for the war effort and was already quite diversified by 1945. With the end of the war, it became necessary to concentrate on civilian production. The central problem was to find markets for existing products and create new products from old ones. The firm began to engage in extensive market research. Luther Reed, the director of trade analysis for the firm, said: "There is an engineering job to do which must establish the same type of scientific management within the art of selling which we today placidly accept within the sphere of production" (*Business Week*, December 13, 1947, p. 72).

This policy was implemented by using a highly decentralized organizational structure. The department general managers were key staff members. They had total responsibility for the development, production, and sales of products. The creation of new products was quite important to the growth of DuPont. But these products were developed in close conjunction with market research, which monitored the uses of current products hoping to identify new markets for them or markets for related products. Market analysis and sales forecasting were the major sources of information in the organization. Upper management demanded that projections be accurate and, in the early postwar era, they were within 5 percent of actual sales (*Fortune*, May 1950, p. 98).

Each product division collected sales reports from sales personnel, analysts, and engineers. With this background material, the department head would determine market possibilities, forecast sales, and direct new product development. The most significant information came from the salespeople. They were highly trained, which enabled them to understand customer problems and advise department heads on possible new markets (*Fortune*, May 1950, pp. 170–171). Decentralization allowed department heads to recommend new markets, direct research in profitable directions, and predict current demand for their products. It also allowed top management some control by monitoring department heads and approving new product lines.

General Electric began an enormous reorganization in 1947. Like DuPont, General Electric was already highly diversified by 1945. Both Gerald Swope and Charles Wilson, who ran the company during the 1930s and 1940s, saw the central problem as organizational (*Fortune*, December 1955, pp. 112–113). The firm had a functional structure in which production and sales were separate. Swope determined that this meant many of the products were designed by engineers without the advice of marketing specialists and that production decisions were made without the input of marketing personnel. Wilson agreed and tried to decentralize authority. But these measures were not enough.

In order to solve the problem, they put Ralph Cordiner to work to devise a plan for reorganization. Cordiner was a longtime General Electric employee who had an engineering background, but had spent most of his career as a merchandiser. In other words, he had a sales perspective on the problems of the firm (*Fortune*, December 1955, p. 114; *Business Week*, December 23, 1950, p. 260). Cordiner's solution revolved around two features: decentralization of decision making and an emphasis on marketing. Decentralization involved changing from a functional form to a multidivisional one. By 1952 the firm was reorganized into twenty product divisions with seventy operating departments. The number of departments grew to one hundred by 1955 (*Fortune*, December 1955, p. 115).

Decentralization gave great authority to the department heads. In order for them to make profitable decisions, the marketing function needed to be more important in the corporation. The marketing director in each department reported directly to the department head and controlled market research and sales. More important, the marketing manager was also responsible for new product development, requesting production schedules, and controlling finished goods inventory. This meant that no new product was introduced without marketing's approval. It also implied that pricing and the flow of production were determined by the marketing plan.

The decentralization of authority simultaneously recognized in General Electric and DuPont the importance of finding new markets and selling to them. Decentralization made marketing the most important function in product development. Without a sense of market size or the demand for a product, new product introduction would not proceed. The highly diversified firm was organized to produce and sell new products. Diversification and decentralization resulted from a sales and marketing conception of the corporation. Firms that were not as large as General Electric and DuPont also came to understand the importance of marketing and diversification.

Stokely-Van Camp, one of the largest producers of processed food, sold 85 percent of its production during the Depression under other company's labels. By 1947 it produced 95 percent under its own labels (*Business Week*, February 15, 1947, pp. 71–72). The president of the firm, William Stokely, Jr., wanted to build a firm that was resistant to price cutting and indifferent to the seasonal ups and downs of the food processing industry.

His strategy involved three tactics. First, the firm spent $3 million in advertising in 1947. Second, it began to produce higher-priced products, particularly frozen foods, to guarantee price stability. The firm also pursued vigorous diversification of its product lines. In 1922 it made only 8 products, but by 1947 the number increased to 112. For year-round stability, the firm entered into the prepared-foods market by producing chili, spaghetti, macaroni, and sausages. It did so by purchasing Van Camp's. The firm managed this diversity by shifting to a multidivisional form.

Bridgeport Brass Company was one of the largest brass producers in the country and sold mainly unfinished products. Because brass is made from copper, the price of copper had an enormous effect on the brass market. If copper decreased in price, then brass prices would drop and users would stockpile the metal. If copper prices rose, then users would cut consumption and use their stockpiles. In 1942 Herman Steinkraus, who had been the vice-president of sales, became president of the company. He approached the problems of the company from a marketing perspective (*Fortune*, July 1949, pp. 70–73).

The war stimulated a demand for brass. But Steinkraus knew that following the war the company would need new markets for continued growth. After studying how the firm could insulate itself from the vagaries of the brass market, Steinkraus decided to diversify. The natural path would have been to begin making finished products out of the brass. The firm did this to a small degree, but decided that if it entered too many markets it would be in competition with its largest customers. Instead, the firm began making a variety of aerosol sprays. The firm enlarged its program of diversification with a series of mergers in the 1960s.

The Heil Company, founded by Julius Heil, began as a maker of riveted tanks but was soon making dump trucks, hoisting equipment, and furnaces. Its strategy of diversification was to produce only related products and ones that could be widely sold. By 1948 sales were $30 million a year. After the war the founder's son, Joseph, took over the firm. His philosophy of growth was simple. "The success of any institution rests upon its willingness and ability to meet changing conditions. The moment we see any of our products decreasing in popularity and usefulness we find a new item to take its place" (*Business Week*, August 14, 1948, p. 68). In the late 1940s the company adopted a new structure that organized the product lines into six divisions. They also entered new product lines, both by internal expansion and merger. The basic outlook of the owners was to increase sales by expanding product lines.

The Ford Motor Company underwent substantial reorganization in the postwar era. The major innovations included a more diversified product line and a multidivisional structure. Ford began to pursue rigorous market analysis and a sales promotion campaign. In 1947 the company set up a market research department, which was headed by a former Time, Inc., sales executive named H. D. Everett (*Business Week*, August 14, 1948, p. 68). The new department concentrated on organizing sales and engaged in extensive consumer surveys to investigate the effectiveness of Ford advertising as well.

Monsanto Company, a large diversified chemical company, adopted the multidivisional form in 1939. The firm was reorganized into seven divisions and eleven staff departments (*Business Week*, December 5, 1952, p. 78). Interestingly, Monsanto's decentralization focused on elaborate financial controls that were used to monitor the firm's divisions. For example, division managers presented top management with plans for sales, costs, and profits, as well as capital expenditures and cash position. These budget controls were used to monitor the divisions' performance on a monthly basis. Division heads were judged by the return on investment. The accounting staff pioneered the use of data processors for keeping track of monthly expenditures, sales, and costs. The firm began using IBM equipment in 1951 to monitor performance more closely.

The Sperry Rand Corporation was formed in 1955 as a combination of the Sperry Company and the Remington Rand Company. Remington Rand was created by James Rand, a seller of office supplies. By 1954 it was a multiproduct firm that produced goods from carbon paper to typewriters and computers, including the original commercial computer, the Univac. Rand had built his firm around a large sales force. When the merger occurred, the firm had a sales force of eight thousand, which was one of the most effective of any firm in the country (*Fortune*, August 1955, p. 89).

Harry Vickers was head of Sperry Corporation, a large diversified producer of electronic and hydraulic equipment, electric controls, and farm and packaging equipment. It was little more than a holding company in 1937 when Vickers joined the firm through a merger with his previous company. The company expanded 3,000 percent during the war and was doing $430 million of business at its peak. When the war contracts lapsed, Vickers helped lead Sperry into an aggressive diversification program that included the purchase of six substantial firms in various industries.

The key to the Sperry-Remington Rand merger was the electronics research team in the Sperry gyroscope division (*Fortune*, August 1955, pp. 89–90). The firms merged because they were complementary. The Remington Rand Company provided a large sales staff and stable nondefense business. The Sperry Company was larger and more technologically advanced. At that time the firm was thought to be a serious competitor to IBM in the computer business.

The Worthington Corporation was a $200 million a year producer of heavy machinery in 1957. The president of the company, Walter Feldmann, had come up through the ranks as a sales executive. In the 1950s the firm had a centralized structure and a diversified product line. As president, Feldmann proposed a two-fold strategy for the firm. First, he put a multidivisional form in place to decentralize control and position related products together. Then, he undertook a campaign to instill the idea of marketing in all levels of the firm (*Business Week*, October 4, 1958, pp. 57–59).

The firm added a market research department and enlarged a product planning group and its staff advertising functions. The decentralized administrative structure allowed its salespeople to specialize in certain product lines and get closer to customers. The basic concern of the campaign was to increase the operating divisions' awareness of customer needs in order to produce goods with ready markets.

The Carnation Company originally was only a producer of evaporated milk. In the 1920s it entered the fresh milk, ice cream, and animal food business through mergers. The firm began an aggressive diversification and marketing campaign in 1953 when Alfred Ghormley became president. Ghormley had worked his way through the organization in a variety of jobs, but had a serious marketing mentality.

> We have new products in every department. Half of the products on grocery shelves 10 years from now will be new. Besides that, in an economy where distribution costs are rising, it's smart to add products that can utilize and share the cost of marketing facilities, particularly when you can trade on a brand name like Carnation. The sales organization is in place; there is an advertising program that with a little added cost can be put to work, and with each new product, the whole brand name image becomes stronger. (*Business Week*, February 22, 1958, pp. 106–107)

The firm chose to expand internally by introducing new products, even though they cost from $3 to 5 million each to develop. A large research facility was essential, but the most important additions were new sales and marketing personnel. After the war Carnation found that its food lines were too concentrated in declining markets. Its new marketing expertise was put to good use in the diversification process.

The sales and marketing conception viewed the corporation as a growth machine powered by new products and modern marketing tactics. Differentiation and diversification of products were two tactics to expand the firm and increase its profitability. The marketing mentality—finding products to meet needs as well as helping to create those needs—permeated the entire organization. The multidivisional structure decentralized authority so that those who were closest to the market could estimate the success of any given product. Even as this conception of the firm triumphed, however, a new conception was emerging.

The Finance Conception Takes Over

The finance conception of control began to emerge in the mid-1950s. From the finance perspective, the firm was a collection of assets earning varying rates of return. The firm's central goal was to allocate capital across product lines in order to increase short-term rates of return. Managers pursued growth through mergers and, when product lines did not perform adequately, divestment. By the mid-1950s, the large firm was already producing multiple products and rapidly becoming organized into the multidivisional form. Managers had been pursuing mergers for diversification since the 1920s. So how was the finance conception different from the sales and marketing conception? What caused the new conception of control to emerge?

The key difference revolved around how each point of view conceived of the firm and its purposes. The sales and marketing conception of control pursued growth by increasing sales. Diversification was one of the tactics utilized. The finance conception pursued growth by ruthlessly evaluating the contribution of each product line to the overall profit and goals of the firm. The finance conception of control viewed the central office as a bank and treated the divisions as potential borrowers. The central office would invest in divisions that showed great potential and divest those in slow-growing markets. Profitable divisions supported mergers of new divisions. From this perspective, mergers were attractive because product lines could be purchased at a lower price than they could be produced internally. The managers of the firm were no longer constrained by major industry because the production of each unit was evaluated solely on its rate of return.

This new conception was not invented by the managers of the largest firms. Indeed, they were generally restricted by their established organizational fields and the power structure of their firms. The new conception was instead the creation of finance-oriented executives who operated mostly outside the established channels. Their firms grew at spectacular rates and often entered stable organizational fields in search of potential mergers. The managers in these fields who followed either the manufacturing or sales and marketing conceptions of control had two choices. They could risk being targets of mergers, and thereby lose their corporate identity, or they could alter their tactics and adopt the finance conception of control.

The overall result of this new conception of control was a shift in the construction of organizational fields. The reference group for the largest firms became the other large firms. Indeed, the 1960s merger movement was a direct result of the spread of the finance conception and strategies to the population of the largest firms. Today, the finance conception of control continues to dominate corporate discourse and the largest firms operate as an organizational field for one another.

The role of antitrust in this reconstruction was important. The innovators of the finance conception knew that the Celler-Kefauver Act was being enforced by the Justice Department and the FTC in the 1950s. They tried to avoid antitrust attention by deliberately staying away from mergers in similar product lines. The farther afield mergers were, the less likely antitrust authorities were to intervene. Growth through merger required that finance-oriented managers choose their merger targets carefully. They sought profitable and growing industries where their capital would earn higher rates of return and avoided mergers where the threat of antitrust prosecution might exist.

The ultimate proof of the validity of the finance conception was the explosive rate of growth achieved by the acquisitive conglomerates. Most of the scholarly work on this subject has focused on the few extremely successful conglomerate firms such as LTV, Textron, Gulf and Western, Litton Industries, and ITT. But there were many others. In the early 1950s multiindustry firms had varying degrees of success. Once a few of them achieved success through mergers, the other largest firms began to pursue mergers for growth. Most of these firms, however, tended to merge into fields related to their major industries.

In 1955 *Business Week* noted a new trend in mergers.

> What we may be seeing is the development of a prevailing business practice—you might define it as "growth by acquisition." And it seems likely to go along, not in feverish jumps, at its own measured pace within the limits of present legislation . . . The mergers are based on the desire to lengthen product lines and to diversify. The first aims to reduce costs and the second to hedge risks—but in many ways they are one and the same. Together, taken as diversification in its broadest sense, they outweigh all other business reasons for current mergers.   (June 4, 1955, pp. 92–94)

Fortune reported that in 1955 one out of four of the largest firms had a "vice president in charge of growth." The magazine listed the following motives for diversification: "1. Nearly all diversifying companies do it as a means to growth. 2. Many companies diversify to offset seasonal or cyclical fluctuations. 3. Many companies diversify to offset a declining or stagnant market. 4. Many companies diversify to take advantage of the tax structure" (September 1955, p. 92). The tax structure favored mergers in three ways. Taxes on capital gains were quite high, so firms who reinvested profits escaped paying taxes. Acquired firms often provided losses so that conglomerates could avoid paying taxes on future profits. The acquired firms' assets could be depreciated immediately, which provided instantaneous profits for the purchasing firm. It took, of course, a finance outlook to look at mergers in this way.

The role of antitrust in diversification was almost always discussed in articles about diversification. A typical comment was: "What is more, business has been acutely aware of what Justice Holmes called the 'brooding omnipresence' of antitrust. Potential diversifiers have their lawyers check the antitrust angles as a matter of routine, and some consult directly with the Federal Trade Commission or the Department of Justice" (*Fortune*, September 1955, p. 208).

By 1954 the business press had already begun to note the rise of "polyglot" corporations. These firms, made of smaller firms, were put together by finance-oriented executives.

> It isn't just their diversity of product line that makes the polyglots peculiar. Today plenty of companies are diversified to a certain extent. The polyglots are not only highly diverse and very new, but don't stick primarily to any one line. They blossomed overnight in response to: management's yen for diversification and growth, the large amounts of confidence and cash in boom times, the indirect pressures applied by existing antitrust and tax laws, and the development of management controls and techniques for handling decentralized operations. (*Business Week*, June 23, 1956, p. 61)

The article identified Textron, Penn-Texas, Glen Alden, Philadelphia and Reading, Ward Industries, Merritt-Chapman and Scott, and Bowser as the leading representatives of this type of firm.

It is useful to explore the tactics of this group in more detail. By 1956 the existence and justification of the purely finance-driven corporation was recognized by the business press.

> Actually, polyglots offer plenty of advantages—growth, perhaps an escape from business cycle profit squeeze, and the development of regular income . . . But these aren't the only pressures

for the creation of polyglots. The present boom, existing antitrust laws, and the tax laws tend to make mergers or acquisitions, usually in an unrelated line, the best way to quick growth. Corporations are afraid to get too large a share of a market for fear of being charged with monopoly or restraint of trade. Hence, to maintain growth, they turn to other fields . . . Polyglots are an offshoot of new organizational concepts. Business has developed both methods for maintaining widespread and diverse operations—through tight accounting and control, growing use of computers, and the use of decentralized structures. (*Business Week*, June 23, 1956, p. 62)

The antitrust authorities remained puzzled by the new corporate forms. "Up to now, they [the antitrust authorities] haven't figured out a way to attack the polyglots. It's pretty hard, they say, to bring companies to court if their merger doesn't eliminate competition, doesn't deprive anyone of raw material, and still leaves plenty of giants around for the mergees to compete with" (*Business Week*, June 23, 1956, p. 63).

These general tactics were established by the mid-1950s. The strategies revolved around finding and buying potential merger candidates. Firms used financial tools to evaluate candidates and often had consultants, or "bird dogs," whose sole function was to find such companies (*Business Week*, October 30, 1954, p. 154, July 14, 1956, pp. 164–168; *Fortune*, October 1956, p. 124). The typical merger candidate was a firm whose stock was selling under its book value. It had a distinct product and an aggressive young management. Because entrepreneurs who bought firms generally were uninterested in running them, they usually tried to retain the existing management.

Some of the early innovators of these finance tactics were Leopold Silberstein (Penn-Texas), Elmer Bobst (Warner Lambert), Royal Little (Textron), Thomas Jones (Daystrom), Tex Thornton (Litton Industries), Norton Simon (Norton Simon), Ben Heineman (Northwest Industries), Max McGraw (McGraw Electric), Thomas Evans (H. K. Porter), and F. M. Davies (FMC). *Business Week* identified about forty firms on the New York Stock Exchange who fit this profile in 1956 (June 13, 1956, p. 91).

Most of the mergers were friendly, but a number of them involved hostile takeovers. A 1955 article in *Fortune* entitled "How Managements Get Tipped Over" had an extremely contemporary ring.

In the past few years, groups of shareholders—usually called raiders—have forcefully demonstrated that the energetic exercise of ownership rights is still capable of standing a corporate management on its ear. The raider is concerned with how cheaply he can get control of a company and how big his capital gains might be. If he is a "good" raider, he will try to get his capital gains by jacking up management, improving profits, and thereby lifting the price of the company's stock. If he is a mere predator, he may liquidate the firm at market prices (October 1955, p. 123).

Ben Heineman, one of the originators of unfriendly takeover tactics, defended the practice: "A professional management really has no incentive to do a good job for the stockholders. But if a group has at least 25 to 30 percent of the stock, its interests are identical with the interests of the rest of the shareholders. Ownership boards will make management utilize the pool of assets they're controlling. Actually what a raid amounts to, when lines of power are drawn, is an effort by a group of investors to take executive directorship into their own hands" (p. 124).

Hostile takeovers would begin when a group of investors slowly purchased the stock of a company whose price they felt was undervalued relative to corporate assets. When the group had a sufficient amount of the stock, they would announce to the management that they wanted representation on the board of directors. If refused, the group would often make a bid for the rest of the stock. If successful, they would attempt to replace existing management.

Many of the polyglots, or, as they came to be called in the 1960s, conglomerates, engaged only in friendly takeovers. They preferred to buy small privately owned firms that had earnings over $1 million a year, a broad product line, and young hungry managers who needed capital to continue to grow. In these situations, it was important to maintain good ties with existing management. Instead of operating the subsidiaries, the conglomerate managers maintained financial control of the newly purchased firms through tight accounting practices and continued aggressive acquisitions.

Royal Little pioneered this strategy at Textron. Initially, Textron was a holding company for a number of textile manufacturers. Little realized that the industry was not growing and decided to enter new businesses. His first major purchases in 1954 were, ironically, textile companies, American Woolen and Robbins Mills, Inc. He used the tax losses from these purchases to invest profits in new firms. Little relied on the advice of Arthur D. Little Inc., a consulting group, to locate companies (*Business Week*, November 5, 1955, p. 81).

Little based his management decisions on three factors:

> First, Textron had the problem of earnings cycles. We felt that by unrelated diversification, we would completely eliminate the one industry cycle and stabilize earnings. Second, we noticed that the Justice Department and FTC were getting tougher on mergers in any one industry. We felt that completely unrelated diversification would avoid any problem whatsoever with Justice. And third, we noticed that in American industry, well-run aggressive single industry companies tended to overexpand their facilities, with resulting excess capacity, price cutting and reduced earnings. We felt that through unrelated diversification, available capital could be used to acquire another business rather than overbuild an existing one.   (*Dun's Review*, May 1968, p. 26)

The company continued to diversify rapidly. By 1960 it had diversified its product mix so that 24 percent was consumer goods, 22 percent industrial goods, 21 percent textiles, 20 percent automotive, and 13 percent defense. The company had a highly decentralized structure which kept its twenty-four divisions somewhat autonomous (*Aviation Week and Space Technology*, April 25, 1960, p. 31). In 1962 Textron divested its textile division because it did not make enough profits.

At that point the company set out to purchase firms that were not the largest in their industry, but instead showed themselves capable of returning 25 percent pretax profit on Textron's investment and 20 percent annually on shareholder equity. Little retired from the firm in 1962 and was replaced by Rupert Thompson, who had previously been a banker (*Business Week*, June 15, 1963, pp. 45–47). Thompson's goal was to tighten financial controls and reduce the firm's debt. He was quite successful and by the mid-1960s the firm had achieved stable growth.

The Warner-Hudnut Corporation, eventually known as Warner-Lambert, was the creation of the Pfieffer family, who had built the firm entirely through mergers from the early 1900s on. Elmer Bobst, the president of the firm in the 1950s when it went on a renewed buying spree, remarked, "The Pfieffers always felt that it was cheaper to buy good will than to create it" (*Fortune*, October

1955, p. 143). When Bobst came to power in 1945, the firm had been in decline for some years. Its primary product was a line of cosmetics that was not very successful. In response, he first reorganized the firm into a multidivisional form.

Bobst's next task was to expand the firm, which he decided to do primarily through mergers. He sought small- and medium-sized enterprises in various parts of the pharmaceutical industry. In looking for merger candidates, the firm had two negative criteria. "As all merger minded executives must, they had to think of the Antitrust Division of the Justice Department. It is true that the company did not have a substantial share of either the drug or cosmetics market. However, the Justice Department quite properly thinks of these as not two markets, but as a great many . . . Bobst and his associates also did not want to buy into any more cosmetics business" (*Fortune*, October 1955, p. 143). In the early 1950s the firm purchased Chilcote Laboratories, a producer of ethical drugs, and the Lambert Company, a producer of many pharmaceutical goods including consumer products. Bobst's basic strategy was to turn over the daily operation of the company to in-house management and then vigorously pursue other mergers as a means to continued growth.

Thomas Jones was a Harvard Business School graduate who specialized in finance. In 1932, he managed a printing equipment manufacturer called American Type Founders (ATF). The firm was almost bankrupt at the time and only recovered when it did defense work during World War II. Jones chose to diversify the firm by entering the electronics field through a merger. After the war, he decided to continue the diversification strategy. "I looked at 300 companies—most of them were overpriced. Then we had the chance to buy Daystrom Co. It made furniture. It was and continues to be a moneymaker" (*Business Week*, December 31, 1955, p. 40).

During the Korean War, Jones changed the name of the firm to Daystrom because he thought it had the ring of a diversified technology firm. He also began to reorganize and decentralize the firm. At that point ATF became one of the divisions. The purchase trend continued into the mid-1950s as Jones bought American Gyro Company, the Heath Company, and Weston Electrical.

Jones described the management structure: "The parent company simply acts as referee, consultant, and judge of results. Its directors do a sort of rotating act through the monthly meeting first as the board of one operating group, then as the board of another. This arrangement approximates a holding company set-up but has the added advantage of keeping a close check on operating results. It also leaves me with time to investigate the purchase of new firms" (*Business Week*, December 31, 1955, p. 40).

Max McGraw was the president and founder of McGraw Electric, a producer of goods for utilities, which had been organized divisionally in the 1930s. In the 1950s he began to add to those divisions, mainly through acquisition. In 1952 the firm bought Edison Electric and changed its name to McGraw Edison. By 1955 the firm was organized into thirty-one divisions and was selling almost $300 million of electrical goods a year.

McGraw's philosophy of management and organization was basically finance centered. "Each division president is responsible. His ingenuity, judgment, and ability are expected to produce profits. He is judged according to his showing. He hires and fires, determines salaries and wage rates within a general acceptable pattern, and he has freedom within reasonable limits to establish his division's organizational pattern" (*Business Week*, December 15, 1955, p. 127). While the division heads had great autonomy, finance was centralized in the main office. All capital spending projects needed approval by the main office. Further, all bank accounts were monitored through the main office. The treasurer reported daily to the president about the cash position of each division.

AMF was another company run by a finance-oriented executive who concentrated on growth through acquisition in the 1950s. Moorehead Patterson became president of the firm, which he had inherited from his father. In 1945 the firm was producing cigarette and packaging equipment and doing only $12 million of business a year. After the war Patterson decided to diversify as a way of expanding the business. His first attempt was internal. For a variety of reasons this failed and Patterson needed cash to keep the firm afloat. As a result he began to purchase privately held firms, mostly in exchange for AMF stock (*Business Week*, October 5, 1957, pp. 197–198).

By the early 1950s AMF had diversified into electronics, power saws, bicycles, fasteners, electric motors, guided missiles, and bowling equipment. By 1955 the firm was producing over $250 million of goods annually. Patterson pursued any company he could, as long as it had good earnings and management that promised to stay on the job. The firm remained unintegrated in the mid-1950s and each of the purchases was operated as a subsidiary.

Ling-Temco-Vought was the creation of James Ling. Ling invented many of the financial manipulations that dominate in large firms today. His goal was to create the largest company on earth and to achieve it he began buying and selling firms. His philosophy is worth quoting. "In the most general sense, my function is to be sure we come up with the most creative use of the assets of the corporation that will build values and increase earnings per share. Redeploying assets in this way is building values and these values are measured on the stock market. And in turn they are useful financially as a means of building new values" (*Fortune*, August 1969, p. 162). When asked what he thought was important in an executive, Ling responded: "I personally believe that the best background for corporate life is that of a financial analyst working in the Wall Street arena—someone who has been exposed to all the technological markets and knows the basic ways of getting good information in and about companies. A man with this background would know the financial values of these operations" (p. 164).

Ling-Temco-Vought started out as Ling Electric Company, which installed electrical systems in new houses. In 1955 Ling decided to take his company public and began to sell stock. After raising $800,000 Ling found that there were limits to the growth that could be achieved by expanding his electrical contracting business (Brown, 1972, pp. 43–51). In order to expand further he began to diversify. He made his first substantial purchase, L. M. Electronics, in 1956 (Sobel, 1984b, p. 81). This venture proved successful and his stock price rose. Ling decided to reorganize his company into Ling Industries, a holding company for Ling Electric and Ling Electronics.

From this point on, Ling followed a purely financial strategy and stopped trying to operate in only one business. Ling purchased United Electronics, Calidyne, Continental Electronics, the Altec Companies, and University Loudspeaking. By 1959 he had greatly increased the size of his company and was already recognized on Wall Street as a powerful man. The businesses he purchased were operating primarily in two fields: military products and consumer products with a concentration in audio equipment (U.S. House, 1970, pt. 6, pp. 614–616).

What is most interesting about Ling's activities is how he financed his purchases. Backed by the assets of the purchased company, Ling would borrow money on short-term notes. He would then sell longer term bonds with lower interest rates and use the proceeds to pay off the loans. To pay off the longer term debt, he would use current earnings and often sell assets.

The effect of this strategy was to reduce short-term debt, though long-term debt was great. But the long-term debt was at lower interest rates and therefore would not place as much of a burden on the firm as long as the firm continued to grow and remain profitable. The other positive effect was that Ling did not have to dilute the stock in order to increase the value of the firm. This meant the stock could continue to show high earnings, in spite of the firm's indebtedness. The stock price in fact soared.

Ling, in essence, perfected the strategy now called the leveraged buyout. He was able to bring together some of the largest purchases ever made and to swallow companies much larger than his own. Ling never became attached to any particular product and would enter or exit an industry in a moment if he felt that there was much to gain by doing so.

By 1959 the name of the company had been changed to Ling-Altec and was doing $48.1 million of business annually. The next big purchase, Temco Electronics, made it a Fortune 500 company in 1960. In 1961 Ling bought a far larger company, the Chance-Vought Aircraft Company, and the new firm was renamed Ling-Temco-Vought (LTV). The takeover created a lot of hostility from both the Temco and Chance-Vought boards of directors and high-level executives. They forced Ling to step down as CEO and chairman of the board when the company began to perform poorly that same year (Brown, 1972, pp. 122–124; Sobel, 1984b, p. 87). Ling, however, returned to power in 1963 and began to bring the company back to financial health.

Ling's plan was to embark on a new merger spree. The purchases were made possible by borrowing against the value of LTV and the undervalued assets of the larger target firms. The large debt would be lowered by selling assets. To increase the value of the firm's stock so that he could purchase other firms, Ling bought back about a one-third of it. Earnings per share increased and the price of the stock rose on Wall Street. Ling also reorganized LTV as a holding company with three divisions, each with its own stock. Both moves provided Ling with new capital and a higher stock price (Sobel, 1984b, pp. 89–91).

The period of greatest merger activity for the firm was the 1960s. Ling obtained Okonite, a wire manufacturer, in October 1965. He sold some of Okonite's assets and essentially gained control of 83 percent of the company without committing any funds. Then he purchased Wilson and Company, which produced meat products but also held a number of companies including a sporting goods manufacturer, a pet food company, a soap company, and a growing pharmaceutical company. Next Ling purchased Greatamerica Corporation, a holding company for several insurance firms, banks, Braniff Airways, and National Car Rental. After selling some of the banks and insurance companies to raise funds to pay some of the loans, Ling was left with the core firms of Braniff, National Car Rental, and two insurance companies. The last company he purchased was Jones and Laughlin Steel. It was at this point that the Justice Department intervened and began antitrust proceedings.

Harold Geneen led ITT's diversification in the early 1960s. Geneen began his career as an accountant with a large firm and later moved into management. His forte was helping unprofitable companies with poor internal financial systems turn around. At Bell and Howell, Jones and Laughlin Steel, and Raytheon he implemented elaborate financial controls and reporting systems that forced managers to account for their costs in detail (Schoenberg, 1985, chs. 3–5). He was chosen for the ITT job because of this skill.

ITT was a holding company of telephone systems in Western Europe and Latin America when Geneen came aboard. The central office did not even know the profitability of the different operations. The subsidiaries operated almost autonomously. As one insider put it, every year "they delivered a bag of money to New York—*maybe*" (Schoenberg, 1985, p. 109). ITT depended on Latin America for one-third of its profits and these were always in jeopardy due to unstable political conditions. In response to these problems, Geneen moved in two directions: he established elaborate financial controls over the subsidiaries and increased the U.S. component of ITT's business through diversification.

Geneen set up headquarters for the firm in Europe and brought the heads of the European subsidiaries together on a monthly basis. This process had the effect of increasing the size and profitability of those businesses (Sobel, 1984b, p. 169; Schoenberg, 1985, pp. 143–145). As part of the general tightening up of ITT's corporate practices, Geneen instituted frequent reviews of the financial records of all the subsidiaries. The central office could then keep track of the performance of each subunit. The firm also began extensive planning. Each division had to submit a yearly forecast of expenditures, production, and profits.

In March 1963 Geneen told the board of directors that he wanted to increase the U.S. share of business by instituting a program of acquisition (Schoenberg, 1985, pp. 161–162). Since ATT held a virtual monopoly on the country's telecommunications market, the firm would have to enter other businesses. Geneen's working group looked for firms in industries with high growth and potential for continued growth. He chose companies that could be nurtured and pumped capital into them as long as the companies could prove that they would grow. He wanted the conglomerate to continue to grow after acquisitions were made. This strategy succeeded because even when ITT stopped engaging in large-scale mergers, the company continued to grow until 1981, well after Geneen's departure.

Geneen's view of antitrust was typical of the other finance-oriented managers.

> As I understand it, the most important aspect here is the concentration of markets within—I repeat—within industries. It is precisely for this reason that horizontal and vertical mergers have virtually ceased. And, it is also for this reason that only the so-called diversified or conglomerate mergers remain to business as a method of seeking more effective forms of management efficiency and growth, which could be translated into stockholder values without concentration of markets within an industry. (*Vital Speeches*, October 23, 1969, p. 149)

Geneen's purchases were generally made with the firm's valuable stock. The only problem with using stock for acquisitions was that profits had to increase to prevent the dilution of earnings per share. Consequently, Geneen had to be sure that the companies that he purchased were growing and profitable and could immediately contribute to the overall profitability of the firm.

Geneen purchased Bell and Gossett, a producer of industrial pumps, first, then General Controls, Cannon Electric, and a number of smaller companies. All of these purchases involved an exchange of stock. Initially, the purchases did not yield the 10 percent increase in growth and profits that Geneen had promised. But by 1964 the performance of the new acquisitions finally improved and Geneen met the five-year goals he had set in 1959: he had doubled the revenues and profits of the company.

In 1965 Geneen prepared to forge ahead with more acquisitions and continued 10 percent growth. But his merger and acquisitions group came to him with a surprising study. While the stock market was enamored of high technology and capital-intensive businesses, service businesses gave higher rates of return. The projected growth in service industries exceeded any projections for manufacturing, so Geneen turned to acquiring companies in the fast growing service sector.

His first purchase was Avis Rent-a-Car, followed by companies in publishing, including Harold Sams. In 1968 he attempted to buy ABC Television, but the deal faltered when the FTC and the FCC dragged out their hearings on the matter. Geneen then bought Levitt and Sons (construction), Sheraton (hotels), Rayonier (chemicals), Continental Baking, and several smaller firms. The peak of ITT's merger activities came in 1968 when the conglomerate acquired Grinnell, Canteen Corporation, and the Hartford Insurance Company (Schoenberg, 1985, p. 163). The merger activity ended when the Justice Department filed suit. In 1971 ITT settled the case by agreeing to make no additional acquisitions over $100 million for ten years as well as to divest itself of Canteen, Levitt, Avis, and part of Grinnell (Schoenberg, 1985, p. 316).

The Spread of the Finance Conception of Control

By the mid-1960s the finance conception of control and its major strategy of growth, diversified mergers, dominated the largest firms. This was because the tactics yielded high rates of growth. The business press was full of stories about firms that had begun to diversify, reorganize into divisions, and use mergers for growth. What held these tactics together was a conception of the firm that stressed close management of assets and strict financial evaluation of the product lines.

In 1961 Ralph Davis, a professor of business, predicted the future of business organization: "A continuing trend toward decentralization and diversification. In industry, this usually requires a product line, profit center, basis for decentralization. It will be accompanied by further dispersion of business operations" (*Dun's Review*, March 1961, p. 73). The importance of finance personnel and financial control was the subject of frequent articles. One argued, "Top financial officers now have a hand in everything from mergers to budgets to personnel and marketing. They also woo bankers and stock analysts. Because they know more about the company than anyone else, they often move, finally, right into the driver's seat . . . Still, it was the production man or engineer who usually ran the show during the Twenties, while the sales chief ran things in the Thirties and Forties. But, in the Fifties, financial executives have come to the fore" (*Fortune*, January 1962, p. 85).

The basis of this new power was their knowledge of the complex financial control systems put in place during the 1950s and 1960s. Financial expertise was necessary to identify merger candidates (*Business Week*, May 20, 1961, pp. 104–110, December 9, 1961, pp. 67–69; *Fortune*, January 1962, pp. 81–85). One indication of this development was that Ralph Cordiner, the president of General Electric and a sales and marketing executive, was followed by Gerald Phillipe, the chief financial officer of the corporation (*Fortune*, January 1962, p. 85). Today General Electric is one of the most diversified large corporations in America.

During the merger boom of the 1960s and into the 1970s, the largest corporations were increasingly controlled by executives whose background or conceptions were finance based. But even when a firm was not led by such people, the finance conception was still influential. Solutions to management problems were framed in finance terms. It is useful to consider how this conception of the firm spread to a great many of the largest corporations in the 1960s.

Donald Kircher became president of Singer Sewing Machine in 1958. The firm was not growing and was losing market share in its core business, sewing machines. Kircher, a lawyer who had worked in a Wall Street firm before joining Singer, approached the firm's problems, which centered on product maturity, with finance tactics.

Kircher initially shored up the sewing machine business by cutting costs, introducing more products, and advertising. He also embarked on a rapid diversification program that included mergers, mainly with firms in electronics and business machines. As part of the reorganization, he decentralized operations into nine divisions. When asked in 1963 about his plans for the firm, Kircher replied: "The sewing machine business continues to have a growing future and Singer intends to expand our preeminent position in it. However, I am aiming at $1 billion a year in sales with half in other fields. The only way to achieve this growth is through continued acquisitions" (*Fortune*, December 1963, p. 117).

Litton Industries was run by Tex Thornton and Roy Ash in the 1960s. Thornton was an organizational genius who had pioneered financial controls and Ash had worked at Bank of America (*Dun's Review*, May 1966, p. 54). Between 1954 and 1966 the company grew from $12 million a year in sales to $1 billion. The rapid growth was due mostly to mergers with firms in the electronics industry. By the early 1960s Litton diversified so much that it was clearly a conglomerate. The firm was organized in autonomous divisions with tight financial controls. Ash ran the firm internally and Thornton externally. Both were involved in the extensive mergers (*Business Week*, April 16, 1966, pp. 174–185).

Even the steel companies participated in the merger movement and the trend toward diversification. Bethlehem Steel purchased Cerro Corporation, a producer of zinc, copper, and lead. Armco acquired titanium, zirconium, and plastic pipe companies. John Lobb, a former ITT executive, became president of Crucible Steel and announced, "If the profit rate for steel can't be increased, you can take cash now and invest it outside steel. We are not going to put our head in the sand and ignore opportunities" (*Business Week*, September 20, 1967, pp. 42–43). Bliss and Laughlin, a producer of cold finished-steel bars, began to diversify in 1962. Fred Robbins reorganized the company into product divisions and bought six firms in the construction and tool industries. Each of the new companies was run as a subsidiary because the firm did not have sufficient management talent to operate the acquisitions itself (*Business Week*, July 15, 1967, pp. 67–68).

The Armour Company started to reorganize its structure in the late 1950s. William Prince took over the firm in 1957. He set out to divide the firm into product divisions. These divisions were given a great deal of control over their product lines, but were forced to meet strict financial goals. The firm then undertook a program designed to acquire more brand name products with higher profit margins (*Business Week*, May 9, 1964, pp. 54–57).

The airplane companies began to diversify in earnest in 1959 because the defense business was too cyclical. When the Pentagon needed arms, business boomed. But in peacetime the loss of a large contract would almost destroy them. An article in *Aviation Week and Space Technology* explained, "There's a tough period ahead for aircraft makers. It's painfully clear that military plane and missile contracts are dwindling in numbers and commercial plane markets won't expand to fill the gap. So they're rushing for new lines to hedge their future—and many will be far different in make-up five years from now" (May 16, 1959, p. 84). Another article suggested, "Virtually all aviation companies are expecting a major share of their future growth to come through diversification of product lines, services, or markets. Most will devote a part of their expansion efforts to establishment or enlargement of civilian and defense business" (*Aviation Week and Space Technology*, June 20, 1960, p. 293).

Most of the diversification that occurred was through mergers. Lockheed Aircraft bought a shipyard and began producing nuclear submarines. North American Aviation bought a steam-generating equipment producer and a builder of petrochemical plants. Chance-Vought began producing electronics for uses other than aircraft. Bell Helicopter moved into production of satellites. Eventually, many of the largest aircraft producers were absorbed in mergers. North American became part of Rockwell. Martin, a producer of missiles, merged with Marietta, a diversified defense contractor. Chance-Vought became part of LTV and Bell Helicopter was purchased by Textron. United Aircraft acquired a number of firms including Pratt and Whitney, Sikorsky Helicopter, and Otis Elevator. In recognition of its diversification, the firm changed its name to United Technologies.

Willard Rockwell assumed control of Rockwell Standard in 1963. The company was primarily a parts producer for the automobile industry. The firm was floundering when the younger

Rockwell succeeded his father. He saw that the management was too decentralized and not held accountable for performance; so he reorganized the firm into product divisions and implemented financial accounting. He also began an extensive diversification program that stressed both internal and external diversification. The goal was to produce $1 billion in sales by 1970. In 1968 the firm bought North American Aviation and changed its name to North American Rockwell. Since that time the firm has continued to diversify and is now known as Rockwell International (*Dun's Review*, June 1966, pp. 28–31, 65–70).

TRW was the product of a 1957 merger between the Thompson Products Company, a major producer of parts for the automobile and aircraft industry, and Ramo-Wooldridge, an electronics firm located on the West Coast. The Thompson Company began as an auto parts company and started producing airplane parts during World War II. After the war John Wright, a lawyer, led the firm. He realized that diversification could help the company achieve continuous growth and balance the cyclical nature of the aircraft and auto businesses. Wright invested in Ramo-Wooldridge, an electronics firm started by two scientists who had worked at Hughes aircraft (*Business Week*, September 24, 1966, p. 90; *Fortune*, October 1966, pp. 154–155).

In the late 1950s TRW had a highly decentralized structure, which unfortunately stunted the firm's growth and profits. When reorganization occurred in 1962, financial controls were set in place. The firm also embarked on a diversification program and merged into high-technology fields. By 1967 the firm had reached $1 billion in sales, about 44 percent defense related and the rest industrial (*Business Week*, June 8, 1968, p. 45).

The Eaton Company was a producer of automotive parts when John Virdon joined the firm as president in 1958. His previous experience was as chairman of the Federal Reserve Bank of Cleveland. Not surprisingly, Virdon thought the company needed to diversify its product lines. Virdon immediately acquired eight relatively small, privately held firms that operated mostly in the automobile industry (*Business Week*, May 28, 1966, p. 101). The largest of these mergers was with Yale and Towne, a large domestic and overseas producer of hardware. The two firms were brought together by the investment banking house of Kuhn, Loeb, and Company, who knew that Eaton was looking to diversify and

felt that the product lines were complementary. Eaton had manufacturing skill and Yale and Towne had extensive multinational
experience. The merged firm was controlled by Eaton's management, but many of the Yale and Towne people occupied key positions. The merger brought about a product-based reorganization
of the firm into thirty-six divisions. At the same time strict financial controls were implemented.

Dun's Review published an article in 1968 about eleven firms
that were in the process of turning their situations around. These
included Allied Chemical, American Motors, American Shipbuilding, Baker Oil Tools, Brunswick, Gould National, Sharon
Steel, Spartans Industries, Standard Packaging, Struthers Wells,
and Swift Foods. Eight of the eleven firms were using diversification to regain profitability and the other three were restructuring
their plants and implementing financial controls (February 1968,
p. 38). Diversification through acquisition and tight financial controls were the accepted treatment for ailing firms.

After the 1969–70 stock market crash some of the firms that had
expanded most rapidly during the boom years of the 1960s lost
their gleam. The 1970s were not good years for the stock market,
nor the American economy in general, so the pace of mergers
slowed until 1975. Mergers never fell below their active 1955
level, however. Many of the firms that had actively pursued
mergers in the 1960s divested themselves of some of their less
profitable acquisitions. After 1975 merger activity increased until
the 1980s witnessed a great resurgence under the Reagan Administration. The bull market, the lax antitrust environment, and the
dominance of the finance conception of control promoted large-
scale mergers. Unfortunately, it is difficult to measure that movement or its direction because Reagan stopped gathering systematic data on mergers in 1981.

One might argue that the finance conception of control went
from boom to bust as the acquisitive conglomerates generally performed poorly in the 1970s. This view, however, misunderstands
the nature of the finance conception. While the conglomerates
practiced the purest form of those tactics, they were only its most
obvious advocates. Indeed, the finance strategy of operating corporations as a set of divisions each responsible for an adequate
contribution to the overall growth and profits of the firm remains
the dominant one for the large corporation. Almost all of the
largest firms are significantly diversified and set up in divisions.

The divestment movement of the 1970s reflects the finance conception. If divisions did not meet the standards, then firms divested themselves of those lines. The decision to divest was usually made as a function of product mix and performance. A multiproduct firm would decide to get rid of divisions that were too distant from its core businesses. Frequently, those divisions had been unprofitable from the beginning and management lacked the expertise to make them profitable.

The price of a firm's stock continued to be its most salient trait in the 1980s. If a firm's worth exceeded its stock price, as was often the case, it was a merger target. The evaluation and selection of merger candidates fueled the stock market throughout the decade. The corporate raiders of the 1980s used strategies developed in the 1950s and 1960s. Their tactics were financially motivated and their behavior, once they acquired firms, closely resembled that of the earlier conglomerate leaders.

One excellent example of the finance conception of control in operation in the late 1970s and early 1980s is U.S. Steel. The steel industry in the United States is mature; the product lines are established and demand is not growing. The industry's problems are compounded by the need for large fixed investment in capital stock in the face of overcapacity and aging plants with obsolete technology. Given the relatively high wage rates in the industry and foreign competition, the steel companies have drifted in and out of profitability for the past thirty years.

U.S. Steel, since its emergence during the turn of the century merger movement, has continued to be one of the largest industrial organizations in the country. But the company's management was always trained in steelmaking and, until 1979, the president was someone who had come up through manufacturing. Its switch to the finance conception of control required that the board of directors recognize the problems of the firm and industry, and act toward their resolution. The board chose David Roderick as chair and CEO in 1979. Roderick had no practical experience in the steel mills and had been finance vice-president in the organization. His point of view on the problems of U.S. Steel was distinctly financial. Roderick made two moves to save the company. He closed all unprofitable facilities so that the steel company shrank in capacity by over 30 percent between 1979 and 1985 (*Industry Week*, February 4, 1985, pp. 34–38). He also embarked on a diversification effort to lessen U.S. Steel's dependence on steel, which he perceived was a declining business (*Fortune*, June 1984, p. 23; *Business Week*, December 2, 1985, p. 82). The board of directors has consistently supported Roderick in his attempts to return U.S. Steel to profitability.

Under Roderick's leadership, the company has divested itself of Universal Cement, its division that manufactures pails and drums, its housing division, real estate scattered over the country, and a substantial amount of its coal properties (*Wall Street Journal*, July 9, 1986, p. 14). Cash from these sales has been used to purchase a number of companies. The first major purchase was Marathon Oil, one of the largest petrochemical companies in the world. The second was Texas Oil and Gas, a major producer of natural gas and owner of an extensive pipeline system. By 1986 only 30 percent of revenues came from the steel division (*Wall Street Journal*, July 9, 1986, p. 14).

On July 9, 1986, the company officially changed its name from U.S. Steel to USX. With the name change came a corporate reorganization. The company is now operating with four major divisions: Marathon Oil, Texas Oil and Gas, USS (the steel division), and U.S. Diversified Group (the company's other assorted businesses). This reorganization isolates the steel group and, according to Roderick, "the steel unit will have to generate its own funds for future modernization. In addition, it will be required to repay the approximately $1.8 billion in steel debt outstanding" (*Wall Street Journal*, July 9, 1986, p. 14). Roderick, in the same interview, added that if the steel group did not return to profitability, it would shrink drastically. It is also possible that the unit will ultimately be sold.

In six years U.S. Steel has been transformed from the largest American steel company, dominated by a manufacturing conception of control with a vertically integrated structure, to a finance-oriented, multidivisional, diversified energy, chemical, and natural resource company. This shift was undertaken by the board of directors and CEO as a self-conscious response to the decline of steel, the firm's basic industry. The original U.S. Steel merger in 1901 marked the new era of monopoly capitalism. U.S. Steel's finance strategies may now cause the firm to abandon its once primary industry. The corporation endures but its identity and product lines have been altered drastically by the implementation of the finance conception of control.

8

Diversification in Large Firms

The interactions between managers and their firms, the state, and the organizational fields in which firms are embedded, are complex. A given element may cause an effect at one time, and at another time, may be transformed by that effect. For instance, sales and marketing presidents were more likely to shift their firms to the multidivisional form in the 1930s. But in the 1940s firms that had the multidivisional form were more likely to select a sales and marketing president. In the first instance, an executive with a certain conception of the firm has the power to enforce that view. Once it is established as a social structure, the multidivisional form continues to be a source of power for certain types of executives and not others.

Similarly, organizational fields can at one moment suppress change and at another promote it. If executives in a group of firms control an organizational field and define what appropriate behavior is in that field, then other executives will conform. When executives in a leading firm alter their conception of control or a new firm enters the field with a different conception of control, the rules shift as the power base shifts, and executives in other firms will follow the new example. Again, understanding the causal forces at work depends on when and where one enters the process.

The way that the finance conception of the firm superseded both the sales and marketing and manufacturing reflects a number of these complex processes. In the postwar era finance executives were successful in pursuing merger strategies for growth. But their ability to do so depended on the existence of an already diversified and divisional corporation. It also depended on an antitrust policy that suppressed the manufacturing and the sales and marketing conceptions. The success of the finance conception for growth and the constraints on other conceptions of growth enabled finance-oriented executives to make claims on the leadership of the large corporations. In the end, large corporations tended to be led by executives who were not tied to any one industry or product. Finance presidents or generalists led the large corporations in the 1980s.

The organizational fields of the largest firms were altered by the conception of control in two interrelated ways. Firms were no longer defined in terms of their major line of business and, since so many firms were operating in so many businesses, the identities of firms changed. Power in firms shifted toward those executives who could manage diversification, which reinforced the change in outlook. Firms that did not diversify were likely to be merger targets of those that did. To protect themselves from takeover, single-product firms had to adopt the finance conception of control and diversify, and take on debt. This development redefined the organizational fields of the largest firms. The finance conception was adopted by managers in order to remain successful and independent.

The finance conception of control continues to dominate the world of the large firms today. The short-run performance of the largest firms measures it efficacy. In multidivisional firms, the return on investment of each division is important because it is an indication of how profitable the firm is. The single most important goal of modern corporate life is keeping the stock price above the book value of the firm. If the stock price falls substantially below the book value, the assets are undervalued and the firm is in danger of being merged. Increasing the profitability of the divisions is one way to increase the stock price. Other financial tactics to prevent being bought out include the repurchase of stock by the company and taking on debt in order to reduce the firm's takeover value. While these two tactics do not significantly improve the ability of the firm to produce goods, they have the general effect of raising stock prices and keeping existing management in power.

The organizational fields of the largest firms have expanded as well. Other large firms, corporate raiders, and the financial community in general are watching their actions. If the executives in charge fail to keep short-run profits and the stock price high, the large corporation may find itself the victim of a buyout. The pressures to continue finance strategies are thus generated both internally by the structure of the organization and externally by the constant monitoring of the organization by other large firms (potential purchasers), the stock market, and the financial sector. This external community is now part of the organizational field of the largest firms.

The Spread of Diversification Strategies

Three major data sets have systematically documented long-run shifts in the product mix of large firms: the data I collected for this study, Gort's (see Chapter 4), and Rumelt's (see Appendixes C and D; Gort, 1962; Rumelt, 1974).

Table 8.1 presents the distribution of diversification strategies of the 100 largest firms at ten-year intervals from 1939 to 1979. A dominant product strategy implied that the firm produced 70 percent or more of its output in a single major industry. One example is a typical steel company. Product-related strategies mean that firms produce in multiple industries that bear some functional relation to one another and no single industry accounts for more than 70 percent of production. An example is a chemical company like DuPont, which produced paint, gun powder, and fertilizers. The final category is labeled product unrelated. In this case, firms produce in multiple industries that bear no functional relation to one another and no single industry accounts for more than 70 percent of the firm's activities. In Appendix C I describe the details of coding.

The measures of diversification mark the product mix of the corporation at a given point in time. This product mix is the result of management's self-conscious policy to create a particular kind of organization. Once in place, a strategy guides the organization's behavior. A decision to alter the product mix reflects a new conception of what the firm ought to be producing.

Table 8.1 Shifts in corporate strategy of the largest corporations (in percentages)

Strategy	1939 (N = 99)	1948 (N = 99)	1959 (N = 99)	1969 (N = 99)	1979 (N = 99)
Dominant	77.8	59.6	37.6	26.0	23.2
Related	22.2	38.4	57.4	54.0	49.5
Unrelated	0.0	2.0	5.0	20.0	27.3

The relationship between the conceptions of control and these strategic actions is important to consider. The sales and marketing conception uses diversification as a way to ensure firm survival by constantly adding new and growing product lines. The natural path for diversification is into products that are related to the main one and the way to diversify is internally. The finance conception treats diversification as a hedge against product cycle swings and as a way to spread risk. The direction of diversification is less important from this perspective but most often occurs through merger or acquisition.

Table 8.1 shows the dramatic reduction in number among the 100 largest firms that operated primarily in one industry. In 1939, 77.8 percent of the firms were classified as product dominant and none of the firms pursued a product-unrelated strategy. By 1948 product-dominant strategies were pursued by only 59.2 percent of the firms and 34.1 percent were in the product-related category. This shift continued and by 1959 firms with a product-related strategy dominated the list of the 100 largest corporations. The major fact to note about this period is that diversification was occurring rapidly in the largest firms before 1950, but clearly accelerated after 1950. From 1959 to 1979 the most rapid growth was in firms with a product-unrelated strategy. By 1979 these firms formed the second largest group on the list. The share of firms with a product-related strategy declined somewhat in that period.

Interpreting these results could be problematic because the table contains only a snapshot of the firms on the list of the 100 largest corporations at each time point. It ignores the issue of whether firms actually shifted their strategies over the decade or whether new firms with new strategies were added to the list. It is important to explore this issue by considering Table 8.2. Data are presented that show whether firms altered their strategies from the beginning to the end of the decade, which is indicated by whether firms stay on the list, enter the list, or exit the list. The percentages show the proportion of firms that had the same strategy at the beginning and the end of the decade. For example, 76.7 percent of the firms that had a product-dominant strategy in 1939 had a product-dominant strategy in 1948. The table should be interpreted somewhat cautiously because the number of cases is small.

Overall, in the period 1939–1948, about 25 percent of the firms changed their strategies. Most of the shifts were from product-dominant to product-related strategies. Those firms that entered the list all had a product-dominant strategy at the beginning of the decade; 30.8 percent of them shifted to a product-related strategy by the end of the period. Of those firms that left the list, most were product dominant and few shifted strategies. One can conclude that diversification was occurring rapidly among the largest firms and mostly among the fast-growing ones, that is, firms that were entering the list. These rapidly growing firms were a role model as well as a threat to the rest of the large firms.

Between 1948 and 1959 almost one-third of the firms with a dominant strategy shift to a product-related strategy. Those firms who stayed on the list tended to shift to a product-related strategy. Those firms that were new to the list were rapid diversifiers to both product-related and -unrelated strategies. One can see quite clearly the rise of the acquisitive conglomerates and the success of the finance conception of control. Again, those who left the list tended to remain with the dominant strategy and not engage in diversification. The 100 largest firms at the end of the decade were either becoming diversified or already diversified. This is evidence that in order to remain in the population of the largest firms, one needed to be diversified.

During the period 1959–1969, the high point of the merger movement, a new pattern began to emerge. A large portion of those firms that stayed on the list, which began the decade with a product-dominant strategy, ended the decade with that same strategy. This pattern was even more pronounced in the 1969–1979 period. These firms tended to be in the metal making and petroleum industries where diversification strategies were never fully implemented. From 1959 to 1969 the firms new to the list that started out as product-dominant firms rapidly diversified. Most of the new firms, however, were already pursuing diversification strategies. Those who left the list were mostly product-related firms.

The last decade shows the least amount of change. Less than 10 percent of the firms altered their strategies, which suggests that by 1979 most firms had already changed course. The diversification phenomenon was so widespread that few firms were left to diversify. It is interesting that the rapidly growing firms continued to be highly diversified. Yet the 1970s were not years of high growth for

Table 8.2 Changes in strategy by decade, by firm status, for the 100 largest firms (in percentages)

1939–1948

Strategy at end of decade	Total			Stayers			Comers			Leavers		
	Dom. (N=90)	Rel. (N=22)	Unrel. (N=0)	Dom. (N=68)	Rel. (N=17)	Unrel. (N=0)	Dom. (N=13)	Rel. (N=0)	Unrel. (N=0)	Dom. (N=10)	Rel. (N=4)	Unrel. (N=0)
Dominant	76.7	9.1	—	75.0	5.9	—	69.2	—	—	100.0	20.0	—
Related	22.3	86.4	—	23.5	88.8	—	30.8	—	—	0.0	80.0	—
Unrelated	1.1	4.5	—	1.5	5.9	—	0.0	—	—	0.0	0.0	—

1948–1959

Strategy at end of decade	Total			Stayers			Comers			Leavers		
	Dom. (N=73)	Rel. (N=40)	Unrel. (N=3)	Dom. (N=48)	Rel. (N=46)	Unrel. (N=1)	Dom. (N=12)	Rel. (N=5)	Unrel. (N=1)	Dom. (N=13)	Rel. (N=7)	Unrel. (N=1)
Dominant	65.8	0.0	0.0	62.5	0.0	0.0	58.3	0.0	0.0	84.6	0.0	0.0
Related	32.9	92.5	0.0	37.5	100.0	0.0	41.7	60.0	0.0	7.1	85.7	0.0
Unrelated	1.4	7.5	100.0	0.0	0.0	100.0	0.0	40.0	100.0	7.1	14.3	100.0

Table 8.2 (continued)

1959–1969

Strategy at end of decade	Total Dom. (N=41)	Total Rel. (N=63)	Total Unrel. (N=11)	Stayers Dom. (N=27)	Stayers Rel. (N=45)	Stayers Unrel. (N=5)	Comers Dom. (N=8)	Comers Rel. (N=8)	Comers Unrel. (N=6)	Leavers Dom. (N=6)	Leavers Rel. (N=10)	Leavers Unrel. (N=0)
Dominant	63.4	6.3	0.0	70.4	6.7	0.0	37.5	12.5	0.0	66.7	0.0	—
Related	29.3	84.1	0.0	25.9	86.7	0.0	37.5	75.0	0.0	33.3	80.0	—
Unrelated	7.3	9.5	100.0	3.7	6.7	100.0	25.0	12.5	100.0	0.0	20.0	—

1969–1979

Strategy at end of decade	Total Dom. (N=28)	Total Rel. (N=63)	Total Unrel. (N=32)	Stayers Dom. (N=21)	Stayers Rel. (N=47)	Stayers Unrel. (N=11)	Comers Dom. (N=3)	Comers Rel. (N=11)	Comers Unrel. (N=4)	Leavers Dom. (N=4)	Leavers Rel. (N=5)	Leavers Unrel. (N=9)
Dominant	89.3	0.0	0.0	90.5	0.0	0.0	66.7	0.0	0.0	100.0	0.0	0.0
Related	7.1	87.3	4.2	9.5	87.2	0.0	0.0	81.8	25.0	0.0	100.0	0.0
Unrelated	3.6	12.7	95.8	0.0	12.8	100.0	33.3	18.2	75.0	0.0	0.0	100.0

the most diversified firms. One can see the failure of a number of the large conglomerates as half of the firms that left the list had a product-unrelated strategy.

Generally, firms that stayed and those that entered the list were the most likely to shift their product mix during the period, while those that left the list were less likely to do so. In the earlier periods, the example of firms that had achieved rapid growth through diversification probably provided some impetus for diversification. After 1948 the product-unrelated firms, that is, the conglomerates, increased spectacularly and their financial tactics spread across the population of the largest firms. Most of the shifts in strategy were from product-dominant strategies to product-related strategies, although a fair number of firms shifted from product-related to product-unrelated strategies. Very few firms that had a diversified strategy shifted back to a nondiversified product mix. By the 1970s shifts in strategy slowed greatly and firms fixed their identities as dominant, related, or unrelated.

Diversification in the largest firms was already in progress by 1939. It continued throughout the 1940s and expanded most rapidly between 1949 and 1969. It is clear from these patterns that firms that chose not to diversify were less likely to grow. The most successful overall strategy for growth was the product-related strategy. In the last decade the unrelated firms left the list at a higher rate than product-related firms. The divestiture movement of the 1970s reflected the awareness of managers that firms built on the merger of unrelated firms were not likely to remain viable. Firms that pursued strategies of growth into products related to their main line of business were most successful at staying on the list of the largest firms. The sales and marketing conception of control is evident in the early periods when managers in the largest firms began to diversify into related fields. Then the finance conception began to gain momentum around 1950 and was strong by 1959. It continued to spread during the 1960s.

I have argued that much of this diversification came about through the use of mergers. Table 8.3 presents the percentage of firms by decade that engaged in the different types of mergers. The data are coded so that firms that participated in more than one type of merger are counted multiple times. The sum of the percentages in the table, therefore, is not 100. The data come from the FTC and refer only to mergers involving assets greater than

Table 8.3 Merger types for entire sample (in percentages)

Type of merger	1939–1948 (N=112)	1948–1959 (N=116)	1959–1969 (N=123)	1969–1979 (N=118)
Horizontal	41.1	17.2	18.7	10.2
Vertical	23.2	15.5	21.1	4.2
Related	10.7	24.1	35.8	24.6
Unrelated	0.0	3.4	22.0	18.6

	1939–1948			1948–1959			1959–1969			1969–1979		
Type of merger	Dom. (N=90)	Rel. (N=22)	Unrel. (N=0)	Dom. (N=73)	Rel. (N=40)	Unrel. (N=3)	Dom. (N=46)	Rel. (N=66)	Unrel. (N=11)	Dom. (N=29)	Rel. (N=65)	Unrel. (N=24)
Horizontal	42.2	36.4	—	21.9	10.0	0.0	19.6	16.7	27.3	17.2	4.6	16.7
Vertical	26.7	9.1	—	13.7	17.5	33.3	13.0	24.2	36.4	6.9	3.1	4.2
Related	10.0	13.6	—	17.8	32.5	66.7	19.6	45.5	45.5	0.0	29.2	41.7
Unrelated	0.0	0.0	—	1.4	1.7	33.3	13.0	22.7	54.5	0.0	21.5	33.3

$10 million and, therefore, the table understates the amount of merger activity.

In the earliest period horizontal and vertical mergers dominate. Over 41 percent of the largest firms executed horizontal mergers during the decade, while 23.2 percent engaged in vertical mergers. Only 10.7 percent of the firms were involved in mergers for diversification. The number of firms that executed vertical or horizontal mergers declined significantly in the 1948–1959 decade, while product-related mergers increased greatly. The increase in diversification strategies and the effects of the Celler-Kefauver Act are quite evident here.

The 1959–1969 period includes the high point of the postwar merger movement. Product-related and -unrelated mergers are the two largest categories. Almost 36 percent of the largest firms executed product-related mergers during the decade and 22 percent executed product-unrelated mergers. Even given the decline in merger activity in the 1959–1979 period, these two categories were the areas of most merger activity for the largest firms.

Overall, merger activity was high during the 1940s, low during the 1950s, high again during the 1960s, and relatively low during the 1970s. The character of mergers for the largest firms changed dramatically. After 1950 the largest firms were much more likely to engage in product-related and -unrelated mergers than before that year when they were more inclined toward horizontal or vertical mergers. Given that a substantial amount of diversification occurred before 1948, it must have been achieved internally and not through mergers. This conclusion is consistent with the view that the sales and marketing conception of control was concerned with product mix, but changed that mix by relying on internal diversification.

Table 8.3 also presents data on the percentage of firms with a particular product mix that executed each type of merger. One would expect that firms with product-dominant strategies would tend to execute vertical and horizontal mergers. Firms with product-related strategies would tend toward related mergers and firms with unrelated strategies would engage in product-related and unrelated mergers. Firms with product unrelated strategies should be most likely to engage in any merger activity.

Generally, these assertions are true. Firms with product-dominant strategies tended toward horizontal and vertical mergers, but after 1948 were less likely to engage in merger activity at all. The highest levels of merger activity occurred among firms with product-unrelated strategies, that is, conglomerates, followed by firms with product-related strategies. Firms with unrelated strategies executed both related and unrelated mergers. Interestingly, firms with product-related strategies merged with related firms. From 1948–1959, 32.5 percent of the largest firms with product-related strategies engaged in product-related mergers and only 1.7 percent of them engaged in unrelated mergers. These results support the contention that diversifying firms grew by acquisition, which was dictated by careful strategizing.

Let us consider the relationship between product mix, merger type, and industry in the postwar era. Table 8.4 presents the diversification strategy by major industry at each time point. For our purposes here, industries are synonymous with organizational fields. Hence, in industries where the manufacturing conception of control dominated, such as metalmaking, mining, and petroleum, one would expect less diversification and mergers. In industries dominated by the sales and marketing conception, such as machinery and chemicals, one would expect more diversification. As the finance conception of control began to break down the organizational fields of the large firms and create a field containing all of the large firms, one would expect some convergence in diversification and mergers.

In 1939 the metalmaking, mining, and petroleum industries were the least diversified. Firms in these industries tended toward vertical integration and away from diversification. The machine-making industry was the most diversified industry and was followed by the miscellaneous group and the chemical industry. In 1948 the food and chemical industries had substantially diversified into product-related industries. The transportation equipment industry was beginning to diversify as well. Metalmaking and mining began to show some diversification, mostly into other metal or mining industries. The petroleum industry remained the least diversified industry.

Rapid diversification came to all industries between 1948 and 1969. The food, chemical, and machine-making industries were all highly diversified by 1959 and many had shifted into unrelated fields. The metalmaking, mining, and transportation industries were all moderately diversified. The one major industry that had

Table 8.4 Strategies by major industry for the 100 largest corporations (in percentages)

Industry	1939			1948			1959			1969		
	Dom.	Rel.	Unrel.	Dom.	Rel.	Unrel.	Dom.	Rel.	Unrel.	Dom.	Rel.	Unrel.
Metal and mining	90.9	9.1	0.0	75.6	24.4	0.0	50.0	38.9	11.1	34.5	50.0	15.5
Petroleum	100.0	0.0	0.0	95.0	5.0	0.0	72.7	27.3	0.0	35.0	60.0	5.0
Food	81.3	18.8	0.0	50.0	50.0	0.0	11.1	88.9	0.0	25.0	50.0	25.0
Chemicals	75.0	25.0	0.0	45.5	54.5	0.0	0.0	86.7	13.3	6.3	81.3	12.5
Machines	40.0	60.0	0.0	25.0	75.0	0.0	0.0	87.5	12.5	0.0	25.0	75.0
Transportation	87.5	12.5	0.0	70.0	20.0	10.0	54.5	18.2	27.3	33.3	41.7	25.0
Miscellaneous	67.3	32.7	0.0	60.0	36.0	4.0	35.0	57.5	7.5	22.7	50.0	27.3

not diversified was the petroleum industry. But by 1969 it had diversified, mainly into petrochemicals. Hence, over the thirty-year period, all of the major industries reached high levels of diversification. These results meet my theoretical expectations and provide evidence that the largest firms began to converge in their product mix strategies during this time. They also indicate that the organizational fields of the largest firms began to be defined in terms of all of the largest firms.

Table 8.5 presents merger data by industry. One would expect that the machine-making, chemical, and food industries would lead the way with product-related and unrelated mergers, while the petroleum, metal, and mining industries would stick to horizontal and vertical mergers. Over time, however, one would expect that firms in all industries would shift away from horizontal and vertical mergers and toward diversified mergers. Generally, the results confirm this view. The firms in the more diversified industries tended toward higher levels of mergers, especially for diversification. The rapid diversification of the petroleum industry between 1959 and 1969 was a function of mergers into product related categories. Indeed, diversification through merger was the major strategy in the postwar era. The miscellaneous category, which contains the purely acquisitive conglomerates, shows a high level of mergers particularly in the related and unrelated categories. In the last two decades most of the mergers were in the product-related and unrelated categories for all industries.

Gort's study ended in 1954, but overlapped my study to a large extent. It was based on three samples: (1) data on industry aggregates from published census materials, (2) a special tabulation from the 1954 Census of Manufacturing, and (3) a data set collected on the product lines of 111 large industrial firms from 1929 to 1954 (Gort, 1961, pp. 14–15). On the basis of this research Gort drew conclusions about the sources and industrial location of diversification.

First, diversification was significant in the 1930s, lower in the 1940s, and highest in the early 1950s. Second, firms in technologically sophisticated industries were the leaders in diversification. In particular, firms in the chemical, machine-making, transportation, and food industries were most likely to diversify (Gort, 1961, ch. 3). Gort found that petroleum and metalmaking firms were the

Table 8.5 Percentage of firms with different merger types (by major industries)

Merger types	Metal and mining	Petroleum	Food	Chemical	Machines	Transportation	Miscellaneous
				1939–1948			
Horizontal	45.2	55.6	43.8	66.7	20.0	0.0	25.0
Vertical	26.8	38.9	.3	41.7	20.0	12.5	16.7
Related	16.7	0.0	12.5	16.7	0.0	37.5	12.5
Unrelated	0.0	0.0	0.0	0.0	0.0	0.0	0.0
				1948–1959			
Horizontal	18.2	42.9	6.7	0.0	0.0	18.2	11.5
Vertical	24.2	14.3	13.3	27.3	25.0	0.0	7.7
Related	18.2	0.0	26.7	63.6	75.0	45.5	19.2
Unrelated	3.0	0.0	0.0	9.1	25.0	9.1	3.8
				1959–1969			
Horizontal	15.0	59.1	0.0	4.3	0.0	8.3	10.5
Vertical	22.5	22.7	11.1	33.3	12.5	16.7	15.8
Related	8.3	31.8	22.2	46.7	37.5	31.6	45.0
Unrelated	8.3	4.5	33.3	20.0	37.5	20.0	42.1
				1969–1979			
Horizontal	11.1	20.0	25.0	11.8	0.0	0.0	0.0
Vertical	5.6	5.0	12.5	5.9	0.0	0.0	0.0
Related	19.4	20.0	37.5	35.3	25.0	16.7	26.1
Unrelated	13.9	15.0	37.5	23.5	0.0	17.4	25.0

least likely to diversify before 1954. These results are consistent with those I have just presented.

Gort argued that after 1950 the pace of diversification increased rapidly. Indeed, the 111 firms in his sample added as many products between 1950 and 1954 as they had during the entire 1939–1950 period. Firms were diversifying most rapidly into products related to their major lines. Gort found that most firms that expanded into related product lines were in high-technology industries with high levels of concentration and low levels of growth. These firms appeared to be searching for new markets in which to grow and chose those with related technologies (1961, pp. 74–78).

These results suggest two important comparisons. First, Gort's data support my data on which industries were diversifying most rapidly up to 1954. Second, they support my argument that the original impetus to diversification was the sales and marketing conception of growth. Firms that diversified tended to enter related lines to find new opportunities for growth. Until the 1950s this was the dominant strategy of diversification (see Appendix D).

Rumelt's results are based on a sample of the 500 largest firms at three points in time: 1949, 1959, and 1969 (1974, pp. 40–43). The final sample continued 246 firms and data were collected for all firms at each time. Rumelt's measure of diversification was similar to mine. Because his data reflected the experiences of the 500 largest firms and mine the 100 largest, it is instructive to compare the two.

Rumelt found that in 1949 his sample was 69.9 percent product dominant, 26.7 percent product related, and 3.4 percent product unrelated (1974, p. 51). In Table 8.1 one can see that my sample included fewer product-dominant firms. In 1969 Rumelt reported that 35.4 percent of his sample was in the product-dominant category, 45.2 percent in the product-related category, and 19.4 percent in the product-unrelated category. Among the 100 largest firms fewer were in the product-dominant category and more were in the related category, again reflecting the sample differences. In all, however, the two samples seem quite comparable. Rumelt concluded that diversified firms moved mainly from product-dominant to product-related categories and from product-related to product-unrelated categories (1974, pp. 55–60). These results confirm mine (see Table 8.2).

The Causes of Diversification

Two major factors were involved in the diversification decision: the role of key managers and the actions of other firms in similar industries. I have argued that executives with a sales and marketing or finance background would be more likely to shift their firms toward related- or unrelated-product mixes than executives with a manufacturing or other type of background. This is because those conceptions of control stressed growth by any means, including diversification.

I have also argued that firms watch one another before deciding on a course of action. In this case, if other firms in an industry began to diversify, and the tactic proved successful, the balance of power in a stable organizational field would be upset. Therefore, in order to keep up with other firms, managers would probably diversify. The age and size of the organization could also be important causes of diversification.

A sales and marketing president made a firm more likely to shift to a product-related strategy between 1919 and 1939 (see Table D.4). From then on, the variable had no effect. But the percentage of firms in an industry with a product-related strategy positively affected the switch to such a strategy. In other words, the first firms to diversify were led by sales and marketing executives. But once their example was set, diversification became an accepted way to grow. Similar results appear for the presence of finance presidents. In the postwar era a finance president influenced the switch to an unrelated product mix, but not to a product-related strategy. Also, firms in industries with unrelated strategies tended to pursue these tactics. This evidence shows the importance of key executives with a certain point of view and how they were able to change the course of their organizations.

A major impetus to this growth in diversification was the antitrust attitude of the government. But equally important were the financial manipulations of the conglomerators who pioneered diversification into unrelated product lines and as a result built firms that experienced spectacular growth. In the antitrust environment of the 1960s, many of the large firms participated in the rush to diversify by merging. The finance conception of control used by the founders of the conglomerates spread across firms and industries. By 1969 most of the largest firms were highly diversified and the economic landscape of corporate America was changed permanently. The following decade was more stable because most firms that were going to adopt new strategies had done so. The largest firms were generally those that had successfully blended related products from multiple mergers.

The Spread of the Multidivisional Form

The role of the multidivisional form in the management of the large modern corporation cannot be underestimated. The decentralized structure made it possible for firms to grow into diverse product lines. Table 8.6 presents a cross-tabulation of product mix by structure at decade intervals from 1939 to 1969. In 1939 only 3.3 percent of the ninety-one firms with a product-dominant strategy had a multidivisional form, while 27.3 percent of the firms with a product-related strategy had that structure. The decision to diversify was generally made first and independently of the ability to reorganize the firm.

The multidivisional form spread from 1949 to 1969 and became the predominant way to organize the diversified enterprise. Firms that were not diversified retained their functional structures. This began to change, however. In the last two periods a majority of even the product-dominant firms had switched to the multidivisional form. The decentralized structure became the conventional way to organize the large firm. Hence, managers felt compelled to divide their firms into divisions whether or not it was necessary.

Appendix D contains a discussion of the causes of the spread of the multidivisional form (see Table D.6). The early adopters of the multidivisional form were older, larger firms with a product-related strategy and were led by either sales and marketing or finance presidents. A product-related strategy meant that firms were having difficulties managing diverse product lines and found it advantageous to switch to the divisional form. The most provocative factor was the presence of a sales and marketing or finance president. In striving to diversify the firm, these executives realized that they needed a new structure. Hence, their leadership implied that a firm was more likely to switch to the multidivisional form.

In the postwar era the presence of a finance president continued

Table 8.6 Cross-tabulation of strategy and structure, 1939–1969

	1939			1948			1959			1969		
	Dom. (N=91)	Rel. (N=22)	Unrel. (N=0)	Dom. (N=74)	Rel. (N=40)	Unrel. (N=3)	Dom. (N=48)	Rel. (N=64)	Unrel. (N=11)	Dom. (N=28)	Rel. (N=67)	Unrel. (N=24)
No MDF	96.7	72.7	—	97.3	50.0	33.3	72.9	37.5	36.4	46.4	19.4	20.8
MDF	3.3	27.3	—	2.7	50.0	66.7	27.1	62.5	63.6	53.6	80.6	79.2

Notes: Variables are defined in Appendix C.
Dom. = product dominant, Rel. = product related, Unrel. = product unrelated, MDF = multidivisional form.
1939: $\chi^2 = 10.81$, 1 d.f., $p < .001$; 1948: $\chi^2 = 18.95$, 2 d.f., $p < .001$; 1959: $\chi^2 = 14.84$, 2 d.f., $p < .001$; 1969: $\chi^2 = 7.91$, 2 d.f., $p < .02$.

to prompt this switch. A product-unrelated strategy and the use of mergers for growth were also related to the implementation of the multidivisional form in firms without finance executives. The last of the significant postwar factors is the mimetic pressure applied by firms in similar organizational fields. As the competition shifted to the multidivisional form, a firm was more likely to shift. The multidivisional form became the accepted organizational structure in the postwar era, even among firms that were still classified as product dominant.

Changes in the Identity of the Largest Firms

Table 8.7 presents the names of firms who entered and exited the list each decade from 1939 to 1979. The 1959–1969 decade was the period of greatest change as twenty-five firms entered and exited the list. In the 1948–1959 and 1969–1979 decades twenty firms moved. The 1939–1948 decade was the period of least turnover.

The 1939–1948 period included the entrance of firms that were mainly in the chemical industries (American Cyanamid, American Viscose, Celanese Corporation, Dow Chemical, Monsanto). Chemical companies embodied the sales and marketing conception of control by engaging in internal diversification of products. There were also firms engaged in motion picture, oil, and cloth production. Those who exited the list were predominantly mining and metal manufacturers (Crucible Steel, Climax Molybdenum, Glen Alden Coal, Koppers) and large-scale retailers (Macy's and Marshall Field's). In the first decade after World War II the entrants to the list of largest firms were concentrated in defense industries (Boeing, Douglas, General Dynamics, United Aircraft, Lockheed), diversified high-technology producers (Sperry Rand, General Telephone and Electric, Borg-Warner), conglomerates (W. R. Grace, ITT), and oil (Sun Oil, Cities Services, Richfield Oil). Those who left the list were a mixed group of manufacturers, including firms engaged in publishing and movie making. The motion picture companies generally ceased to grow as television replaced movies. They were also forced to divest their movie theater chains in a series of antitrust decisions in the late 1940s thereby reducing their control over the industry.

The 1959–1969 period included the rise of conglomerates

Table 8.7 Shift in identities of the 100 largest firms

	1939–1948		1948–1959
Enter	**Exit**	**Enter**	**Exit**
Allied Stores	American Sugar	Boeing	Allied Stores
American Cyanamid	Climax Molybdenum	Borg-Warner	American Car and Foundry Industries
American Viscose	Corn Products	Caterpillar	American Standard
Burlington Industries	Crane	Cities Service	American Viscose
Celanese Corp.	Crucible Steel	Corn Products	Borden
Dow Chemical	Marshall Field's	Douglas Aircraft	Coca-Cola
May Department Stores	General American Transportation	General Dynamics	Consolidated Coal
Monsanto	Gimbel's	General Telephone and Electric	Hearst Publications
National Distillers	Glen Alden Coal	Grace, W. R.	International Nickel
Owens-Illinois	International Shoe	International Telephone and Telegraph	S. S. Kresge
Paramount Pictures	Koppers	Kaiser Aluminum	Loew's
Skelly Oil	R. H. Macy's	Kaiser Steel	National Biscuit
Standard Oil (Ohio)	United Shoe Machinery	Lockheed	National Lead
Twentieth Century Fox	Wilson	Olin-Mathieson Chemical	Paramount Pictures
		Reynolds Metal	Pullman
		Richfield Oil	Skelly Oil
		Safeway	J. P. Stevens
		St. Regis Paper	Twentieth Century Fox
		Sperry Rand	United Fruit
		Sun Oil	Warner Brothers
		United Aircraft	Wheeling Steel

1959–1969	
Enter	**Exit**
American Standard	Allis Chalmers
Avco	American Cyanamid
Boise Cascade	Armour
Borden	Borg-Warner

Burroughs
Control Data
Federated Department Stores
Georgia-Pacific
Getty Oil
Gulf & Western
Honeywell
Illinois Central Industries
International Industries
Ling-Temco-Vought
Litton Industries
McDonnell Aircraft
Minnesota Mining and Manufacturing
Minnesota Ontario Paper
National Cash Register
Occidental Petroleum
Rapid American
Signal Co.
Tenneco
U.S. Plywood-Champion Papers
Xerox

Corn Products
Crown-Zellerbach
Douglas Aircraft
Great Atlantic & Pacific
Jones & Laughlin Steel
Kaiser Aluminum
Kaiser Steel
Kraftco
Liggett & Myers Tobacco
May Department Stores
National Distillers
Phelps Dodge
Pure Oil
Richfield Oil
St. Regis Paper
Schenley Industries
Seagram's
Sinclair Oil
Sunray Oil
Swift
Tidewater Oil

1969–1979

Enter	Exit
American Metal Climax	American Standard
Amerada Hess	Anaconda
American Cyanamid	Avco
Ashland Oil	Boise Cascade
Beatrice Foods	Borden
Coca-Cola	Burlington Industries
Dresser Industries	Burroughs
Johnson & Johnson	Celanese Corp.
S. S. Kresge	Control Data
J. Ray McDermott	General Dynamics
Merck	B. F. Goodrich
Phillip Morris	International Industries
Northwest Industries	Lockheed
Pepsico	Minnesota & Ontario Paper
Pfizer Chemical	Montgomery Wards
Rockwell International	Olin-Mathieson Chemical
Superior Oil	Rapid-American
Thomson-Ramo-Woolridge	Singer
Union Pacific	U.S. Rubber
Warner Lambert	Youngstown Steel

Note: Firms entered or exited sometime during the decade.

(Avco, Gulf and Western, Illinois Central Industries, International Industries, LTV, Litton Industries, 3M, Rapid American, and Tenneco) and the continued importance of diversified defense and high-technology firms (Burroughs, Control Data, Honeywell, McDonnell Aircraft, National Cash Register, and Xerox). Firms that left the list were usually old manufacturing firms in single industries such as steel and meat packing (Armour, Jones and Laughlin, Kaiser, Swift, and Phelps Dodge). The large number of oil firms that exited the list (Pure Oil, Richfield Oil, Sinclair Oil, Sunray Oil, Tidewater Oil) did so mainly through merger.

Firms that entered the list in the 1969–1979 period continued to be multiproduct firms (Coca-Cola, Johnson and Johnson, Merck, Pepsico, and Warner Lambert), conglomerates (Beatrice Foods, Dresser Industries, Union Pacific, Northwest Industries, Rockwell International, and TRW), and oil companies (Amerada Hess, Ashland Oil, J. Ray McDermott, and Superior Oil). The oil companies grew on the strength of oil prices. Those that left the list were conglomerates (Avco, Rapid-American, and International Industries), some high-technology firms whose growth had slowed (Burroughs, Control Data, and General Dynamics), and a variety of less diversified manufacturers (Boise Cascade, Minnesota and Ontario Paper, U.S. Rubber, and Youngstown Steel).

Aside from the oil industry, the major winners since World War II have been diversified defense, high-technology firms, consumer product firms, and conglomerates such as ITT, Gulf and Western, TRW, and Beatrice Foods. The losers have been firms in mining, metalmaking, movies, and single lines of manufacturing. Those firms that stayed on the list throughout the period, such as General Electric and Westinghouse, came to be multiproduct firms by engaging in diversification.

The Careers of Corporate Presidents

The experiences of executives are important in shaping their careers and the types of policies they implement. In this regard, I consider three issues: the educational background of the presidents, the moves they made between organizations during their careers, and the jobs they held in those organizations before they became presidents.

Table 8.8 presents data on the education of the presidents of the

Table 8.8 Educational backgrounds of presidents of the 100 largest firms (in percentages)

President's degree	1919		1929		1939		1948		1959		1969		1979	
	(1)[a]	(2)[b]	(1)	(2)	(1)	(2)	(1)	(2)	(1)	(2)	(1)	(2)	(1)	(2)
BA or less	66	98.7	71	98.6	76	100	72	97.2	69	92.2	67	81.4	69	77.5
Harvard MBA	0	0	0	0	0	0	1	1.4	5	6.5	10	12.6	13	14.6
Other MBA	1	1.3	1	1.4	0	0	1	1.4	1	1.3	5	6.0	7	7.8
Missing data	33		28		24		26		25		17		11	

Note: See Appendix B for discussion of sampling and data source.
a. In columns headed (1), percentages are calculated with missing data.
b. In columns headed (2), percentages are calculated without missing data.

100 largest corporations at ten-year intervals from 1919 to 1979. I use the term president but the data refer to presidents or CEOs. In the earlier periods there were no CEOs, just presidents and chairmen of boards of directors. Since World War II upper management functions became differentiated and many firms have had a chairman of the board, vice-chairman, CEO, and a president. In order to maintain some consistency I use the term to mean the person who was the executive in charge. In the later period, however, this was the CEO. My data were gathered from descriptions provided by presidents in *Who's Who in America* and *Who's Who in Business and Industry*. The first important fact to note is that substantial data on the education of presidents are missing. This limits the usefulness of the data, but the patterns across time are consistent and thus can suggest what the experiences of top executives were.

Generally, the vast majority of presidents do not have MBAs. In fact, before 1959 no more than two of the presidents of the 100 largest firms held such degrees. Since that time, however, the number of presidents with MBAs has rapidly increased. By 1979, 20 of the 100 largest corporations had presidents with MBAs. Of these, thirteen were from the Harvard Business School.

While this may not seem like many, the number is deceptively small. The Harvard Business School graduated about two hundred students a year before World War II and no more than three or four hundred each year after the war. My consideration of only the 100 largest industrial firms means that the graduates who went to work for other than Fortune 100 firms were not counted. Further, in any given period only a few executives hold the top office in these firms. Together, these facts suggest that the odds were slim that very many of these people would become president of one of the 100 largest corporations, yet thirteen of them did.

What accounts for this phenomenon? Business schools attract people who are obviously interested in becoming top managers and the best business schools select the most motivated candidates. These motivated individuals use their training and credentials to get into the largest firms. Contacts made in school also help to further one's career. Finally, many of the top business schools explicitly prepare students to assume roles as top leaders.

Table 8.9 presents data on the career moves of presidents. Data are missing but the table still suggests trends. One assumption

Table 8.9 Employment history of presidents of the 100 largest firms (in percentages)

President's employment history	1919		1929		1939		1948		1959		1969		1979	
	(1)[a]	(2)[b]	(1)	(2)	(1)	(2)	(1)	(2)	(1)	(2)	(1)	(2)	(1)	(2)
Worked for other firms	32	54.2	50	64.9	42	53.8	43	54.5	45	55.6	47	56.6	46	53.5
Worked for competitors	13	21.7	29	37.7	17	24.6	14	20.0	12	16.4	10	12.0	14	16.3
Worked for another 100 largest firm	5	8.5	16	20.8	10	13.0	10	13.0	6	7.5	14	16.9	26	30.2

a. In columns headed (1), percentages are calculated with missing data.
b. In columns headed (2), percentages are calculated without missing data.

about corporate presidents is that executives used to work their way up through one firm and now switch firms as a strategy to reach the top. In my data there is little evidence to support this view.

The top column of Table 8.9 shows the percentage of presidents who reported ever working for another firm. Except for 1929 the amount, excluding the missing data, was 50 to 55 percent. This implies that presidents of large firms have always had a fair amount of mobility. There do not appear to be any clear trends toward increased movement over time. The middle panel shows the percentage of presidents who actually worked for a competitor at some previous time. There was a slight decrease in this category over time. The way to the top for most presidents, therefore, was not by working for competitors.

The bottom panel of Table 8.9 presents data on the percentage of presidents who once worked for one of the other 100 largest firms. This percentage increased over time, which is the only evidence that presidents of large firms tend to move more now than in the past. Such an increase is probably the result of the homogenization of management strategies and practices over time. As the organizational fields of the largest firms expanded across industry boundaries, the search for an appropriate executive to lead the firm extended to executives from other industries. Sales and marketing and finance expertise are not industry specific skills, so CEOs were probably hired increasingly for their functional specialization rather than their industrial experience. This practice would also lead firms over time to resemble one another more closely because the executives they exchanged would have similar notions about what constituted appropriate firm behavior (DiMaggio and Powell, 1983, pp. 147–160).

Table 8.10 presents data on functional specialization of presidents (see Appendix C for information on coding and sources). Their backgrounds were coded by function to get a sense of how different subunits in the organization were important to the overall management over time. The large modern firm has evolved from a vertically integrated functional form to a highly diversified, multidivisional form. I have tried to explicate this transformation by understanding how forces within organizations, their environment, and their interactions with the government have changed. It follows that those who control large firms have

Table 8.10   Backgrounds of presidents of the 100 largest firms
(in percentages)

President's background	1919	1929	1939	1948	1959	1969	1979
Manufacturing	26	36	34	29	30	26	22
Sales	6	9	16	26	24	19	16
Finance	8	8	7	13	13	20	31
General	7	6	6	8	11	12	17
Entrepreneur	27	19	17	9	8	6	4
Lawyer	14	11	12	7	12	10	7
Missing data	12	11	8	8	2	7	3

also changed. The bases for these shifts are two-fold: authority and ownership.

Early in the century many of the largest firms were run by their founders. They ran their firms with iron fists and controlled by virtue of their ownership. As power in large firms shifted to managers, control meant commanding enough authority to direct the organization. The basis for this authority was expertise in understanding the internal problems of the organization, the external constraints, and the implications of the actions of the state. Individuals from various functional specializations could rise to power by making claims on authority given new shifts in the environment.

The types of expertise are relatively easy to catalog. One is based on knowledge of the production process, that is, a manufacturing background. Sales and marketing became a source of expertise as large firms discovered the need to market their products in order to continue to grow. This involved paying attention to the product cycle, differentiating products from competitors', and growing into new markets, both national and multinational. A finance background was another form of expertise. Those who could evaluate the growth prospects of the firm by analyzing financial data on disparate product lines began to control the firm. Recently, more people with experience in different functional units have become chief executives. They claim to be generalists with knowledge of many of the firm's operations. Finally, those with a law background can help the firm in its dealing with the government.

The success of certain executives to achieve positive results for their organizations led to a succession of functional specializations in leadership roles. Manufacturing presidents rose as firms vertically integrated and tried to form oligopolies. Sales and marketing executives rose as they aided their firms growth during the Depression and the early postwar era. Finance executives organized the spectacular growth of the conglomerates. Their counterparts claimed control of other firms. Basically, my theoretical assertions are confirmed in Table 8.10.

While the patterns of who led the large modern corporation conform to my theoretical expectations, it is important to model how certain factors favored these executives. Choosing a top leader for an organization is an important political decision. It reflects who is in control of the organization and the bases for that control. When a leader is chosen it is a chance to observe whether there is continuity in the control of the organization or whether new forces are gathering to alter its direction by recognizing new internal or external circumstances.

A model of control in the corporation must focus on the role of internal and external conditions. Internally, the product mix and structure of a firm would favor one set of actors over another. More specifically, a functional structure and product-dominant strategy would favor manufacturing personnel. A multidivisional structure would favor sales and marketing and finance presidents. A related-product mix would favor sales and marketing presidents and an unrelated-product mix or merger strategy would favor finance presidents. Externally, the types of presidents who have come to dominate the firms of competitors provide a model for other firms because of pressures to conform.

One would also expect different industries to favor different types of presidents. Steel making and petroleum should favor manufacturing presidents, while food, chemical, machines, transport, and miscellaneous industries will favor sales and marketing and finance presidents. As the strategies and structures of firms shift toward diversification and decentralization, the power of manufacturing executives will decrease and the power of sales and marketing and finance presidents will increase. Appendix D presents a model of the causes of who controls the corporations (see Table D.5).

Generally, the results of my study confirm this point of view.

Product-related strategies favor sales and marketing executives while product-unrelated and merger strategies favor finance executives. The multidivisional form selects sales and marketing and finance executives. The petroleum and metalmaking firms are dominated by manufacturing personnel and the miscellaneous industries tend toward sales and marketing and finance personnel. The organizational field also plays a significant role in the selection of a top executive. In fields where manufacturing executives dominate, a firm is more likely to choose such an executive. A similar pattern holds for sales and marketing and finance presidents. As firms have altered their strategies and structures in accordance with shifts in their fields, the basis for power in those organizations also shifted. Who controls the large firm is not just a question of ownership, but of structural position in the organization.

The Growth and Profitability of the Diversified Firm

The model of firm success proposed here can be summarized in the following way. The leaders of firms have developed, through trial and error, various conceptions of control. These conceptions of control imply different views of how to organize a corporation internally and in relation to its organizational field and the state. Indeed, they define an organizational field by specifying the rules by which interaction will be guided. When these conceptions have led to strategies that produce stable outcomes for firms, they and the organizational fields they help organize tend to get locked into place. The high-level executives in any firm owe their power to the success of these strategies and to upset them is to court individual and collective disaster. By definition, success implies that strategies produce stable growth and profits for the firm. Once such success appears, one would expect that other firms in the organizational field would adopt the innovative conception of control and implement its strategies. It also follows that for an organizational field dominated by a particular conception of control to be altered requires an enormous crisis or an invasion by outside firms.

In this section I will show that the sales and marketing and finance conceptions of control and their strategies of diversification and mergers initially provide growth for the firms that pioneered them. For innovators there was tremendous risk. If they were successful, they could gain great advantage; if they failed, they could face going out of business. One would expect first movers to new conceptions of control to benefit greatly and those who followed to benefit less as everyone would operate with a similar conception. Certain conceptions and strategies could also succeed under one set of conditions and fail under another. For instance, the acquisitive conglomerates grew at high rates in the 1950s and 1960s, but underperformed in the 1970s.

The performance of strategies is not absolute, but relative to others'. A firm may earn a perfectly adequate level of profit and achieve some rate of growth in sales or assets, but still not perform as well as another firm operating with a different conception of control. It is this relative performance that is most important, especially for the large firms. If a firm is one of the largest, it needs to continue to grow in order to maintain its position. If its rate of growth falls behind the other large firms, its management risks losing that position.

From my perspective there are a number of hypotheses that can be framed concerning the causes of growth. The most obvious is that the growth of a firm will be tied to the growth of its main industry. As the assets of the industry increase, one would expect that a given firm would grow. The conception of control and the strategies it implies should strongly affect the performance of any given firm. One would expect that following the Depression and in the postwar era firms with a related and unrelated product mix at the beginning of the decade would perform better than firms with a single major product. Similarly, firms that were significantly vertically integrated would perform less well than firms that were not vertically integrated. As the product-related and -unrelated strategies spread, their effects on growth would lessen because the gains would be shared by all.

One would expect that mergers executed in the previous decade would contribute to overall growth. The reader should note that this is not a tautological definition of growth. The measure refers to the number of mergers in the past decade and the assumption is that those merged firms are sufficiently integrated into the company that they contribute to is overall growth. The last measure of strategy was the presence of substantial multinational activity at the beginning of the decade. Such a presence would affect growth by allowing firms to find new markets worldwide. One would expect this strategy to be most effective before World War II as it reflected a sales and marketing conception of control.

The early adopters of the multidivisional form should also experience growth. The form allowed firms to more easily manage various lines of business by decentralizing authority and one would expect that that would give firms a spurt of growth. As the form spread, however, one might expect its contribution to diminish as most of the firms would have reaped its benefits. The final variable included is the functional background of the president at the first time point. One might expect that the effect of sales and marketing and finance presidents might be more directly mediated through diversification strategies and the existence of the multidivisional form. But these presidents' conceptions of control imply more than just diversification. For instance, it is possible that they may be more oriented toward growth in that sales and marketing presidents would encourage advertising to increase growth, while finance presidents might implement financial controls that would allow the central office to solve problems more quickly.

The results of the analysis appear in Table D.2. Three dependent variables are considered: the change in assets, sales, and profits. All amounts are in 1967 dollars to correct for inflation and a weighted least squares technique was used to correct for heteroscedasticity. Details of the technique and model are in Appendix D.

The growth of assets in a firm's major industry was a consistent predictor of a firm's performance from 1939 to 1979. In every decade, if an industry grew, a firm in that industry experienced growth in sales, assets, and profits. The measures of strategy performed in interesting ways. If a firm was at all vertically integrated, it was less likely to grow in sales and assets from 1939 to 1969. In the 1939–1949 period, a vertically-integrated firm grew less in profits. The manufacturing conception of control that dictated the vertical integration of production failed to produce gains in sales, assets, or profits.

A product-related strategy produced growth in sales and profits relative to firms with a product-dominant strategy in every decade except 1969–1979. It was a less consistent cause of growth in assets. This confirms my view that product-related diversification was sales motivated and indeed helped the bottom line as well. The product-unrelated strategy, which reflected the finance conception of control, produced spectacular growth in sales and assets from 1948 to 1969, but actually caused a small decrease in growth from 1969 to 1979. The rise of the acquisitive conglomerate produced enormous growth rates and profits for two decades until the 1970s. Mergers in the 1960s were a consistent source of growth in assets and sales, but less so of profits. Finally, multinational activity did not substantially influence growth in any of the categories.

The multidivisional form produced growth in all three measures in the 1939–1948 period and growth in assets from 1948 to 1959. The form was then so sufficiently spread among the firms that it produced no advantages to the late adopters. There were only two decades in which the background of the president positively affected the performance of the firm: 1939–1948 and 1959–1969. Sales and marketing presidents helped their firms grow in assets and sales net of strategy and structure from 1939 to 1948 while finance presidents increased the assets of their firms during the merger movement of the 1960s.

The results of my analysis confirm the historical view discussed earlier. Diversification generally positively affected the growth of large firms. The product-unrelated strategy produced enormous growth from 1948 to 1969 and performed less well in the 1970s. The only measure of strategy that produced any growth in the 1970s was the level of previous mergers. Indeed, during those years a firm's strategies and structures had little effect on its performance reflecting the generally stagnant economic conditions. The multidivisional form aided the early adopters while maintaining vertical integration slowed growth.

The sales and marketing and finance conceptions of control and their strategies of diversification, divisionalization, advertising, financial controls, and mergers proved to be superior ways to achieve growth relative to the manufacturing conception of control and its strategies of vertical integration and producing in only one industry. The innovators of these new tactics gained the most. As the tactics spread, their effects diminished. This is clear evidence that the new conceptions of control provided more growth. Those who stayed with the old conceptions declined and were more likely to fall off the list of the largest firms.

It is important to compare my results with those of similar

studies. The first issue concerns the actual relationship between merger strategies and growth. In a recent study done for the FTC, Scherer and Ravenscraft (1984) utilized a data set that records the product lines of the 200 largest firms in 1950 and 1975. Their goal was to analyze whether or not diversification in those firms was achieved mainly through internal growth or through mergers.

Their findings are quite instructive. All of the firms had rapidly diversified over the period. Their major conclusion was that those firms that grew aggressively through diversification stayed on or entered the list. Those that did not diversify left the list or were merged. The most interesting calculation they performed concerned the means of diversification. Overall, only 14 percent of the new lines of business entered by new firms came from internal growth. Fully 86 percent were entered through mergers (Scherer and Ravenscraft, 1984, p. 13). This remarkable result confirms both my arguments and the implications of the tables in this chapter. Scherer and Ravenscraft conclude by saying that "much entrepreneurial activity in large U.S. corporations consists of bringing about diversified growth through the acquisition of other corporations, large and small" (1984, pp. 14–15).

Given that the largest firms grew primarily through mergers, it is of great interest to determine whether this activity was profitable. The evidence I provide suggests that mergers aided growth in assets and sales, but not in profits. There is substantial evidence from other studies that the diversification movement greatly increased the size of large firms in sales and assets.[1] The profit record of the large diversified acquisitive firm is, however, mostly negative. Most studies on the performance of conglomerates show that these firms do not outperform firms that are product dominant or product related. They show instead that, if anything, conglomerates underperform firms of a similar size with different strategies.[2] The most successful firms in terms of profitability appear to be those firms who engage in product-related strategies, although studies often find that firms with product-dominant strategies also perform well. These results would seem to contradict mine, but they can be rectified to some degree when one considers that most of such studies were done in the 1970s. My conclusions show that the major gains for the conglomerates were during the 1950s and 1960s, but during the 1970s they produced poor results.

These conclusions require some interpretation. Highly profitable firms with product-dominant strategies were often targets of mergers. These firms grew in one line of business and reached a certain size class (assets in the $10–50 million range). They tended to be profitable and well-run corporations that were subsequently swallowed up by larger more diversified firms. Those firms that remained in related businesses were better able to manage an array of smaller businesses.

The acquisitive conglomerates were not built to maximize profits. Instead, most of them pursued asset growth. Their financial activities were oriented toward building larger and larger organizations based on the accumulation of debt. The only way that the debt could be supported was through further acquisitions. In relatively short periods of time enormous agglomerations of capital were built, yet the firm was more like a holding company than an integrated organization. When the firm stopped acquiring other firms, the debt remained and it was often difficult to make money. Conglomerates experienced spectacular growth with low profitability. Many of the acquisitive conglomerates of the 1960s failed when they stopped buying other firms. Many had to divest some of their product lines and a number of the survivors have since pursued more focused product strategies.

Other firms experienced similar problems. When large firms began to purchase firms in any line of business they frequently discovered that they could not make a profit because they lacked expertise in the production and marketing of the new product line. As a result there have been some divestitures of firms bought during the merger boom of the last fifteen years. Any claim that all mergers are for efficiency cannot be sustained in the face of abundant data which show that most mergers have produced growth in assets and sales, but have also created great problems for the merged firm. Generally mergers create debt, lower profitability, and other problems for the acquiring firm as it tries to integrate the new company into its operation.

Why have mergers persisted, and indeed increased, even though the efficiency claims cannot be sustained? One would think that rational managers in the 1980s would realize that the divestitures of the 1970s were the result of the excesses of the 1960s. The answer is complex and reflects the expansion and dominance of the finance strategy. First, firms who engage in mergers are able to expand their firm size instantly. Managers, who are confronted by shareholders and boards of directors, are under pressure to show that the firm is growing. Mergers can enable large firms to show spectacular growth rates in any given year. Further, profits are generally the creation of accounting systems. By manipulating tax losses and interest payments large firms can sustain acceptable levels of profitability in the short run. Since profits are more erratic than assets and depend to a large degree on the overall state of the economy, managers pay more attention to growth figures than profitability.

Other factors that promote mergers concern the financial markets themselves. When large-scale mergers occur, investment banks, law firms, and brokerage firms make enormous sums of money. Bankers generally support mergers as they often lend money to the acquiring firm to buy the target firm. Often they get stock or guarantee of assets as collateral. Another important factor is that many firms have higher book value than the value of their stocks. In this situation mergers are profitable because even if the merged firm is divided and sold the buyer makes money.

The finance conception of control cannot be exclusively identified with the acquisitive conglomerates. The theory of the firm implicit in the finance conception still dominates corporate discourse today, even though the conglomerate strategy is not in vogue. This is because the use of financial tools to evaluate firms has firmly entrenched itself in the corporate community. In the past ten years, mergers have become the province of financial entrepreneurs who are often uninterested in actually managing firms. Carl Icahn, Saul Steinberg, Ted Turner, the Bass brothers, Boone Pickens, Henry Kravis, and others have captured the imagination of the business community by pursuing undervalued firms through elaborate financial maneuvers. It should be noted that none of their strategies are new, although there have been a few variations. For instance, the creation of "junk bonds" to finance leveraged buyouts is a product of the 1980s.

While the conglomerators worked from the framework of a large diversified firm, the current group of corporate raiders treat their investments as a stock portfolio. Their interest is in driving up the value of their holdings. The banks and financial community have willingly aided in helping these actions. In response, managers in many firms have bought up shares of their stock in order to drive stock prices up. They do this by borrowing money creating additional debt. With a higher stock price and more debt, they become unattractive targets of potential takeovers. Entrenched managements have also taken to using leveraged buyouts rather than letting corporate raiders take control. While the tactics have shifted somewhat, the finance conception of the corporation still dominates.

It has been estimated that 25 percent of the stock disappeared from the New York Stock Exchange between 1980 and 1985 due to mergers and stock buybacks. The overall result of this activity for the economy should be obvious. If capital is being diverted toward mergers and preventing mergers, then it is not being used to invest in new businesses. This means that the largest firms are not likely to be the leading entrepreneurial sector of the economy, that is, producing new products and technologies. The actual number of persons working for Fortune 500 firms has in fact declined in the past ten years even though the asset concentration has increased.

The largest firms and the financial community are creating enormous debt, with capital that could be used to create jobs, and accelerating the concentration of capital. The finance conception of control that was pioneered by the conglomerates is still driving the large-scale corporate sector of the economy. New financial investors have emerged who are not associated with large firms. Instead they buy and sell large firms for short-run gain which is achieved by breaking up those firms. The overall result is profit for these individuals and instantaneous growth for the large firms that remain independent and engage in mergers. But the overall economy suffers from fewer new jobs or productive activities.

Schumpeter praised the large modern firm as an engine of change in capitalism. The firm as he knew it has disappeared and been replaced by the diversified firm that is run totally on the basis of financial criteria. This new modern firm is not likely to be an engine of change. Instead it absorbs smaller, successful enterprises. The limits on size for the large modern firm have not yet been reached. Utilizing financial criteria and divisionalized forms, the large firm can continue to prosper in the indefinite short run.

9

The Social Construction of Efficiency

Efficiency can be defined as the conception of control that produces the relatively higher likelihood of growth and profits for firms given the existing set of social, political, and economic circumstances. This definition takes into account the three most important factors necessary for the firm to prosper: a conception of control held by its top managers, the existence of a stable organizational field, and a political system that does not question the legality of the courses of action taken in the organizational field.

This view provides a model as to how and why different courses of action are established by large firms, how they are maintained, and what forces are likely to produce their transformation. Conceptions of control are world views that define one firm's relationship with others, what appropriate behavior is for firms of that type, and how those kinds of organizations ought to work. They imply certain strategies and structures. In essence, conceptions of control and the organizational fields they create define how markets are structured for firms. They are efficient in the sense that they provide firms with growth and profits relative to other conceptions of control. To the degree that firms in established fields continue to prosper, the fields remain stable. New conceptions of control which are legal and produce more growth and profits than the existing system will spread. They will do so because of their relative success, but also because they provide a threat to systems of existing power in other organizational fields.

The motive to find new conceptions of control with appropriate courses of action is always present. But there have been very few conceptions of control. The difficulty of establishing a new conception of control is that managers must construct it in the context of the existing social world. The problem is compounded by the fact that organizations already profit from a given conception of control and the power arrangement of the existing organizational field. Managers are also constrained by their organizations, which have selected them on the basis of their allegiance to a certain view of the firm, by their own world views, and by their organizational field.

The state maintains the institutional conditions for stable organizational fields and can provide the stimulus for change. Since it defines what the rules are for the existence of organizations and their relationships with other firms, it encourages and discourages different conceptions of control. The central theme of this book has been that the conceptions of control and socially constructed organizational fields of large firms have emerged through interaction with the political and legal system in the United States. Managers and entrepreneurs have tried to impose their view of the sociologically efficient organization of markets on others. Then the government has decided which of these is legal given the popular political and economic ideologies. If the state disapproves of the conception of control, it is no longer efficient and the organizational field that defines the market must be reconstructed. The direct, manufacturing, sales and marketing, and finance conceptions of control were alternative ways to produce higher rates of growth and profits for large firms. The emergence and spread of these conceptions depended on their relative success and their eventual displacement depended on the institutional structure of state-firm relations.

From this perspective, the key problem of direct control was that it was illegal. Predatory trade practices, cartels, and monopolies preserved profits and kept organizations in existence. As ways to organize markets, they created the possibility of growth and profits. But because they were illegal in the United States forms of direct control could not guarantee profits or growth for large firms. The manufacturing conception of control proved acceptable to government agencies. It aided in the creation of organizational fields with leading firms that enforced prices by focusing on indirect forms of control: vertical integration of suppliers and customers, public pricing decisions, and the threat of ruinous competition. Hence managers in firms in these organizational fields were assured of profits and growth. The Depression brought limits to the manufacturing conception of control. In industries dominated by this conception, managers favored moving toward more formal price arrangements and maintaining prices by cutting production. Instead of trying to expand and grow, firms tried to preserve what they could and guarantee themselves at least short-term profits.

The sales and marketing conception shifted attention away from the control over price and production toward market share as a measure of how well the firm was doing. Sales and marketing managers realized that to guarantee any profits at all, a firm needed growth. An efficient firm was one that was growing in its main markets or diversifying into new and more rapidly growing markets. These strategies were efficient relative to the manufacturing ones because, given the existing political situation and definition of markets, they made money. The realization of managers after the Depression that concentration on production alone would not guarantee survival meant that they had a much different sense of efficiency. The relative advantage of the sales and marketing view of efficiency was that even in bad economic times firms could enhance their survival prospects by finding markets for their goods.

The organizational fields of the large corporation consequently were redefined in terms of entire industries. More important, the relations between firms became less directly competitive. Managers in firms fought over market share, not the right to exist. Product lines were diversified and managers concentrated on differentiating their products in order to avoid continued direct competition. Firms and organizational fields driven by sales and marketing executives were generally not prosecuted by antitrust authorities because the antitrust laws were intended to prevent the lessening of competition by direct control. If managers in firms avoided direct confrontation, they were not violating the law.

The finance conception of control took the sales and marketing conception one step further. If growth and profits were the essential goals of the corporation, they could be best achieved by financially evaluating all firm activities. Because firms were already significantly diversified and the antitrust authorities were renewing their efforts against concentration and vertical and horizontal mergers, finance managers were able to improve their growth and profits by using financial tools to evaluate, buy, and sell assets in many industries. The finance conception of control destroyed some organizational fields defined in single industry terms because the leading firms in those industries were bought and made part of a larger firm. Managers in firms operating with finance strategies changed the rules no matter what the managers in firms in a given organizational field wanted. The finance view of efficiency dominates the corporate world today. It proved its relative success by taking advantage of the antitrust climate and diversification to produce spectacular rates of growth.

Of course, the ability to measure financial performance is itself a social construction. The common belief is that the ultimate measure of a corporation's worth is its stock price or price/earnings ratio. When managers in both corporations and the financial community become more aware of those numbers, their importance increases. For instance, if CEOs spend most of their time attempting to manipulate stock prices, then they are less likely to worry about the underlying fundamentals of their firms. Such an orientation can produce an obsession with short-run profits and fluctuations of the stock price and a lack of attention to replacing capital stock and investing in future products. The finance conception of efficiency that focuses narrowly on financial data results in a socially constructed view of the firm as assets which are used to obtain short-run returns and keep the stock price high.

It is useful to contrast the view I propose here with the dominant historical view, which emphasizes the market as the key to understanding change in large-scale corporations. There are three kinds of economic efficiency to consider. First, efficiency implied the need to achieve economies of scale and lower costs to compete in markets. This was done by implementing the newest production technology and increasing the scale of production. Second, managers built integrated organizations as they took over the role of markets in making decisions regarding the allocation of resources, the production of inputs, and control over outputs. Managers who created hierarchies were able to show higher profits than those who used markets because they were less susceptible to the vagaries of markets that were unreliable and more costly in providing suppliers and customers. Finally, the multiproduct firm was efficient as it used the capital of the firm to spread risks across product lines thereby increasing the stability of the corporation. Together, these different efficiencies increased the scale of corporate enterprise (Chandler, 1962, 1977; Williamson, 1975).

The cause of all three forms of efficiency was the market. The market generally refers to how the price of a given commodity is determined by the balance of the supply and demand. The social organization surrounding this price mechanism is the dependent variable that determines that efficient organizations—those that produce at low cost—survive and inefficient organizations die. All organizational innovations are reactions to the market.

This view of the market gives rise to the following story of the history of the large modern corporation. Around 1860 national markets for commodities came into existence. These markets were possible because of canals, railroads, and the telegraph system. Once they were built the transportation costs for commodities dropped significantly which allowed firms to increase their scale of operation. Firm size expanded and costs decreased as competition intensified. The largest producers became the most efficient producers. The term efficiency here refers to economies of scale.

But the large scale of production required enormous amounts of capital. If supply of inputs or sale of outputs was halted the firm could not take advantage of possible economies of scale. This uncertainty in the market caused the organization to expand. Firms began to control their suppliers and customers by absorbing more functions (Chandler, 1977, ch. 1). Hence the large modern firm was the model of efficiency in two senses: it maximized productive capacity by using the best and cheapest technology and by guaranteeing itself suppliers and customers.

The next stage in achieving more efficiency was the redeployment of capital to create the multidivisional, multiproduct firm. The market was influential in this transformation because it provided firms with the opportunity to produce multiple related products and thereby enter new markets. In order to control the new multiproduct firm, the multidivisional form was invented. The multidivisional, multiproduct firm was efficient in a new sense: it insured the growth and profitability of the firm by spreading risk to many businesses.

At first glance the market-driven efficiency theory seems parallel to mine. But there are a number of major differences. The key problem is that these theoretical notions suggest that market processes are outside of social processes and therefore require no explanation. They do not involve the setting up of social institutions that reflect the interests of powerful groups. Instead, this view assumes that the price mechanism is constantly encouraging more and more efficient forms of social organization. The types of efficiency that get called into play from this perspective are a result of interactions between producers and consumers in the market. The efficiency demands of markets operate in a functionalist, seamless manner. Opportunities are recognized by rational managers and entrepreneurs whose actions are oriented toward the exploitation of profitable possibilities and organizational forms follow. Even in accounts that stress the failure of the market to provide resources and stability, the institutional response of managers and entrepreneurs is to create efficient social organization (Williamson, 1975).

From my perspective, once powerful interests legitimized capitalistic institutions in the United States they constructed markets to aid private gains. Sociological efficiencies resulted because of these institutional interactions between firms, organizational fields, and the state. The structuring of markets to produce growth and profits was limited by the existing conceptions of control, the strategies they implied, and their legality. Instead of markets calling forth efficient forms of social organization, political and social interactions produced the structuring of sociologically efficient markets.

A social organization that produced efficiency replaced another only when the former was illegal or in crisis. The social structure of markets and its relation to the state caused changes in their organization. In other words, the forms of social organization produced the market, not the reverse. The central mistake made in traditional accounts of the history of the large corporation is that by reading history backwards economic historians have known how things turned out and thereby were able to impute what kind of social institutions must have been called forth by efficient markets. By beginning with how managers, entrepreneurs, and politicians in each historical epoch constructed their worlds, one understands that the development was in the opposite direction. The institutions created markets that were dominated by a given conception of control that produced relatively more growth and profit and were legal.

Since the courses of action taken by managers and entrepreneurs were framed in worlds with quite different rules and understandings, it is difficult to see how economic arguments can account for what happened historically. The plausibility of economic efficiency stories rests more on their abstract character and ability to round off the edges of historical evidence and provide a pleasing and simple version of what occurred. Most of the evidence presented here is hard to rectify with such a view. One could account post hoc for this evidence, but that would not be scientific.

The basic economic argument about competitive markets is that the firms that produce the most cheaply will dominate. It is also asserted that such markets will reach a point at which production stops when the most efficient producer no longer makes money. Both of these claims are problematic. Historically, the problem has been that there are often a number of firms with similar technologies and hence similar levels of efficiency. Firms with similar technologies begin to lose money if they continue to allow prices to drop. But instead of discontinuing production of that line, they lose money until they go out of business.

This creates a paradox. If competitive markets are enforced, firms of similar efficient technologies will eventually drive one another out of business. If that occurs throughout the economy, the result is economic recession or depression. The so-called efficient market results in large-scale economic dislocation and the destruction of efficient producers.

The result of the cutthroat competition in the nineteenth century, however, was to create powerful organizations that sought direct control of competitive markets and to act efficiently from a sociological point of view. In order to account for the historical events of this period, the economic analyst has to ignore the overwhelming evidence that the conceptions of control of managers and entrepreneurs from 1880 to 1920 were oriented toward controlling competition. I have already shown that the best predictor of whether or not an industry engaged in the turn of the century merger movement was whether or not the industry had attempted to form cartels. In spite of abundant evidence that the owners and managers of large corporations were engaged in such efforts, the conventional wisdom asserts that such efforts were doomed to failure and that the search for economies of scale motivated managerial decisions (Chandler, 1977, ch. 1).

Because the economic model already assumes that market processes will dominate social interaction, the only possible outcome from that perspective is economic efficiency. Hence, economic accounts have to downplay the social and political search for stability and focus on arguments concerning economies of scale. They also have to ignore the role of the state in defining what behavior is acceptable from firms. The only reason that direct forms of control did not work was because they were illegal. In a different political system, for instance Western Europe and Japan before World War II, direct forms of control produced more stable outcomes.

The central ideas of the efficiency approach also require an unrealistic view of the motives and actions of managers and entrepreneurs. In the context of the competitive market, managers and entrepreneurs are actors who choose courses of action that conform to the rules of markets by acting only to improve their situations in those markets. The theory of action, one that stresses rationality or bounded rationality, requires actors to know and behave in ways that have little to do with how courses of action were constructed. The interpretation of the history of the corporation that stresses efficiency ignores the central fact that managers and entrepreneurs were constantly trying to escape or control competition, not engage in it. These actors were also well aware that markets were social constructions that revolved around systems of power, both private and public. As such, the rules of markets could be changed by powerful corporate actors and the government.

The central argument I propose here is that managers rarely know what is economically efficient. They have a sense of controlling a market or market share and to some degree can control costs. But the driving force for managers, just as it is for any kind of social actor, is to preserve their organizations and further their individual and collective interests. To do so they must define their situations, including what constitutes a market. In that process, they construct a conception of control that includes strategies and structures and helps to define their organizational fields.

Economists have tended toward two views of managers: omnipotent or irrelevant. These views account for the alleged efficiency and rationality of the firm. From the omnipotent perspective of the microeconomics of the firm, managers and entrepreneurs understand their markets and production processes quite well. They respond to markets by expanding and contracting production and utilize the best technology and the fewest labor inputs to achieve results. The firm is efficient because of the actions taken by managers and entrepreneurs. Inefficiency is caused by managers who do not act rationally, that is, they do not mix the factors of production to maximize outcomes.

The other perspective suggests that markets select successful firms, technologies, and products. The actions of managers and entrepreneurs are almost irrelevant. In an economy with few barriers to entry, no firm will be able to prevent others from entering a successful market nor prevent more efficient producers from emerging. In essence, no matter what managers do the market will encourage efficiency. The market is the final arbiter of efficiency and managers who are successful are efficient because the market is efficient.

The problem with these views is that they place either too much or too little weight on the two central constructs, managerial autonomy and the market. In my opinion managers must construct views about what constitutes efficient action that are historically determined. There have been very few conceptions of control yet each reflects the thinking of the period and the problems managers perceived. The goal of their actions has been to produce social conditions that stabilized their organizations. Managers' actions are highly constrained; they tend to go with what has worked in the immediate past or with the conventional wisdom guiding their organizational fields. When they innovate, it is to gain, preserve, or recover an advantage in some organizational field.

The problem with relying on the market to determine what is efficient is that all markets are comprised of a social structure or set of rules which preserve the power and interests of the largest organizations. When the rules no longer produce positive results for those in control, the rules are changed. In the case of competitive markets, the managers and entrepreneurs in the largest firms have tried to opt out of them because their existence implies competition that will end in the ruin of them all.

The point of view I provide here has a number of improvements over the traditional economic view of the various transformations of the large corporation. First, it does not assume the rationality of action or some absolute standard of efficiency. There is not one most efficient mode of organization, nor is there only one way in which organizational goals can be pursued.

Instead, my view requires that one understand the rationale for an action. Second, it implies that the social construction of the world is as important as the "objective" character of the world. In this sense, managers are neither more nor less intelligent than any other social actors.

Additionally, it allows for the rules by which worlds are constructed to be negotiated and changed. Organizational conceptions, structures, fields, and performance are the outcome of the key interactions between managers, their organizations and fields, and the actors who control government agencies. The market as the driving force of economic history is replaced by the variety of constructions of institutional arrangements in the economic and political sphere and the dynamics of those arrangements. The market and the rules that govern it are the product of those interactions.

The most important feature of this point of view is that it does not rely upon the functionalism implied by the economic point of view expressed earlier. Since it is often difficult to tell who the winners and losers are, and hence what the winning and losing strategies are, there can be no one best way to achieve profitability. By dropping the notion that the most efficient economic solution is the predominant one and accepting that efficiency is a social construction, one can then see how the transformation of conceptions of control and their strategies rely on organizational dynamics and the interaction between organizations, their leaders, and the state.

A Comparative Consideration

To prove the difficulty of the functionalist position exemplified by the use of market logic, let's consider some other cases. If the economists are right, the most efficient form will emerge in every market society either because the market will select that form or because managers will adopt it. Factors such as the intervention of the state, conceptions of control, and organizational strategies and structures should not have an impact on the shape of the large modern firm. There should be convergence in form across societies of roughly equal levels of development in the conceptions of control and the strategies and structures of the largest firms. If economic theory is correct and the market selects the most efficient form, the large, multiproduct, multidivisional firm that grows through mergers should be the dominant social organization across nation states. Hence, the Japanese, German, British, and French large firms will mirror the large American firms.

In contrast, if the view that markets are constructed in the context of strategic interactions between firms and states is correct, such convergence should not be observed. This brief consideration of other countries is intended to illustrate and suggest that an organizational theory of the economy grounded in a view of how managers and entrepreneurs construct actions and how they spread to other organizations will bring us more understanding of large American firms than an approach that assumes that the most efficient form will emerge either through market processes or by managerial choice.

There are a number of problems in considering the evidence. The measurement of product mix and mergers in different countries is uneven and cannot always be compared. The role of the state in the postwar era was complex and differed by country. Before the war, the Japanese, German, French, and British governments encouraged cartels to varying degrees. After the war, the American occupation forces tried to break up the large Japanese trading companies and German cartels. The United States forced its antitrust laws on both of these countries. Generally, these laws did not change the cooperation between firms or between the government and the firms. But the philosophy of open international markets pushed on these countries by U.S. policymakers encouraged the firms and governments to pursue policies that blended competition and cooperation. Another problem that makes comparison difficult is that the U.S. firms were used as role models for some countries. The French and British governments thought that the large size of U.S. firms was most responsible for their effectiveness so they encouraged mergers. Some of the convergence of these countries reflects this conscious policy rather than the workings of the market.

The British government supported cartel arrangements in the prewar era and suppressed them afterward. The Monopolies and Restrictive Practices Act of 1948 created a tribunal to consider possible anticompetitive practices. Between 1956 and 1973 four pieces of legislation were passed that made it increasingly difficult to restrain trade (George and Joll, 1975, pp. 10–14). The British approach allowed some restrictive trade practices if positive competitive effects on international markets could be shown. This differed from the American antitrust laws which condemned all restrictive trade practices (George and Joll, 1975, p. 15).

The 1956 legislation made cartels illegal. Cartels were thought to prevent competition and reward inefficient producers. At the same time, the British government began to promote mergers and both Conservative and Labour parties embraced the policy. They argued that in order to compete effectively both domestically and internationally, economies of scale were needed. They thought mergers were the most effective mechanism to achieve those economies most rapidly (Hannah, 1976, pp. 150–181).

Not surprisingly, a large-scale merger movement began in the mid-1950s and continued until 1973. The aggregate concentration in the British economy increased greatly as the 100 largest British manufacturing firms increased their share of output from 21 percent in 1949 to almost 41 percent in 1970. Concentration within industries also increased substantially during that time (Prais, 1976, p. 5). Most of these increases in concentration were due to mergers. The 100 largest manufacturing firms in the United States increased their aggregate share from about 20 percent in 1950 to roughly 32 percent in 1970 and there was little increase in concentration within product lines. One can conclude that the British merger movement created more aggregate industrial concentration than this country's. It brought about marked increases in concentration within product lines as well. It is interesting to note that at the same time the British economy suffered greatly.

As these increases in aggregate and product market concentration became evident, new legislation was passed. The Monopolies and Mergers Act of 1965 set up administrative machinery to evaluate the effects of mergers on competition and prevent anticompetitive mergers. Between 1965 and 1973, 83 percent of the mergers investigated were horizontal in character (Utton, 1975, pp. 96–98). In 1964, only 16.2 percent of the mergers undertaken by the 159 largest British firms were product related or unrelated. By 1969, 63.6 percent of these mergers were in these categories (Jacquemin and deJong, 1977, pp. 106–108). The British merger policy worked like the Celler-Kefauver Act: it encouraged firms to diversify and shy away from vertical and horizontal mergers that would attract the attention of antitrust authorities.

The overall result of British policy toward mergers in the postwar era can be seen in the following figures. In 1950, 80 of the 100 largest British manufacturing enterprises were product dominant compared to 62 in the United States in 1948. By 1970, 38 of the 100 largest firms in Great Britain were primarily producing one product, 56 were producing related products, and only 6 were conglomerates (Channon, 1973, p. 67). In the United States in 1969, 24 were product dominant, 56 were product related, and 20 were product unrelated. British firms diversified substantially during the period, but they remained less diversified than their American counterparts. It could be argued that these differences reflect the differences in the antitrust laws. In this country horizontal and vertical mergers were consistently shunned after the war. In Britain such mergers were encouraged. Even when public policy turned somewhat against them, they remained a substantial component of overall mergers. The purest form of the finance conception, the acquisitive conglomerate, was not as important in the British context as in the American.

The German case shows more clearly the differences in national policies. In prewar Germany, cartels dominated the economy. The Allied forces instituted an ordinance prohibiting cartels and monopolies in 1947. This law became the 1957 Act against Restraint of Competition. The main target of the act was cartels, but substantial numbers of cartel situations were excluded from it including agreements related to rebates, standardization, specialization, rationalization of production, foreign trade, patents, and industrial secrets (Cable et al., 1980, p. 114). The 1973 amendments to the act brought abuse of market position under the law. Such abuses were left undefined and the laws were much weaker than the Sherman or Clayton acts in specifying what constituted restraints of trade. In 1974 an antimerger act went into effect that required clearance for mergers by an agency call B Kart A. The agency decides whether a merger helps or hurts competition in the relevant markets and prevents anticompetitive mergers (Cable et al., 1980, p. 115).

The German antitrust laws operated to encourage economic cooperation between firms. But that cooperation was directed toward export markets, economies of scale, and new technology. The cartel arrangements were used most effectively to promote these strategies. The German banks played a central role as

German firms relied on banks for most of their financing. In 1965 German firms relied on internal funds for 32 percent of financing, banks for 44 percent of their financing, the bond market for 20 percent, and the stock market for only 8 percent (Dyas and Thanheiser, 1976, p. 57). The typical merger in Germany was vertical or horizontal and not oriented toward diversification. In the 1950s it was common for a producer to purchase stock in other firms, but not to merge the two firms. Managers in German firms have never engaged in merger for growth.

The 1950s and 1960s were periods of low merger activity in Germany. Mergers picked up in 1969 and peaked in 1977 (Cable et al., 1980, pp. 110–115). During the 1970s vertical and horizontal mergers comprised between 83 and 89 percent of the largest mergers in the German economy. Vertical mergers increased from 7.9 percent of the total in 1971 to 24 percent in 1977 and outnumbered the 1976 and 1977 mergers for diversification. At the same time industrial concentration increased in Germany both in aggregate and product terms (Dyas and Thanheiser, 1976, p. 50).

These results suggest that the strategies of German firms were quite unlike those of their American and British counterparts. The German government and banking system worked with firms to increase their international competitiveness. The managers of German firms were not highly rewarded for increasing their stock prices or the size of their firm. Instead, their system promoted cooperation between firms to increase the scale of production and compete effectively in the world economy. The institutional system produced results markedly different from the American system.

The French case shows a different dynamic than the German one. Whereas the German government left the economy in the hands of the private sector and offered incentives to that sector, the French state has taken a more active role in promoting corporate transformation. Many of the largest French firms are publicly owned and many of the private firms are profoundly affected by the French government. It has been estimated that the French government owns half of the capital stock in France and controls firms in the tobacco, coal mining, railway, airlines, utilities, communications, automobile, oil, chemical, shipping, aircraft, banking, insurance, and advertising industries (Dyas and Thanheiser, 1976, p. 168). The French government exerts control over the economy through its control over investment and regulation of various industries.

The industrial policy of the French government in the 1960s greatly affected the number and types of mergers that occurred. The French government passed an anticartel law in 1956 and amended that law to include monopolistic practices in 1963 (Jenny and Weber, 1980, pp. 141–142). Generally, the law was not enforced. Instead, the government decided that to compete with American firms, French firms needed to imitate their American counterparts. Since French firms were smaller than American firms, it was thought that they needed to be larger to generate economies of scale and increase innovation. The French government therefore began to encourage mergers by directly engineering various mergers and cartel arrangements in both the private and public sectors. In 1965 the government tried to promote mergers by reducing taxes on firms that engaged in them (Jenny and Weber, 1980, pp. 142–143).

The effects of these policies became evident throughout the 1960s and early 1970s. Mergers picked up in 1963 and remained high until 1973. The peak of the movement coincided with the tax incentives that existed from 1965 to 1969. Industrial concentration increased, particularly from 1965 to 1969. Between 1970 and 1972, 48 percent of the mergers were classified as horizontal, 23 percent as vertical, and 29 percent as product related and unrelated. Using broad definitions of diversification, it has been estimated that 48 of the 100 largest French firms were product dominant, 42 product related, and 10 product unrelated in 1970. While there was some diversification in the French economy, the large French firm was less diversified than large firms in the other countries.

The Japanese case is perhaps the most interesting. The largest Japanese firms are diversified and rival American firms in size. In 1980, 37 of the 102 largest Japanese firms were classified as product dominant, 59 as product related, and 6 as product unrelated (Kono, 1984, p. 80). These levels of diversification are less than the United States, particularly in terms of product-unrelated firms. However, the Japanese firms have one important quality that distinguishes them from the American firms. The expansion into new product lines is almost always done through internal growth, not mergers.

The emergence of the modern Japanese corporation is the subject of much speculation. Its development most parallels the German situation. Before World War II Japan's economy was dominated by a small group of large holding companies, each owned by extended families, that were called Zaibatsu (Yoshino, 1969, pp. 118–119). The American Occupation Force tried to break up the power of the Zaibatsu and establish a competitive market system based on the U.S. model. Four steps were undertaken to achieve this: the Zaibatsu organizations were dissolved and their component parts became independent firms; attempts were made to break up concentration in large-scale industry; senior executives of the Zaibatsu were removed; and an antimonopoly act was passed (Yoshino, 1969, p. 123). The only part of this program that was at all effective was the breaking up of the Zaibatsu and the replacement of their chief executives. By the early 1950s efforts at deconcentration bogged down and the Zaibatsu resumed as loose coalitions of firms.

Cooperation within the Japanese economy was encouraged throughout the 1950s and 1960s. Three distinct forms of industrial groupings appeared. First, loose federations of firms that were former members of the Zaibatsu began to buy stock in one another's corporations. They created informal associations that promoted cooperation and competition. Members of the group relied on the banks within the group for financing as well as one another for joint ventures into new products. Second, coalitions of firms began to gravitate toward large banks for their capital needs. The banks played the major role in the postwar era in terms of financing firms and owning stock. Like German firms, Japanese firms relied on banks for the bulk of their outside funds to fuel expansion. The banks also became major shareholders and exerted great control over the firms. Banks often encouraged their corporate customers to cooperate on new ventures. Third, large firms organized their subsidiaries and suppliers into loose groups. These associations would sometimes involve ownership and sometimes just long-term supplier relations (Yoshino, 1969, pp. 139–148).

The Japanese government also played a role in this development. The Ministry of International Trade and Industry (MITI) encouraged cooperative efforts among Japanese firms, particularly in developing and implementing technology for goods for foreign export. But MITI's efforts could not have worked without a structure of industry that promoted cooperation. The development of new products in Japan tended not to occur through mergers. Although some mergers were encouraged in order to create more efficient firms, especially in the 1960s, the general tendency has been to produce new products internally or through joint ventures.

The focus on the internal generation of ideas can be seen more clearly when one considers the backgrounds of Japanese executives. In 1978 it was found that about 50 percent of Japanese top management came up through the production ranks while 26 percent came up through marketing and only 5 percent came up through finance or accounting (Kono, 1984, p. 33). Almost 76 percent of the new products were developed from ideas that were internally generated as opposed to ideas brought in from the outside (Kono, 1984, p. 219). The focus of Japanese top managers, even in diversified firms, is on product development and production first, marketing second, and finance last.

Japanese firms are able to make long-term investments in new industries for a number of reasons. First, the financial community does not impose rigid standards on short-term rates of profit and growth. The Japanese bankers view their loans and investments on a more long-term basis. This means that managers are rewarded for long-term performance and have less need to opt for measures that increase only short-run profitability. Second, the Japanese government has encouraged firms to cooperate on the creation of new products, especially on those that could result in substantial export markets. It has also encouraged investment in new industries and aided in exiting from older industries. Finally, the Japanese firms compete strenuously with one another in domestic and foreign markets. While cooperation exists within groups, competition is the rule between them. The result is that the large Japanese firm is able to create new products, adopt the most modern manufacturing processes, take a number of years to enter a market, and achieve success.

The finance conception, which dominates the largest American firms, does not drive the largest Japanese firms. The interaction between Japanese firms and their government has produced a large diversified corporation that grows, not through acquisition, but through internal expansion. The institutional milieu that produced the Japanese firms may be one of the primary reasons that they have an advantage over American firms.

The most diversified large firms in the world are American, followed by the British, Japanese, German, and French firms. The American firms are substantially more diversified, particularly the product-unrelated ones. Underlying these levels of diversification, however, are quite different conceptions of growth. The British firms have taken the American example of mergers for growth the most seriously and their largest firms most resemble the large American firms. The Japanese and German firms are in an institutional setting that encourages them to grow internally and cooperate with other firms, particularly in the development of products for export. Banks play important roles in these societies as providers of funds for expansion. Their stock markets have lesser roles. The French case is the most anomalous because the French government is the most intrusive in the organization of its economy. The large French firms are the least diversified, but more highly concentrated than their counterparts.

While this cursory review is partially speculative, there does not exist strong evidence for a convergence of the conceptions of control across societies. Indeed, the evidence suggests that unique interactions between the state and the largest firms in the economies of various advanced countries has resulted in different organizational forms driven by different sets of actors operating with different conceptions of control. There exists no abstract market that disciplines firms to one and only one efficient standard. Instead, industrial organization reflects the unique experiences of national economies.

The Future of the Large American Corporation

The problems of the American economy can be understood in the context I outline here. The finance conception that dominates the large American corporation is the product of a complex set of institutional structures. It maintains its advantage because it has been more successful than other tactics in guaranteeing the existence and growth of the largest firms in the unique context of the American economic and political system. Any change of the structure of American business will, thus, have to be a more successful tactic to preserve the power, size, and growth of the largest firms.

It is not just its relative success that holds the finance conception in place. The world of top managers is now more concerned with the firm's position in the stock market and with its accounting records. The finance conception evaluates the consequence of any course of action in purely financial terms. Any possible shift in that view will require an alternative world view that challenges the financial perspective by creating firm growth more predictably. A shift is also dependent on a crisis in the current point of view.

One could argue that such a crisis exists today. The 1970s were not good years for the largest firms and the 1980s have forced them to expand their view of organizational fields to encompass the international market. The large firm is in crisis because it cannot meet the competitive challenge of firms in other countries. The finance conception has been used throughout the 1980s as the solution to this problem. Mergers, acquisitions, and divestitures have been tried to encourage efficiency by eliminating unproductive product lines and ineffective managements. Their success remains to be seen. The short-run financial perspective of American managers is even more reinforced by the restructuring and increase of American business debt.

The effect on conceptions of control will depend on the ability of the managers of the largest firms to construct new solutions to this current crisis. Any new view must overtake the power of the stock market and finance executives to dictate a concern with short-run profits. Investment will need to be made for the long run. Such a structural change will probably require increased cooperation between firms to create and implement new technology. That cooperation will in turn require a radical shift in antitrust philosophy. Consequently the federal government's role in this transformation may be pivotal. One could speculate that an American industrial policy would allow more cooperation and joint ventures and discourage mergers that only create highly leveraged firms. In any case, these changes would have to produce spectacularly successful examples. The examples may be among the firms that are somewhat smaller than the largest firms because they are able to take advantage of changed conditions. These firms would also, at least initially, have to stay out of the stock market where the pressures to produce short-run profits would overwhelm long-run plans.

An alternative scenario would be the continuation of already existing tendencies. Smaller firms could continue to innovate and larger firms then purchase their assets. While this would continue to fuel the growth of the largest firms, its long-run effects on the economy might be continued decline. American firms have already exited from a number of important markets, leaving them to foreign competitors. Much depends on how the federal government changes the rules by which capital is depreciated, mergers are executed, and cooperation between firms is allowed. Any shift will require structural changes that produce advantages for a new conception of the corporation and disadvantages for the finance conception.

In this book I have traced the transformation of the large American firm from its inception to its current state. I have tried to show the complex interactions between organizations, the state, and the actors who have altered the conceptions of control guiding the strategies and structures of the largest firms. The results of these interactions have produced the large, modern corporation in its American form. This form is driven by financial considerations, is highly diversified, and uses mergers and divestitures to expand and restrict product lines. Its future will be determined by further unique interaction between the large corporations and the state.

Appendixes
Notes
Bibliography
Index

Appendix A

Industrial Location of Cartels and Mergers

Here I provide multivariate models to specify the causes of cartel and merger behavior in the late nineteenth and early twentieth centuries. The data used were originally collected by Naomi Lamoreaux (1985). They are based on tables from the 1900 *Census of Manufactures* (Tables 1, 2). I added certain pieces of data for additional analyses, in particular, variables measuring capital intensity in 1879 and participation in cartels at the industry level. The source for the former was the same census tables mentioned above while the latter sources can be seen in Table 2.1.

The original data set contained information on 272 manufacturing industries. In the data analysis of the determinants of cartels, all industries were used. In the study of the determinants of mergers, the sample was restricted to the 230 industries that did not have significant mergers prior to 1895. Lamoreaux imposed this restriction in her analysis. Models for the entire and the restricted samples for both dependent variables were run and the results were substantially the same.

Table A.1 contains the descriptive statistics for the model containing the determinants of cartels. The independent variables used were the total dollars of capital in an industry in 1879, the average capital investment per plant in 1879, the number of establishments in the industry in 1879, the marginal rate of return on capital, and the percent change in capital in an industry from 1879 to 1889. While some of the cartels were formed in the 1880s, most were formed later in that decade. The time order of variables is potentially a problem only for the growth measure. The basic hypothesis was that industries that engaged in cartels tended to be in newly emerging production markets characterized by high rates of capital investment, low rates of return, and rapid growth. The

Table A.1   Means and standard deviations of variables for analysis of
              determinants of cartels (N = 272)

Variable[a]	Mean	Standard deviation
Cartel	.17	—
Capital 1879[b]	11,256.4	46,667.2
Growth	153.0	1097.9
Capital/Noestab	84.0	137.9
Noestab	865.2	3326.9
Margin	.22	.08

a. Cartel: 0 = no cartel, 1 = cartel; Capital 1879 = capitalization of industry in
1879 in thousands of dollars; Growth = [(Capital 1889) − (Capital 1879)]/(Capital
1879); Noestab = number of establishments in the industry, 1879; Margin: see note
to Table A.3 for definition.

b. *Sources*: Lamoreaux (1985; U.S. Bureau of the Census, *Census of Manufactures*
(1900), tables 1, 2.

number of establishments measured the difficulty of organizing a
cartel. If there are more establishments, presumably it was more
difficult to organize a cartel.

Table A.2 presents the result of a series of logistic regression
analyses predicting the presence or absence of a cartel. The computer program used was the logistic regression routine in BMDP.
The first two columns use the total capital in an industry as a
measure of its size and capital intensiveness. High amounts of
capital positively affect the likelihood of a cartel. The higher the
marginal rate of return, the less likely the industry was to engage
in cartel behavior. The growth of an industry and number of
establishments do not have statistically significant effects on the
likelihood of a cartel. The third and fourth columns present
results with an alternative measure of capitalization, the average
capital per establishment. They produced the same conclusions.

The effect of cartels on the likelihood of an industry partici-
pating in the 1895–1904 merger movement can be seen in Tables
A.3 and A.4. These tables concern only the 230 industries where
there were no significant mergers before 1895. The variables are
defined differently than in the first models, although there is substantial overlap. The variables in these models are identical to
Lamoreaux's measures.

Table A.3 presents the means and standard deviations of the
variables used in the analysis. Table A.4 presents the results from

Table A.2 Results of a logistic regression predicting whether or not an industry had a cartel, 1885–1895 (N = 272)

Independent variable[a]	b	SE(b)	b	SE(b)	b	SE(b)	b	SE(b)
Capital 1879	.00013*	.00005	.00014**	.00006	—	—	—	—
Growth	-.0006	.001	-.0006	.0011	.00001	.001	.00007	.0002
Noestab	—	—	-.00002	.0005	—	—	.00005	.0003
Capital/Noestab	—	—	—	—	.0035**	.0013	.0037**	.0013
Margin	-8.43**	2.43	-8.25**	2.46	-7.21	2.49	-7.43**	2.47
Constant	-1.84**	.18	-1.82**	.18	-2.11**	.22	-2.18**	.23

Note: *p < .05, **p < .01.
a. See Table A.1 for definitions of variables.

Table A.3 Means and standard deviations of variables for analysis of
determinants of significant merger activity, 1895–1904
(N = 230)

Variable[a]	Mean	Standard deviation
Capout	.36	.48
Growth	11.11	15.50
Margin	.23	.08
Size 1	71.18	100.76
Interact	4.9	11.3
Cartel	.15	—
Mergers	.21	—

Note: See text for definition of sample.

a. Capout: 1 if industry's capital/output ratio was above the mean, 0 if below; Growth = [(value of capital 1899) − (value of capital 1889)] / [(value of capital 1899) + (value of capital 1889) × .5]; Margin = [(annual value of output) − (annual wage bill + annual cost of materials + annual miscellaneous expenses)] / (annual value of output); Size 1 = (value of capital invested) / no. of establishments; Interact = Growth × Size 1; Cartel: 0 if no cartels, 1 if cartels existed (see Lamoreaux 1985, pp. 89–96).

Table A.4 Results of a logistic regression predicting whether or not an industry
engaged in mergers, 1895–1904 (N = 230)

Independent variable[a]	Lamoreaux results		Reproduced results		Results with cartel variable	
	b	SE(b)	b	SE(b)	b	SE(b)
Capout	1.22*	.55	1.10*	.50	.52	.70
Growth	−.0007	.004	.001	.02	.02	.02
Margin	−8.64**	2.85	−7.44**	2.79	−2.44	3.53
Size 1	.05**	.02	.05**	.02	.003	.002
Interact	.01	.0056	.006	.02	−.01	.03
Cartel	—	—	—	—	2.43**	.40
Constant	NR	NR	−.79	.63	−.08	.91

Note: See text for description of sample. * $p < .05$, ** $p < .01$. NR = not reported.
a. See Table A.3 for definition of variables.

the logistic regression, again utilizing the routine in BMDP. The first column of Table A.4 presents Lamoreaux's results (1985). Lamoreaux's basic hypothesis was that mergers were more likely to occur in highly capitalized, fast-growing industries. Her measures reflect different aspects of those factors. Capout, margin, size

1 are measures of capital intensivity, while growth directly indexes growth. The term interact is used to assess the hypothesis that the simultaneous conditions of fast growth and high assets per establishment resulted in a greater likelihood of merger.

The second column is an attempt to reproduce her results using her data. While there are slight differences in the parameters, her results are substantially reproduced. The major difference is that she reports an almost statistically significant relation between the interaction term and the dependent variable. That interaction proved to be difficult to reproduce. The differences in results may be caused by one or all of four factors: differences in data coding; slightly different samples; slightly different estimates from different computer programs; or no constant in her results which may alter the parameter estimates.

One effect worth noting is the parameter estimate for the variable margin. Lamoreaux interprets this effect in two ways. First, she suggests that lower profit firms were in mass production industries and hence the measure includes what I call production markets. Second, the effect literally implies that low-profit industries engaged in mergers more frequently. Hence, they could have undertaken those mergers in order to raise profits. Both explanations are consistent with my argument.

The most important results are in the last column of Table A.4, where the cartel measure is added. Cartels were created in order to control production and prices. Since they failed to do so, we would expect that the motivation for controlling production and prices remained. If industries in which cartels were attempted and failed are more likely to engage in mergers, we can infer that they engaged in mergers for the same reason they engaged in cartels, to control production and prices. The variable has a substantial effect on the likelihood of mergers in an industry and at the same time makes the other coefficients in the model insignificant.

These results lend substantial plausibility to the market control motive for the merger movement. The universal failure of cartels to stem the problems of overproduction in newly emergent production markets did not end the desire of managers and owners to lessen price competition. When cartels were tried and failed, other mechanisms became necessary to control such competition. The merger movement reflected the desire of managers to achieve some price stability by controlling production through the concentration of an industry's assets.

Appendix B

Survival of Merged Firms, 1895–1919

I will describe here the data and statistical model used to generate the results reported in Chapter 3. The basic goal of this analysis is to explain the probability of a firm surviving from its initial consolidation during the merger movement until 1919. The year 1919 was chosen for two reasons. First, it is sufficiently distant in time from the events at the turn of the century that one can evaluate the relative success or failure of those consolidations. Second, it is an arbitrary choice that is partially dictated by the fact that the other major data source used here begins in 1919. This appendix has a three-part structure. First, the relevant sample definitions, data sources, and variable codings will be reviewed. Then the specification of the statistical model will be presented. Finally, the results of the analysis will be described and appropriate conclusions drawn.

The sample of firms is the 317 consolidations that occurred between 1895 and 1904, the generally agreed-upon dates for the merger movement. These data are from Ralph Nelson's original worksheets (1959). An industrial consolidation is defined as the creation of a new firm that did not previously exist. Mergers that were initiated by existing firms that did not create new firms were excluded from the analysis. The goal was to determine the probability of success for a new consolidation.

Nelson's worksheets contained data on the date of consolidation, the name of the newly consolidated firm, the names and number of companies involved in the consolidation, the level of capitalization of the consolidation, four-digit Standard Industrial Classification scores describing the major industry of the consolidation, and the motive for consolidation. Motives included horizontal integration, vertical integration, both horizontal and vertical integration, and unknown. Concentration ratios for the industries in which the consolidations occurred were taken from Ralph Nelson (1959) and G. Warren Nutter (1951). These ratios refer to concentration just after consolidation occurred.

Information about the industry in which firms operated was coded from tables in the *Census of Manufactures*, 1900 and 1910. The other major source for industrial information was the *Historical Statistics of the United States* (1960). The number of establishments in an industry, the number of workers in an industry, and the total capital invested in an industry were coded for 1899 and 1909. These data measured the capital intensiveness of an industry and the growth of an industry.

A measure of integration of firms was constructed from two sources, Chandler (1977) and *Moody's Industrials* (1920). This measure was coded to assess Chandler's hypothesis that firms that created a separate sales and marketing division were more likely to survive than those without such a division. This hypothesis is discussed more thoroughly in Chapter 3.

The final variable of importance is whether or not the firm survived to 1919. These data came from two sources, *Moody's Industrials* (1920) and the *Handbook of Industrial Statistics* (1904–1916). All firms were studied from 1900 on. Of the total 317 firms, 145 (45.7 percent) survived until 1919. Ninety-five of the remaining firms (30.4 percent) were involved in mergers and 65 (20.5 percent) went bankrupt. The remaining 12 firms disappeared and, for the sake of the data analysis, I have assumed that they were either absorbed or went bankrupt.

The variables were coded as follows. The dependent variable is whether or not a firm survives until 1919. The variable is coded "0" if the firm did not survive and "1" if it did. Firms that were merged, went bankrupt, or disappeared were treated as nonsurvivors.

The independent variables in the analysis attempted to capture some of the hypotheses in Chapter 3. These hypotheses can be organized into four distinct ideas. First, the size of the firm could affect survival. Larger firms, for instance, would survive merely because of their size. The firm's capital in millions of dollars was used as the indicator of size. Second, the market power of the firm would be important to the firm survival. Firms with high degrees of market power could be more likely to survive. Here I used the same concentration ratios discussed above. The third hypothesis

comes from Chandler. He argues that firms that vertically integrated and created sales and marketing departments experienced
reductions in transaction costs and were thus more likely to survive. This measure was coded using two dummy variables. The
first dummy variable is coded "0" if the firm was not integrated
and coded "1" if the data were missing because substantial data
were missing on this measure. The second dummy variable was
coded "0" if the firm were not integrated and coded "1" if it was.

The largest number of measures were constructed in an effort to
capture the effects of the various industries of the firms. Industry
was measured with the two-digit Standard Industrial Classification. All measures are based on that level of detail. The information for these measures comes from the *Census of Manufactures,*
1900 and 1910. The size of the industry in 1899 was included as
an independent variable and it was measured in millions of dollars of assets. The growth of the industry was coded by constructing the following measure:

$$\frac{\text{industry assets in 1909} - \text{industry assets in 1899}}{\text{industry assets in 1899.}}$$

This variable will be interpreted as the percentage growth in assets
over the decade. One would expect that firms in large growing
industries would be more likely to survive than firms in industries
that were small or not growing. A measure of capital intensiveness
of the industry was constructed in the following way:

$$\frac{\text{number of workers in the industry in 1899}}{\text{number of establishments in the industry in 1899.}}$$

This measure would reflect the average size of establishments. In
Chapter 3 it was hypothesized that one cause of the survival of
large firms was the barriers to entry in an industry. The size of
establishment is a rough measure of that variable.

Finally, a series of dummy variables were constructed to reflect
major industries. Firms were coded into the following industrial
groups: chemical, petroleum, metals, mining, textiles, food products, tobacco, transportation equipment, machine-making, electrical machine-making, and miscellaneous. The left-out category
in the regression analysis was mining. One could argue that the
results of the logistic regression might underestimate the industry
effects on the outcome because the industry dummy variables

absorb variation that might otherwise be called industry effects. Models were run without the industry variables and the parameter estimates were nearly identical. The lack of effects of the industry-level variables, therefore, is not due to the industry dummy variables.

The statistical technique I utilized was a logistic regression. I chose this technique because the dependent variable in the data analysis was a dichotomy. The computer program used to generate the estimates was BMDP. The procedure specifies deletion of variables where data is missing. Only 12 cases were eliminated on this basis for the logistic regression, which means that there were 305 usable cases.

Table B.1 presents the means and standard deviations of the various variables in the data analysis. No standard deviations are reported for dummy variables. The numbers reported for dummy variables can be interpreted as the percentage of the population in

Table B.1   Means and variances of variables used in analysis of the causes of survival of large firms, 1895-1919 ($N = 305$)

Variable	Mean	Standard deviation
Success	.457	—
Capitalization	53.64[a]	566.68
Industry assets, 1899	671.25[a]	404.78
Change assets	1.14	2.46
Worker/establishments	35.65	48.01
Concentration	14.41[b]	28.82
Integrated	.33	—
Missing on integrated	.39	—
Petroleum	.019	—
Textiles	.032	—
Chemical	.041	—
Metals	.218	—
Transport	.050	—
Food	.164	—
Machines	.088	—
Electrical equipment	.019	—
Mining	.129	—
Tobacco	.044	—
Miscellaneous	.177	—

Note: See text for definition and coding.
a. In millions of dollars
b. This variable ranges from 0 to 90.

that category. From 1904 to 1919, 45.7 percent of the firms survived. The average capital of all firms formed in the period was $53.64 million, and there was a wide variation around that mean (the standard deviation was $566.68 million dollars). From 1899 until 1909, industries grew by an average of 114 percent. The average size of industry assets in 1899 was $671.25 million. The average number of workers per establishment was 35.65 and the average concentration level for firms in their major industry was 14.41 percent of the market. The dummy variables for industries represent the percentage of all mergers in each industry. The metal-making, miscellaneous, food, and mining industries contained the most consolidations. The last descriptive statistic of great interest concerns the variables that index whether or not a firm had a sales and marketing unit. Thirty-three percent of the firms had established such a unit, while 28 percent of the firms had not. For 39 percent of the firms, this information was not available.

Table B.2 presents the results of a logistic regression model predicting whether or not the firm survived until 1919. A positive parameter implies that the firm had higher odds of survival, while a negative parameter implies that the firm had lower odds of survival. There are only four statistically significant effects in the regression. First, the level of concentration is strongly associated with survival over the period. If a firm was consolidated in an industry and controlled a large market share, it was more likely to survive. Second, both parameters indexing whether or not a firm had a sales and marketing unit indicated the likelihood of survival. If a firm had such a unit, it was more likely to survive than a firm without such a unit. Third, those firms with missing data on this variable were less likely to survive, which suggests that the inability to measure this variable was strongly related to the lack of data on the organization. Finally, firms who merged during this period in the petroleum industry were less likely to survive.

The lack of statistically significant effects for all of the variables measuring industry size, firm size, industry growth, and average size of establishment (or capital intensiveness) is quite interesting. It shows that industrial location, capital investment, and large size were no guarantees of success.

In sum, two plausible hypotheses are confirmed in these data regarding the causes of success for industrial consolidations. First,

Table B.2 Results of a logistic regression predicting whether or not a firm continued to exist in 1919 (0 = nonexistence, 1 = existence) (N = 305)

Variable[a]	b	SE(b)
Capitalization	−.003	.006
Concentration	.021**	.006
Industry assets, 1899	−.003	.004
Change assets	.16	.34
Worker/establishments	−.0003	.006
Integrated	.33*	.16
Missing on integrated	−.51**	.17
Petroleum	−3.97**	1.72
Textiles	−.12	.43
Chemical	.61	.40
Transport	−.23	.37
Food	.04	.27
Machines	.51	.31
Electrical equipment	−.78	.69
Metals	.22	.25
Tobacco	−.69	.41
Miscellaneous	.24	.23
Constant	−4.48	—

Note: Goodness of fit chi-square *p*-value = .065. * p < .05, ** p < .01.
a. See text for definition of variables.

concentration in an industry implied that a firm could control its environment by setting prices. (See various strategies of price setting in Chapter 3.) Second, firms that guaranteed their ability to sell their output by creating sales and marketing divisions were also able to achieve some stability in the market.

Appendix C

The Data Set

The data for this book came from a variety of sources. Given the long time period I studied, there were serious problems of data comparability and measurement. Much of the measurement required coders to make judgments, many of which were further reduced to crude levels of classification. The measures have been used in a number of causal studies. Further, the patterns of important variables have been compared to similar studies that gathered independent data sets. The descriptive statistics from this study compare quite favorably with other studies, suggesting face and concurrent validity. The results from the causal models are quite strong, meaning that the measures may have predictive validity.

The basic data were collected from the 100 largest firms at intervals beginning in 1919. The list of the 100 largest firms for the years 1919–1948 was taken from Collins and Preston (1961) and for the years 1959–1979 from *Fortune*'s list of the 500 largest firms (1960, 1970, 1980). The criterion for inclusion on the list was that the firm needed to be one of the 100 largest in assets. Asset size was chosen over sales or number of employees for two reasons. The available lists were based on assets and asset size was more generally and reliably reported in the past.

The *Fortune* lists contain only firms engaged in manufacturing for more than 50 percent of their revenue. The Collins and Preston lists include all nonfinancial corporations, with the bulk of the nonmanufacturing firms being engaged in retail trade or entertainment. The lists were made compatible by continuing to use the Collins and Preston definitions. It was easier to find data on the largest nonfinancial companies in the postwar era than to impose the *Fortune* definition on earlier records. Table C.1 presents the names of the 100 largest firms at each time point.

The data reported have the following structure. For every firm that appears, data were collected for the time point before the firm entered the list, if the firm entered the list after 1919, and for the time point after the firm left the list, if the firm exited. Table C.2 contains the number of firms that entered and exited the list in each decade. When firms left the list, their reason for exiting were coded. For convenience, many of the tables I have reported are organized into decades in order to assess how patterns changed: 1919–1929, 1929–1939, 1939–1948, 1948–1959, 1959–1969, 1969–1979. The year 1948 was used because Collins and Preston's list refers to that year. Their major data source was a 1948 FTC report. Collins and Preston also use 1935 instead of 1939. I have utilized the 1935 and 1948 panels and done an exhaustive search of the 1940 volume of *Moody's Industrial Manuals* in order to construct a 1939 list.

The variables I have reported were coded in the following way. Two coders independently coded the measures from the various sources. In case of disagreement, I went back to the source to make a judgment. Tables C.3 and C.4 present distributions for strategies and structures over time. Table C.5 presents the industrial breakdown of firms over time.

The organizational form data were coded into four categories: unitary/functional, holding company, multidivisional, and unable to ascertain. The data were coded from a number of sources: *Moody's Manuals*, Chandler (1962), and Rumelt (1974). *Moody's Manuals* describe corporate organization by defining the legal form of the company (for instance, holding company), if the corporation operates through subsidiaries, and if the company is organized divisionally. When the corporation is organized divisionally, *Moody's* describes these divisions by listing their heads and their titles. From this information, one can ascertain whether the divisions are functional, geographic, or product based. For instance, in 1929 U.S. Steel had divisions described as "mining operations," "shipping lines," and "smelting and refining." These divisions imply a functional form of organization.

Strategies were coded into the following categories: product dominant, product related, and product unrelated. Rumelt (1974) and *Moody's Manuals* were used to code these variables. Product dominant implies that the firm is producing primarily one type of product (at least 70 percent of its output), even though different end products might result. Product-related strategies imply sub-

Table C.1 Companies in firm sample and years when they were on the list of the 100 largest companies

Company	1919	1929	1939	1949	1959	1969	1979
1. Allied Chemical and Dye		x	x	x	x	x	x
2. Allied Stores				x			
3. Allis-Chalmers	x .		x	x	x		
4. Aluminum Company of America	x	x	x	x	x	x	x
5. AMAX							x
6. Amerada Hess							x
7. American Agricultural Chemical	x						
8. American Can	x	x	x	x	x	x	x
9. American Car and Foundry Industries	x	x	x	x			
10. American Cotton Oil	x						
11. American Cyanamid				x	x		x
12. American Express	x						
13. American Locomotive	x	x					
14. American Radiator and Standard Sanitary		x	x	x		x	
15. American Smelting and Refining	x	x	x	x	x		
16. American Sugar Refining	x	x	x				
17. American Tobacco	x	x	x	x	x	x	x
18. American Viscase				x			
19. American Woolen	x	x					
20. Anaconda	x	x	x	x	x	x	
21. Armco Steel		x	x	x	x	x	x
22. Armour and Company	x	x	x	x	x		
23. Ashland Oil							x
24. Associated Oil	x						
25. Atlantic Gulf and West Indies Shipping Lines	x						
26. Atlantic Refining	x	x	x	x	x	x	x
27. Avco						x	
28. Baldwin Locomotive Works	x						
29. Beatrice Foods							x
30. Bethlehem Steel	x	x	x	x	x	x	x
31. Boeing Airplane					x	x	x
32. Boise Cascade						x	
33. Borden	x	x	x	x		x	
34. Borg-Warner					x		
35. Burlington Industries				x	x	x	
36. Burroughs						x	x
37. Calamet and Hecla Consolidated Copper	x						

Table C.1 (continued)

Company	1919	1929	1939	1949	1959	1969	1979
38. Caterpillar Tractor					x	x	x
39. Celanese Corp. of America				x	x	x	
40. Chile Copper	x						
41. Chrysler	x	x	x	x	x	x	x
42. Cities Service					x	x	x
43. Climax Molybdenum			x				
44. Coca-Cola			x	x			x
45. Colorado Fuel and Iron	x						
46. Consolidation Coal (original)	x						
47. Consolidation Coal (Pittsburgh)	x	x	x	x			
48. Continental Can			x	x	x	x	x
49. Continental Oil		x	x	x	x	x	x
50. Control Data						x	
51. Corn Products Refining	x	x	x		x		
52. Crane	x	x	x				
53. Crown-Zellerbach		x	x	x	x		
54. Crucible Steel Co. of America	x	x	x				
55. Cuba Cane Sugar	x	x					
56. Cudahy Packing	x						
57. Deere and Company	x	x	x	x	x	x	x
58. Douglas Aircraft					x		
59. Dow Chemical				x	x	x	x
60. Dresser Industries							x
61. DuPont de Nemours	x	x	x	x	x	x	x
62. Eastman Kodak	x	x	x	x	x	x	x
63. Federated Department Stores						x	x
64. Marshall Field		x	x				
65. Firestone Tire and Rubber	x	x	x	x	x	x	x
66. Ford Motor Company	x	x	x	x	x	x	x
67. General American Transportation			x				
68. General Dynamics					x	x	
69. General Electric	x	x	x	x	x	x	x
70. General Foods			x	x	x	x	x
71. General Motors	x	x	x	x	x	x	x
72. General Telephone and Electronics					x	x	x
73. Georgia-Pacific						x	x
74. Getty Oil						x	x
75. Gimbel Brothers			x				
76. Glen Alden Coal		x	x				
77. Goodrich, B.F.	x	x	x	x	x	x	
78. Goodyear Tire and Rubber	x	x	x	x	x	x	x
79. Grace, W. R.					x	x	x

Table C.1 (continued)

Company	1919	1929	1939	1949	1959	1969	1979
80. Great Atlantic and Pacific Tea		x	x	x	x		
81. Great Northern Iron Ore Props	x						
82. Greene Cananea Copper	x						
83. Gulf Oil	x	x	x	x	x	x	x
84. Gulf and Western Industries						x	x
85. Hearst Consolidated Publications			x	x			
86. Honeywell						x	x
87. Illinois Central Industries						x	x
88. Inland Steel		x	x	x	x	x	x
89. International Business Machines			x	x	x	x	x
90. International Harvester	x	x	x	x	x	x	x
91. International Match		x					
92. International Mercantile Marine	x						
93. International Nickel	x	x	x	x			
94. International Paper	x	x	x	x	x	x	x
95. International Shoe		x	x				
96. International Telephone and Telegraph					x	x	x
97. International Utilities						x	
98. Johnson and Johnson							x
99. Jones and Laughlin Steel	x	x	x	x	x		
100. Kaiser Aluminum and Chemical					x	x	x
101. Kaiser Steel					x		
102. Kennecott Copper	x	x	x	x	x	x	x
103. Koppers		x	x				
104. Kresge, S.S.		x	x	x			x
105. Lackawanna Steel	x						
106. Lehigh Coal and Navigation	x						
107. Lehigh Valley Coal		x					
108. Libby, McNeill and Libby	x						
109. Liggett and Myers Tobacco	x	x	x	x	x		
110. Ling-Temco-Vought						x	x
111. Litton Industries						x	x
112. Lockheed Aircraft					x	x	
113. Loew's		x	x	x			
114. Long-Bell Lumber		x					
115. Lorillard, P., Company	x	x					
116. Macy, R. H.			x				
117. Magnolia Petroleum	x						
118. May Department Stores				x	x		
119. McDermott, J. Ray							x

Table C.1 (continued)

Company	1919	1929	1939	1949	1959	1969	1979
120. McDonnell Aircraft						x	x
121. Merck							x
122. Mexican Petroleum	x						
123. Midvale Steel and Ordnance	x						
124. Midwest Refining	x						
125. Minnesota Mining and Manufacturing						x	x
126. Monsanto Chemical				x	x	x	x
127. Montgomery Ward	x	x	x	x	x	x	
128. Morris	x						
129. National Biscuit	x	x	x	x			
130. National Cash Register						x	x
131. National Dairy Products		x	x	x	x		
132. National Distillers and Chemical				x	x		
133. National Lead	x	x	x	x			
134. National Steel		x	x	x	x	x	x
135. Northwest Industries						x	
136. Occidental Petroleum						x	x
137. Ohio Oil	x	x	x	x	x	x	x
138. Olin Mathieson Chemical					x	x	
139. Owens-Illinois Glass				x	x	x	x
140. Packard Motor Car	x						
141. Paramount Pictures		x	x	x			
142. Penney, J. C.			x	x	x	x	x
143. Pepsi Co.							x
144. Pfizer Chemical							x
145. Phelps Dodge	x	x	x	x	x		
146. Philadelphia and Reading Coal and Iron		x					
147. Philip Morris							x
148. Phillips Petroleum		x	x	x	x	x	x
149. Pittsburgh Plate Glass		x	x	x	x	x	x
150. Prairie Oil and Gas	x	x					
151. Prairie Pipe Line	x	x					
152. Procter and Gamble	x	x	x	x	x	x	x
153. Pullman	x	x	x	x			
154. Pure Oil	x	x	x	x	x		
155. Radio Corporation of America		x	x	x	x	x	x
156. Rapid-American						x	
157. Republic Steel	x	x	x	x	x	x	x
158. Reynolds Metals					x	x	x
159. Reynolds, R. J., Tobacco	x	x	x	x	x	x	x
160. Richfield Oil		x			x		

Table C.1   (continued)

Company	1919	1929	1939	1949	1959	1969	1979
161. Rockwell International							x
162. St. Regis Paper					x		
163. Safeway					x		x
164. Schenley Industries			x	x	x		
165. Seagram, J. E. and Sons			x	x	x	x	
166. Sears, Roebuck	x	x	x	x	x	x	x
167. Shell Oil		x	x	x	x	x	x
168. Signal Companies						x	x
169. Sinclair Crude Oil Purchasing		x					
170. Sinclair Oil	x	x	x	x	x		
171. Singer Manufacturing	x	x	x	x	x	x	
172. Skelly Oil				x			
173. Socony Mobil Oil	x	x	x	x	x	x	x
174. Sperry Rand					x	x	x
175. Standard Oil (Calif.)	x	x	x	x	x	x	x
176. Standard Oil (Indiana)	x	x	x	x	x	x	x
177. Standard Oil (New Jersey)	x	x	x	x	x	x	x
178. Standard Oil (Ohio)				x	x	x	x
179. Steel and Tube Company of America	x						
180. Stevens, J. P.				x			
181. Studebaker	x	x					
182. Sun Oil			x	x	x	x	x
183. Sunray Mid-Continent Oil					x		
184. Superior Oil							x
185. Swift	x	x	x	x	x		
186. Tenneco						x	x
187. Texas Co./Texaco	x	x	x	x	x	x	x
188. Thomson-Ramo-Woolridge							x
189. Tidewater Oil		x	x	x	x		
190. Twentieth Century Fox		x		x			
191. Union Carbide	x	x	x	x	x	x	x
192. Union Oil Company of California	x	x	x	x	x	x	x
193. Union Pacific							x
194. United Aircraft					x	x	x
195. United Cigar Stores		x					
196. United Drug		x					
197. United Fruit	x	x	x	x			
198. United Shoe Machinery	x		x				
199. U.S. Leather	x						
200. U.S. Plywood-Champion Papers						x	x
201. U.S. Rubber	x	x	x	x	x	x	

Table C.1 (continued)

Company	1919	1929	1939	1949	1959	1969	1979
202. U.S. Smelting, Refining and Melting	x						
203. U.S. Steel	x	x	x	x	x	x	x
204. Utah Copper	x						
205. Vacuum Oil	x	x					
206. Virginia Carolina Chemical	x						
207. Warner Brothers		x	x	x			
208. Warner Lambert							x
209. Western Electric	x	x	x	x	x	x	x
210. Westinghouse Electric	x	x	x	x	x	x	x
211. Weyerhaeuser Timber				x	x	x	x
212. Wheeling Steel	x	x	x	x			
213. Wilson	x		x				
214. Woolworth, W. F.	x	x	x	x	x	x	x
215. Xerox						x	x
216. Youngstown Sheet and Tube - Lykes	x	x	x	x	x	x	

Table C.2 Number of firms staying on, coming to, or leaving list of 100 largest, 1919–1979

	1919–29	1929–39	1939–48	1948–59	1959–69	1969–79
Stayers	69	82	86	79	75	80
Comers	31	18	14	21	25	20
Leavers	31	18	14	21	25	20
Total	131	118	114	121	125	120

stantial multiple-product lines that are related. For instance, chemical companies produced paint and explosives. No single product line can account for more than 70 percent of output. Product unrelated implies that firms are engaged in unrelated businesses for a substantial proportion of their revenue. Again, no one product line accounts for more than 70 percent of output. For instance, LTV produced steel, guided missiles, and owned a rent-a-car company.

Table C.3 Strategies and structures of the 100 largest firms by decade, 1919–1979 (in percentages)

	1919	1929	1939	1948	1959	1969	1979
Strategy							
Dominant	89	85	78	62	40	24	22
Related	11	15	22	36	55	56	53
Unrelated	0	0	0	2	5	20	25
Structure							
Holding company	31	25	16	5	5	7	4
Unitary/functional	69	73	75	75	43	20	10
Multidivisional	0	2	9	20	52	73	86
Multinational							
No	59	47	35	33	23	13	7
Yes	41	53	65	67	77	87	93

The 70 percent rule was chosen following Rumelt. In his study, he found that firms were either well above or well below the 70 percent line. This is a somewhat arbitrary dividing point, but it allows for comparison across data sets and time. I would have liked to have more detailed product line data. Unfortunately, no such systematic data exist for the early twentieth century. Further, the product division data for older firms is scarce so judgments as to strategy were made based on the descriptions of products.

Table C.4 Strategies and structures of firms leaving and arriving over each decade, 1919–1979 (in percentages)

	1919–1929 (N = 31)		1929–1939 (N = 17)		1939–1948 (N = 14)		1948–1959 (N = 21)		1959–1969 (N = 25)		1969–1979 (N = 20)	
	Leaver	Comer	Leaver	Comer	Leaver	Comer	Leaver	Comer	Leaver	Comer	Leaver	Comer
Strategy												
Dominant	93.5	94.8	94.1	92.9	64.3	100.0	61.9	66.7	48.0	34.8	20.0	20.0
Related	6.5	4.2	5.9	7.1	35.1	0.0	33.3	27.8	52.0	39.1	35.0	55.0
Unrelated	0.0	0.0	0.0	0.0	0.0	0.0	4.8	5.6	0.0	26.1	45.0	25.0
Structure												
Holding company	22.6	19.0	29.4	21.4	7.7	25.0	9.5	33.3	12.0	13.0	20.0	10.0
Unitary/functional	77.4	81.0	70.6	78.6	69.2	75.0	85.7	44.4	48.0	52.2	5.0	15.0
Multidivisional	0.0	0.0	0.0	0.0	23.1	0.0	4.8	22.2	40.0	34.8	75.0	75.0
Multinational												
No	71.0	77.4	64.7	76.5	35.7	78.6	47.6	52.4	36.0	48.0	25.0	10.0
Yes	29.0	22.6	35.3	23.5	64.3	21.4	52.4	47.6	64.0	52.0	75.0	90.0

Table C.5 Industry representation of the 100 largest corporations, 1919–1979

Background	1919	1929	1939	1948	1959	1969	1979
Mining	18	6	2	6	4	0	0
Lumber	0	2	1	1	1	4	2
Stone, clay, glass	0	1	1	2	2	2	2
Primary metals	8	5	8	10	12	12	10
Fabricated metals	4	12	12	3	3	3	5
Machinery	7	2	5	3	6	3	2
Electrical equipment	3	2	5	5	5	10	8
Automobiles	5	4	3	3	3	3	3
Other transportation	3	5	5	2	5	8	8
Instruments	1	3	2	1	2	4	5
Food	13	9	15	13	7	4	6
Tobacco	4	4	3	3	3	2	2
Textiles, apparel	1	2	1	5	1	1	0
Paper	1	2	2	2	3	2	2
Chemicals	3	6	5	7	11	9	8
Petroleum	18	18	16	18	19	17	22
Rubber	3	4	4	4	4	4	2
Leather	1	0	0	0	0	0	0
Retail	2	7	7	7	7	5	6
Miscellaneous	5	6	3	5	2	7	7

Appendix D

Models for the 100 Largest Firms, 1919–1979

The data discussed in Appendix C have been used extensively in recently published papers (Fligstein, 1985, 1987, 1989a, 1989b). It is useful to present the basic empirical results of those analyses because they inform the historical materials in this book. Four different outcomes have been studied using this data: the causes of different forms of growth of the largest firms; the shift in strategies toward greater product diversification; the shifts in the subunit background of CEOs in the largest corporations; and the shift to the multidivisional form.

The basic theoretical conception motivating this work revolves around the organizational field. Once organizational fields stabilized in the 1920s, they became the context of various organizations' actions. For any corporation, the field defined successful strategies and structures. It also provided presidents of the largest firms with a reference group and role model for appropriate courses of action. Since what was most efficient was not apparent, most actors in organizations spent a fair amount of time watching one another and evaluating the performance of those firms in their field.

The source of change for any given organization could originate in the field or the state. If the state rewrote the rules of any given organizational field, circumstances would change and actors in firms would respond. General economic conditions could greatly affect the actions of other firms. Those firms that innovated because of a crisis in the field helped redefine what was appropriate behavior in the field. But for change to occur in an organization, it was always necessary for key actors to interpret the crisis and propose a solution to the crisis. Once a set of actors in a field altered their course of action, then other actors would come under pressure to follow suit.

Change in these organizational fields was therefore a complex set of diffusion processes that revolved around new points of view coming to dominate the field. One time it would require innovative actors to produce change, while at another those very same actors could resist innovations. In the initial stages of any change some actors had to have the power to enforce their view on the course of their organization. Once that course of action was interpreted as successful, others followed.

In all of the analyses there are three sorts of mechanisms that produce change. First, the organizational field and the state provide impetus to change. Second, certain key actors are able to impose innovation. Third, once a set of actions is defined as successful in the field, other organizations are encouraged to change. Claims on power by certain presidents with different subunit backgrounds will also be a consequence of these factors.

The basic logic of these analyses is similar. The data cover the 100 largest firms at ten-year intervals. Firms that leave the list and arrive on the list are included in the data analysis. For three of the analyses, the data are organized into panels that are divided into the following periods: 1919–1929, 1929–1939, 1939–1948, 1948–1959, 1959–1969, and 1969–1979. One of the analyses combines the data into twenty-year periods: 1919–1939, 1939–1959, and 1959–1979. This allows us to examine how certain practices at the initial time point affect practices at subsequent time points as well as viewing the causes of why firms entered, exited, or stayed on the list in a given decade.

The use of variables was relatively consistent throughout the studies. The measures fall into distinct categories: strategies, structures, subunit background of the president, organizational demography, characteristics of the organizational field, and technology. (For a discussion of data sources, see Appendix C.)

Measures of strategy were coded on the basis of product mix and the number of mergers a firm engaged in over the decade. The measure refers to the previous decade in all of the analyses. Mergers were coded from *Moody's Manuals* before 1948 and from the *Federal Trade Commission's Report on Mergers* (1981) thereafter.

Two other measures of strategy were coded. First, a dummy variable was created to indicate whether or not the firm had a significant multinational presence. This was indexed by the presence of an international unit in the firm or a description of the firm as engaged extensively in overseas markets. The source for this data was *Moody's Manuals*. The final measure used was a dummy variable signifying whether or not a firm was vertically integrated. This refers to elements of integration backward toward raw materials, not the presence of a sales and marketing subunit. This variable was coded on the basis of the description of the firm in *Moody's Manuals*.

Structure was indexed by a dummy variable indicating whether or not a firm had a multidivisional form. These data were collected from a variety of sources including Chandler (1962), Rumelt (1974), and *Moody's Manuals*.

The subunit background of the president of the firm is the measure of cognition in the field and the power to act. There are three important subunits in large firms: manufacturing, sales and marketing, and finance. These three subunits have strategies that are consistent with their views of the world and their power base in the organization. The best indicator of who is in control of the firm is the subunit background of the president of the firm. We will use the president's background to measure the likely change in the firm, the shifts in power, and as a dependent variable.

The data were collected by first identifying the president or CEO for each firm at all relevant times. These were found in *Moody's Manuals*. Then, from *Who's Who in America, Who's Who in Business and Industry*, and other sources, the description of each president's career was analyzed to determine how the person came up through the organization. The following categories were coded: manufacturing, sales and marketing, finance, general management, entrepreneur, lawyer, and unable to ascertain. The general management category implied that a person held positions across subunits, such as plant manager and vice-president in charge of finance. In the data analyses, various codings were used. Sometimes, a large set of dummy variables were created using the manufacturing presidents. Other times, the contrasts were limited to manufacturing, sales and marketing, finance, and other.

There were a number of measures of organizational demography. The age of the firm was calculated by subtracting the year of the firm's founding from the first year of each decade in the panel study. A firm founded in 1900 would be coded as nineteen years old in the earliest panel, twenty-nine in the second panel, and so forth. Founding dates were taken from *Moody's Manuals*. Firms that were consolidations of a number of firms aged from when the consolidation occurred. Firms that engaged in mergers were considered to have been founded when they were incorporated, even though the mergers could have substantially altered product mix.

Several measures of size and growth were utilized. Size was indexed by assets, sales, and profits at the first time point. All measures of size were standardized to 1967 dollars to adjust for the effects of inflation. Growth was indexed in two ways. When growth was the dependent variable, it was coded as the simple difference in assets, profits, or sales over the decade. In other models where growth was an independent variable, it was indexed by the percent change in assets, the most consistent measure of size reported over time. These data came from *Moody's Manuals*.

The most difficult data to obtain were those indexing the organizational field. The two-digit Standard Industrial Classification score was used as a proxy for the organizational field. A variety of measures was calculated within a field to indicate the effects of that field on the actions of a given organization. For instance, if one is interested in the effect of the field on the likelihood of a firm to adopt the multidivisional form, an adequate measure might be the percentage of other large firms in that field that had adopted the new structure. Similarly, measures could be constructed for the percent of firms in a given field that had adopted a product-related or -unrelated strategy and the percent that had a manufacturing, sales and marketing, and finance president. These measures do not include the firm to which they apply and all refer to the condition of the organizational field at the first time point in the panel. For the study of growth, a measure was included that indexed the percentage change in an industry's assets over the decade.

The measure of technology employed varied from study to study. Often crude measures of industry level were employed. These were dummy variables coded into major industry groups.

The Causes of Growth

The growth of the largest firms has been the outcome of complex processes of organizational, demographic, and economic factors. Growth is defined here as change in assets, sales, and profits. I choose to analyze all three possible sources of growth because all are theoretically interesting. In the panels I model the causes of firms entering, exiting and staying on the list of the 100 largest companies in the United States. The causes of growth shift as growth strategies change. For a historical and theoretical discussion of these causes, see Fligstein (1989b).

Table D.1 presents the means and standard deviations for the variables used in this analysis. Table D.2 presents the results of a weighted least squares regression attempting to explain this growth decade by decade. A weighted least squares procedure was chosen because there was evidence of heteroscedasticity. Growth is measured as discussed previously and all three sources of growth are considered. In general, what causes one source of growth is related to changes in the other measures.

In the 1919–1929 period, vertical integration of production was positively related to changes in all three sources of growth. This implies that the manufacturing strategy that focused on integrating production toward suppliers was a successful one. Firms that had shifted to a product-related strategy, executed mergers, and contained a substantial multinational presence also experienced growth. The sales and marketing strategy of diversification that began in the 1920s was already successful. Finally, if a firm was located in an industry that experienced growth, it was likely to increase its size on all three measures.

In the Depression most firms did not grow very much. The only effect of strategy on growth was by firms with a product-related strategy. Here, diversified firms had higher sales and profits than firms that maintained a product-dominant strategy. Firms that shifted to the multidivisional form also grew at higher rates than firms operating with a functional form. Another important factor that led to growth was the presence of a sales and marketing president. One could argue that such presidents were more likely to aid their organizations in a downturn by concentrating on various ways to sell. Finally, the expansion and contraction of a firm's major industry positively affected growth.

During World War II the presence of vertical integration was related to negative growth. The decline of this strategy in the post-Depression era is quite striking. Product-related and merger strategies again were positively related to growth. Firms that adopted the multidivisional form continued to experience higher than

Table D.1 Means and standard deviations of variables in the data analysis

Variable	1919–1929		1929–1939	
	X̄	S.D.	X̄	S.D.
Strategies				
Vertical	.51		.69	
Product related	.13		.14	
Product unrelated	.00		.00	
Multinational	.40		.52	
Mergers	2.06	3.93	3.45	5.81
Structure				
Multidivisional form	.00		.02	
Subunit control				
Manufacturing	.26		.33	
Sales and marketing	.07		.09	
Finance	.09		.07	
Organizational demography				
Assets, t_1	323.7	480.4	533.6	627.5
Change in assets	196.0	361.0	74.9	306.4
Age	20.89	18.85	21.29	18.12
Sales, t_1	332.2	489.4	531.8	669.2
Change in sales	155.9	393.2	133.6	261.2
Profits, t_1	18.1	28.7	26.7	42.4
Change in profits	11.0	22.9	−8.1	20.5
Industry growth	.65	.86	.13	.19

Source: Fligstein (1989b), table 3.

1939–1948		1948–1959		1959–1969		1969–1979	
$\overline{X}$	S.D.	$\overline{X}$	S.D.	$\overline{X}$	S.D.	$\overline{X}$	S.D.
.79		.82		.73		.68	
.20		.34		.54		.51	
.01		.08		.11		.21	
.61		.62		.75		.88	
2.22	4.04	.82	1.39	1.51	2.11	.87	1.75
.08		.19		.50		.73	
.35		.26		.26		.25	
.14		.22		.23		.19	
.06		.11		.17		.22	
608.6	761.0	619.1	723.6	1197.1	1560.0	2251.5	2388.9
23.2	193.1	590.5	849.2	978.8	1188.2	653.4	1330.8
29.45	13.41	38.21	15.08	43.2	17.5	51.1	19.9
583.1	516.5	827.4	962.5	1443.0	1766.9	2323.1	2848.4
387.0	488.8	575.0	976.8	951.6	1375.6	1671.5	3205.9
15.25	22.4	48.5	61.5	81.1	124.9	159.3	227.98
31.7	43.8	28.3	72.6	70.3	125.3	307.6	470.2
.80	.33	.66	.45	.51	.19	.52	.51

Table D.2 Results of a weighted least squares regression analysis predicting growth in assets, sales, and profits (in millions of dollars) by decade, 1919–1979

Independent variables	1919–1929 (N = 102) Assets b	SE(b)	Sales b	SE(b)	Profits b	SE(b)	1929–1939 (N = 104) Assets b	SE(b)	Sales b	SE(b)	Profits b	SE(b)
Vertical	91.5**	40.3	63.0*	31.4	1.98**	.49	-2.1	4.6	-19.1	10.5	.77	1.7
Related	15.1*	.07	158.3*	80.3	1.11*	.54	59.2	48.6	111.4**	43.4	2.6*	1.2
Unrelated	—	—	—	—	—	—	—	—	—	—	—	—
Mergers	13.4**	5.2	5.1	6.5	.89**	.33	2.6	3.4	5.1	4.0	-.1	.1
Multinational	137.4*	60.1	76.3	60.1	5.9*	2.8	15.9	9.7	20.7	15.8	.30	.91
MDF, t_1	—	—	—	—	—	—	.92*	.45	.32*	.15	.84	.65
Assets, t_1	-.04	.10	—	—	—	—	-.10*	.05	—	—	—	—
Age	1.43	1.3	.64	1.4	-.03	.07	.54	.51	-.45	1.6	-.01	.03
Sales, t_1	—	—	.28	.24	—	—	—	—	-.20**	.04	—	—
Profit, t_1	—	—	—	—	.37	.26	—	—	—	—	-.49**	.12
Manuf. president	23.7	38.8	-118.4	71.8	2.9	6.1	7.6	5.5	52.5	50.5	-.24	2.6
Sales president	21.1	26.4	76.6	79.4	6.6	6.0	73.5*	30.8	85.9*	41.6	7.0*	3.4
Finance president	61.7	52.1	84.5	79.8	7.7	4.6	35.8	39.5	81.9	54.8	-1.2	2.7
Industry growth	111.5**	47.9	92.3*	45.8	7.5*	3.2	91.4*	42.3	291.7**	98.6	11.3*	5.3
Constant	-67.9	78.4	87.8	96.7	-2.38	3.84	-140.9	92.1	88.9	75.8	.97	4.0
R^2	.20		.25		.22		.31		.20		.28	

Source: Fligstein (1989b), table 5.
Note: * $p < .05$, ** $p < .01$.

Table D.2 (continued)

Independent variables	1939–1948 (N = 102)						1948–1959 (N = 104)					
	Assets		Sales		Profits		Assets		Sales		Profits	
	b	SE(b)	b	SE(b)	b	SE(b)	b	SE(b)	b	SE(b)	b	SE(b)
Vertical	-40.1*	19.8	-101.4*	50.6	-9.8*	4.7	-78.4**	26.2	-72.8*	34.4	-54.6	26.1
Related	15.7	8.6	29.3**	7.5	2.6**	.98	40.9*	18.7	8.6	7.4	5.8*	2.6
Unrelated	—	—	—	—	—	—	279.5**	41.5	235.6**	71.3	21.6*	10.1
Mergers	7.7*	3.7	11.9*	5.7	.91	.87	93.8**	27.6	65.9**	20.6	2.8	4.8
Multinational	25.5	31.9	-16.0	14.2	2.8	4.6	6.2	8.1	.76	.82	7.4	9.5
MDF, t_1	14.7*	7.2	125.6*	61.4	17.7*	8.4	87.2*	43.3	19.8	18.6	1.8*	.51
Assets, t_1	-0.7*	.04	—	—	—	—	.23**	.07	—	—	—	—
Age	1.6	1.2	.46	1.7	-.05	.20	-1.9	2.6	-.47	.61	.26	.36
Sales, t_1	—	—	.82**	.07	—	—	—	—	.58**	.16	—	—
Profit, t_1	—	—	—	—	1.5**	.26	—	—	—	—	.07**	.01
Manuf. president	4.1	3.3	-1.8	1.8	6.7	7.7	-15.1	9.9	-16.9	20.8	-2.4	1.5
Sales president	191.5*	91.7	133.4*	63.2	21.0*	10.1	15.9	8.7	2.7	2.0	1.8	1.3
Finance president	92.9	67.7	13.2	7.2	2.3	3.7	17.5	10.6	30.5	21.0	1.1	1.2
Industry growth	13.9*	6.8	70.3*	34.9	16.3*	7.9	223.1**	90.6	427.1**	149.3	28.5**	10.1
Constant	55.4	91.3	91.4	87.2	12.3	14.6	131.7*	62.1	515.9	484.2	15.5	8.6
R^2	.18		.45		.51		.60		.32		.43	

Table D.2 (continued)

Independent variables	1959–1969 (N = 102)						1969–1979 (N = 104)					
	Assets		Sales		Profits		Assets		Sales		Profits	
	b	SE(b)	b	SE(b)	b	SE(b)	b	SE(b)	b	SE(b)	b	SE(b)
Vertical	−166.8*	76.7	−959.2*	487.6	−8.6	7.3	−46.2*	22.3	−72.6	48.8	−9.6	7.2
Related	199.7*	96.8	142.9*	64.8	12.6*	6.1	29.9	28.9	43.4	54.7	1.9	4.2
Unrelated	1073.6**	396.3	959.2**	327.8	41.4*	20.6	79.9	63.4	−24.2	56.4	−12.3	10.1
Mergers	161.1**	53.4	230.9**	40.1	9.6**	2.6	63.5**	22.8	58.8**	28.8	19.8*	9.6
Multinational	−32.1	25.5	−55.1	32.4	−2.3	2.8	49.3	42.7	29.3	31.7	−9.9	9.4
MDF, t_1	13.8	18.7	25.4	24.6	1.8	4.8	34.6	34.8	23.3	41.5	30.6	28.4
Assets, t_1	.46**	.08	—	—	—	—	.19**	.07	—	—	—	—
Age	−.04	.03	−1.35	4.4	.37	.35	12.8*	5.6	5.9	3.2	1.7	1.5
Sales, t_1	—	—	.58**	.06	—	—	—	—	.64**	.20	—	—
Profit, t_1	—	—	—	—	.68**	.14	—	—	—	—	.26**	.08
Manuf. president	−63.1	76.3	−22.8	27.0	−25.6	19.4	−85.1	48.1	−25.1	28.2	−16.7	9.6
Sales president	22.8	26.2	27.0	35.1	15.9	16.5	30.6	29.3	22.2	21.8	−7.7	8.0
Finance president	86.3*	36.2	70.0	99.1	19.8	23.6	24.9	31.9	27.3	24.7	7.6	7.4
Industry growth	1047.6**	314.5	964.9**	363.8	83.9*	40.3	1052.4*	225.1	2898.7**	663.2	19.8**	5.9
Constant	63.7*	30.8	108.3**	42.1	−34.6	31.5	−712.0*	350.8	−1612.1*	834.6	25.6**	8.4
R^2	.37		.56		.41		.33		.56		.54	

average growth. At this time the presence of a sales and marketing president promoted growth regardless of strategy. If a firm was in a growing industry, it was also more likely to experience growth.

The product-unrelated or conglomerate strategy produced enormous growth in the 1948–1959 period. The effect of product-related diversification was still a cause of growth, albeit at a lower level. Mergers continued as a growth strategy. This demonstrates that the financial strategy of firms buying and selling other firms was a spectacular source of growth for those firms that pioneered it. The multidivisional form continued to boost firm growth. Again, the growth of an industry was a major cause of growth in firms.

The product-unrelated and merger strategies continued as causes of growth in the 1960s. By this time most of the largest firms had already adopted the multidivisional form and therefore any gains were shared by all. The fact that the overall economy was rapidly growing was also a major cause of firm growth. The 1970s were a period of lower growth. The only successful strategy then was mergers. The growth of a firm's industry had the most substantial effect on firm growth.

A number of overall patterns are worth noting. First, as new strategies emerged, they began to cause growth in their firms. Once those strategies spread all firms gained equally from them. The first to employ the diversification strategies and multidivisional form gained greatly from their innovations. Second, mergers were a constant source of growth in the ten years after they were undertaken. Third, industry location was an important source of growth. It is most interesting that the only successful tactic for growth in the Depression was a product-related strategy and the dominance of a sales and marketing president. It is also important to see that the manufacturing strategy declined in importance by World War II and in fact contributed to negative firm growth. Together these results support my theoretical and historical arguments.

The Causes of Diversification

One important question that these tables leave open is how diversification spread. There are two possibilities: first, new corporations could come into existence with the new strategy and

Table D.3 Changes in corporate strategy by decades, 1919-1979 (in percentages)

1919–1929

Status in 1929	Total sample, 1919			Stayers, 1919			Leavers, 1919			Comers, 1919		
	Dom. (N = 100)	Rel. (N = 15)	Unrel. (N = 0)	Dom. (N = 61)	Rel. (N = 9)	Unrel. (N = 0)	Dom. (N = 23)	Rel. (N = 1)	Unrel. (N = 0)	Dom. (N = 16)	Rel. (N = 5)	Unrel. (N = 0)
Dominant	92.0	40.0	0.0	96.7	12.2	0.0	95.6	0.0	0.0	68.75	20.0	0.0
Related	8.0	60.0	0.0	3.3	87.2	0.0	4.4	100.0	0.0	31.25	80.0	0.0
Unrelated	0.0	0.0	0.0	0.0	0.0	0.0	0.0	0.0	0.0	0.0	0.0	0.0

1929–1939

Status in 1939	Total sample, 1929			Stayers, 1929			Leavers, 1929			Comers, 1929		
	Dom. (N = 93)	Rel. (N = 16)	Unrel. (N = 0)	Dom. (N = 69)	Rel. (N = 14)	Unrel. (N = 0)	Dom. (N = 10)	Rel. (N = 1)	Unrel. (N = 0)	Dom. (N = 14)	Rel. (N = 1)	Unrel. (N = 0)
Dominant	92.4	6.3	0.0	95.6	7.0	0.0	100.0	0.0	0.0	71.4	0.0	0.0
Related	7.6	93.7	0.0	4.4	93.0	0.0	0.0	100.0	0.0	28.6	100.0	0.0
Unrelated	0.0	0.0	0.0	0.0	0.0	0.0	0.0	0.0	0.0	0.0	0.0	0.0

1939–1948

Status in 1948	Total sample, 1939			Stayers, 1939			Leavers, 1939			Comers, 1939		
	Dom. (N = 90)	Rel. (N = 22)	Unrel. (N = 0)	Dom. (N = 68)	Rel. (N = 17)	Unrel. (N = 0)	Dom. (N = 9)	Rel. (N = 5)	Unrel. (N = 0)	Dom. (N = 13)	Rel. (N = 0)	Unrel. (N = 0)
Dominant	76.7	9.5	0.0	75.0	5.9	0.0	100.0	20.0	0.0	69.2	0.0	0.0
Related	22.1	85.6	0.0	23.5	88.2	0.0	0.0	80.0	0.0	30.8	0.0	0.0
Unrelated	1.1	4.8	0.0	1.5	5.9	0.0	0.0	0.0	0.0	0.0	0.0	0.0

Table D.3 (continued)

1948–1959

Status in 1959	Total sample, 1948			Stayers, 1948			Leavers, 1948			Comers, 1948		
	Dom. (N = 73)	Rel. (N = 40)	Unrel. (N = 3)	Dom. (N = 48)	Rel. (N = 28)	Unrel. (N = 1)	Dom. (N = 13)	Rel. (N = 7)	Unrel. (N = 1)	Dom. (N = 12)	Rel. (N = 5)	Unrel. (N = 1)
Dominant	65.7	0.0	0.0	62.5	0.0	0.0	84.6	0.0	0.0	58.1	0.0	0.0
Related	32.7	92.5	0.0	37.5	100.0	0.0	7.7	85.7	0.0	41.1	60.0	0.0
Unrelated	1.4	7.5	100.0	0.0	0.0	100.0	7.7	14.3	100.0	0.0	40.2	100.0

1959–1969

Status in 1969	Total sample, 1959			Stayers, 1959			Leavers, 1959			Comers, 1959		
	Dom. (N = 41)	Rel. (N = 63)	Unrel. (N = 11)	Dom. (N = 26)	Rel. (N = 46)	Unrel. (N = 5)	Dom. (N = 6)	Rel. (N = 10)	Unrel. (N = 0)	Dom. (N = 8)	Rel. (N = 8)	Unrel. (N = 6)
Dominant	63.4	6.4	0.0	70.4	6.7	0.0	66.6	0.0	0.0	37.5	12.5	0.0
Related	29.2	84.0	0.0	25.9	86.6	0.0	33.3	80.0	0.0	37.5	75.0	0.0
Unrelated	7.3	9.6	100.0	3.7	6.7	100.0	0.0	20.0	0.0	25.0	12.5	100.0

1969–1979

Status in 1979	Total sample, 1969			Stayers, 1969			Leavers, 1969			Comers, 1969		
	Dom. (N = 28)	Rel. (N = 63)	Unrel. (N = 24)	Dom. (N = 21)	Rel. (N = 47)	Unrel. (N = 11)	Dom. (N = 4)	Rel. (N = 5)	Unrel. (N = 9)	Dom. (N = 3)	Rel. (N = 11)	Unrel. (N = 4)
Dominant	89.2	0.0	0.0	90.5	0.0	0.0	100.0	0.0	0.0	66.6	0.0	0.0
Related	7.2	87.3	4.2	9.5	87.2	0.0	0.0	100.0	0.0	0.0	81.8	25.0
Unrelated	3.6	12.7	95.8	0.0	12.8	100.0	0.0	0.0	100.0	33.3	18.2	75.0

Source: Fligstein (1989a), table 2.

Note: Status refers to status over the decade. Stayer implies that firm appears on list of 100 largest firms at both time points; leaver implies firm leaves list at second time point; comer implies firm enters list at second time point.

displace corporations with the old strategy and second, old corporations could shift their strategies to achieve continued growth. It is important to model this process as support for the growth models.

Table D.3 presents the change in strategies by status with respect to the list of the 100 largest corporations. In the earliest periods new firms to the list were more likely to have been diversified and those that left the list were less likely to have been so. The firms that stayed on the list were somewhere in between. Further, between 1919 and 1948 those firms that arrived on the list were more likely to have shifted their strategy toward a diversification strategy over the decade, implying that their ability to grow was an outcome of their diversification. There was also a substantial amount of shift in strategies among those firms that stayed on the list, implying that diversification as a strategy for growth was generally a property of the fastest growing large firms. The firms that dropped off of the list of the 100 largest corporations were, quite simply, not diversifying.

In the postwar era these patterns continued. Firms that were growing tended to engage in diversification, both product related and unrelated. Those firms that left the list appeared to be shifting strategies at lower rates than those that remained or arrived on the list. By 1979 almost all of the firms were substantially diversified.

While these descriptive patterns show that diversification was certainly related to growth, they do not allow one to assess the causes of diversification for those firms that actually shifted strategies. Indeed, some firms diversified and grew and others did not. The causes of diversification can be located in the organizational view presented earlier. Organizations are systems of power that are dominated by certain interest groups. These groups benefit from the distribution of valued goods in those organizations and, therefore, have little incentive to alter their organization. The remarkable fact is that organizations shift strategies at all (see Fligstein (1989a) for a more detailed discussion).

Hence, one would expect that organizations tend to reproduce their strategy as that strategy itself reflects a particular system of power. What, then, causes actors to change the outputs of their organization? A necessary condition would be some objective crisis in the organization or the organizational field. Such a crisis could reflect general economic conditions, the actions of the state, the actions of particularly aggressive competitors, or even a succession struggle within the organization. I have already argued that the depressions of the 1890s and 1930s, as well as the enforcement of the Sherman, Clayton, and Celler-Kefauver acts, are examples of such crises.

In a crisis there have to be actors in firms who can perceive the problem and prescribe a course of action to solve it. Here I identify those key actors by their subunit background in the largest firms. Those who come from manufacturing backgrounds are likely to stick to vertical integration, product-dominant, and leading firm strategies. Their view of the organization and its problems is centered on control of production. Sales and marketing presidents are likely to favor strategies that focus on selling more goods by differentiating products from competitors, expanding markets nationally and multinationally, and diversifying into related product lines. Finally, finance presidents are likely to favor strategies that result in steady and increasing profitability for the firm. They will tend toward mergers as a strategy for growth and use diversification without regard for product mix or fit.

The success of these varying tactics requires a crisis to show clearly how the dominant new strategy is superior. The product-related approach began in the 1920s, but it took the Depression to prove that it was viable. After the war the product-related strategy and the sales and marketing techniques that buttressed it were accepted practice. Similarly, the ability to put together conglomerate firms was available after the 1920s. But the antitrust environment of the 1940s and 1950s produced a lot of antipathy toward product-dominant and even product-related strategies. This opened the door for purely financial tactics. When mergers of unrelated firms began to skyrocket in the 1950s, the product-unrelated strategy of mergers became the dominant point of view.

A final mechanism was at work through these processes. Once a set of actors had taken control of a firm and shifted its strategy, the other firms in the organizational field were more likely to follow suit. This diffusion of strategy was likely to result from actual and perceived pressures. If competitors were doing quite well with a new strategy, one probably had to do equally well to hold one's position. Further, actors also felt the pressure to conform because they needed to appear to be abreast of the latest trend in business.

Table D.4 demonstrates the validity of these views. The table

Table D.4 Results of a logit regression predicting strategy by decade for the largest corporations

| Variables | 1919–1929[a] (N = 102) | | 1929–1939 (N = 108) | | 1939–1948 (N = 112) | | 1948–1959 (N = 117) | | | |
| | | | | | | | (1)[b] | | (2) | |
	b	SE(b)	b	SE(b)	b	SE(b)	b	SE(b)	b	SE(b)
Age	-.001	.04	.01	.021	.03*	.014	-.01	.01	-.36	.31
Asset	-.004	.005	.005	.005	.006*	.003	-.005	.006	-.018	.015
Related strategy	1.08*	.48	1.12**	.42	2.04**	.567	1.05**	.41	.99	.58
Unrelated strategy	—	—	—	—	—	—	.02	.42	2.02**	.83
% Related strategy	.045*	.023	.02*	.01	.14*	.06	.16*	.07	-.06	.08
% Unrelated strategy	—	—	—	—	—	—	-.22*	.09	.87**	.38
Manuf. president	.156	.645	-.137	.497	-.35	.30	.51	.66	-.22	.57
Sales president	.957*	.418	.694**	.144	.44	.23	.20	.72	-.77	.86
Finance president	-.562	.912	.637	.423	.63	.98	-.89	.94	1.09**	.41
Constant	-.446		.18		.55		.04		-.28	

Table D.4 (continued)

| | 1959–1969 (N = 114) | | | | 1969–1979 (N = 115) | | | |
| | (1) | | (2) | | (1) | | (2) | |
Variables	b	SE(b)	b	SE(b)	b	SE(b)	b	SE(b)
Age	.02	.03	.009	.04	.002	.002	-.005	.02
Asset	-.002	.003	-.002	.001	-.003	.002	-.000	.000
Related strategy	2.08**	.68	.67	.56	.85**	.25	.08	.06
Unrelated strategy	.009	.38	1.45**	.64	-.02	.08	.94**	.21
% Related strategy	-.007	.02	.04	.04	.08*	.04	-.07	.10
% Unrelated strategy	-.08	.06	.12*	.06	-.02	.02	.16*	.08
Manuf. president	-.11	.28	-.33	.28	-.06	.07	.03	.08
Sales president	.41	.74	.68**	.33	-.10	.08	.13*	.06
Finance president	-.10	.32	.98**	.34	-.06	.07	.42*	.20
Constant	.11		.006		.09		.06	

Source: Fligstein (1989a), table 3.

Note: * $p < .05$, ** $p < .01$.

a. Results from logistic regression: dominant strategy = 0; related strategy = 1.

b. Results from multinomial logit: dominant strategy = left-out category; related strategy = 1; unrelated strategy = 2.

presents the results of logistic regressions predicting firm strategy at the second time point. Logistic regressions were chosen because the variables were dichotomous and trichotomous in character. If one examines the table, one can observe that over time there is quite a bit of inertia in strategy. The best predictor of strategy at the second time point is the strategy at the first time point.

The most interesting effects are those associated with the presence or absence of presidents with certain backgrounds. In the earliest panels a sales and marketing president clearly affects a shift toward a product-related strategy. Once that shift has occurred, the effects disappear. Similarly, the presence of a finance president is related to a shift toward a product-unrelated strategy in the postwar era. This is evidence that the role of actors with alternative views of the organization is crucial in causing a shift in an organization's basic strategy.

The effects of the organizational field are also quite stunning. The presence of other firms in the organizational field with the new strategy is a strong predictor of any given firm's shift to that strategy. Here is clear evidence that firms watch one another and mimic what they perceive to be successful behavior.

The spread of diversification appears to match both theoretical and historical expectations. Diversification required a crisis in the organizational field, often caused by macroeconomic conditions or the enforcement of antitrust laws by the federal government. Key actors in certain firms were able to take advantage of these situations and provide their firms with new tactics in their fields. The success of these tactics therefore informed other firms and caused them to alter their product mix.

The Shift in Presidential Backgrounds

Manufacturing, sales and marketing, and finance presidents succeeded in the different eras to varying degrees. It is worthwhile to explore the successes of these various groups and how the successes of one enabled others with similar backgrounds to rise to the top.

The subunit background of the president may seem to be an odd indicator of conceptions of control, but this background tells us a number of things about the people who lead the largest firms. First, the subunit background can be thought of as an ideology. All organizational actors must analyze their situation. That analysis will be focused on the major problems of the organization and courses of action that will solve them. This implies a totalizing world view. This is different from more familiar notions of bounded rationality. The idea here is that actors' points of view will cause them to see the same problem in different ways. Thus, Henry Ford recognized the maturation of the automobile market in the 1920s and dealt with it by cutting prices and integrating production, a continuation of his original tactics. Alfred Sloan saw the same problem and realized that the solution was to differentiate products and offer more choices thereby increasing the possibilities for profit. These intelligent, successful actors both perceived the same problem, but their analysis of that problem led them to quite different solutions precisely because they saw the world differently. Ford had a manufacturing approach and Sloan a marketing approach.

These ideologies emerge in the experiences key actors have in their organizations and organizational fields. A person who has been concerned with the process of manufacturing will tend to see all of the problems of the organization as related to manufacturing. If sales drop, then sales can be stimulated by cutting prices and costs from the manufacturing point of view. If people have spent their life attempting to market products, then their central concern will be tactics that will increase the sale of products. From their perspective a drop in sales should be accompanied by an attempt to differentiate a product from the competitors', create style and qualitative differences between products, increase advertising, find new markets nationally and multinationally, and manufacture new products related to the old product, relying on one's existing reputation to expand sales. Finally, those who have spent their careers analyzing balance sheets and scrutinizing profits will tend to see the problems of the organization as financial. If sales fall off in a certain product, the solution is to disinvest in that product line and diversify into some more profitable activities. Having spent careers analyzing business problems in a certain way, managers come to view all problems through a certain theoretical lense.

The subunit background, however, is not just an ideology but also a power base. The organization contains more or less integrated divisions. One's position in that divisional structure will

Table D.5   Results of a logit model predicting a manufacturing, sales and marketing, and finance president versus all others for the decades 1919–1939, 1939–1959, and 1959–1979

1919–1939 (N = 192)

Independent variables[a]	Manufacturing				Sales and marketing				Finance			
	b	SE(b)	b	SE(b)	b	SE(b)	b	SE(b)	b	SE(b)	b	SE(b)
Assets, t_1	.003	.003	.002	.002	.004	.004	.006	.005	-.001	.006	-.005	.09
% change in assets	-.20	.22	-.18	.21	-.16	.27	-.09	.29	.21	.30	.11	.41
Age	.01	.01	-.05	.05	-.01	.02	-.01	.02	.04	.03	-.04	.03
Comer	-.60	.74	-.47	.74	1.59*	.73	1.44	.74	-.72	1.22	-.40	1.29
Leaver	-.30	.51	-.30	.52	-.75	.88	-.68	.90	-.56	.93	-.68	1.03
MDF, t_1	—	—	—	—	—	—	—	—	—	—	—	—
Conglomerate												
Related	.45	.52	.42	.55	1.17*	.59	1.22*	.60	-1.07	1.27	.05	1.25
Mergers	-.05	.05	-.01	.02	-.03	.06	-.03	.06	-.05	.09	-.07	.10
% in industry with:												
Manuf. president	4.76**	1.11	3.83**	1.20	.31	.48	.34	.46	.34	.46	.36	.59
Sales president	.83	.76	.87	.74	4.61	3.47	4.60	3.38	-.73	.54	-.70	.44
Finance president	.24	.58	.32	.56	.37	.55	.37	.55	2.67**	1.09	1.65	.86
Food	—	—	-1.48**	.57	—	—	.42*	.20	—	—	—	—
Machines	—	—	-.86	.64	—	—	.24*	.11	—	—	—	—
Chemical	—	—	-.28	.60	—	—	.06**	.01	—	—	—	—
Petroleum	—	—	.48*	.23	—	—	.78	1.16	—	—	—	—
Transport	—	—	-1.32*	.62	—	—	1.14	.80	—	—	—	—
Miscellaneous	—	—	-.42	.43	—	—	.12	.23	—	—	—	—
Dec. 1929	-.60	.42	.01	.01	.30	.59	.30	.64	-.18	.72	-.09	.86
Dec. 1949	—	—	—	—	—	—	—	—	—	—	—	—
Dec. 1969	—	—	—	—	—	—	—	—	—	—	—	—
Constant	-1.37**	.58	-1.10*	.54	-3.60**	.90	-4.27**	1.11	-2.51*	1.28	-4.18*	2.09

Table D.5 (continued)

1939–1959
(N = 218)

Independent variables[a]	Manufacturing				Sales and marketing				Finance			
	b	SE(b)	b	SE(b)	b	SE(b)	b	SE(b)	b	SE(b)	b	SE(b)
Assets, t_i	.008	.0045	.008	.0047	.001	.03	.001	.02	-.001	.01	-.000	.000
% change in assets	-.32	.26	-.29	.27	.02	.015	.05	.04	-.58	.54	-.38	.53
Age	-.01	.01	-.01	.01	-.02	.02	-.02	.02	.03	.02	.04	.021
Comer	.51	.71	.45	.73	-.48	.71	-.61	.73	-.44	1.05	-.65	1.07
Leaver	-1.03*	.51	-1.08*	.52	-1.025*	.51	-.88*	.43	-2.65**	1.18	-2.64**	1.20
MDF, t_i	-.10*	.04	-.12*	.06	.62*	.30	.41	.23	1.15*	.68	1.44**	.54
Conglomerate												
Related	.28	.54	.37	.74	.44*	.21	.40	.24	.09	.08	.27	.35
Mergers	-.03	.08	-.05	.08	.01	.05	.01	.04	.08*	.04	.06*	.03
% in industry with:												
Manuf. president	3.98**	1.11	3.29*	1.51	.39	.98	-.09	.88	.55	.97	.75	.99
Sales president	.55	.37	.59	.41	3.11**	1.3	3.09**	1.12	-.17	.22	-.60	.42
Finance president	.24	.28	.22	.29	3.05	2.19	1.51	2.06	4.39**	1.63	4.11*	1.96
Food	—	—	-.14	.10	—	—	1.43**	.57	—	—	2.31*	1.11
Machines	—	—	-.43	.48	—	—	.53*	.26	—	—	.19	.58
Chemical	—	—	.29	.19	—	—	1.56**	.62	—	—	1.97*	.89
Petroleum	—	—	.36*	.16	—	—	.26	.96	—	—	1.63	1.44
Transport	—	—	.17	.13	—	—	.87	1.06	—	—	2.43*	1.21
Miscellaneous	—	—	-.61*	.30	—	—	.13	.11	—	—	.68	.79
Dec. 1929												
Dec. 1949	.70	.53	.60	.54	-.16	.48	-.07	.50	.63**	.24	.55*	.21
Dec. 1969												
Constant	-2.29**	.76	-1.83	1.01	-.67	.62	-.85	.90	-3.09**	1.00	-5.03**	1.73

Table D.5 (continued)

		1959–1979 (N = 218)										
Independent variables[a]	Manufacturing				Sales and marketing				Finance			
	b	SE(b)	b	SE(b)	b	SE(b)	b	SE(b)	b	SE(b)	b	SE(b)
Assets, t_1	.001	.001	.001	.001	.001	.001	.001	.001	.001	.001	.001	.001
% change in assets	−.32	.25	−.42	.29	.005	.004	.004	.005	−.001	.001	−.001	.001
Age	−.01	.008	−.01	.01	.01	.01	.01	.01	−.01	.01	−.01	.01
Corner	−.47	.76	−.38	.77	−.37	.24	−.42	.64	−.71	.56	−.62	.58
Leaver	−.19	.56	−.17	.58	−.75*	.33	−.73*	.35	−.56*	.28	−.50*	.24
MDF, t_1	.05	.45	−.11	.42	.29	.18	.22	.15	.40*	.17	.51*	.24
Conglomerate	.14	.67	.05	.07	−.25*	.10	−.52	.33	.20**	.08	.18	.12
Related	.79	.51	.91	.55	.72*	.34	.51	.27	.90*	.44	.58	.37
Mergers	−.20*	.09	−.21*	.08	−.08	.09	−.09	.08	.03*	.014	.06*	.03
% in industry with:												
Manuf. president	2.06**	.89	1.12*	.43	−1.88	1.64	−1.47	1.02	.50	.98	.81	.60
Sales president	−.92	.77	−.21	.23	2.60**	1.04	1.77*	.86	1.62	1.67	.85	.89
Finance president	−.25	.46	−.46	.29	.61	.39	.94	.61	3.61**	1.44	1.88**	.71
Food	—	—	1.27*	.61	—	—	.96*	.44	—	—	.62	.54
Machines	—	—	.50	.74	—	—	.91*	.42	—	—	1.58*	.71
Chemical	—	—	.07	.07	—	—	.42	.79	—	—	.57	.70
Petroleum	—	—	.56	.68	—	—	.14	.76	—	—	−.58	.33
Transport	—	—	.08	.92	—	—	−.30	.88	—	—	1.14*	.53
Miscellaneous	—	—	−1.01*	.45	—	—	−.54	.77	—	—	1.40*	.68
Dec. 1929												
Dec. 1949												
Dec. 1969	−.17	.45	−.21	.48	−.01	.01	−.05	.01	.52*	.24	.54*	.24
Constant	.35	.89	1.21	1.19	−2.26**	.99	−1.69	1.11	−1.48	.88	−2.28*	1.12

Source: Fligstein (1987), table 4.   Note: * $p < .05$, ** $p < .01$.   a. See text for operationalization.

allow one to claim the ability to solve the organization's problems. To the degree that the subunit or function is perceived as crucial to organizational success, that subunit will have the power to direct the organization. Of course, existing strategy and structure are great sources of power for subunits and they are quite difficult to dislodge. Organizations that are highly vertically integrated are dominated by manufacturing personnel because they can claim production expertise. Those organizations will be difficult to change because of the fusion of strategy and structure and the obvious claims of manufacturing personnel over the power to produce the output.

The multidivisional form, however, reflects the dominance of a new strategy: diversification. Once diversification takes hold, the claims of manufacturing personnel are lessened. After all, their expertise revolves around one set of products, not all of the products. In this situation sales and marketing and finance personnel have an advantage because their expertise extends across the operations of the organization.

Once a new strategy and structure are in place in some firms, often through the efforts of a sales and marketing or finance president, they prepare the way for those of a similar point of view. As a certain view of the organizational field becomes dominant, one would expect that actors in other organizations could promote their careers internally by appealing to what is occurring in the field. If sales presidents are pressing forward in other firms with diversification strategies, and these tactics prove successful, then sales personnel throughout the field can press their claim on power by arguing for what is occurring elsewhere. The sources of power open to the various subunits are thus both internal and external and will revolve around perceived crises and solutions. (For further elaboration of these arguments, see Fligstein (1987).)

Table D.5 contains a logistic regression predicting whether or not a firm is led by a manufacturing, sales and marketing, or finance president. In the earliest time period the strongest predictor of the presence of a manufacturing president is the percentage of those presidents in the organizational field. This shows the early dominance of manufacturing presidents and their strategies. The only predictor of a sales and marketing president is the presence of a product-related strategy, as one would theoretically expect.

In the middle period, the rise of sales and marketing presidents is a function of the multidivisional form, the product-related strategy, and the percentage of sales presidents in the organizational field. Finance presidents emerged in firms that engaged in mergers and in industries where there were already concentrations of finance presidents. Finance presidents increased in the last period when firms engaged in diversification and merger strategies. They also emerged in industries where concentrations of finance presidents existed. Sales and marketing presidents continued to dominate in industries where they dominated previously and in firms with product-related, but not product-unrelated, strategies.

These results show how the organizational field and the internal strategies and structures of firms favor different types of presidents. Manufacturing presidents dominate in certain industries. Sales and marketing presidents rise on the basis of product-related strategies and a trend toward sales and marketing presidents. Finance presidents rise as mergers are used as tactics for expansion and firms diversify to unrelated product lines. All three types of presidents are more likely to lead in certain organizational fields where their leadership is already dominant. One interesting result is that the multidivisional form provides a structure that is more conducive to takeover by sales and marketing and finance presidents.

The Spread of the Multidivisional Form

The final aspect of organizational change that I document is the spread of the multidivisional form. I have already shown that the multidivisional form is a source of growth for its early adopters. Further, the multidivisional form works to diminish the power of manufacturing presidents and encourages the power of sales and marketing and finance presidents. It is useful to explore the implementation of the multidivisional form as a function of shifts in strategy and who controls the largest firms.

The multidivisional form takes advantage of the fact that large firms tend to produce in numerous product lines. Whereas the functional form organized the firm according to the flow of materials, the multidivisional form organizes the firm by product divisions. Each product division is thereby responsible for its own

Table D.6 Results of a logit model estimating whether or not a firm adopted the multidivisional form over the decade as a function of various factors (0 = nonadoption, 1 = adoption)

Variables	1929–1939 (N = 108)		1939–1948 (N = 98)		1948–1959 (N = 91)		1959–1969 (N = 57)		1969–1979 (N = 31)	
	b	SE(b)	b	SE(b)	b	SE(b)	b	SE(b)	b	(SE)b
Related strategy	1.39**	.47	2.52**	.72	.76*	.32	.14	.65	1.10*	.47
Unrelated strategy	.76	.90	.21*	.10	.15	.38	.88*	.39	.67*	.32
Mergers				.10	.49	.58	.38*	.16	1.26*	.60
Indmdf[a]	.48	.53	.23*	.10	.05**	.02	.15*	.08	.062*	.03
Age	.14**	.06	.034*	.016	-.007	.20	.06*	.03	-.004	.004
Assets, t_1	.0006	.001	.001*	.0005	.0004	.0005	.0003*	.0001	.0008	.0009
% change in assets	1.46	2.32	.89	.89	1.23*	.53	.03	.08	-.07	.08
Sales president	2.71**	1.04	1.12*	.54	.68	.45	1.12*	.58	.26	1.16
Finance president	2.44**	.99	2.62	2.12	.67*	.32	2.11*	1.01	2.05	1.21
Lawyer president	-.12	.28	.15	.60	-.42	.61	-.73	.64	.19	1.04
Entrepreneur president	.26	.72	-.17	.74	-.25	.47	-.30	.83	.14	.47
Manager president	-.67	.39	1.40	.87	.16	.51	.70	.64	.40	.82
No data on president	2.40	2.10	.57	.90	-.54	.63	-.54	.34	.18	.30
Comer	-.31	.73	.33	.73	-.86	.58	1.28	.88	.84	.57
Leaver	.16	.24	-.43	.29	-.25	.49	.38	.74	.18	.30
Constant	-1.82	1.61	-8.70**	6.68	-7.39	5.18	-1.82	3.36	-1.23	4.61

Source: Fligstein (1985), table 4.

Note: * $p < .05$, ** $p < .01$.

a. Indmdf = percentage of firms in industry that made the transition to MDF by the first point.

manufacturing, marketing, and finance, and the central office assumes planning and coordination functions for the entire organization. The original impetus for the form was the recognition by certain executives that diversified products could not be produced efficiently in functional organizations.

Here I discuss the introduction of the multidivisional form as a function of three factors. First, the strategy of a firm will determine its structure. The more the firm engages in product-related or -unrelated diversification, the more likely it is to shift to the multidivisional form. Second, to the degree that sales and marketing and finance personnel control the large firm, they will introduce the form in order to promote and control their diversification strategies. Third, as organizations in a given field come to adopt the form, other organizations will follow suit. As I have shown, the multidivisional form provided an impetus for growth. Actors in other firms in the field will be more likely to follow that innovation if they perceive it to be successful. (For a more in-depth discussion of these issues, see Fligstein (1985).)

Table D.6 contains the results of a logistic regression to predict the adoption of the multidivisional form. Strategy consistently predicts the shift to the multidivisional form. The presence of product-related, product-unrelated, and merger strategies make the firm more likely to shift to the multidivisional form. Similarly, the effect of the organizational field is evident. Those firms embedded in fields that are adopting the form are more likely to do so themselves.

The final important result is that the presence of sales and marketing and finance presidents makes the firm more likely to shift to the multidivisional form. The sales and marketing presidents are more likely to have this effect in the early panels and the finance presidents in the middle panels. This conforms to my theoretical expectations.

Appendix E

Antitrust Enforcement and Mergers, 1950–1980

The antitrust environment of the late 1940s intensified diversification in the largest firms. Here I will show how the enforcement of the Celler-Kefauver Act encouraged firms to engage in product-related and -unrelated mergers as opposed to the horizontal or vertical mergers during the postwar era. I will also show how the Nixon Administration's antitrust policy was a major contributing factor to the decline of the 1960s merger movement. There are two major dependent variables: change in the types and number of mergers. I will examine the patterns of mergers by type in the postwar era and attempt to relate them to a number of variables that might explain the trends.

A substantial proportion of all mergers were engaged in for diversification before 1950 and that pattern accelerated after 1950 (see Chapter 6). Presumably, this shift reflected two forces: the presence of diversification strategies in large firms and the antitrust environment of the period. By the 1960s merger for diversification was the most common. My basic hypothesis is that the period of strict enforcement of the Celler-Kefauver Act, beginning in 1962 with the U.S. v. Brown Shoe decision and ending with the 1974 U.S. v. Marinebankcorp decision, was a period when firms were more likely to engage in product-related and -unre'ated mergers and less likely to engage in vertical or horizontal mergers. My second hypothesis concerns the relationship between changes in the overall merger rate and antitrust enforcement. I argue that the Nixon Administration's antitrust policy from 1969 to 1973 provided a great shock to the merger market and slowed the merger movement considerably. An alternative hypothesis is that rising interest rates and a slowdown in the stock market made mergers less attractive.

The data for this analysis came from a number of sources. The merger time series was collected by the FTC (1981). Four dependent variables were coded: the total number of mergers, the number of large mergers (large is defined as a purchase of over $10 million in assets) that were vertical or horizontal, the number of large mergers that were product related or unrelated, and the percentage of large mergers that were horizontal or vertical. The merger time series begins in 1947, however, because all of the independent variables lag one year, the analysis is from 1948 to 1980.

A number of hypotheses are specified about the causes of different types of mergers. First, the value of the dependent variable in the previous year is placed in the equation. The regressions answer the question of what caused changes in the year-to-year totals or mix of mergers. By lagging the dependent variable, the current level of merger activity is also controlled. The measure of Celler-Kefauver enforcement is a set of two dummy variables, one coded "0" for all years except 1962 to 1974 (coded "1" in those years) and the other coded "0" for all years except 1975 to 1980 (coded "1" in those years). The expectation is that the first dummy variable will statistically predict a decline in horizontal and vertical mergers relative to product-related and -unrelated mergers, while the second will be unrelated to that decline. Once the enforcement of Celler-Kefauver is negated, the behavior of large firms should shift back somewhat to horizontal and vertical mergers. A third dummy variable was coded "0" for all years except 1969 to 1973 (coded "1" in those years). This variable reflects the effect of the Nixon antitrust policy on the overall merger rate.

One might argue that a better measure of antitrust activity would be the number of lawsuits in a given year or the number of victories. the basic problem with these measures is that they do not accurately reflect the perception of the business world of the importance of antitrust enforcement. Once antitrust decisions were made and lawyers could decipher the strategies of the antitrust authorities, they could advise their clients about what were likely to be legal and illegal courses of action. This perception probably remained stable until new decisions or new patterns of enforcement were announced by antitrust authorities. The number of lawsuits is not an accurate measure whereas period effects seem to have greater face validity.

Before the U.S. v. Brown Shoe decision in 1962, for instance, the actual meaning of the Celler-Kefauver Act was unclear. From 1962 to 1974 the Supreme Court continuously ruled in favor of the government. I argue that the executives in the largest firms understood this practice and chose to undertake product-related and -unrelated mergers instead of vertical and horizontal mergers. Therefore, in this era of strict enforcement, horizontal mergers should have been less likely to occur. One would expect that the later period would show no reduction of horizontal mergers as the enforcement of the law diminished. The Nixon Administration's antitrust policy had the effect of making mergers less attractive because of potential antitrust lawsuits (see Chapter 6). The pursuit of acquisitive conglomerates stopped firms from making purchases. It is useful to see if the intensity of that policy affected the total number of mergers and if it contributed to the end of the merger movement.

Two other variables regarding mergers are in the analysis. First, the *Standard and Poor's Index of Average Stock Prices* was included. Generally, mergers occur when stock prices are on the rise and occur less frequently when stock prices drop. The second variable was the average Federal Reserve discount rate in the previous year. This measure indexes how easy it was to borrow money. In an era of high interest rates, one would expect fewer mergers. Indeed, the rising interest rates and declining stock market are often thought to be the major causes of the end of the 1960s merger movement. The following data came from the *Historical Abstract of the U.S.* (1981).

The data analysis involved running an ordinary least squares regression on time series data. The computer program LIMDEP was used to estimate the models. Given that the data were a time series, a Durbin-Watson statistic was estimated for each model. For the models presented in Table E.2, none of the tests are in the significant range. In the regression where the total level of mergers is the dependent variable (Table E.3), the Durbin-Watson statistic is in the indeterminate range and a generalized least squares approach with a first-order autocorrelation correction was used to produce the estimates.

Table E.1 presents the means and standard deviations of the various variables. Vertical and horizontal mergers made up an average of 36 percent of all large mergers during the period. Large

Table E.1   Means and standard deviations of variables used in the analyses, 1948–1980 (N = 32)

Variables	X̄	S.D.
% horizontal and vertical mergers, t	0.36	0.17
% horizontal and vertical mergers, $t-1$	0.38	0.16
Number of horizontal and vertical mergers, t	19.0	9.03
Number of horizontal and vertical mergers, $t-1$	19.6	8.80
Number of related and unrelated mergers, t	44.1	34.97
Number of related and unrelated mergers, $t-1$	44.2	34.90
Number of mergers, t	798.84	513.25
Number of mergers, $t-1$	786.97	522.25
Interest rate, $t-1$	4.31	2.65
Standard and Poor's stock index, $t-1$	72.75	35.35
Period effect, 1962–1974	0.41	—
Period effect, 1975–1980	0.19	—
Period effect, 1969–1973	0.16	—

horizontal and vertical mergers averaged about nineteen per year, while product-related and -unrelated mergers averaged about forty-four per year. The overall merger rate averaged almost eight hundred a year with a substantial standard deviation.

Table E.2 presents the results of an ordinary least squares equation estimated for the three dependent variables. The first column shows the results for the change in the percentage of all large mergers that are vertical and horizontal. Only two variables have a statistically significant effect on this shift: the overall interest rate and the period of Celler-Kefauver enforcement. As interest rates increase, the percentage of vertical and horizontal mergers decrease. More interesting, the period of greatest enforcement of Celler-Kefauver sees a drop in horizontal and vertical mergers relative to product-related and -unrelated mergers. Also, the 1975–1980 period does not statistically significantly effect the change in the percentage of horizontal and vertical mergers. This confirms my central hypothesis.

The change in the number of horizontal and vertical mergers is related to the change in stock prices and the interest rate. As stock prices increase and the interest rate decreases, horizontal and vertical mergers increase. It is interesting to note that during the period of Celler-Kefauver, horizontal mergers tended to decrease substantially, as the hypothesis predicted, and, in the period following Celler-Kefauver, there is not a statistically significant effect on large vertical and horizontal mergers. The third column contains the predictors of change in product-related and -unrelated large mergers. The interest rate is a strong predictor of these mergers. During the years of Celler-Kefauver, product-related and -unrelated mergers increased substantially, again as I hypothesized.

The results show quite clearly that the enforcement patterns of the Celler-Kefauver Act during the merger movement of the 1960s was a strong predictor of the shift from horizontal and vertical mergers to product-related and -unrelated mergers. After 1974 the enforcement of the law was no longer effecting the merger choices of large firms.

Table E.3 presents a regression analysis of the causes of the overall merger rate. The stock average almost had a statistically significant effect on changes in overall mergers. The coefficient implies that as the market rose, mergers increased and, as the market contracted, mergers decreased. The interest rate had a strong effect on changes in the number of mergers in the expected

Table E.2 Regression analysis of the causes of large merger types, 1948–1980

Variables	% horizontal and vertical mergers		No. of horizontal and vertical mergers		No. of related and unrelated mergers	
	b	SE(b)	b	SE(b)	b	SE(b)
% horizontal mergers, $t-1$	.25	.18	—	—	—	—
Number of horizontal and vertical mergers, $t-1$	—	—	.40**	.13	—	—
Number of related and unrelated mergers, $t-1$	—	—	—	—	.78**	.17
Interest rate, $t-1$	−.04*	.01	−3.89**	.72	−6.48*	2.95
Standard and Poor's stock index, $t-1$	.001	.001	.34**	.08	.11	.30
Period 1962–1974	−.13**	.04	−5.59**	1.41	29.11*	13.04
Period 1975–1980	−.12	.10	−2.95	2.45	11.10	10.21
Constant	.39**	.11	6.36*	2.81	15.11	10.68
R²	.64	—	.69	—	.68	—
Durbin-Watson statistic	1.91	—	1.96	—	1.87	—

Note: * $p < .05$, ** $p < .01$.

Table E.3 Regression analysis of the change in all mergers, 1948–1980
(GLS results)

Variables	No. of all mergers	
	b	SE(b)
All mergers, $t-1$	.92**	.15
Interest rate, $t-1$	4.60+	2.70
Standard and Poor's stock index, $t-1$	−60.83*	30.52
Period 1969–1973	−383.72*	190.0
Constant	61.11	136.3
R^2	.78	—
Durbin-Watson statistic	1.38	—

Note: + $p < .1$, * $p < .05$, ** $p < .01$.

direction. As the interest rate fell, mergers rose. But neither of these variables completely accounted for the decline of mergers in the late 1960s. The dummy variable for the years of the Nixon antitrust policy shows a strong negative effect on changes in the numbers of mergers.

From these results one can see that antitrust policy had an important impact on mergers. During the 1960s merger movement the enforcement of the Celler-Kefauver Act encouraged firms to engage in product-related and -unrelated mergers. The Nixon Administration's merger policy led to a radical decline in the number of mergers and indeed must be considered one of the most important causes of the end of that movement. The antitrust laws had a profound effect on mergers that did occur.

Notes

1. Introduction

1. The following discussion owes a great debt to Chandler, 1962, 1977; DiMaggio and Powell, 1983; Hannan and Freeman, 1977, 1984; Meyer and Rowan, 1977; Meyer and Scott, 1983; Perrow, 1970; Pfeffer, 1981; White, 1981; and to my earlier papers, Fligstein, 1985, 1987, 1990a, 1990b; and Fligstein and Dauber, 1989.

2. Direct Control, the State, and the Large Firm

1. U.S. v. Trans-Missouri Freight Association, 1897, F. 53, p. 456.
2. U.S. v. Joint Traffic Association, 1898, 217 U.S., p. 507.
3. See the Report on Committee of Manufacturers, 1889, H. Rep. 4165, and Whiskey Trust Investigation, 1893, H. Rep. 2601.
4. U.S. v. Addyston Pipe, Cir. 498, pp. 194–195.
5. Ibid., pp. 263–264.
6. Ibid., p. 94.
7. U.S. v. DuPont, Government Exhibit no. 6, vol. 1, p. 95.
8. Ibid., Government Exhibit no. 7, vol. 1, p. 114.
9. Central Ohio Salt v. Guthrie, 35 Ohio 666, 1880, p. 672.
10. See Lamoreaux, 1985, ch. 2, and Bittlingmayer, 1985, pp. 107–110.
11. Bittlingmayer, 1985, is the most recent advocate of this view.
12. U.S. v. Knight, 1895, 156 U.S., p. 16.
13. See, for example, von Halle, 1896; Clark, 1898; Ely, 1900; Jenks, 1900; Kales, 1918; Jones, 1921.

3. The Manufacturing Conception of Control

1. U.S. Federal Trade Commission, 1919, vol. 1, p. 52; Federal Trade Commission Packer Consent Decree, 1924, pp. 18–19; U.S. v. Swift and Co. et al., 1931, Brief for the U.S., p. 36.
2. U.S. v. Standard Sanitary Manufacturing Company, 1912, Opinion of the Court, p. 9.
3. Ibid., Government Exhibit no. 3, vol. 2, pp. 4–5.
4. Ibid., Petition in Equity, pp. 44–46, 51, 62–66.
5. U.S. v. General Electric, 1911, Cir. Petition in Equity, pp. 12–18.
6. Ibid., pp. 25–28.
7. U.S. v. Standard Oil, 1911, vol. 2, pp. 428–500.

8. Ibid., vol. 2, pp. 432–436.

9. U.S. v. DuPont, 1911, Testimony of F. J. Waddell, Brief, vol. 2, p. 60.

10. U.S. v. National Cash Register, 1916, vol. 2, p. 985.

11. Ibid., Petition in Equity, pp. 14–15.

12. U.S. v. Motion Patents Company, 1916, Exhibit 3, p. 55.

13. U.S. v. General Electric, 1911, Petition in Equity, pp. 25–30.

14. U.S. v. DuPont, 1911, Testimony of F. J. Waddell, vol. 2, pp. 58–60.

15. U.S. v. Standard Oil, 1912, Brief for the U.S., vol. 2, p. 520.

16. For an interpretation that stresses the shippers' victory, see Martin, 1971, esp. ch. 4. Kolko (1965, pp. 127–150) has argued that the railroads got what they wanted. Kerr (1968, ch. 2) has taken a middle position and argued that both sides won something.

17. U.S. Attorney General, 1938, discussions of Standard Oil, pp. 97–98; American Tobacco, p. 101; International Harvester, p. 129; American Sugar, p. 107; DuPont, p. 102; General Electric, p. 113.

18. Ibid., discussions of U.S. Steel, p. 122; American Can, p. 144.

19. U.S. v. Addyston Pipe, 1898, 85 F. 271, pp. 293–298.

20. U.S. v. U.S. Steel, 1920, 251 U.S. 417.

21. Ibid., Brief for the U.S., vol. 2, p. 147.

22. Both Dewing and Livermore studied only firms continuously in existence. Hence, their results are positive in part because they limited themselves to successful firms. I avoid this problem because my study covers causes of firm survival, not growth in profits for survivors.

23. This is Baruch's account of the War Industries Board. A general history was written by Cuff (1973).

24. See Seager and Gulick, 1929, pp. 491–495; Handler, 1932, pp. 179–271; Martin, 1959, pp. 118–120. The important decisions regarding open price trade associations were U.S. v. American Lumber, 1921, 257 U.S. 377; U.S. v. American Linseed Oil, 1923, 262 U.S. 271; U.S. v. Maple Flooring Manufacturers, 1925, 268 U.S. 563; U.S. v. Trenton Potteries, 1927, 273 U.S. 392.

4. The Sales and Marketing Conception of Control

1. For a number of different versions, see Thorp and Crowder, 1941, pp. 243–244; Chandler, 1962, pp. 114–163, 1964, p. 98, 1979; Katz, 1977; Thomas, 1977; Nevins and Hill, 1954; Cray, 1980; Pound, 1934; Crabb, 1969. For an insider's view, see Sloan, 1964.

5. The Emergence of the Celler-Kefauver Act

1. *Vital Speeches*, October 1, 1938, p. 567; March 1, 1939, pp. 291–293; *Fair Fights and Foul*, 1951, p. 137.

2. *Vital Speeches*, March 1, 1939, pp. 291–293.

3. *Business Week*, May 7, 1938, pp. 13–14; May 28, 1938, pp. 13–14; March 25, 1939, pp. 14–15.

4. U.S. Federal Trade Commission, Official Minutes of the Commissioners, Record Group 122, vol. 78, 1944, pp. 174–176.

5. Ibid., vol. 79, 1944, pp. 259–260.

6. Ibid., pp. 259–270.

7. Ibid., vol. 80, 1945, pp. 497–498.

8. Ibid., pp. 675–678.

9. Ibid., vol. 86, 1947, p. 628.

10. Ibid., vol. 81, 1946, p. 323.

11. Ibid.

12. Ibid., vol. 84, 1946, p. 213.

13. Ibid., p. 58.

14. Ibid., vol. 85, 1947, p. 58.

15. Ibid., p. 498.

16. *Congressional Record* vol. 14, September 12, 1914, p. 14314.

17. Papers of E. Celler, Manuscript Collection, U.S. Library of Congress.

18. See H. Reps. 1820 and 1480, 79th Cong., 1946.

19. Papers of E. Celler.

20. Ibid.

21. U.S. Federal Trade Commission, Official Minutes of the Commissioners, vol. 91, 1949, p. 5.

22. Papers of E. Celler.

23. Ibid.

24. *Congressional Record*, vol. 18, August 15, 1949, p. 11484.

25. Ibid., p. 11507.

26. Ibid., 1950, pp. 8320, 11978, 14697.

27. Ibid., 1950, p. 16404.

28. Ibid., 1950, pp. 16433, 16508.

29. Ibid., 1950, p. 17138.

6. The Impact of the Celler-Kefauver Act

1. Antitrust Division, U.S. Department of Justice, "1968 Merger Guidelines," Memorandum.

2. In the matter of Pillsbury Mills, FTC Docket no. 6000, June 16, 1952.

3. Ibid., December 28, 1953.

4. In the matter of Crown Zellerbach, FTC Docket no. 6180, February 15, 1954.

5. For a complete listing of cases as of 1977, see Mueller, 1977, app. C.

6. U.S. v. Brown Shoe, Opinion of the Court, 1962, p. 296.

7. "Significant new antitrust developments," Address to the Antitrust Section of the American Bar Association, August 6, 1962.

8. FTC v. Procter and Gamble, 386 U.S., 1967, p. 568.

9. Neal Commission Report was published in *Congressional Record*, vol. 115, November 27, 1969, pp. 6472–6945.

10. Stigler Commission Report was published in *Congressional Record*, vol. 115, June 17, 1969, pp. 1812–2346.

11. Kleindienst, 1985, pp. 94–95. This account was confirmed and extended in a personal conversation with Kleindienst in November 1987.

12. Nixon Presidential Papers, Memorandum, April 17, 1969.

13. Ibid.

14. Ibid., Memorandum for attorney general, March 25, 1969.

15. Ibid., Memorandum from John Ehrlichman to Arthur Burns, April 28, 1969, on the subject of conglomerates.

16. Ibid., Minutes of a meeting of the Cabinet Committee on Economic Matters, May 7, 1969, p. 7.

17. Ibid., p. 10.

18. personal communication with Kleindienst, November 1987.

19. Nixon Presidential Papers, Presidential news summary, September 20, 1969, p. 20.

20. Ibid., Memorandum to John Ehrlichman, September 22, 1969.

21. Ibid., Memorandum from Richard McLaren to John Ehrlichman, October 9, 1969.

22. Ibid., Memorandum from Peter Flanigan to Staff Secretary, June 7, 1971, subject log no. P–1589.

23. U.S. v. Marine Bankcorporation, 1974, 418 U.S. 602.

24. This point was made to me during a visit to the Antitrust Division, Department of Justice, July 1985.

25. Antitrust Division, U.S. Department of Justice, "Guidelines for Mergers," 1977, 1982, 1984, Memoranda.

26. Documents filed with the Supreme Court, U.S. v. Brown Shoe, U.S. Department of Justice Archives.

27. Some of the leading advocates of this position were Armentano, 1973; Posner, 1975; Bork, 1978; and Brozen, 1982.

28. These results are presented in NERA, Inc.'s "The antitrust climate: mergers," no. 2, January 1966.

29. Antitrust Division, U.S. Department of Justice, "1968 Merger Guidelines," pp. 9–10.

30. Ibid., p. 12.

31. Ibid., p. 20.

32. Ibid., 1984, esp. pp. 7–9, 35–36.

8. Diversification in Large Firms

1. Mueller, 1986, chs. 10, 11, presents a review of this literature.

2. A partial listing includes Narver, 1967; Lynch, 1971; Vance, 1971; U.S. Federal Trade Commission, 1972; Andreano, 1973; Markham, 1973; Winslow, 1973; Rumelt, 1974; Steiner, 1975; Biggadike, 1976; Mueller, 1977, pp. 314–347, 1980; Scherer, 1980.

Bibliography

Adelman, M. A. 1961. The antimerger act, 1950–1960. *American Economic Review* 51(2): 236–254.

American Management Association. 1924. Coordination of sales, production, and finance, no. 7. New York.

———1926. Marketing policies and sales methods that stabilize business, no. 36. New York.

Andreano, R. L., ed. 1973. *Superconcentration/Supercorporation.* Boston: Warner Modular Publications.

Armentano, D. T. 1982. *Antitrust and Monopoly: Anatomy of a Policy Failure.* New York: John Wiley & Sons.

Arnold, T. 1965. *Fair Fights and Foul.* New York: Harcourt, Brace.

Auerbach, J. S. 1899. The legal aspects of trusts. *North American Review* 169: 375–398.

Bain, J. S. 1956. *Barriers to New Competition.* Cambridge, Mass.: Harvard University Press.

Baruch, B. M. 1941. *American Industry in the War.* New York: Prentice-Hall.

Belush, B. 1975. *The Failure of the NRA.* New York: Norton.

Benson, L. 1955. *Merchants, Farmers, and Railroads.* Cambridge, Mass.: Harvard University Press.

Biggadike, E. R. 1976. *Corporate Diversification: Entry, Strategy, and Performance.* Boston: Harvard Business School.

Bittlingmayer, G. 1985. Did antitrust policy cause the great merger wave? *Journal of Law and Economics* 28: 77–118.

Blair, J. M. 1976. *The Control of Oil.* New York: Pantheon Books.

Bork, R. 1978. *The Antitrust Paradox.* New York: Basic Books.

Brown, S. 1972. *Ling: Rise, Fall, and Return of a Texas Titan.* New York: Antheum.

Brozen, Y. 1982. *Mergers in Perspective.* Washington, D.C.: American Enterprise Institute.

Burns, A. R. 1936. *The Decline of Competition.* New York: McGraw-Hill.

Cable, J. R., J. P. R. Palfrey, and J. W. Runge. 1980. Federal Republic of Germany, 1962–74. In *The Determinants and Effects of Mergers*, ed. D. Mueller. Cambridge, Mass.: Oelgeschlager, Gunn, and Hain.

Campbell, E. G. 1938. *Reorganization of the American Railroad System, 1893–1900.* New York: Columbia University Press.

Carnegie, A. 1889. The bugaboo of trusts. *North American Review* (February): 141–142.

Caves, R. 1967. *American Industry: Structure, Conduct, Performance.* Englewood Cliffs, N.J.: Prentice-Hall.

Chandler, A. D., Jr. 1962. *Strategy and Structure*. Cambridge, Mass.: MIT Press.

———1964. *Giant Enterprise*. New York: Harcourt, Brace & World.

———1965. *The Railroads*. New York: Harcourt, Brace & World.

———1977. *The Visible Hand*. Cambridge, Mass.: Harvard University Press.

———1979. *Managerial Innovation at General Motors*. New York: Arno Press.

Chandler, A. D., Jr., and S. Salsbury. 1971. *Pierre S. du Pont and the Making of the Modern Corporation*. New York: Harper & Row.

Channon, D. F. 1973. *The Strategy and Structure of British Enterprise*. Boston: Harvard Business School.

Clark, B. C. 1895. *The Cordage Industry*. Boston: Ginn.

Clark, J. B. 1898. *Control of Trusts*. New York: Macmillan.

Clark, J. D. 1931. *Federal Trust Policy*. Baltimore: Johns Hopkins University Press.

Clark, V. S. 1928. *History of Manufactures in the U.S.: 1860–1914*. Washington D.C.: Carnegie Institution.

Collins, N., and L. Preston. 1961. The size structure of the largest industrial firm, 1900–1958. *American Economic Review* 51: 986–1011.

Copeland, M. 1929. Marketing. In *Recent Economic Changes*, ed. Hoover Commission. New York: McGraw-Hill.

Cornish, W. R. 1979. Legal control over cartels and monopolization, 1880–1914. In *Law and the Formation of the Big Enterprises in the Nineteenth and Twentieth Centuries*, eds. N. Horn and J. Kocka. Gottingen: Vandenhoeck und Ruprecht.

Crabb, R. 1969. *Birth of a Giant*. Philadelphia: Chilton Book Co.

Cray, E. 1980. *Chrome Colossus*. New York: McGraw-Hill.

Cuff, R. 1973. *The War Industries Board*. Baltimore: Johns Hopkins University Press.

Daubman, J. R. 1924. The modern sales manager and his developing technique. *The Annals of the American Academy of Political and Social Science* 115: 174–182

de Chazeau, M. G., and A. E. Kahn. 1959. *Integration and Competition in the Petroleum Industry*. New Haven, Conn.: Yale University Press.

Denison, H. S. 1929. Management. In *Recent Economic Changes*, ed. Hoover Commission. New York: McGraw-Hill.

Dewing, A. S. 1914. *Corporate Promotions and Reorganization*. Cambridge, Mass.: Harvard University Press.

———1922. A statistical test of the success of consolidations. *Quarterly Journal of Economics* 36: 84–101.

DiMaggio, P., and W. Powell. 1983. Institutional isomorphism. *American Sociological Review* 48: 147–160.

Dodd, E. 1954. *American Business Corporations until 1860*. Cambridge, Mass.: Harvard University Press.

Dooley, C., G. Hughes, P. White, and W. Heusner. 1948. Marketing research in American industry. *Journal of Marketing* 12: 338–353.

Dyas, G. P., and H. T. Thanheiser. 1976. *The Emerging European Enterprise*. London: Macmillan.

Eddy, A. 1901. *The Laws of Combinations Embracing Monopolies*. Chicago: Callaghan.

Edgerton, C. E. 1897. The Wire Nail Association. *Political Science Quarterly* 11: 246–272.

Eis, C. 1978. *The 1919–1930 Merger Movement in American Industry*. New York: Arno Press.

Ely, R. 1900. *Monopolies and Trusts*. London: Macmillan.

Fligstein, N. 1985. The spread of the multidivisional form. *American Sociological Review* 50: 377–391.

———1987. The intraorganizational power struggle: The rise of finance presidents in large corporations, 1919–1979. *American Sociological Review* 52: 44–58.

———1990a. The structural transformation of American industry. In *The New Institutionalism in Organizational Theory*, eds. W. Powell and P. DiMaggio. Chicago: University of Chicago Press.

———1990b. Organizational, demographic, and economic determinants of the growth patterns of large firms. In *Research on Organizations*, ed. C. Calhoun. Greenwich, Conn.: JAI Press.

Fligstein, N., and K. Dauber. 1989. Changes in corporate organization. In *Annual Review of Sociology*, ed. W. R. Scott. Palo Alto: Annual Reviews.

Fontenay, C. 1980. *Estes Kefauver: A Biography*. Knoxville: University of Tennessee Press.

Ford, H. 1922. *My Life and Work*. Garden City, N.Y.: Garden City Publishing.

Fortune. 1960, 1970, 1980. *The 500 Largest Corporations*. July.

Freese, J., and J. Judd. 1985. *Business and Government*. New York: Sleepy Hollow Press.

Friedman, L. 1973. *A History of American Law*. New York: Simon and Schuster.

Galambos, L. 1975. *The Public Image of Big Business in America: 1880–1940*. Baltimore: Johns Hopkins University Press.

George, K. D., and C. L. Joll. 1975. *Competition Policy in the U.K. and the E.E.C.* Cambridge: Cambridge University Press.

Gilchrist, D. T. 1960. Albert Fink and the pooling system. *Business History Review* 34: 24–49.

Goodnow, F. 1897. Trade combinations at common law. *Political Science Quarterly* 12: 212–245.

Goolrick, R. M. 1978. *Public Policy toward Corporate Growth*. Port Washington, N.Y.: Kennikat Press.

Gorman, J. B. 1971. *Estes Kefauver: A Political Biography*. New York: Oxford University Press.

Gort, M. 1962. *Diversification and Integration in American Industry*. Princeton, N.J.: Princeton University Press.

Haber, L. F. 1971. *The Chemical Industry: 1900–1930*. Oxford: Oxford University Press.

Handler, M. 1932. Industrial mergers and the antitrust laws. *Columbia Law Review* 32: 179–271.

Haney, L. H. 1914. *Business Organizations and Combinations.* New York: Arno Press.

Hannah, L. 1976. *The Rise of the Corporate Economy.* London: Methuen.

Hannan, M., and J. Freeman. 1977. The population ecology of organizations. *American Journal of Sociology* 82: 929–966.

———1984. Structural inertia and organizational change. *American Sociological Review* 49: 149–164.

Hartz, L. 1948. *Economic Policy and Democratic Thought.* Cambridge, Mass.: Harvard University Press.

Hawley, E. W. 1966. *The New Deal and the Problem of Monopoly.* Princeton, N.J.: Princeton University Press.

———1981. Three facets of Hooverian associationalism: Lumber, aviation, and movies, 1921–30. In *Regulation in Perspective*, ed. T. McCraw. Boston: Harvard Business School.

Hennessy, E. L., Jr. 1984. *Allied Corporation: Strength Through Diversification.* New York: Newcomen Society.

Hidy, R. W., and M. E. Hidy. 1955. *Pioneering in Big Business: 1882–1911.* New York: Harper & Row.

Himmelberg, R. 1976. *The Origins of the National Recovery Administration.* New York: Fordham University Press.

Hirschl, A. J. 1896. *Consolidations, Combinations, and the Succession of Corporations.* Chicago: Callaghan.

Hoffmann, C. 1970. *The Depression of the Nineties.* Westport, Conn.: Greenwood Publishing Corp.

Hogan, W. T. 1971. *Economic History of the Iron and Steel Industry in the U.S.* Lexington, Mass.: D. C. Heath and Co.

———1984. *Steel in the U.S.: Restructuring to Compete.* Lexington, Mass.: Lexington Books.

Horwitz, M. 1977. *The Transformation of American Law, 1780–1860.* Cambridge, Mass.: Harvard University Press.

Hurst, J. W. 1956. *Law and the Conditions of Freedom in the Nineteenth Century United States.* Madison: University of Wisconsin Press.

———1970. *The Legitimacy of the Business Corporation in the Law of the United States, 1780–1970.* Charlottesville: University Press of Virginia.

Jacquemin, A. P., and H. W. deJong. 1977. *European Industrial Organization.* London: Macmillan.

Jeans, J. S. 1894. *Trusts, Pools, and Corners.* London: Methuen.

Jenks, J. W. 1888. The Michigan Salt Association. *Political Science Quarterly* 3: 78–98.

———1889. The development of the whiskey trust. *Political Science Quarterly* 4: 296–319.

———1900. *The Trust Problem.* New York: McClure, Phillips & Co.

Jenny, F., and A. P. Weber. 1980. France, 1962–1972. In *The Determinants and Effects of Mergers*, ed. D. Mueller. Cambridge, Mass.: Oelgeschlager, Gunn, and Hain.

Johnson, A. 1985. The FTC: The early years, 1915–1935. In *Business and Government*, eds. J. Freese and J. Judd. New York: Sleepy Hollow Press.

Jones, E. 1921. *The Trust Problem in the United States.* New York: Macmillan.

Kales, A. M. 1918. *Contracts and Combinations.* Chicago: Callaghan.

Kaplan, A. D. H. 1964. *Big Enterprise in a Competitive System.* Washington D.C.: Brookings Institution.

Katz, H. 1977. *The Decline of Competition in the Automobile Industry: 1920-1940.* New York: Arno Press.

Keasbey, E. J. 1899. New Jersey and the great corporation. *Reports of the American Bar Association* 22: 379-413.

Keller, M. 1981. The pluralist state. In *Regulation in Perspective*, ed. T. McCraw. Boston: Harvard Business School.

Kerr, K. A. 1968. *American Railroad Politics.* Pittsburgh: University of Pittsburgh Press.

Kirsh, B. S. 1928. *The Trade Associations.* New York: Central Book Co.

Kleindienst, R. 1985. *Justice.* Ottawa, Ill.: Jameson Books.

Kolko, G. 1963. *The Triumph of Conservatism: 1900-1916.* New York: Free Press.

————1965. *Railroads and Regulation.* Princeton, N.J.: Princeton University Press.

Kono, T. 1984. *Strategy and Structure of Japanese Enterprises.* London: Macmillan.

Kovaleff, T. 1980. *Business and Government during the Eisenhower Administration.* Athens: Ohio University Press.

Lamoreaux, N. R. 1985. *The Great Merger Movement in American Business: 1895-1904.* New York: Cambridge University Press.

Letwin, W. 1965. *Law and Economic Policy in America.* New York: Random House.

Lindahl, M. L., and W. A. Carter. 1959. *Corporate Concentration and Public Policy.* Englewood, N.J.: Prentice-Hall.

Little, R. 1979. *How to Make and Lose $100,000,000.* Boston: Little, Brown.

Livermore, S. 1936. The success of industrial mergers. *Quarterly Journal of Economics* 28: 68-96.

Lynch, H. H. 1971. *Financial Performance of Conglomerates.* Boston: Harvard Business School.

Lyon, L. S., P. T. Homan, L. L. Lorwin, G. Terbough, C. L. Dearing, and L. C. Marshall. 1935. *The National Recovery Administration.* Washington, D.C.: Brookings Institution.

Markham, J. W. 1973. *Conglomerate Enterprise and Public Policy.* Boston: Harvard Business School.

Markovits, R. S. 1983. The Burger Court, antitrust, and economic analysis. In *The Burger Court*, ed. V. Blasi. New Haven, Conn.: Yale University Press.

Martin, A. 1971. *Enterprise Denied.* New York: Columbia University Press.

Martin, D. D. 1959. *Mergers and the Clayton Act.* Berkeley: University of California Press.

McCraw, T. 1981. *Regulation in Perspective.* Boston: Harvard Business School.

———1985. *Prophets of Regulation.* Cambridge, Mass: Harvard University Press.

McCurdy, C. W. 1979. The Knight sugar decision of 1895 and the modernization of American corporation law: 1869–1903. *Business History Review* 13: 304–342.

McLean, J. G., and R. W. Haigh. 1954. *The Growth of Integrated Oil Companies.* Boston: Harvard Business School.

Meade, E. S. 1912. The economies of concentration. *Journal of Political Economy* 18: 358–372.

Meyer, J., and B. Rowan. 1977. Institutionalized organizations: Formal structure as myth and ceremony. *American Journal of Sociology* 83: 340–363.

Meyer, J., and W. R. Scott. 1983. *Organizational Environments.* Beverly Hills: Sage.

Moody, J. 1904. *The Truth about the Trusts.* New York: Moody Publishing.

Moody's. 1920–1980. *Moody's Manual of Industrials.* Selected years.

Morrison, E., and R. Craswell. 1980. *Papers on Business Strategy and Antitrust.* Washington, D.C.: Federal Trade Commission.

Mueller, D. C. 1977. The effects of conglomerate mergers: A survey of the empirical evidence. *Journal of Banking and Finance* 1: 315–347.

———1980. *The Determinants and Effects of Merger: An International Comparison.* Cambridge, Mass: Oelgeschlager, Gunn, and Hain.

———1986. *The Modern Corporation.* Sussex: Wheatsheaf Books.

Mueller, W. 1979. *The Celler-Kefauver Act: The First Twenty-seven Years.* 96th Cong. Washington D.C.: Government Printing Office.

Narver, J. C. 1967. *Conglomerate Mergers and Market Competition.* Berkeley: University of California Press.

Neale, A. D. and D. G. Goyder. 1980. *The Antitrust Laws of the U.S.A.* Cambridge: Cambridge University Press.

Nelson, R. L. 1959. *Merger Movements in American Industry: 1895–1956.* Princeton, N.J.: Princeton University Press.

Nevins, A., and F. E. Hill. 1963. *Ford.* New York: Scribners.

Nutter, G. W. 1951. *The Extent of Enterprise Monopoly in the U.S.: 1899–1939.* Chicago: University of Chicago Press.

Perrow, C. 1970. Departmental power and perspectives in industrial firms. In *Power in Organizations,* ed. M. Zald. Nashville: Vanderbilt University Press.

Pfeffer, J. 1981. *Power in Organizations.* Marshfield, Mass.: Pitman Publishing.

Posner, R. A. 1970. A statistical study of antitrust enforcement. *Journal of Law and Economics* 11: 365–419.

———1976. *Antitrust Law.* Chicago: University of Chicago Press.

Pound, A. 1934. *Turning Wheel.* New York: Doubleday, Doran & Co.

Prais, S. 1975. *The Evolution of Giant Firms in Britain.* Cambridge: Cambridge University Press.

Pratt, J. 1980. The petroleum industry in transition: Antitrust and the decline of monopoly. *Journal of Economic History* 15: 815–837.

Ripley, W. Z. 1905. *Trusts, Pools and Corporations: Selections and Documents in Economics.* Boston: Ginn.

——1913. *Railroads, Rates, and Regulation.* New York: Longmens, Green, and Co.

Roosevelt, T. 1926. *Works of Theodore Roosevelt,* vol. 15. New York: Scribners.

Rumelt, R. 1974. *Strategy, Structure, and Economic Performance.* Boston: Harvard Business School.

Sampson, A. 1973. *The Sovereign State of ITT.* New York: Stein and Day.

Scheiber, H. N. 1975. Federalism and the American economic order, 1789–1910. *Law and Society Review* 10: 57–118.

Scherer, F. M. 1980 *Industrial Market Structure and Economic Performance.* Chicago: Rand McNally.

Scherer, F. M., and D. Ravenscraft. 1984. Growth by diversification. Working paper no. 113, Bureau of Economics. Washington, D.C.: Federal Trade Commission.

Schoenberg, R. J. 1985. *Geneen.* New York: Norton.

Seager, H. R., and C. A. Gulick. 1929. *Trust and Corporation Problems.* New York: Harper & Row.

Skocpol, T. 1979. *States and Social Revolutions: A Comparative Analysis of France, Russia, and China.* New York: Cambridge University Press.

——1985. Bringing the state back in. In *Bringing the State Back In,* eds. T. Skocpol and P. Evans. New York: Cambridge University Press.

Sloan, A. P. 1964. *My Years with General Motors.* Garden City, N.J.: Doubleday.

Sobel, R. 1984a. *The Age of Giant Corporations.* Westport, Conn.: Greenwood Press.

——1984b. *The Rise and Fall of the Conglomerate Kings.* New York: Stein and Day.

Steiner, P. O. 1975. *Mergers: Motives, Effects, Policies.* Ann Arbor: University of Michigan Press.

Stevens, W. S. 1912. The powder trust. *Quarterly Journal of Economics* 16: 445–481.

——1913. A group of trusts and combinations. *Quarterly Journal of Economics* 17: 593–643.

——1917. *Unfair Competition.* Chicago: University of Chicago Press.

Stigler, G. J. 1966. The economic effects of the antitrust laws. *Journal of Law and Economics* 10: 225–258.

——1968. *The Organization of Industry.* Homewood, Ill.: Richard D. Irwin.

Stone, A. 1977. *Economic Regulation and the Public Interest.* Ithaca, N.Y.: Cornell University Press.

Sullivan, J. 1924. The contribution of the Association of National Advertisers to better present business practices. *The Annals of the American Academy of Political and Social Science* 115: 116–123.

Taylor, G., and P. E. Sudnik. 1984. *Du Pont and the International Chemical Industry.* Boston: Twayne.

Temin, P. 1964. *Iron and Steel in Nineteenth-Century America*. Cambridge, Mass.: MIT Press.

Thomas, R. P. 1977. *An Analysis of the Pattern of Growth of the Automobile Industry, 1895–1929*. New York: Arno Press.

Thorelli, H. B. 1955. *Federal Antitrust Policy*. Baltimore: Johns Hopkins University Press.

Thorp, W. L. 1924. *The Integration of Industrial Operation*. Census Monograph no. 3. Washington D.C.: Government Printing Office.

Thorp, W. L., and W. Crowder. 1941. *The Structure of Industry*. Monograph no. 27, Temporary National Economic Committee. Washington D.C.: Government Printing Office.

Turner, D. 1965. Conglomerate mergers and section 7 of the Clayton Act. *Harvard Law Review* 78: 1313–95.

U.S. Antitrust Division, Department of Justice. 1968, 1977, 1982, 1984. Merger guidelines. Mimeo.

U.S. Attorney General, Department of Justice. 1895–1903. *Annual Report of the Attorney General*. Washington, D.C.: Government Printing Office.

——1938. *The Federal Antitrust Laws*. Washington, D.C.: Government Printing Office.

——1955. *Report of the Attorney General's National Committee to Study the Antitrust Laws*. Washington, D.C.: Government Printing Office.

U.S. Bureau of the Census. 1900. *Census of Manufactures*. Washington, D.C.: Government Printing Office.

——1910. *Census of Manufactures*. Washington, D.C.: Government Printing Office.

——1920. *Census of Manufacturing*, vol. 10. Washington D.C.: Government Printing Office.

——1960. *Historical Statistics of the U.S.* Washington D.C.: Government Printing Office.

U.S. Commissioner of Corporations. 1904, 1906, 1908. *Annual Report*. Washington, D.C.: Government Printing Office.

——1907. *Report on the Meat Packing Industry*. Washington, D.C.: Government Printing Office.

——1911. *Report on the Steel Industry. Washington, D.C.: Government Printing Office.*

——1912. *Report on the Tobacco Industry*. Washington, D.C.: Government Printing Office.

——1913. *Report on the International Harvester Co.* Washington, D.C.: Government Printing Office.

U.S. Congressional Hearing Index. 1985. *Part 1*. Washington, D.C.: Congressional Information Service.

U.S. Department of Commerce. 1923. *Trade Association Activities*. Washington D.C.: Government Printing Office.

U.S. Federal Trade Commission. 1918–1944. *Commission's Annual Report*. Washington, D.C.: Government Printing Office. Selected years.

——1919. *Report on the Meat Packing Industry*. Washington, D.C.: Government Printing Office.

————1928. *Petroleum Industry: Prices, Profit and Competition.* Doc. 61, 70th Cong., 1st sess.

————1929. *Open-price Trade Associations.* S. Doc. 226, 70th Cong., 2nd sess.

————1939. *Report on the Motor Vehicle Industry.* Washington, D.C.: Government Printing Office.

————1944–1947. *Official Minutes of the Commissioners,* vols. 78–86.

————1949a. *Official Minutes of the Commissioners,* vol. 91.

————1952–53. In the matter of Pillsbury Mills, docket 6000.

————1954–1957. In the matter of Crown Zellerbach, docket 6180.

————1972. *Merger Performance: An Empirical Analysis of Nine Corporations.* Washington, D.C.: Government Printing Office.

————1981. *Report on Mergers and Acquisitions.* Washington, D.C.: Government Printing Office.

U.S. House of Representatives. 1889. *Report on Committee of Manufacturers.* H. Rep. 4165, 52nd Cong.

————1893. *Report on Whiskey Trust Investigation.* H. Rep. 2601, 54th Cong.

————1912. *Trust Legislation Serial No. 2, Patent Legislation.* Hearings before the House Judiciary Committee, 62nd Cong.

————1945. *Hearings on H.R. 2357.* Subcommittee no. 3 of the House Judiciary Committee, 79th Cong.

————1946. *House of Representatives Report No. 1820, and 1480.* 79th Cong.

————1947a. *Hearings on H.R. 515.* Subcommittee no. 2 of the House Judiciary Committee, 80th Cong.

————1947b. *House of Representatives Report No. 596.* 80th Cong.

————1947c. *House of Representatives Report No. 1171.* 80th Cong.

————1949a. *House of Representatives Report No. 1191.* 81st Cong.

————1949b. *Hearings on H.R. 2734.* Subcommittee no. 3 of the House Judiciary Committee, 81st Cong.

————1950–51. *A Study of Monopoly Power.* Hearings before a subcommittee of the House Judiciary Committee. 82nd Cong.

————1957. *Congress and the Monopoly Problem.*

Report to the House Select Committee on Small Business, 84th Cong.

————1970. *Investigation of Conglomerate Operations.* Antitrust Subcommittee, House Judiciary Committee, 91st Cong.

U.S. Industrial Commission. 1900. *Trusts and Industrial Combinations,* vols. 1–19. Washington, D.C.: Government Printing Office.

U.S. Senate. 1886. *Report of the Senate Select Committee on Interstate Commerce.* 48th Cong.

————1903. *Reply of the Attorney General.* Senate Judiciary Committee. 57th Cong., 2nd sess.

————1912. *Investigation of the U.S. Steel Corporation.* Hearings before the Senate Judiciary Committee. 62nd Cong. 2nd sess.

————1949–50. *Hearings on H.R. 2734.* Hearings before a subcommittee of the Senate Judiciary Committee, 81st Cong.

————1950. *Senate Report No. 1775.* 81st Cong.

————1969. *Statement of Richard McLaren.* Confirmation Hearings, Senate Judiciary Committee, vol. 1951(1).

U.S. Temporary National Economic Committee. 1941. *Investigation of Concentration of Economic Power,* vols. 1–43. Washington, D.C.: Government Printing Office.

Utton, M. A. 1975. British merger policy. In *Competition Policy in the U.K. and the E.E.C.,* eds. K. D. George and C. L. Joll. Cambridge: Cambridge University Press.

Vance, S. C. 1971. *Managers in the Conglomerate Era.* New York: Wiley-Interscience.

von Halle, E. 1896. *Trusts.* London: Macmillan.

Walker, A. H. 1980. *History of the Sherman Law.* Greenwood, Conn.: Greenwood Press.

Watkins, M. W. 1927. *Industrial Combinations and Public Policy.* Boston: Houghton Mifflin.

Weaver, S. 1977. *Decision to Prosecute: Organization and Public Policy in the Antitrust Division.* Cambridge, Mass.: MIT Press.

Weinstein, J. 1968. *The Corporate Ideal in the Liberal State, 1900–1918.* Boston: Beacon Press.

Weston, J. F., and S. I. Ornstein. 1973. *The Impact of Large Firms on the U.S. Economy.* Lexington, Mass.: Lexington Books.

White, H. 1981. Where do markets come from? *American Journal of Sociology* 87: 517–547.

Whitehead, D. 1968. *The Dow Story.* New York: McGraw-Hill.

Whitney, E. B. 1905. The Addyston Pipe Company. In *Trusts, Pools, and Corporations,* ed. W. Z. Ripley. Boston: Ginn.

Whitney, S. N. 1934. *Trade Associations and Industrial Control.* New York: Central Book Co.

Williamson, H. F., and A. R. Daum. 1959. *The American Petroleum Industry,* vols. 1–2. Evanston, Ill.: Northwestern University Press.

Williamson, O. E. 1975. *Markets and Hierarchies: Analysis of Antitrust Implications.* New York: Free Press.

Winslow, J. F. 1973. *Conglomerates Unlimited.* Bloomington: Indiana University Press.

Yoshino, M. 1968. *Japan's Managerial System.* Cambridge, Mass.: MIT Press.

Index

DISCARD